CLASSICAL HOLLYWOOD, AMERICAN MODERNISM

Classical Hollywood, American Modernism charts the entwined trajectories of the Hollywood studio system and literary modernism in the United States. By examining the various ways Hollywood's industry practices inflected the imaginations of authors, filmmakers, and studios, Jordan Brower offers a new understanding of twentieth-century American and ultimately world media culture. Synthesizing archival research with innovative theoretical approaches, this book tells the story of the studio system's genesis, international dominance, decline, and continued symbolic relevance during the American postwar era through the literature it influenced. It examines the American film industry's business practices and social conditions, demonstrating how concepts like anticipated adaptation, corporate authorship, systemic development, and global distribution inflected the form of some of the greatest works of prose fiction and nonfiction by modernist writers, such as Anita Loos, F. Scott Fitzgerald, William Faulkner, Patsy Ruth Miller, Nathanael West, Parker Tyler, Malcolm Lowry, and James Baldwin.

JORDAN BROWER is Assistant Professor of English at the University of Kentucky. He coedited *American Literature in the World: An Anthology from Anne Bradstreet to Octavia Butler* (Wai Chee Dimock et al., 2016). His work has appeared in journals such as *Critical Inquiry*, *ELH: English Literary History*, *Historical Journal of Film, Radio and Television*, *James Joyce Quarterly*, and *Modern Language Quarterly*.

CLASSICAL HOLLYWOOD, AMERICAN MODERNISM

A Literary History of the Studio System

JORDAN BROWER
University of Kentucky

Shaftesbury Road, Cambridge CB2 8EA, United Kingdom

One Liberty Plaza, 20th Floor, New York, NY 10006, USA

477 Williamstown Road, Port Melbourne, VIC 3207, Australia

314–321, 3rd Floor, Plot 3, Splendor Forum, Jasola District Centre, New Delhi – 110025, India

103 Penang Road, #05–06/07, Visioncrest Commercial, Singapore 238467

Cambridge University Press is part of Cambridge University Press & Assessment,
a department of the University of Cambridge.

We share the University's mission to contribute to society through the pursuit of
education, learning and research at the highest international levels of excellence.

www.cambridge.org
Information on this title: www.cambridge.org/9781009419154

DOI: 10.1017/9781009419192

© Jordan Brower 2024

This publication is in copyright. Subject to statutory exception and to the provisions
of relevant collective licensing agreements, no reproduction of any part may take
place without the written permission of Cambridge University Press & Assessment.

First published 2024

A catalogue record for this publication is available from the British Library

A Cataloging-in-Publication data record for this book is available from the Library of Congress

ISBN 978-1-009-41915-4 Hardback

Cambridge University Press & Assessment has no responsibility for the persistence
or accuracy of URLs for external or third-party internet websites referred to in this
publication and does not guarantee that any content on such websites is, or will
remain, accurate or appropriate.

For Carol, Murray, and Zack

Contents

List of Figures		*page* viii
Acknowledgments		x
	Introduction: Hollywood Signs	1
1	Paramount Pictures and Transmedial Possibility	21
2	MGM Modernism	54
3	The Motion Picture Industry's Coming of Age	84
4	Global Hollywood: Parker Tyler and Malcolm Lowry, between Myth and System	113
5	The Scenes of an Ending: Adaptation, Originality, and the New Authorship of Hollywood Pictures	143
6	Conclusion: Read Anything Good Lately?	178
Notes		192
Index		236

Figures

I.1 Dramatis Personae of *Camille: or, the Fate of a Coquette* (Ralph Barton, 1926), title card one of four   *page* 15
I.2 Charlie Chaplin, channeling Oscar Wilde and Alla Nazimova. *Camille: or, the Fate of a Coquette* (Ralph Barton, 1926)   17
I.3 Anita Loos, *But Gentlemen Marry Brunettes*, New York: Penguin 1998 [1928], 138   18
I.4 Paul Robeson as Alexandre Dumas *fils* in *Camille: or, the Fate of a Coquette* (Ralph Barton, 1926)   19
1.1 Famous Players emphatically announcing its ownership of the rights to George Du Maurier's bestseller *Trilby* (1894)   26
1.2 Elliott Service Company advertisement, presenting Warner Bros.' "Screen Classics" campaign (featuring F. Scott Fitzgerald)   29
1.3 The transmedial flow of intellectual property neatly depicted in the trailer for *The Great Gatsby* (Herbert Brenon, Paramount, 1926)   47
2.1 MGM advertising its corporate voice (*Variety*, April 14, 1930)   65
4.1 Parker Tyler's movie screen in *The Granite Butterfly: A Facsimile Edition*, unnumbered photograph insert page 3   127
4.2 The myth of Pygmalion and Galatea referenced in *Mad Love* (Karl Freund, MGM, 1935)   134
4.3 Dr. Gogol (Peter Lorre) reads Elizabeth Barrett Browning's *Sonnets from the Portuguese* in *Mad Love* (Karl Freund, MGM, 1935)   134
4.4 Psychoanalysis satirized in *Mad Love* (Karl Freund, MGM, 1935)   135
5.1 Holly Martins fumbling a question about James Joyce in *The Third Man* (Carol Reed, London Films, 1949)   150

List of Figures

5.2	*Untitled Love Story*, an original tragedy by Joe Gillis and Betty Schaefer. *Sunset Boulevard* (Billy Wilder, Paramount, 1950)	155
5.3	Paramount picturing its own demise. *Sunset Boulevard* (Billy Wilder, Paramount, 1950)	156
5.4	Darryl F. Zanuck on the cover of *Time* magazine, June 12, 1950	159
5.5	Twentieth Century-Fox's Advertisement of "Scheduled Performances" of *All About Eve* (*Boxoffice*, October 7, 1950)	165
5.6	*Sarah Siddons as the Tragic Muse* (Sir Joshua Reynolds, 1784). *All About Eve* (Joseph L. Mankiewicz, Fox, 1950)	167
5.7	Norma and the profusion of portraits. *Sunset Boulevard* (Billy Wilder, Paramount, 1950)	168
5.8	Laurel's Modernist portraits and *In a Lonely Place*'s anticlassicism. *In a Lonely Place* (Nicholas Ray, Santana/Columbia, 1950)	168
5.9	Margo, framed. *All About Eve* (Joseph L. Mankiewicz, Fox, 1950)	170
5.10	Eve, framed. *All About Eve* (Joseph L. Mankiewicz, Fox, 1950)	170
5.11	All about TV. *All About Eve* (Joseph L. Mankiewicz, Fox, 1950)	171
5.12	Classicism dissolved. *Sunset Boulevard* (Billy Wilder, Paramount, 1950)	174
5.13	Classicism preserved at its limit. *All About Eve* (Joseph L. Mankiewicz, Fox, 1950)	175
5.14	"Source Material of Feature-Length Pictures Approved by Production Code Administration," *1956 Annual Report*, Motion Picture Association of America, Inc, 17 (Margaret Herrick Library, Academy of Motion Pictures Arts and Sciences)	176
6.1	"*The Far Away Mountain* ... three studios tried to lick it and failed." *The Bad and the Beautiful* (Vincente Minnelli, MGM, 1952)	187
6.2	"Read anything good lately?" *The Bad and the Beautiful* (Vincente Minnelli, MGM, 1952)	188
6.3	James Lee Bartlow, author of *Proud Land*. *The Bad and the Beautiful* (Vincente Minnelli, MGM, 1952)	190

Acknowledgments

Four mentors deserve first mention. Jack Cameron, my undergraduate adviser, taught me how to read Joyce and watch movies; this all started with him. I cannot overstate the influence of my dissertation advisers Joe Cleary and J.D. Connor, and I'm lucky to have had the chance to learn from their examples. No one has committed more time to the many drafts of these chapters than Michael Trask, and no one has made me feel more at home in Lexington.

At Yale, I enjoyed the guidance of Dudley Andrew, Jane Bordiere, Wai Chee Dimock, Katherine Germano, McKenzie Granata, Langdon Hammer, David Kastan, John MacKay, Charlie Musser, Erica Sayers, Katie Trumpener, John Williams, and Ruth Bernard Yeazell. Claudia Calhoun, Paul Franz, Josh Glick, Seo Hee Im, Jess Matuozzi, Chris McGowan, and Palmer Rampell read and improved chapters at various points over the past decade; in countless conversations and arguments during that span, Aaron Pratt, Andrew Willson, and Joe Stadolnik read and improved my mind. These friends were joined by many others—Kim Andrews, Annie Berke, Kirsty Dootson, Danny Fairfax, Sam Fallon, Dave Gary, Len Gutkin, Leana Hirschfeld-Kroen, Ed King, Tom Koenigs, Brian Meacham, Lukas Moe, Matt Rager Sarah Robbins, Zelda Roland, Justin Sider, and Elena Torok—in making my time in New Haven a joy. I apologize to any others I've forgotten. And no accounting of my grad school debts would be complete without acknowledging Paul Fry and Brigitte Peucker, the directors of study of English and Film Studies, who allowed me to complete a joint Ph.D. following the James Franco ad hoc degree plan. In a very real sense, this literary history of the studio system depended on a Hollywood adventure in literary history.

Two years teaching in Harvard's History and Literature concentration went quickly, but my colleagues there left their mark on these pages. I'm especially grateful to Emily Lasse and Jessica Shires for herding the actual and metaphorical cats, to coteachers Paul Adler and

Briana Smith for holding me to account daily, to officemate Emily Pope-Obeda for bearing with the disordered desk of a disordered mind, and to Angela Allan, René Carrasco, Chris Clements, Thomas Dichter, Maggie Doherty, Reed Gochberg, Ernest Hartwell, Alan Niles, Mark Sanchez, Debbie Sharnak, and Duncan White for the many educations in interdisciplinarity. And, on the other side of the Barker Center basement in the English department, I found old friend and Amherst College Writing Center cohort Kelly Rich, who, with her famous kindness, lent her expertise as a modernist and let me housesit for her when I was between apartments.

The University of Kentucky has proven to be an ideal place to teach and write. Chairs Jonathan Allison and Jill Rappoport have been unstintingly supportive. Peter Kalliney and Alan Nadel commented on multiple portions of this work and, as coordinators alongside Michael Trask of the 20/21 Working Group, offered a venue for me to test its merits. Fred Bengtsson, Jeff Clymer, Andrew Milward, Kristen Pickett, Hannah Pittard, Robin Rahija, and Emily Shortslef welcomed me with open arms, and Kamahra Ewing, Regina Hamilton, and Jap-Nanak Makkar have been wonderful junior faculty peers. Emily also helped me polish the manuscript in its final stages, bringing her early modernist's eye for style to bear on some tenaciously ungainly prose. As directors of the International Film Studies program, Molly Blasing, Pearl James, and Jeff Peters have made UK an increasingly exciting place to think about movies, as have present and past graduate students including Amanda Salmon, Matthew Wentz, and Ben Wilson, and former undergrads Jorden Keator and Jessica Miller.

A project that attempts to speak equally to two fields exposes one's ignorance at least doubly. In an attempt to ameliorate my own, I emailed Mark Lynn Anderson, Steven Cohan, Pardis Dabashi, Sarah Gleeson-White, Richard Godden, Catherine Jurca, Peter Lev, Will Scheibel, and Stefan Solomon asking for help, and they responded with unfailing generosity. Further help was offered in working groups at Yale, Harvard, and the University of Kentucky, and at the Modernist Studies Association and American Comparative Literature Association conferences. Despite all their best efforts errors surely remain, and it goes without saying that they're all mine.

Old friends have influenced this book in profound ways. Jeff Lawrence has been a constant interlocutor for half my life and has helpfully fought with me through all the iterations of these arguments. John Babbott, Hallie Davison, Scott and Amy Ganz, Will Havemann, Tessa Kelly, Chris Parkinson, Maggie

Roth, Andrew Rubinstein, and Karti Subramanian have suffered my excesses and corrected my mistakes, just as a chosen family should.

Numerous institutions supported this project both monetarily and in kind. At the beginning, a summer stipend from the Beinecke Library gave me the time to rummage through papers and get the project off the ground; at the end, a manuscript review grant from the Cooperative of the Humanities and Social Sciences of the University of Kentucky College of Arts and Sciences helped me prepare the book for submission. In between, I've received invaluable aid from many librarians, including Genevieve Maxwell at the Margaret Herrick Library, Tara Craig and Vianca Victor at the Columbia University Rare Book & Manuscript Library, and the many workers at the University of Kentucky Libraries. This book would simply not have been possible without the massive scanning initiative undertaken by Eric Hoyt and the Digital Media History Library.

Ray Ryan at Cambridge responded enthusiastically to the manuscript and secured truly helpful reports from Catherine Jurca and another anonymous reviewer. Edgar Mendez ably shepherded the book through production. An early version of the first chapter appeared in *Modern Language Quarterly* in 2017 and was edited expertly by Marshall Brown. I'm grateful to *MLQ* for permission to use that material here.

And then, of course, there's Ellen Song, who's given me so much happiness, not to mention so much of her time to the improvement of this work, that the least I can do is give her a paragraph of her own.

My father, Murray, and my mother, Carol, always believed in me despite the very real possibility things wouldn't work out, and they expressed enthusiasm for whatever arcane interest or idea I obsessed over at any given time. One summer morning in 2017, I received an email from Dad containing a link to a Paramount Newsreel segment from February 28, 1941 (see it for yourself: www.gettyimages.com/detail/video/exterior-of-farm-building-close-up-of-cow-maisie-and-news-footage/502484911). The thirty-three second clip celebrated some local color: Maisie, a six-year-old Holstein cow on a dairy farm in Lindenhurst, New York, had given birth to triplets, an event, the voiceover exclaims, as rare as human sextuplets. The young man leading Maisie along is my grandfather, Albert, and the baby boys playing with the calves are great uncles Ivan and Joel (Itzsie and Hishy, as they were called in Yiddish). Miriam Hansen couldn't have identified a better example of the way that Hollywood shaped regular people and ushered them into modernity, made their lives momentous and at the same time a sideshow (this on the eve of World War II). How odd and yet totally banal that my family is, in the smallest way, part of Hollywood history, and how marvelous and yet surely common it is to see in your grandfather's lanky lope the moving image of yourself at twenty-three. "Just thought you'd like to see it," Dad wrote. Indeed. Murray passed away just after he learned that I got the job at UK that would let me complete this book. It's dedicated to him, and to Carol, and to my brother Zack, my dearest friend.

Introduction
Hollywood Signs

...if for no other, still for an audience upon the stage, one could make those delicate cross-references that are now the discoveries of the learned.

—William Empson, *Seven Types of Ambiguity*, 1930[1]

The Big Picture

Classical Hollywood, American Modernism traces the arc of the Hollywood studio system from 1912 to 1952—its genesis, consolidation, global extension, and self-understood demise—by way of shifting understandings of literature and the literary within the American film industry. "Literary" here encompasses three distinct but overlapping concepts. Most narrowly, the term names the forms of writing produced within the studio system, principally prose fiction but also poetry, drama, and the screenplay. More broadly, it refers to the intellectual property that furnishes the raw materials for much film production. And, most abstractly, it constitutes the rarefied antithesis of "entertainment"—entertainment being Hollywood's métier at least since the Supreme Court's 1915 decision in *Mutual Film Corp. v. Industrial Commission of Ohio*, which ruled that the moving picture was not a form of expression protected by the First Amendment. This study begins at the moment when writers in the *Moving Picture World* trade newspaper began to ask what a studio was, when the Townsend Amendment to the Copyright Act of 1909 codified moving picture rights to literary works, and when Adolph Zukor founded the Famous Players Film Company, which quickly led the industry in producing pictures based on copyrighted literary properties. It concludes just after the Supreme Court mandated the disintegration of the vertically integrated oligopoly in *United States v. Paramount Pictures, Inc.*, and when the landmark *Miracle* decision (*Joseph Burstyn, Inc. v. Wilson* [1952]) established moving pictures as protected speech, allowing the studios as well as independent filmmakers to reorient the movies toward a diminished and fragmented filmgoing audience.

At the same time, *Classical Hollywood, American Modernism* describes the permutations of North American and primarily United States based literary modernism as they occur within a literary profession adjusting to an increasingly commodity-driven and transmedial culture. This book thus also posits the studio system as a dynamic set of conditions among which literary experimentation occurred alongside and dialectically engaged with the writing of popular literature (and especially the genre of Hollywood fiction). It thereby integrates two lineages of scholarship developed within the New Modernist Studies. The first is interested in modernist literature's relation to information technologies (cinema, phonography, print, radio). The second is committed to reading the aesthetic preoccupations and formal strategies of ostensibly inward-facing, autotelic fiction as deriving from and responding to changes in the professional life of letters within broader economic, legal, and political transformations. Because the studio system had a more or less determinate origin, developed and declined somewhat rapidly, responded to internal and external pressures, and had the features both of a geographic area ("Hollywood is in Southern California") and of a "mere" collection of rules and mores ("Hollywood is a state of mind") without being reducible to either, its history provides an ideal opportunity by which to track the various ways a complex set of institutions, interacting at various scales, affect literary production.

To be sure, mine is not the first book to explore these intersecting issues. There have been many such studies—of Hollywood fiction; of authors' often harrowing, occasionally risible experiences writing for this or that studio; of the way modernists modeled their formal experiments on cinematographic and editing techniques—and from many angles, ranging from the formalist to the feminist, the Adornian to the Žižekian. *Classical Hollywood, American Modernism* draws on a century of criticism and scholarship in light of recent parallel developments in the studies of American cinema and twentieth-century literature that make possible a new synthesis of the two fields, a synthesis that in turn offers novel insights to each. Thus, and at the risk of being needlessly explicit and vulgarly self-regarding—of imitating the best and worst aspects of studio system-era Hollywood films—a preliminary sketch of those developments in the evolving accounts of the "studio system" and of "modernism" is in order.

Studio System

In its most basic and least controversial sense, the "studio system" describes the industrial organization of the American movie business, including its many institutional features, from the star system and the norms of continuity editing to the Motion Picture Producers and Distributors of America (MPPDA), the industry's trade association, and the Production Code Administration (PCA).[2] Although the term can be found in trade journals as early as 1911 to refer to an individual studio's operations (its system of management), "studio system" takes on its more familiar meaning in the mid-1920s, when organizations began the process of vertical integration—that is, coordinating companies specializing in production, distribution, and exhibition through interlocking boards of directors—and, in response to bad publicity, created the MPPDA to protect the industry's interests.[3] The studio system settled into its mature oligopoly form with the massive capital investment required by the transition to sound cinema production around 1930, with a dominant Big Five that integrated production, distribution, and exhibition—Metro-Goldwyn-Mayer (MGM), Paramount Pictures, RKO Radio Pictures (RKO), Fox Film Corporation (Twentieth Century-Fox after the 1935 merger), and Warner Bros.—and a Little Three that integrated production and distribution—Columbia Pictures, United Artists, and Universal Pictures. Remaining space was occupied by upmarket independent producers (e.g., Samuel Goldwyn, David O. Selznick, Walter Wanger) and the underfunded Poverty Row producers of the lower-budget B pictures that populated the bottom half of the double bill (e.g., Republic Pictures, Monogram Pictures). This scheme would remain relatively stable until the Supreme Court's decision in *Paramount* mandated the divorcement of the Big Five's respective theater chains from their production and distribution arms. Beyond this basic consensus, film historians have disagreed about the relative importance of criteria employed to characterize the era. Where Thomas Schatz prioritizes the management of facilities in Southern California and privileges powerful producers like MGM's Irving Thalberg, Douglas Gomery prefers to emphasize the financial control of the interrelated businesses in the New York offices and focuses on executives like Loew's president Nicholas Schenck.[4]

Of course, though the film industry is a commercial one, even the most cynical would agree that it produces aesthetic objects. David Bordwell, Janet Staiger, and Kristin Thompson's *The Classical Hollywood Cinema* (1985) marked the first major attempt to extrapolate and formalize an aesthetics from Hollywood's industrial organization. That book presents a neoformalist account of what its authors call classical style, a concept they derive from the art history of E. H. Gombrich and the aesthetic theory of Jan Mukařovský. According to this foundational argument, the oligopoly established protocols that both optimized production efficiency and guaranteed narrative and spatiotemporal coherence and comprehension. As a consequence, the "typical" Hollywood film, they argue, followed the principles of "decorum, proportion, formal harmony, respect for tradition, self-effacing craftsmanship, and cool control of the perceiver's response."[5]

Where *The Classical Hollywood Cinema* assigned a style to the studio system's mode of production, subsequent research has sought to describe the relationship between the studio system and the meanings of the films produced within it. Scholars interested in this issue have supplemented (and argued with) Bordwell, Staiger, and Thompson's indifference to interpretation by devising what could broadly be called a textualist approach inspired by models of expression in anthropology, literary criticism, and systems theory. If for Bordwell, Staiger, and Thompson Hollywood is principally an industry, for later scholars it is also—and equally importantly—a highly ordered social body with internal signifying practices. In his influential *Production Culture* (2006), a study of contemporary film and television production work inspired by the anthropological theory of Clifford Geertz, John Thornton Caldwell reads the "deep texts" of the industry (e.g., trade show iconography) as "imaginative means that help create and maintain ... craft- or discipline-specific communities."[6] Following from Caldwell to a greater or lesser degree, scholars like Jerome Christensen, J.D. Connor, Catherine Jurca, and Denise Mann consider motion pictures produced during the era of the studio system as texts that communicate *within* the industry at the same time that they perform their more evident function as the world's most popular form of entertainment.[7]

Christensen's version merits special mention. His theory of corporate authorship, which posits the studio as the primary engine of meaning in Hollywood films, not only privileges the studio as a person capable of addressing its employees, its rivals, and its audiences, but also conceives of movies as allegorical expressions of studio intentions. By establishing a comprehensive alternative to both *The Classical Hollywood Cinema*'s meaning-agnostic stylistics and the auteur theory, which prioritizes the director and thus cannot account for the importance of multiple contributors within a highly capitalized and hierarchical organization, this radically new theory has enabled recent scholars like Connor, Jurca, and Jeff Menne to synthesize industrial-economic analysis and moving image hermeneutics to rewrite Hollywood's history from the studios' points of view. *Classical Hollywood, American Modernism* continues that project of rewriting by returning to writers the allegorical capacity extended to the studios, reading their works of literature as deep texts produced within the social and economic fields of the system. By "returning," I mean that I approach writers working in the film industry the way Christensen treated Romantic authors before shifting his attention to American cinema. In briefly rehearsing the origins of his theory, we can see the justification for the extension I propose.[8]

Christensen's film theory derives from the particular view of Romantic authorship he developed in the wake of the New Historicists' uptake of Michel Foucault's critique of power and Paul de Man's rhetorical reading. In *Lord Byron's Strength* (1993), Christensen takes a cue from Nietzsche, who, he argues, "revived a conception of aristocracy as eventful deed rather than as a class united by interest[.]" Central to Nietzsche's conception was the claim that "[s]trength does not await the conferral of credit; it commands it."[9] In an era of ascending commercial culture, when aristocracy was "no more than nominal," Byron took credit for his lordship through the poetic acts of *Childe Harold's Pilgrimage* and *Don Juan*. This lordship was, crucially, a poetic construction, a persona distinct from the empirical George Gordon.

Similarly, according to Christensen, MGM claimed its status as the "Tiffany's of Hollywood" in movies like *Singin' in the Rain* (Gene Kelly and Stanley Donen, 1952), "the most self-reflexive of all MGM pictures," a movie fundamentally "about credit: who gives it, who receives it, who takes it, and incidentally who deserves it."[10] The theory of corporate authorship, like the theory of the Romantic career, is not only a theory of expression but moreover a theory of assertion, of the author's power to assert. For MGM, which made "art" a century after Byron in a moment of mass entertainment, credit takes on its most vulgar economic connotations: the studios' revolving credit with investment banks; the attributions of responsibility for all of the tasks involved in the filmmaking process. Nevertheless, those connotations do not elide the studio's self-credited ability to make meaning. In other words, the vertically integrated studio within the system's oligopoly claimed the power to monopolize the expressive capacity of the movies it made (an exclusive power the studios would forfeit after the *Paramount* decision, resulting in "jurisdictional conflicts" over the meanings of Hollywood movies produced ever since).[11] By way of allegory, the studio may address multiple audiences, "may," Christensen writes, "admonish its employees and punish its stars ... exhort the president of the United States to alter a policy ... [or] allegorize its formidable institutional power to appease its creditors and dismay its competitors."[12] So, a movie like *Dinner at Eight* (1933) could tout the unparalleled glamour of MGM's galaxy of stars to its paying customers while at the same time (as I will argue in Chapter 2) assuring the studio's employees of its ongoing might even after Louis B. Mayer effectively deposed Irving Thalberg, the boy-genius head of production who took the company to the apex of the system after the transition to sound.

According to this theory, Hollywood movies are ambiguous just as Shakespeare's plays are for William Empson. Empson, the source of this introduction's epigraph, saw "the deposit of cross-reference and incidental detail" across the text of *King Lear* as the subtle means through which the playwright could speak to his actors—his "audience on the stage"—and maintain their interest and commitment while they repeatedly perform their parts.[13] Empson here describes, in a very different idiom, the production culture of the Jacobean stage, and I invoke his *Seven Types of Ambiguity* (1930), a hallmark of modernist literary criticism, as a precedent for my own attempt to make sense of fictions that speak to multiple, distinct addressees: to persons behind and before the screen, on and off the lot, and, crucially, both corporeal and corporate.

Aside from the innuendo institutionalized by the Production Code (a matter of importance in Chapter 4), the critical difference between the ambiguity of Shakespeare's plays and that of MGM's movies is in the different conditions required for the corporation, that novel person, to make meaning. Christensen formulates those conditions thus: "There is no interpretation without meaning, no meaning without intention, no intention without an author, no author without a person, no person with greater right to or capacity for authorship than a corporate person."[14] What the man of letters accomplishes by great effort—"a strategy for achieving immunity or exemption from the forces of decay and death"—the corporate author, legally distinct from any individual and existing in perpetuity, has by definition.[15] But while the corporeal poet endeavors to transcend mortality in a career of artworks that instantiate a persona, the corporation requires artworks, and thus flesh-and-blood makers or "agents," to assert its existence and its intentions to multiple audiences: there is "no corporation," Christensen finally observes, "who can act without an agent."[16] That pattern of intentions comprises the corporation's strategy, its "career." The successful agent, whether a head of production like Adolph Zukor (Chapter 1), a director like Edmund Goulding of MGM (Chapter 2), or a star like James Cagney of Warner Bros. (Chapter 3), identifies and extends the corporation's career. The studios' agents are therefore not only mechanisms for the continued production of corporate allegories but also Empsonian close readers, astute interpreters of those messages.[17]

Classical Hollywood, American Modernism proceeds from this insight, identifying and interpreting the ambiguous address of Hollywood films (a literary reading of the movies) while also construing the same ambiguity in literature written by authors working and living within the studio system. Because the studio system is a social field in which flesh-and-blood individuals and corporations vie discursively for prestige and power, both Hollywood pictures and the fictions of industry personnel, from *Dinner at Eight* to William Faulkner's *Absalom, Absalom!*, from Selznick's *A Star is Born* to Horace McCoy's *I Should Have Stayed Home*, may be interpreted as deep texts of the movie colony in conversation with each other. Taking this approach as its ground, *Classical Hollywood, American Modernism* offers two contributions to the study of the studio system's history. First, through readings of these deep texts, this book plots the arc of the system by examining how three studios, Paramount, MGM, and Twentieth Century-Fox, leveraged different ideas of and relations to literature and the idea of literariness in order to stake a claim to leadership of the industry. Because these efforts exerted pressure on and motivated responses from writers, this book also argues that developments in literary style and form constitute events in the history of Hollywood.

Modernism

At the same time, these developments in literary style and form are part of the history of modernist writing as it was practiced in North America in the first half of the twentieth century.

Since 2000, scholars of modernism have begun to study the consequences of corporate personhood for literature and culture in the United States during the twentieth century. Following Walter Benn Michaels's argument that the emergence of the corporate form helped shape the epistemology and aesthetics of literary naturalism, critics such as Michael Szalay, Donal Harris, and Lisa Siraganian have analyzed the various cultural and aesthetic ramifications of the legal concept and social existence of the corporation at a time when big business came to dominate the American psychic landscape.[18] Siraganian's *Modernism and the Meaning of Corporate Persons* is especially pertinent to this study, not only because it explicitly asserts a "genetic connection" between naturalism and modernism, but also because it observes the consequences of corporate speech in the context of the most extravagant corporate speakers, the studios that began producing talkies in the late 1920s.[19] Her case study is F. Scott Fitzgerald, who worked on and off and almost wholly unsuccessfully for MGM during the decade that it dominated the industry.

Before I clarify where my thinking agrees with and departs from Siraganian's, allow me to linger on what the "modernism" in *Modernism and the Meaning of Corporate Persons* means. Readers of *Classical Hollywood, American Modernism* whose disciplinary training is in cinema and media studies may be somewhat less familiar with the array of uses of that term that have emerged under the expansive and pluralizing research program of the New Modernist Studies, a movement named and practiced predominantly by literary scholars. Where Old Modernism, following Clement Greenberg's "Towards a Newer Laocoön," emphasized "an aesthetic of pristine self-regard and hypertrophied opacity that denies the historical conditions and politics of the period," the New Modernist Studies reintroduces those conditions by privileging the myriad transformations associated with the concept of modernity.[20] Along with increased attention to literatures by underrepresented groups along the axes of gender, sexuality, race, ethnicity, and nationality, this reframing has prompted investigations of relations between different forms of media: the fine arts media of painting and sculpture; and the mass media of print, photography, phonography, radio, and perhaps most intently, film. Most intently, in part, because "film" compresses several related but distinct meanings into a single term: an audiovisual narrative form; a medium of communication and artistic creation; a set of production practices; a sociocultural field; a purveyor of cultural values; and an experience (i.e., moviegoing) comprising unique material and psychological conditions. As Steven G. Kellman implies in his survey of the multiple semantic valences at play in "the cinematic novel," the particular understanding of "film" an author, critic, or scholar privileges coordinates with their particular understanding of modernism and modernity.[21] Here are six such correspondences, briefly presented, for clarity's sake, in table form. Note that the examples I cite are more interesting and complex than the capsule form in which I present them, and that I set aside for the moment the massive subfield of adaptation studies, which has seen its own calls for extension, diversification, and renewal (Table I.1). To this table, we might add, per Christensen, "film" understood as a commodity produced by an authoring corporate person.

This plurality of approaches can be seen as a synecdoche of the New Modernist Studies itself; the richness of the resulting criticism is a warrant for continued research. In my view, however, the numerous inquiries undertaken along each line of "literature and film" have not been

Table I.1 *Conceptions of "Film" in the New Modernist Studies*

Film understood as…	Meaning in modernist studies scholarship	Uses in literary criticism
Movie	Manipulations of mise-en-scène, cinematography, editing, and sound.	Critics of modernist literature have long identified analogies between literary experimentation and filmmaking techniques, whereby formally self-conscious works emphasize their literariness by mimicking the movie-ness of movies. This form of criticism dates at least as far back as Sinclair Lewis's praise of John Dos Passos's use of the "technique of the cinema … its flashes, its cutbacks, its speed" in *Manhattan Transfer* (1925).[1]
Film (celluloid)	The photographic medium: a mechanically produced, indexical representation of the world.	Traces of attention to these features can be found at least as early as 1948 in Claude-Edmonde Magny's *The Age of the American Novel: The Film Aesthetic of Fiction Between the Two Wars*, which, in part, emphasizes the affinities between the camera's registration of external reality and objective narration.[2] Magny saw this sensibility at work most evidently in Dashiell Hammett, the master of "the aesthetics of the stenographic record," but operating in "almost every American novelist" since the end of World War I. While also concerned with the qualities of the medium, this approach to modernist writing differs from the one described above because it refers not to autotelism but rather to film-inspired writing's fitness to the purpose of representing contemporary life. Magny explains the modernism (though she doesn't use the term) of American fiction by way of contrast to continental literature: "French writers too often give us an image of modern life as incongruous as a daguerreotype of a skyscraper would be."[3]
Filmmaking	Writers' engagements with the industry in the form of the sale of subsidiary rights or employment, either by the studios or in the para-industry of journalism.	Scholars have considered these conditions with respect to (a) endorsing, combatting, or modifying the Hollywood-the-destroyer myth, whereby authorial careers are ruined by contact with philistine film production, and/or (b) treating modernist writers as artist-critics whose formal difficulties derive from, resist, and criticize the Culture Industry.[4]

Table 1.1 (cont.)

Film understood as…	Meaning in modernist studies scholarship	Uses in literary criticism
The movie colony	A variant of "Filmmaking." Writers who participated in film production also observed and participated in the culture of the highly ordered social world of the Hollywood community, resulting in fictions set in, and often disdainful of, the industry.	Numerous studies of authors' experiences working as screenwriters in the 1930s and 1940s offer accounts of fiction set in or about Hollywood. Some of the best works of this kind, such as Walter Wells's *Tycoons and Locusts: A Regional Look at Hollywood Fiction of the 1930s* (1973), have construed these narratives as allegories of impending national dissolution amidst the poverty of the Depression and the yet more general havoc wrought by industrial modernity.[5]
Hollywood cultural values	The qualities and values—from story types to star personae—that Hollywood movies purvey.	From this vantage, the industry's myth-making elucidates the epistemological and aesthetic investments of modernists, as when, in Mark Goble's study of Gertrude Stein's "social poetics," the numerous cameo appearances that comprise *The Autobiography of Alice B. Toklas* are juxtaposed with the galaxy of stars in MGM's *Grand Hotel* (Edmund Goulding, 1932).[6]
Moviegoing	The experience of spectatorship within a given *dispositif*; the conjunction of cultural, economic, ideological, social, and technological conditions that comprise the situations of filmmaking and viewership.[7]	"Modernism" here can be understood in two ways: either as a form of transgression of norms, as when, in *Native Son* (1940), Richard Wright depicts Bigger Thomas masturbating in a movie theater, or as an analogy for a formal principle, as when Jonathan Foltz reads the impersonality of Henry Green's narration alongside the novelist's reflections on dissolving into a cinema audience.[8]

[1] Sinclair Lewis, "Manhattan at Last!," *Saturday Review of Literature*, December 5, 1924, 361. For discussions of Lewis's analogy, see, for instance, Gretchen Foster, "John Dos Passos' Use of Film Technique in *Manhattan Transfer* and *The 42nd Parallel*," *Literature/Film Quarterly* 14, no. 3 (1986): 186–194; David Seed, *Cinematic Fictions: The Impact of the Cinema on American Fiction up to World War II* (Liverpool, UK: Liverpool University Press, 2009), 128–150; and Alix Beeston, *In and Out of Sight: Modernist Writing and the Photographic Unseen* (Oxford, UK and New York: Oxford University Press, 2018), 108–146.

[2] Claude-Edmonde Magny, *The Age of the American Novel: The Film Aesthetic of Fiction between the Two World Wars*, trans. Eleanor Hochman (New York: Frederick Ungar Publishing Company, 1972 [1948]), 39.

3   Magny, *American Novel*, 40, 38.
4   On William Faulkner: John T. Matthews, "Faulkner and the Culture Industry," *The Cambridge Companion to William Faulkner*, ed. Philip M. Weinstein (New York and Cambridge, UK: Cambridge University Press, 1995), 51–74; Richard Godden and Pamela Knights, "Forget Jerusalem, Go to Hollywood—'To Die. Yes. To Die': (A Coda to *Absalom, Absalom!*)," in Richard Godden, *Fictions of Labor: William Faulkner and the South's Long Revolution* (Cambridge, UK and New York: Cambridge University Press, 1997), 179–232; Peter Lurie, *Vision's Immanence: Faulkner, Film, and the Popular Imagination* (Baltimore: Johns Hopkins University Press, 2005). On Nathanael West: Rita Barnard, *The Great Depression and the Culture of Abundance: Kenneth Fearing, Nathanael West, and Mass Culture in the 1930s* (New York and Cambridge, UK: Cambridge University Press, 1995); Richard Keller Simon, "Between Capra and Adorno: West's *The Day of the Locust* and the Movies of the 1930s," *Modern Language Quarterly* 54, no. 4 (December 1993): 513–544; and William Solomon, *Literature, Amusement, and Technology in the Great Depression* (Cambridge, UK and New York: Cambridge University Press, 2002), 140–177. Early traces of the Hollywood-the-destroyer criticism can be found in Edmund Wilson's seminal study *The Boys in the Back Room: Notes on California Novelists* (San Francisco: The Colt Press, 1941). In *Some Time in the Sun* (1976), Tom Dardis seeks to revise what he calls this "most commonly held assumption that all the time they [i.e., Agee, Faulkner, Fitzgerald, Huxley, and West] spent in Hollywood was lost, wasted time," by taking a more charitable view of the screenwriting work itself as well as the literary work produced during their stints at the studios (Dardis, *Some Time in the Sun* (New York: Penguin, 1981 [1976]), 9). Neither as dismal as Wilson nor Pollyannaish as Dardis, Tom Cerasulo's *Authors Out Here* studies the careers of Fitzgerald, Dorothy Parker, Budd Schulberg, and West with a more explicit eye on institutions—the studio, the publishing industry, the Screen Writers' Guild. Tom Cerasulo, *Authors Out Here: Fitzgerald, West, Parker, and Schulberg in Hollywood* (Columbia: University of South Carolina Press, 2010). See also Richard Fine, *West of Eden: Writers in Hollywood, 1928–1940* (Washington, D.C. and London: Smithsonian Institution Press, 1993), and Ian Hamilton, *Writers in Hollywood, 1915–1951* (New York: Harper, 1990).
5   See also Geneva Gano, "Nationalist Ideologies and New Deal Regionalism in *The Day of the Locust*," *Modern Fiction Studies* 55, no. 1 (Spring 2009): 42–67. Generally, works of criticism in the "movie colony" mode focus on the genre of the Hollywood novel; these range from Jonas Spatz's *Hollywood in Fiction* (1969) to Bruce Chipman's *Into America's Dream-Dump: A Postmodern Study of the Hollywood Novel* (1999), John Parris Springer's *Hollywood Fictions: The Dream Factory in American Popular Literature* (2000), and Chip Rhodes's *Politics, Desire, and the Hollywood Novel* (2008). A slightly different species of studies takes a somewhat broader approach, surveying works by authors who had spent time at the studios; novels like James M. Cain's *The Postman Always Rings Twice* would, for instance, fall in this second, broader group. Studies in this lineage include David Fine's *Imagining Los Angeles: A City in Fiction* (2000) and *The Cambridge Companion to the Literature of Los Angeles* (2010).
6   Goble, *Beautiful Circuits*, 85–148.
7   For an elaboration of the value of a genealogical approach to cinematic *dispositifs* that updates and revitalizes the "apparatus theory" developed in the 1970s, see Thomas Elsaesser, "The Cinematic Dispositif (Between Apparatus Theory and Artists' Cinema)," in *Film History as Media Archaeology: Tracking Digital Cinema* (Amsterdam: Amsterdam University Press, 2011), 101–136.
8   Jonathan Foltz, *The Novel after Film: Modernism and the Decline of Autonomy* (New York and Oxford, UK: Oxford University Press, 2017), 135–166.

synthesized according to a logic more refined than that of abstract competition between media (e.g., the death of the novel at the hands of film) or of grand economic transformation (e.g., the cultural logics of capitalism in its different phases). Miriam Hansen's vernacular modernism thesis, which rebuts *The Classical Hollywood Cinema* by construing the "entwine[ment of the] concepts of modernity and aesthetic modernism in an *institutionally specific mode*," furnishes the theory necessary for that synthesis.[22] By denying Bordwell, Staiger, and Thompson's cognitivist understanding of the normative viewer and introducing exhibition and reception into an analysis of the industry, Hansen reconceives the American cinema as one that achieved success "not because of its presumably universal narrative form but because it meant different things to different people and publics, both at home and abroad." As the products of an industry founded by immigrants attempting to sell images to a nation of immigrants, Hollywood movies, more ably than any other artform, "mediat[ed] competing cultural discourses on modernity and modernization ... because [they] articulated, multiplied, and globalized a particular historical experience"—all, I would add, while selling "Hollywood."[23] Hansen's Classical Hollywood, extant from the 1920s through the 1950s, is thus a congeries of institutions, internally organized and desirous of autonomy from local, national, and foreign governments and other forms of geopolitical interference, yet operating according to a capitalist logic that required sensitivity to markets of every conceivable scale. In her conception, it was Hollywood's institutional organization, its status as a quintessentially modern industry mediating and disseminating a quintessentially modern experience, that gave rise to its worldwide hegemony.

Following Hansen's reframing of Classical Hollywood, when I take up the issue of MGM's corporate authorship in Chapter 2, I do so not only to emphasize the corporation's presence in the modernist literary imagination, as Siraganian does, but also to understand how the studio leveraged its particular persona, and specifically its "voice," to position itself as the leader of the industry in the wake of the transition to sound cinema. Fitzgerald, like just about everyone else within and outside of Hollywood, understood MGM as a corporation apart—*primus inter pares* reigning under the banner *Ars Gratia Artis*. How did *that* bear on the writers working within its unique screenwriting system, instituted by Thalberg, the model for Fitzgerald's tragic hero Monroe Stahr? I'll attempt to answer that question through readings of fiction by Fitzgerald, Aldous Huxley, and William Faulkner. I see their MGM-era works as syntheses of a neo-naturalist critique of corporate personhood and a modernist self-consciousness that each author devised in response to the way the studio made movies, how it exceeded and contained its geniuses, and how it continued to make and tell stories after those geniuses passed through (or, in the cases of Thalberg and Fitzgerald, away).[24]

The larger point I want to make, however, is that all of the concepts drawn from cinema and media studies that I'll consider—transmedial possibility (Chapter 1), corporate authorship (Chapter 2), industrial reflexivity (Chapters 3 and 5), and vernacular modernism (Chapter 4)—should be seen as in play in each chapter. I isolate them both to demonstrate the particular hermeneutic value of this or that theoretical coinage and to indicate novel concerns that arose within the industry over the course of its trajectory, as new challenges arose and studios took turns as self-nominated leaders. Thus, Chapter 1 tells the literary history of how Paramount came to dominate American film by leveraging moving picture rights, and how that legal novelty gave birth to transmedial possibility, the capacity of and motivation for authors to consider the filmic afterlives of their fiction at the moment of composition. Movie rights never cease to matter to authors; indeed, in our era of intellectual property-driven cinematic universes, they matter more than ever. But with the transition to sound, and the ascension of MGM, the emergent issue of corporate voice moves to the fore. Industry-wide concerns may, however, take precedence over studio-specific ones. Hence Chapter 3 focuses on Hollywood's coordinated attempt, in the late 1930s, to win back its audiences by pushing a narrative of industrial and aesthetic maturity, captured in the slogan "Motion Pictures' Greatest Year." Similarly, the onset of World War II forced the studio system to manage its global presence in new ways, not least in having to adjust to the closing of European markets and having to accommodate the Office of War Information's oversight, "the most systematic governmental effort to regulate content that has been seen in any American medium of popular culture."[25] Finally, Chapter 5 returns to the concept of industrial reflexivity in order to analyze the studio system's late-1940s attempt to shore itself against ruinous antitrust action, political witch hunting, and medium obsolescence under the self-consciously historicist slogan "Movies are Better than Ever."

In brief, then, I argue over this book's five chapters that several varieties of the North American transformation of the Anglo-European avant-garde's aesthetic preoccupations and formal strategies occurred not only alongside exposure to the medium of cinema and to popular literature about the movies, but specifically among the evolving emphases of the studio system: that is, under the sign of Hollywood.

A Great Superfeature

To get a sense of how this book's approach illuminates the dark corners that remain in modernist studies, consider that one of the most comprehensive visual documents of 1920s American and European intellectual and artistic interchange, Ralph Barton's short film *Camille: or, The Fate of a Coquette* (1926), has hidden from scholars in plain sight as a special feature on a set of Charlie Chaplin DVDs and subsequently on YouTube.[26] The creation of this unburied treasure began with requests for participation like this one, from Barton to H.L. Mencken, the preeminent American cultural critic at the time, in late December 1926: "We are filming ... a great superfeature production of *Camille* with Anita in the title rôle and with a cast which includes well-known film stars, the Queen of Romania, the Sultan of Morocco and the Mayor of New York.... You must be in it. Your part is all written and experts predict a great future for you."[27] The "we" comprises Anita Loos, the film scenario writer, playwright, and author of the best-selling novel *Gentlemen Prefer Blondes: The Illuminating Diary of a Professional Lady* (1925), and Barton, the illustrator of *Blondes* and a prominent figure among the East Coast literati. Barton's seemingly hyperbolic and tongue-in-cheek description of his cast in fact undersells the number and the range of leading lights who participated in his thirty-three-minute home movie adaptation of Alexandre Dumas *fils*'s *La Dame aux camélias*.[28] Although the Queen of Romania and the Mayor of New York are regrettably absent from the production, the list of dramatis personae does include Americans such as Paul Robeson, Sinclair Lewis, Theodore Dreiser, Sherwood Anderson, Clarence Darrow, Alfred A. Knopf, the director Rex Ingram, and various actors including Richard Barthelmess, Dorothy Gish, Aileen Pringle, and Patsy Ruth Miller[29]; Englishmen Charlie Chaplin, W. Somerset Maugham, and actor Robert Young; French artists including Paul Claudel, Bernard Boutet de Monvel, and Yvonne Printemps; the German theatrical producer Max Reinhardt; the Russian conductor Serge Koussevitzky; the Hungarian actress Lili Darvas; and, though briefly and surely unknowingly, the Sultan of Morocco (Figure I.1).[30] As Barton's letter indicates, Loos plays the titular Camille; she is the center of gravity powerful enough to order a galaxy of stars so large and luminous as to make even the glitziest studio gawk. She could occupy that central position because she commanded respect in the fields of both American film and American literature, having, on the one hand, won the admiration of D. W. Griffith and cowritten numerous successful scenarios with her husband John Emerson, and, on the other, authored *Blondes*, which earned

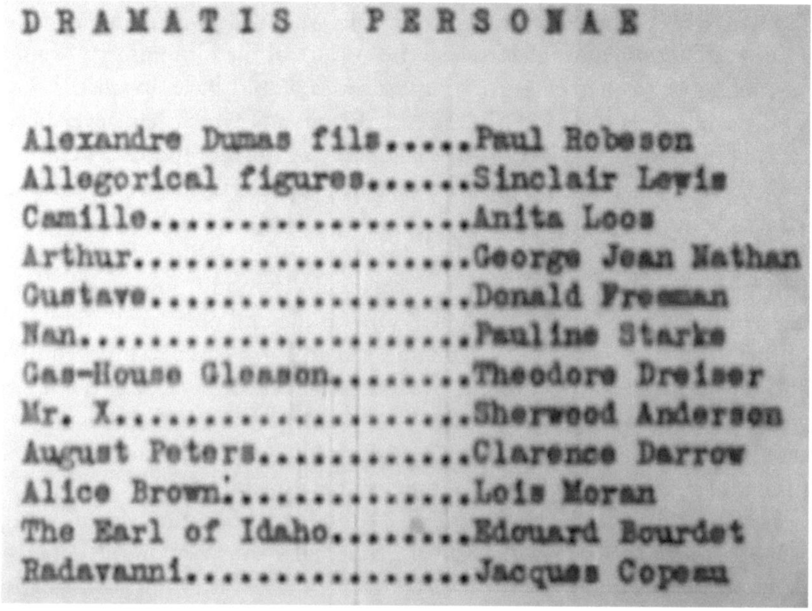

```
DRAMATIS         PERSONAE


Alexandre Dumas fils......Paul Robeson
Allegorical figures.......Sinclair Lewis
Camille...................Anita Loos
Arthur....................George Jean Nathan
Gustave...................Donald Freeman
Nan.......................Pauline Starke
Gas-House Gleason.........Theodore Dreiser
Mr. X.....................Sherwood Anderson
August Peters.............Clarence Darrow
Alice Brown...............Lois Moran
The Earl of Idaho.........Edouard Bourdet
Radavanni.................Jacques Copeau
```

Figure I.1 Dramatis Personae of *Camille: or, the Fate of a Coquette* (Ralph Barton, 1926), title card one of four

high praise from William Faulkner, James Joyce, and Edith Wharton (the last of whom, however wryly, called it "the great American novel").[31]

As in *Camille*, which Loos cowrote with Barton and which features intertitles in both English and French, the horizon of *Gentlemen Prefer Blondes* (1925) extends beyond the geographic bounds of the United States. Beautiful, naïve, tossing off malapropisms, Loos's Lorelei Lee sets sail, courtesy of her suitor Mr. Eisman, for the cultural capitals of Europe where she will "broaden out and improve [her] writing."[32] London, to Lorelei, is nothing compared to New York; Paris is "devine" because "the French are devine [sic]," presumably because their customs agents wear gold braids and can be shut up for five francs (*GPB* 51); Munich, "very full of art, which they call 'kunst' … is very, very educational" (*GPB* 81); Vienna offers a meeting with "Dr. Froyd" (*GPB* 88–90) and a trip to the Prater, which "is really devine because it is just like Coney Island but at the same time it is in the woods" (*GPB* 92). After all that education, though, Lorelei returns to the States, where the happiest possible ending could take place: a marriage to the wealthy and genteel Mr. Spofford, who provides the financial backing for films that she will produce and co-author with the writer H. Gilbertson Montrose, and in which she will star. *Blondes* is a satire, of course, and the idea that the culture of the film industry would be preferable to that of Europe's great cities would have appalled Loos, who proudly "belonged to the elite of the cinema which has never been fond of Hollywood."[33] But the dismal quality of the film industry's culture isn't the only or even the most important point Loos makes. By putting Hollywood up against New York, London, Paris, Munich, and Vienna, she demonstrates a truth that lies at the core of this study: for better or (from Loos's vantage) probably for worse, Hollywood's power and allure are world-shaping forces. As Lorelei notes at the end of her narrative, "all of the Society people in New York and Philadelphia came to my wedding and they were all so sweet to me, because practically every one of them has written a senario [*sic*]" (*GPB* 121). (One can argue, as I will in Chapter 1, that *Blondes* itself was something of a proto-senario, and that Loos was a master of maximizing literature's transmedial possibility.)

Hollywood inflects the world of Barton and Loos's movie in many senses. Ironically, Dumas *fils*'s tale of a tubercular courtesan in the Parisian demimonde became a favorite source text for the industry during the early days of the feature film and the height of the Progressive-era sanitization and embourgeoisement of the movies. Between 1915 and 1926, four studios adapted the novel, the most recent of which starred Loos's dear friend Norma Talmadge. Like Lorelei, who planned to produce her movies with the help of her husband, Talmadge made *Camille* with her own husband, Joseph Schenck, with whom she established the Norma Talmadge Film Company; critics found the modernized, bowdlerized version of the story forgettable save for Talmadge's magnetic screen presence. For Norma, *Camille* was an opportunity to display herself and her autonomy—to speak, as it were, through her company's pictures—at a time when stars typically worked under long-term contracts, a norm that contributed significantly to the studio system's stability. In her own film, Loos could pay homage to her pal and at the same time claim authorship apart from her unproductive but fragile-egoed husband John Emerson, with whom she had habitually deigned to accept co-authorship credit.

This "superfeature," with star power enough to match high-wattage backstage pictures like *A Trip to Paramountown* (Jack Cunningham, Paramount, 1922) or its remake *Hollywood* (James Cruze, Paramount, 1923), could best the industry at its own game. But where those movies sought to recuperate the image of a Paramount studio rocked by a series of scandals, Barton and Loos joyfully flouted the industry's attempts to achieve respectability. Much of the content of their *Camille* directly contradicts the

Figure I.2 Charlie Chaplin, channeling Oscar Wilde and Alla Nazimova. *Camille: or, the Fate of a Coquette* (Ralph Barton, 1926)

wishes of Will H. Hays, the head of the MPPDA, who in 1924 issued The Formula, the first version of what would become the infamous Production Code in 1930. That the film essentially portrays a boozy bacchanal, replete with frank depictions of forbidden sexuality and desire, marks it as a work in direct opposition to acceptable Hollywood fare. *Camille*'s centerpiece presents Chaplin, then the world's biggest star, impersonating Salomé in drag, a reference to both Oscar Wilde and Alla Nazimova, whose rendition of the Biblical antiheroine in 1923 preceded the moral crackdown. Chaplin bests his forebears in synthesizing the movie's various transgressions in a single gesture, making love to the severed head of Jokanaan played superbly by a cocktail shaker (Figure I.2). As the movie's indecorous images sought to shock the sensibility promoted by Hays, so, in another sense, does its editing: an extended montage of poorly lit closeups with vignettes of chaotic New York, a tip of the hat perhaps to Paul Strand and Charles Sheeler's avant-garde city symphony *Manhatta* (1921). Loos and Barton would transfer the drunken carousing of *Camille* more or less directly to *But Gentlemen Marry Brunettes* (1928), the sequel to *Blondes*, in which Lorelei's raven-haired foil

"So finally all the geniuses were present and the way the conversation worked out was remarkable."

Figure I.3   Anita Loos, *But Gentlemen Marry Brunettes*, New York: Penguin 1998 [1928], 138

Dorothy goes to meet the "High Brows"—"H.L. Mencken, Theadore Dreiser, Sherwood Anderson, Sinclare Lewis, Joseph Hergesheimer, and Ernest Boyd"—at "a literary party that was being held by George Jean Nathan at a place in Jersey that is noted for serving the kind of beer that is made without ether" (Figure I.3).[34]

No less remarkable is the film's frame narration. At a time when Black men and women were and would continue to be caricatured as shuffling help or comic relief, *Camille* begins with the radiant face of Robeson, playing Dumas *fils* in a nod to the author's racially mixed heritage. A Rutgers valedictorian, bass-baritone singer, All-American football player, and theatrical actor—a renaissance man if there ever was one—Robeson had only appeared onscreen once before, playing two roles in Oscar Micheaux's *Body and Soul* (1925). Robeson wouldn't act in another movie until 1930 when he starred in *Borderline*, a story of an interracial love triangle in an Alpine town written and directed by Kenneth Macpherson and involving H.D. and Bryher, the three members of the

Figure I.4   Paul Robeson as Alexandre Dumas *fils* in *Camille: or, the Fate of a Coquette* (Ralph Barton, 1926)

avant-garde Pool Group that created the seminal modernist film criticism magazine *Close Up*. Where the more famous *Borderline* presents Robeson's hands as aesthetic objects unto themselves, allowed only to gleam and, once, ball into a hurling fist, *Camille* not only puts them to aesthetic work but also allows them to work themselves, that is, to produce art; Robeson plays the humanist artist-genius he was and could not be in a Hollywood production (Figure I.4). With an early intertitle that reads "His inspired pen dealt out to us even as the player deals out cards—all the elements that control the Destiny of Man," the film celebrates the abilities of Dumas *fils* and Robeson, but it also, in hindsight, points up an ugly truth about the institutional absence of Black talent among the ranks of Hollywood's writers, and therefore of the relative lack of attention to Black authors in this study. That absence will be only partially ameliorated in this book's final passages, when I turn to the writings of James Baldwin and Ralph Ellison. There I will suggest that, through their trenchant criticisms of Hollywood's racist projections and their remarkable figurations of the movies in their fiction, Baldwin and

Ellison join an array of authors whose works mark the end of the eras of both Classical Hollywood and American Modernism.[35]

This is finally to say that this literary history of the studio system is ambivalent about Hollywood's effects but absolutely clear on its power. In this regard, it is much like Loos herself and the *Camille* she made. In its queer sexuality and celebration of dipsomania, its empowerment of a Black actor onscreen and a diminutive female screenwriter-cum-novelist off, Barton and Loos's adaptation of Dumas *fils*'s 1848 novel resists contemporary industry trends; its unabashed emphasis on star power and ability to unite citizens of the world through montage, on the other hand, couldn't be more Hollywood. But whether aligning or resisting, the film takes the protocols of the studio system as a baseline. Like *Blondes* and *Brunettes*, *Camille*, a synecdoche of the cultural field at the height of the Modernist moment, would not have existed as it does without Hollywood, the force shaping all of this home movie's features. Simply put, the studio system is, for all three works, a superfeature.

Observing the functions of that superfeature and the literary forms that follow is the work of the pages to come.

CHAPTER 1

Paramount Pictures and Transmedial Possibility

> Have you noticed the trend of recent literature? ... More and more plots are being written *with the movies in mind*. Authors are becoming canny. Why not kill three birds with one rock, they say, as they proceed to write with the serial rights, the book rights, and last but not least the *movie rights* in mind.
> —William Lord Wright, *Hints for Scenario Writers*, 1919[1]

Near the end of *Manhattan Transfer* (1925), John Dos Passos introduces a hex of a character into the charmed lives of the Merivale family, cousins of protagonist Jimmy Herf. It's of course too late in the narrative to introduce such an important figure, but that lateness is precisely the point. The Merivales, comfortable and conservative upper-middle class Manhattanites, have no real idea how to make sense of Jack Cunningham, a new kind of man: a publicity man for Paramount Pictures. Patriarch James "hope[s] he's as good a fellow as he seems to be," but the properly attuned reader knows that the Merivales have little more than hope.[2] The conversation between James and his wife begins with a discussion of Paramount's fortunes:

> The diningroom smelled of toast and coffee and the New York *Times*. The Merivales were breakfasting to electric light. Sleet beat against the windows. "Well Paramount's fallen off five points more," said James from behind the paper.
> "Oh James I think its horrid to be such a tease," whined Maisie who was drinking her coffee in little henlike sips.
> "And anyway," said Mrs. Merivale, "Jack's not with Paramount any more. He's doing publicity for the Famous Players."
> "He's coming east in two weeks. He says he hopes to be here for the first of the year."
> "Did you get another wire Maisie?"

> Maisie nodded. "Do you know James, Jack never will write a letter. He always telegraphs," said Mrs. Merivale through the paper at her son.
> "He certainly keeps the house choked up with flowers," growled James from behind the paper.
> "All by telegraph," said Mrs. Merivale triumphantly.

The bourgeois sophistication indicated by the electric light and the *Times* stock report heightens, by contrast, the family's ignorance of the fact that the Famous Players-Lasky Corporation (FPL) and Paramount Pictures were one and the same; in 1919, the company boasted that it was the only studio whose shares were publicly traded on the New York Stock Exchange.[3] The Merivales' confusion is especially meaningful given that, in the years leading up to *Manhattan Transfer*'s publication, FPL and its founders Adolph Zukor and Jesse Lasky had consistently and notoriously appeared in the paper of record for malfeasances both professional and personal. Beginning with a substantial writeup in September 1921 and followed by blow-by-blow reportage of the hearings from November 1922 to July 1923, the *Times* chronicled the federal government's antitrust suit against the corporation, a situation that would have appealed to Dos Passos, a leftist intellectual (at the time) and illegitimate son of a pro-trust corporate lawyer. More interesting to the general public, however, might have been the numerous scandals plaguing the company: Fatty Arbuckle's arrest and trial for manslaughter following the death of Virginia Rappe; Wallace Reid's death from complications related to morphine addiction; the Boston-area roadhouse spree attended by Zukor and Lasky that resulted in attempts by the Massachusetts District Attorney to extort $100,000 to drop charges; and the suicide of actress Zelda Crosby after "being jilted by a motion picture director" that, as film historian Mark Lynn Anderson has noted, "was widely known to have been Zukor."[4] All of this is to say that behind the apparent difference between the two companies lies a continuity that the Merivales don't understand.

Dos Passos's reference to Paramount conjures not only the infamy of its executives' salacious behavior; the fact that the corporation maintained a multimillion-dollar production facility in Astoria since 1921 and its headquarters in Times Square since 1922; or even Paramount's reputation as the biggest and best studio in the American film industry, with Zukor having "established the first principles of the studio system."[5] It also calls forth the fact that Paramount, more than any other film producer since Zukor's and Lasky's respective entrances into the industry, was famous for purchasing the rights to works of drama and literature. Indeed, the company proudly claimed this superlative as it flaunted both its unparalleled stable of past and present literary and dramatic talent, and the way it treated those authors' works. "Because writers know that this company can give to their works an ideal production," the studio boasted in its autobiographical *The Story of the Famous Players-Lasky Corporation*,

> they are enthusiastic rather than hesitant about selling them.
>
> Sir J. M. Barrie first reached the screen through this company. So did Maurice Maeterlinck. Other great authors whose works have been screened by the company are Hall Caine, Louisa M. Alcott, Robert W. Chambers, Edward Sheldon, Booth Tarkington, William J. Locke, Sir Gilbert Parker, Henry Arthur Jones, Granville Barker, David Graham Phillips, Rupert Hughes, Edgar Selwyn, Mark Twain, Charles Dickens, Mrs. Humphrey Ward, Elinor Glyn, and hundreds of others.
>
> No good story is ever passed by because there is no present need for it. It is the policy of the production department to buy options on the best of the world's material, for the organization has the facilities and the individuals for the perfect presentation of any kind of subject.[6]

By the 1920s, Paramount was so powerful and, thanks to its accumulation of theaters, so pervasive, and its reputation as an additional and robust source of income for writers so secure, that a self-consciously literary novelist like F. Scott Fitzgerald could tell his agent, "I must try some love stories with more action this time. I'm going to try to write three that'll do for Famous-Players [sic] as well as for the [*Saturday Evening*] *Post*."[7]

Both Paramount's investment in literary properties and Fitzgerald's hopeful accommodation of the studio's desires are, if not generally known, then certainly easy to grasp in light of our familiarity with the "adaptation industry," Simone Murray's term for the complex of literary agents, book fairs, film festivals, and prizes that supports contemporary transmedial convergence culture.[8] But the adaptation industry has not always existed; it was fundamental neither to the origins of filmmaking in the mid-1890s nor even to the "cinema of narrative integration," Tom Gunning's term for the mode of storytelling cinema that replaced the spectacle-oriented "cinema of attraction."[9] Rather, the adaptation industry can be understood to begin with the extension of copyright protection to motion pictures following Harper Brothers' successful suit against the Kalem company for its unauthorized 1907 adaptation of Lew Wallace's bestselling *Ben Hur: A Tale of the Christ* (1880), which, according to Peter Decherney, fundamentally changed the modus operandi of the American film industry. Before 1911, film companies had adapted works of fiction, poetry, and drama unencumbered by the law of copyright; after that point, the studios had to obtain the rights to properties before adapting them. The ruling in the case, and the 1912 Townsend Amendment to the Copyright Act of 1909 that quickly followed, enabled individual production companies to attain a monopoly on screen material, leading them to prioritize works under copyright and original ideas.[10]

Kalem Co. v. Harper Brothers (so named after Kalem's appeal was decided in Harpers' favor by the Supreme Court) spurred the rise of independent production companies like Zukor's and Lasky's, which established exclusive alliances with publishing houses and theatrical production companies, and contributed to the demise of the Motion Picture Patents Company (also known as the Edison Trust), which did not adapt well enough to the new dispensation.[11] The production and four-year legal battle over *Ben Hur* came at the start of what early cinema scholars like Charlie Keil and Shelley Stamp call the Transitional Era (1908–1917), a period that begins with the formation of the Edison Trust and concludes at the onset of the Classical Hollywood period. "No other decade in U.S. film history encompasses such broad ranging transformation," including the emergence of the multireel feature film, the establishment of continuity editing as the basis for longer and more elaborate narratives, and the exploitation of stars. The Transitional Era was also characterized by attempts to bootstrap film into cultural respectability via the production of quality films often drawn from classical literature, the replacement of store-front nickelodeons by theaters, and the disciplining of movie content and of filmgoer behavior alike.[12]

Alongside these many developments, the modern concept of the "studio" emerged in intra-industry discourse as distinct, in the words of leading *Moving Picture World* columnist W. Stephen Bush, from a "factory":

> In the plants of some manufacturers the studio seems to be more of a factory. In a factory, "goods, wares and merchandise are produced by mechanical process or the skill of the human hand." In the studio, art is the dominant factor. Either the studio is built for the factory or the factory is made for the studio. As soon as the making of pictures is reduced to a more or less mechanical function, art flees from the studio and the result is a film which just reaches the level of the "nickel-in-the-slot" standard.[13]

For Bush and even more so for his colleague Louis Reeves Harrison, who penned a series of profiles entitled "Studio Saunterings," the word "studio" began to perform two contradictory but equally essential functions. First, it described the complex interaction of corporate organization, technology, and aesthetic sensibility; and second, it identified a brand, occluding the business of production and fostering a belief in a consistent and unique sense of value for easy identification and consumption.[14] In Catherine Kerr's estimation, Zukor, above all others, "succeeded in combining the new film aesthetic with a coordinated corporate structure." While Kerr attributes Zukor's ascendance to his investment in stars (the advertised "Famous Players"), her argument that his studio spearheaded the shift "from an undifferentiated volume output offered by competitive firms to a highly differentiated consumer product" works just as well for copyrighted source material (the advertised "Famous Plays"), since the exploitation of a star and a story each depends on the exclusive control of a property.[15] Where the Edison Trust based its power in the accrual of hardware patents, the independents, led by Zukor and Lasky, depended on brand uniqueness along the vectors of story, star, and style. If Paramount established the first principles of the studio system, one of those principles was that film production existed within a competitive media ecology dependent on the adaptation of literature. The protection of motion picture rights is therefore among the best indices of the moment when the studios became "the studios," the necessary precondition of the emergence of a studio system (Figure 1.1).

However, the influence of *Kalem* and subsequent cases and legislation was yet more widely felt, as the emergence of copyright protection for motion pictures contributed to a profound transformation in the economic, institutional, and aesthetic constitution of the literary field. The burgeoning hegemony of narrative cinema, which led to the emergence and then dominance of the feature film, created a practically insatiable need for story material. Scenario writing departments at film studios soon followed, as Janet Staiger has demonstrated, thus giving rise to the profession of the scenario writer.[16] At the same time, film adaptation became a financial boon for writers of novels, short stories, serials, and plays.[17] The lure of this new source of income brought with it the threat of mistreatment by the legal counsels of publishers and production companies. The Authors' League of America formed in 1912 to support writers in their negotiations with the businesses, including film companies, that exploited their work. The inaugural issue of the Authors' League's *Bulletin* alerted its constituents to the new world *Kalem* opened: "Moving-pictures," the warning read, "in their relation to authorship may not sound particularly interesting or important to those fiction writers who are not given to writing plays, if there be any such. But that is because most authors do not realize the future significance of recent developments in this rapidly growing infant industry."[18] Arthur C. Train, the League's general counsel, continued this discussion in the *Bulletin*'s next issue, speculating that

Figure 1.1 Famous Players emphatically announcing its ownership of the rights to George Du Maurier's bestseller *Trilby* (1894)
Source: *Moving Picture World*, April 19, 1913

dramatic rights and moving-picture rights would henceforth count as separate properties subject to assignment by the holder of copyright.[19] His hunch proved accurate less than a year later, in February 1914, when Judge Learned Hand of the US District Court in the Southern District of New York issued his opinion in *Photo Drama Motion-Picture Co., Inc.* v. *Social Uplift Film Corporation*:

> A man having general statutory dramatic rights ... might make a publication, or he might copyright the play, and he would still not have copyrighted or published his moving-picture rights. If he wrote such a scenario and made his film, he could get a separate copyright upon that. Of course, he could sell his statutory or common law copyright of the play and keep the moving-picture copyright, or he could sell each. It seems to me clear that if he could do this, he could sell separately the right to make a moving-picture

play, dividing his statutory dramatizing rights and thus giving each assignee the right when he had exercised those rights to get his own copyright for a drama or for a moving-picture show.[20]

On January 12, 1915, Judge Emile Henry Lacombe of the Second Circuit Court of Appeals upheld Hand's decision: "If a book can be copyrighted; if a drama giving the story of the book can be copyrighted; if a moving picture showing such story pictorially also can be copyrighted, then each of these copyrights can be separately assigned and must be recorded to avail of the constructive notice which the section [i.e., Section 44 of the Copyright Law] contemplates."[21] Hand and Lacombe thus established the condition for fiction writers to imagine the possibility of adaptation when they conceived their work. With the full panoply of rights now available—book publication, serialization, dramatic, and, crucially, motion picture—writers were in a position to write with the movies in mind. That is, for the first time on a large scale, authors could imagine the afterlives of their fiction at the moment of composition.

The newfound ability of writers to determine the distribution of rights to their works after *Kalem* led to the widespread consideration of what I would call the *transmedial possibility* of literary fiction: its capacity to be "translated" into other forms. Transmedial possibility names a quality distinct from adaptability, though both concepts concern the adaptation of a work. "Adaptability" describes a studio prerogative: Film studios determine the adaptability of a work by buying the rights to it and turning it into a movie, thereby "[converting] the cultural capital of the novel [or other work of fiction] back into the economic capital of a successful motion picture."[22] Transmedial possibility, on the other hand, describes an anticipatory position taking into account both expectations of adaptation and bids for either literary popularity or prestige. The concept I develop here should be understood as a means to integrate textualist and sociological approaches to adaptation, a desideratum repeated frequently in film studies over the past forty years.[23] In theoretical terms, transmedial possibility nuances and complements Jay David Bolter and Richard Grusin's influential theory of remediation, a "representation of one medium in another."[24] According to Bolter and Grusin, media interactions are understood by a logic of response and antagonism, a logic that therefore misses the way works in one medium anticipate and potentially accommodate uptake by works in another.[25] Moreover, because their remediation is conceived in a McLuhanite abstract sense ("the content of a medium is always another medium"), Bolter and Grusin dismiss adaptation, considering it to be "simple repurposing" where "[t]he content has been borrowed, but the medium has not been appropriated or quoted."[26] They make their distinction because they understand the representation of a medium as a special subset of the general category of representation. In a sense, they are obviously right: Depicting a television set on film is different from depicting, say, a banana or a rock. However, this conception of representation is constrained by its literalism. That is, Bolter and Grusin's theory does not account for the ability of one medium to represent another by nonliteral means, such as by allegory or manipulations of form. If we grant this possibility, then the distinction between content and medium breaks down in a way the theory of remediation does not anticipate.

In the remainder of this chapter, I will demonstrate, through the testimony of both prominent studio executives and journalists in the trade presses of both the filmmaking and literary professions, that concern for transmedial possibility in fact existed. I will then argue that the range of attitudes toward the concept can be glimpsed most clearly in Anita Loos's, Dos Passos's, and Fitzgerald's respective approaches to Paramount's drive to acquire source material.

Inventing Transmedial Possibility

After the *Photo-Drama* decision, the effects of the new adaptation regime registered on both sides of the fault line between the literary and film fields.[27] On the literary side, by 1918, film rights departments were endemic among publishers.[28] On the film side, production companies capitalized on the marketing value of famous authors as well as on the entertainment value of their works. In June 1919, Samuel Goldwyn partnered with Rex Beach, onetime president of the Authors' League and writer of popular adventure novels, to form Eminent Authors Pictures, a new arm of Goldwyn Studios with the exclusive rights to the past and future works of some of the most famous writers of the day, such as Gertrude Atherton, Mary Roberts Rinehart, Rupert Hughes, Basil King, Gouverneur Morris, and Leroy Scott.[29] Metro advertised its stable of writers as early as 1920, and FPL followed in 1921 by hiring sixteen authors of repute, including Elinor Glyn, W. Somerset Maugham, Samuel Merwin, and Gilbert Parker, to write original scenarios.[30] Warner Bros., an upstart concern in the early 1920s, made a bid for both respectability and popular success during the 1922–1923 season by embarking on a campaign called "Classics of the Screen," featuring adaptations of Sinclair Lewis's *Main Street* (1920) and F. Scott Fitzgerald's *The Beautiful and Damned* (1922), among other novels. Their promised good taste only went so far, however,

Inventing Transmedial Possibility 29

Figure 1.2 Elliott Service Company advertisement, presenting Warner Bros.' "Screen Classics" campaign (featuring F. Scott Fitzgerald)
Source: *Film Daily*, October 1, 1922

as Warners advertised "Classics of the Screen"/"Screen Classics" with a float containing enormous facsimiles of the adapted books that traveled from 42nd Street and Fifth Avenue in New York City to the West Coast (Figure 1.2).

Production companies and publishers went further than buying the rights to well-known fiction and drama by encouraging authors to render their narratives ready for the screen. In a May 13, 1919 letter to Joseph Moore, his Cosmopolitan Pictures chief financial officer, William Randolph Hearst demanded that his magazine editors "make sure that every story will be fit for moving pictures." Hearst reasoned that doing so would preclude "any question of whether a magazine story would be adaptable to moving pictures. It would be adapted not after it was written and printed *but while it was being written and before it was printed.*"[31] Whitman Bennett, production manager for FPL, similarly wrote in an October 18, 1919 letter to Charles Eyton, the general manager of the company,

> What we now seek to do is not so much to encourage authors to write originals as to encourage them to write the kind of stories and plays that will later be good film. In this we believe we are having great success. It is on this account that we feel our venture into the play producing business is already a success—we have helped managers to produce only such plays as are positively film material and thus we supply ourselves with more subjects at less cost than if we bought a few successes outright. It is on this account that we are considering the acquisition of a great publishing house—which will always consider film values when selecting books, short stories and serials for publication. The idea is to let the author express himself according to his natural inclination—in play, novel or story form—but to make it essential that his plot shall have an underlying picture value.[32]

Clearly, both production companies and publishing houses augmented the already strong economic pressure exerted on authors to prepare potentially transmedial fiction. So great was the demand to produce literature suitable for adaptation that it inspired a backlash by the Authors' League in favor of medium specificity. Even for writers of popular fiction, the perceived proscription against literariness created by the possibility of adaptation was too much to countenance. In May 1921, the Executive Committee of the Authors' League issued a resolution urging fiction writers, on aesthetic grounds, to resist selling to film companies the rights to their work. Louis Joseph Vance, the chairman of the committee, asserted:

> Writing and motion pictures are two different arts and to combine them one must be subordinated to the other. If the sale of fiction is contingent upon its moving-picture possibilities the art of fiction will suffer and perhaps be destroyed.
>
> The motion picture is an art; but it is different from the fiction story. By its very nature there is no literary form or style embodied in the picture, so if a story is written with its moving-picture possibilities in mind letters must suffer.[33]

By mid-1921, then, the literary field comprised two poles of transmedial possibility in fiction: at one pole, the purely literary, which possesses minimal transmedial potential, and at the other, the story with "picture value," ready for translation to the screen or stage.

As Whitman Bennett's letter suggests, Zukor and Lasky were at the center of such concerns; indeed, in 1920, the critic Walter Prichard Eaton singled out the company for corrupting the theater in pursuit of profit.[34] On behalf of FPL and the industry more broadly, Lasky fired back: "although we hear a great deal about the high ideals of our drama, as a whole its standards are too low for the motion picture to accept."[35] Instead of buying a publishing house in an early version of media industries synergy, as

Bennett suggested they might, Famous Players seems to have decided to limit its capital investment and follow a different path toward the same end. In 1923, the studio funded the First International Congress on Motion Pictures Arts, a two-day cosponsored event run by the Authors' League. Held in the Waldorf-Astoria Hotel in New York City on June 7 and 8, the bombastically titled conference realized FPL's desire to "[bring] writer and producer closer in their aim to improve the quality of the motion-picture play." The studio made sure, however, to stress the closeness that already existed; during one of the Congress's sessions, FPL's general production manager Robert T. Kane asserted that "25 per cent of their productions were written directly for the screen, 50 per cent were taken from novels and the other 25 were from magazine stories."[36]

As intriguing as Hearst's, Bennett's, and Vance's comments are, they offer little insight into the characteristics of literature's transmedial possibility. Bennett acknowledged the challenge of determining the influence of film adaptation on the form of prose fiction: "it is obvious that writers have ample inducement to produce books and shorter stories that have the 'film quality.' It is equally obvious that the influence of the picture, though difficult to trace definitely in specific instances, must be very great indeed." He defended his claim by explaining that, in 1919, he spent a million of Famous Players' dollars on film rights.[37] What qualifies as "film quality" (or the "picture germ," as he calls it), remained undefined. Bennett comes closest to clarifying the idea by suggesting that

> it is not the length of a story or play that determines its availability for pictures; it is the breadth of the underlying conception and the possibilities it affords for further development. A pregnant short story that is only an incident means nothing; the short story that is a slice out of life, presupposing action before and action to follow, is quite sufficient for scenario-writers to begin upon.[38]

More than anything, here Bennett seems to imply the appropriate artistic temperament toward adaptation rather than the appropriate form a source text ought to take. Given authors' grousing about the perceived butchering of their literary efforts, he sounds as though he wished to preempt consternation by indicating the need to adjust works for filming.

Slightly more thorough theorizations of the effect that authorized adaptation had on literary form can be found in various kinds of writing on the border between the film industry and the literary field: film fan magazines that ostensibly offered inside information to a general public, literary journals devoted to the business of authorship and publishing, and fiction written by authors who had either worked in Hollywood or sold their film rights to production companies. Not content merely to encourage authors to consider transmedial possibility as they wrote, William Lord Wright of *Picture-Play Magazine* enumerated how they might accommodate the studios' expectations:

> The popular novelist now writes *action*. He knows well, from dire experience, perhaps, that the movies consider action as essential and word paintings as nonessential.... Harold O'Tush, author of one of the six best sellers, disposes of the movie rights to his latest serial, which just appeared in the *Wednesday Evening Gazette*, for ten thousand ducats! The authors of the other five best sellers hear about it and rush to study Harold's serial to see just what it was that brought so fat a sum from the movies. They discovered the action was packed in, pressed down, and running over; that there was a deal of love interest; that there was business either for a young male or a young female star, as the case may have been. They see how Harold wrote his serial directly *at* the movie industry, and having done so, sat back, awaiting results which were not long in coming. And so they all pitch in and do the same thing.[39]

If writing with an eye toward the movies was a "trend" in Wright's estimation in 1919, by the end of 1920, it was, according to *The Bookman*, an established, pervasive tactic. "Some of these days," mused the columnist of "The Gossip Shop," "someone ought to write a book upon the invasion of the field of literature by the moving picture, for there has been an invasion and no one can tell what the end will be. It is a common impression nowadays that every author writes with a feeling that the moving-picture director is looking over his shoulder." To Wright's qualities of action, romance, and star potential, "The Gossip Shop" columnist adds: "characters created with a view to their presentation on the screen," dialogue that "has no other excuse for being than its use as 'cut-ins' between pictures," and "a tendency among authors to regard literature merely as a means to an end."[40] The risks were outlined by the critic Burton Rascoe: "the purely commercial writers" rendered narrative "reduced to its lowest elements of continuous action, devoid of comment, observation, and philosophic content, and stripped of the factors requiring cerebration for appreciation."[41]

Popularity versus prestige and transmedial possibility versus medium specificity are thus the coordinates of the movie-minded literary field. However, the matrix is historically contingent, for what constitutes transmedial possibility at any given moment depends on the capacities and competencies of the studios.[42] "The Gossip Shop's" proscription against dialogue, for instance, or the need to avoid subtle psychological shading, developed as a consequence of the limits of technology and technique (acting, directing, editing, etc.) during the era of silent cinema. As of 1924, the film-readiness of a book depended on its adherence to the recently instituted "Formula," a set of criteria established by the Motion Picture Producers and Distributors of America (MPPDA) that adjudicated the moral character of movie material (the Formula was a prelude to the "Don'ts and Be Carefuls" of 1927 and the Production Code of 1930). On July 19, 1924, the MPPDA, headed by Will H. Hays, passed a resolution damning the contemporary adaptation situation. It began:

> WHEREAS, the members of the Motion Picture Producers and Distributors of America, Inc., in their continuing effort "to establish and maintain the highest possible moral and artistic standards of motion picture production" are engaged in a special effort to prevent the prevalent type of book and play from becoming the prevalent type of picture; to exercise every possible care that only books or plays which are of the right type are used for screen presentation; to avoid the picturization of books or plays which can be produced only after such changes as to leave the producer subject to a charge of deception....[43]

This resolution was affirmed two days later at a special meeting of the Association of Motion Picture Producers (AMPP). M.C. Levee, president of United Studios, predicted that the Formula would dramatically affect literary production, saying:

> I believe the entire field of modern fiction will soon undergo a radical change....
>
> Authors frequently realize more money on the film rights to their books or plays than from any other source. Writers of modern fiction will very shortly begin to realize that unless their stories are without objectionable situations or themes a very lucrative avenue of revenue is closed to them.
>
> The effect of the ban on salacious material in photoplays by the producers and distributors of motion pictures, headed by Will H. Hays, is bound to react upon the field of fiction. I predict a marked change in the type of book and play which has seemed so popular during the last year, as a direct result of Mr. Hays's idea.[44]

Whether or not literary production adjusted to the Formula—though it's difficult to imagine writers not accommodating the new morality regime—in 1925, the Hays Office nonetheless succeeded in barring from the screen 160 "prevalent books and plays" whose rights would have been worth between two and three million dollars.[45]

At least as early as 1924, then, popularity did not necessarily equate to fitness for adaptation. Books written the same way—emphasizing action and romance, limiting psychological investigation and philosophical speculation—would have fared differently at the studios because of their perceived decency or indecency. Then again, moral quality or lack thereof in a given work could imply its bid for sophistication and, hence, for literary prestige. The highbrow work—the work written for a restricted audience—marked itself as such by emphasizing its literary specificity, its divergence from mainstream morality, or both, thereby resisting adaptation. Among the four possible extremes—the popular-adaptable, the popular-unadaptable, the prestigious-adaptable, and the prestigious-unadaptable—there existed a vast middle ground in which authors on the border between the film and literary fields registered in their works the tension between resistance to and invitation of adaptation.[46]

One way this tension manifested in the early and mid-1920s was in the self-conscious acknowledgment of the distinction between literature proper and a mere plot vehicle ready for film translation. For instance, in the 1924 Hollywood novel *On the Lot and Off*, George Randolph Chester and Lilian Chester, a scenario writing and directing team, put this discrimination in the voice of minor character Gifford Lane Jones, an accomplished author brought to financial precarity after suffering injuries during World War I: "A story requires a harmony of word and expression and a subtlety of thought which pictures can't use. It requires polish and finesse, and bubble! I'll get those all back soon, but in the meantime…." In the meantime, Jones looks to sell a scenario for a quick buck.[47] By featuring an aspiring producer-mogul protagonist instead of the aspiring star more typical of Hollywood fictions, and by offering keen insight into the social and financial machinations—both the backstabbing intrigue and the contractual and accounting nitty-gritty—of the industry, the Chesters formulated their work as adaptation-resistant literature. At a time when representations of Hollywood had achieved a kind of vogue among production companies—in the wake of the scandals of the early 1920s, the studios itched for positive depictions of the industry, resulting in *A Trip to Paramountown* (Jack Cunningham, Paramount, 1922), *Hollywood* (James Cruze, Paramount, 1923), *Souls For Sale* (Rupert Hughes, Goldwyn, 1923), and *Merton of the Movies* (James Cruze, Paramount, 1924)—*On the Lot and Off* was conspicuously absent from the screen.

Other novels, such as Harry Leon Wilson's *Merton of the Movies* (1922), tell stories of their protagonists' successful incorporation into the film industry as allegories of their embrace of adaptation potential. *Merton of the Movies* is the archetypal Hollywood novel: it follows a Midwestern screen hopeful named Merton Gill, who travels to Hollywood and suffers many setbacks before finally achieving success. Merton's absolute credulity leads him to be exploited by his friend Sarah Montague and the slapstick director Jeff Baird; while Merton thinks he's being filmed in serious roles, he actually stars in lowbrow comedies. Merton begins with a naïve, pseudo-highbrow sensibility and dislikes the movies of popular taste, and the novel punctures his pretensions by alerting him to his status as a straight man. *Merton* concludes, essentially, with a reconciliation with and submission to the film industry; though Merton intends to bring refinement to the movies, he ultimately accepts his position, albeit ambivalently, within the status quo of popular film. The novel pokes just enough fun at the industry to score laughs before succumbing to the industry's prerogatives. *Merton* can thus be read as an allegory of the journey to maximal transmedial possibility in its protagonist's gradual drift toward a popular sensibility, and moreover, an allegory of remarkable prescience: though respected by Gertrude Stein, *Merton of the Movies* embraced its mass appeal, transitioning smoothly from popular novel to successful play to well-reviewed, Paramount-produced film.[48]

Paramount Concerns

As I intimated in this book's Introduction, no writer had a greater command of the protocols of Hollywood film production than Anita Loos, and no writer was in a better position to devise work that both anticipated adaptation and is ironically critical of that very disposition. From the late 1910s into the 1920s, Loos and her husband John Emerson produced comedies for Paramount. Even after kissing Hollywood goodbye and heading for New York to write plays, the pair continued to contribute to numerous Paramount pictures. The play they finally produced, *The Whole Town's Talking: A Farce in Three Acts* (1923), demonstrates the canniness and ease with which competent authors incorporated Hollywood into their plots and allegorized the intended passage of their work from one medium to another. *The Whole Town's Talking* is, to riff on a famous coinage of Loos's beloved H.L. Mencken, a comedy of booboise manners on the model of *The Importance of Being Earnest*. Where Oscar Wilde's bored aristocrats go Bunburying, creating a life that imitates art by passing themselves off as different personae, Emerson and Loos's characters lie profusely to alleviate the petty pressures of the Midwestern middle class. In order to prevent his daughter Ethel from marrying Jack Shields, an insufferable, pretentious fop, and at the same time to solidify his paint business, Henry Simmons creates a backstory to entice Ethel to pursue his trusted junior partner, the sweet and awkward Chester Binney: he invents an affair between Binney and Letty Lythe, a movie star. Simmons's confabulation works too well. Lythe becomes outrageously popular in Sandusky, Ohio because of her rumored dalliance with the local boy (hence the play's title) and visits the town to meet her adoring fans, travelling with Donald Swift, her director and fiancé as well as a prizefighter. Discovering Simmons's ruse, Shields connives to get his retribution against Simmons and Binney with the help of Lythe herself, who is eager to make her naïve and jealous fiancé anxious.

From the latter half of the play's second act until its conclusion, as Simmons and Shields attempt to outmaneuver each other, the play becomes increasingly explicit in its thematization both of film production and of the ease with which ways of life can be transformed. Moments before the curtains fall, the play roasts the pugilistic Swift (and the intellectual capacity of workaday movie men more generally) by having Simmons remind the director of the morally salutary lesson of one of his own films in order to persuade him to spare Binney: "The chords of the eagle's heart melted, and a flood of forgiveness burned the barriers between them."[49] The barrier between the real world and the dream factory dissolves as roles reverse: the paint manufacturer becomes an impresario, the moving-picture director a credulous viewer. During the play's madcap conclusion, after Shields has convinced Swift to again threaten Binney, the meek junior partner becomes the savviest director of the bunch. Binney convinces Swift to fight him in the dark, which results in Shields and Swift accidentally bludgeoning each other as Binney hangs from a chandelier. This climactic scene, after which the play resolves neatly, abides formally by the dictates of the silent screen; in a play dependent on verbal dexterity, it stands out as the show's most explicitly visual moment and the only one without dialogue. Binney's triumph is the success of slapstick cinema. When Lythe asks with obvious sexual interest, "Why, Mr. Binney, did you do this?" he replies, "with an exclamation of indifference" (according to the stage directions), "Why not"?[50] Binney's indifference to what he did—it doesn't matter whether the "this" means the physical beating of the two other men or the hatching of the plan that allowed them to beat each other, since both result in his victory—is also the play's ultimate indifference to its medium. Unsurprisingly, Universal bought the rights to the play, releasing it (with or without tongue in cheek) on Boxing Day 1926.

Loos's much more famous *Gentlemen Prefer Blondes: The Illuminating Diary of a Professional Lady*, serialized in *Harper's Bazaar* before becoming a bestseller for Boni and Liveright, also played lucratively on both stage and screen. Like Wilson's Merton and the Ohioans of *The Whole Town's Talking*, *Blondes*' protagonist Lorelei Lee hails from the country's interior, in this instance Little Rock, Arkansas. Also like Merton, Lorelei is associated with the movies. Having worked on the same lot as Charlie Chaplin before her diary-narrative begins, she winds up a writer-producer-star. Just as, according to "Dr. Froyd," Lorelei is a "famous case," lacking inhibitions and dreams, *Blondes* has no hang-ups about its eventual translation into other media (*GPB* 90). Susan Hegeman is therefore exactly right when she calls *Blondes* "a literary object that seems to presuppose its replicability" and argues that "in producing the sequel and the various *Gentlemen Prefer Blondes* spin-offs that followed, Loos did what her most basic training as a screenwriter had taught her to do: to adapt material like *Gentlemen Prefer Blondes* into new usable venues."[51] Loos would in fact play a significant role in realizing the adaptation of her work: producer Edgar Selwyn hired her in 1925 to write the theatrical adaptation and Paramount not only followed suit in 1927 but moreover gave her the authority "to prepare the final scenario, select the cast, have a hand in supervising the production and then write the titles."[52] Though she distanced herself from her dumb blonde in her preface to the novel, Loos would end up as her creation's counterpart, paving the way off-screen for her professional lady Lorelei's transmedial triumph.[53]

Where Loos's writing circa 1925 can be understood as a canny instance of maximal transmedial possibility, Dos Passos's *Manhattan Transfer* comes into focus as the opposite, a work of fiction that emphasizes its literariness by mimicking film techniques and limiting its appeal to story departments. Thus, while Sinclair Lewis's comparison of the novel's style to the "flashes, cutbacks, [and] speed" of movies is well known, his more crucial observations are of *Manhattan Transfer*'s specificity as prose fiction:

> Large numbers of persons are going to say that it is the technique of the movie. But it differs from the movie in two somewhat important details. It does not deal only with the outsides of human beings; and Dos Passos does not use the technique to acquire a jazz effect, but because, when he has given the complete inwardness of a situation, he will not, to make a tale easy to 'drool out,' go on with unessentials.[54]

The Nobel Prize winner shrewdly observed that medium analogy and medium specificity are complementary for the author of *Manhattan Transfer*. Dos Passos would fail, in Lewis's estimation, if he stuck to the surfaces of people (the quality of *USA* that Jean-Paul Sartre would later praise) and would compromise his humanism by hewing too closely in his analogy (the "jazz effect"), or, alternatively, if he allowed himself to indulge in spectacle or sentimentality ("unessentials"), the qualities not of film per se but of American commercial cinema.[55]

Indeed, Dos Passos reviled superficiality and meretriciousness in art and in people, and in the principal character Ellen Thatcher, the author merged his moralist's disdain for economic and political pragmatism and his aesthete's revulsion at the vulgarity of cheap art. Her rise, corresponding to her shift from name to name and lover to lover—from Ellen Thatcher to Ellen Oglethorpe to Helena Oglethorpe Herf to, lastly, Ellen Baldwin—signals Dos Passos's horror at the unchecked transformation of a person without a core identity. Ellen's off-putting mutability registers in her own distaste for urban masses and urban filth, which the novel conflates as a sludgy underground flow: "Under all the nickelplated, goldplated streets enameled with May, uneasily she could feel the huddling smell, spreading in dark slow crouching masses like corruption oozing from broken sewers, like a mob." Her uneasiness arises from a too-close identification with and subsequent rejection of both the "huddling smell" of the rank stifled bodies in the subway and the oozing waste of the congested sewers, and she asserts her difference from both by "walk[ing] briskly down the crossstreet" (*MT* 335). Ellen differs from the anonymous faces and feces in her ability to move about freely, to become whatever she chooses to be. If this moment is, as Kate Marshall suggests, representative of the way *Manhattan Transfer* tropes infrastructure as media and thus "thematizes its own participation in the communication systems of modern sociality," the novel's attitude toward that participation—and thus toward participation in that particularly modern communication system of film adaptation—would be one characterized by disgust.[56] As if to eliminate all doubt about his aversion to Ellen's protean nature and the fluid translatability she represents, Dos Passos emphasizes her philistine rejection of art and idealism and the devotees of each, all of which she perceives as juvenile. "I'm so sick of all that stuff," she tells eventual husband George Baldwin, a wealthy lawyer and budding politician, over the phone after they stymie a police raid of an avant-garde party. "Oh just everything like that aesthetic dancing and literature and radicalism and psychoanalysis.... Just an overdose I guess.... Yes I guess that's it George ... I guess I'm growing up" (*MT* 292). As usual, "growing up" means replacing abstract commitments with economic and political pragmatism; Ellen embodies everything wrong with New York, including the films FPL produced in its Astoria facilities.

Unsurprisingly, then, of the scores of minor characters in the novel, Ellen most resembles Jack Cunningham, in whom all the slipperiness and business acumen of the Famous Players is concentrated. Cunningham appears as a master of translatability, a character who not only transfers easily within the FPL-Paramount corporate structure but who, as a publicity man, is the magician of the studio system's commodity fetish, one who translates art objects into sales. Moreover, this mastery has a particularly medium-technological valence, evidenced by his suave wooing of Maisie Merivale via telegraph. While *Manhattan Transfer*'s earnest, honest protagonist Jimmy Herf succumbs to the emotional beating he receives in New York, losing Ellen to George Baldwin and ultimately leaving the metropolis for parts unknown, Cunningham rises at the expense of those he willingly consigns to a previous life. Mere pages before the novel ends, a tabloid column headline announces, "Mr. and Mrs. Jack Cunningham Hop Off for the First Lap of Their Honeymoon on his Sensational Seaplane Albatross VII" (*MT* 330), which is then followed by the collateral damage of that success, the wife he left behind in Wisconsin: "Mrs. Cunningham heaved a deep sigh and settled herself among the pillows. Outside churchbells were ringing. 'Oh Jack you darling I love you just the same,' she said to the picture. Then she kissed it. 'Listen, deary the churchbells sounded like that the day we ran away from the High School Prom and got married in Milwaukee'" (*MT* 331). Like Merton Gill and Lorelei Lee, Jack Cunningham ascends from inconspicuous flyover origins to coastal success. We will soon see, in Chapter 2, how MGM figures the publicity man Space Hanlon as the mentally and verbally gymnastic hero of the proto-screwball backstudio picture *Bombshell* (1933), whose anonymity and flexibility make him the perfect dummy for that studio's corporate voice. But for Dos Passos, Jack, the Famous Players publicity man, is the most despicable modern Manhattanite, with less backstory than Ellen and thus no compensatory qualities or explanatory youthful experiences. His brief story is the kernel of a Hollywood novel that *Manhattan Transfer* refuses to be, a rejection that dovetails with the novel's movie technique to ward off adaptation in advance.

Gatsby's Ghost of Filmic Future

Like Nick Carraway, his famously ambivalent and compromised participant-narrator, F. Scott Fitzgerald found his vision split between the strategies of Loos and Dos Passos, simultaneously enchanted and repelled by the chance of a windfall from some studio for the rights to *The Great Gatsby*. The critic John M. Kenny, writing in *Commonweal*, suspected as much when the book was initially released:

> It is not beyond probability that Mr. Fitzgerald may have had one eye cocked on the movie lots while writing this last novel. The movie type of wild Bacchanalian revel, with the drunken ladies in the swimming-pool

> and the garden fêtes that just drip expensiveness, are done to perfection—
> and who knows but that they will offer some soulful Hollywood director
> a chance to display his art? But for a writer in whom there is the spark at
> least of real distinction to be so palpably under suspicion of catering to
> Hollywood is a grievous thing.[57]

Kenny was righter than his melancholy barb suggests. As Michael North has explained, Fitzgerald's fame rests on his ability to conjure a "feeling of possibility and, almost in the same breath, its utter disappointment." That contradictory response results, I suggest, from the writer's decision to nest Gatsby's narrative of "hope" and "romantic readiness" within Nick's disillusioned retrospective narrative that can, in turn, be mapped onto warring positions in the literary field: between wholesome and popular stories with maximal transmedial possibility and sophisticated, literary fictions with minimal transmedial possibility.[58] The novel's internal conflict between the romantic Gatsby and the cynical, realist Nick encodes the broader conflict between the dictates of the MPPDA's recently instituted Formula and the demands of high literary fiction.

In the years leading up to the composition of *Gatsby*, Fitzgerald had his finger on the pulse of the film industry, though he was never an insider in the way Loos was. In 1920, the year he started writing *The Beautiful and Damned*, he had sold the film rights to three of his stories—"Head and Shoulders" (to Metro for $2500), "Myra Meets His Family" (to Fox for $1000), and "The Off-Shore Pirate" (to Metro for $2250)—and signed an option contract with Metro for $3000.[59] Fitzgerald had such an acute awareness of the adaptation potential of his short stories that he considered *In One Reel* as a title for what became the 1922 collection *Tales of the Jazz Age*.[60] However, he was conflicted about this new source of income. Just as George and Lillian Chester would do in *On the Lot and Off*, Fitzgerald expressed his ambivalence about transmedial possibility in *The Beautiful and Damned* through the professional writer Dick Caramel:

> In the two years since the publication of 'The Demon Lover,' Dick had made over twenty-five thousand dollars, most of it lately, when the reward of the author of fiction had begun to swell unprecedentedly as a result of the voracious hunger of the motion pictures for plots. He received seven hundred dollars for every story, at that time a large emolument for such a young man—he was not quite thirty—and for every one that contained enough 'action' (kissing, shooting, and sacrificing) for the movies, he obtained an additional thousand. His stories varied, there was a measure of vitality and a sort of instinctive technic in all of them, but none attained the personality of 'The Demon Lover,' and there were several that Anthony [Patch] considered downright cheap. These, Dick explained severely, were

to widen his audience. Wasn't it true that men who had attained real permanence from Shakespeare to Mark Twain had appealed to the many as well as to the elect?[61]

By denigrating stories readily translatable to film, the novel separates itself from them while also capitalizing on the vogue of behind-the-scenes narratives. Yet Fitzgerald continued to accept money from the studios: in 1922, $2,500 plus a $1,500 bonus from Warners for *The Beautiful and Damned*; in 1923, $10,000 from FPL for *This Side of Paradise*; and, in 1926, $13,500 from FPL for *Gatsby*.[62] Because Fitzgerald would receive his bonus for *The Beautiful and Damned* if the film grossed more than $250,000, the deal with Warners remained in the ever-impecunious author's thoughts until *Gatsby*'s completion. The displeasure he expressed to his agent Harold Ober over the low sum the novel brought, his suspicion that the studio was flimflamming him ("Heaven knows they got it cheap and it was one of their own men who told me how it was packing them in on the coast"), and his distaste for William Seiter's adaptation ("I'm determined to make Warner Bros pay up more because they so mutilated the picture than for the money itself") all suggest that the problem of film adaptation was very much on his mind through at least January 1925, during which time he wrote *Gatsby*, his "consciously artistic achievement."[63]

In touting such an achievement, Fitzgerald implicitly distinguished between the aesthetic merits of his nascent third novel and the potboiling efforts of his commercial literary work. But this, Fitzgerald scholar Matthew J. Bruccoli might say, was an act of self-mythology: "The popular notion that [Fitzgerald] squandered his genius on lavishly paid hackwork persists with the legends of his orgiastic irresponsibility. In actuality Fitzgerald functioned for twenty years as a professional writer and as a literary artist—but he did not have two separate careers. He had one career to which everything he wrote connected."[64] For an American writer of the 1920s, managing a literary career involved taking into account the transmedial possibility of one's writing. Writing *Gatsby* with an eye toward film adaptation both explicitly and implicitly factored into Fitzgerald's thinking about the novel's commercial and aesthetic strategy. In an October 25, 1924 dispatch to Ober about the possible serialization of *Gatsby*, he wrote, "Needless to say whether [*Gatsby*] serializes or not I will refer any and all moving picture bids on the book to you and will tell Scribners to let you know about any moving picture bids that come through them. Of course this is looking pretty far ahead."[65] At the beginning of the same letter, Fitzgerald assured Ober that *Gatsby* "is a love story and it is sensational," which underscores Fitzgerald's belief that FPL was in the market for romantic subjects. Thus, he was keenly aware of the tension produced by the opposing pressures to produce a purely literary work and profitable, adaptable material.

Just as the ghosts of future adaptation followed Fitzgerald during the writing of *Gatsby*, the unsubstantial presence of the film industry haunts the text, manifesting at narratively and symbolically crucial moments in the form of indirect reference and semantic resonance. The first of these moments occurs within the doors of the Merton College library, when Nick wanders away from his first foray into a Gatsby party and finds himself confronted with the bespectacled Owl Eyes. Any soothsayer worthy of the name sees beyond mere appearances, and if Owl Eyes counts as one—and the general consensus holds that he does—then his remark "this fella's a regular Belasco" indicates more than Gatsby's gift for naturalistic dissimulation or even his ambiguous ethnic origins.[66] Owl Eyes voices his appreciation for the "thoroughness" and "realism" of Gatsby's theatrical efforts, but his inspired comparison has a more temporally local allusion than the set design for which the Bishop of Broadway was famous at the turn of the twentieth century. At the beginning of January 1923—six months after Gatsby's first party, a year-and-a-half before Fitzgerald began writing the novel—Belasco was in the news for ending a nine-year hiatus from film production, which he had begun with Jesse Lasky, and agreeing with Warner Brothers to bring *Daddies, Deburau,* and *The Gold Diggers* to the screen. In exchange for the rights to the plays and assistance in casting and designing the films, Belasco received $250,000.[67] Being a "regular Belasco" therefore entails, in one sense, the ability to see one's work proliferate in film for hefty remuneration. Here, Fitzgerald follows the path trodden by Wilson and Loos, embedding in the narrative a prediction of *Gatsby*'s transmedial success. But "a regular Belasco" is ambiguous, referring not only to the producer himself but also to an instance of his work (i.e., "a Belasco production"). Understood as a production, Gatsby is, to adapt Rebecca Walkowitz's term, born-filmic, struck from the mold of contemporary American cinema and ready to be filmed.[68] Nick's declaration that Gatsby served a God whose "business" is "vast, vulgar, and meretricious beauty" thus comes into focus (*GG* 98); Gatsby is made in the image of His Father, what Fitzgerald would, a decade later, call "a more glittering, a grosser power": the Hollywood movie.[69]

Gatsby, therefore, is not *like* a director or *like* a star, as Joss Lutz Marsh would have it, but, more radically, *is* an instantiation of American film.[70] When Daisy confesses her love for Gatsby to Tom, she does so not in explicit terms but in the language of temperature; in the midst of the sweltering August day, Daisy marvels at Gatsby's coolness:

> "Ah," she cried, "you look so cool."
> Their eyes met, and they stared together at each other, alone in space. With an effort she glanced down at the table.
> "You always look so cool," she repeated.
> She had told him that she loved him, and Tom Buchanan saw. He was astounded. (*GG* 119)

Only a few pages later, during the drive into Manhattan, Jordan proposes a possible place to rest: "Those big movies around Fiftieth Street are cool" (*GG* 125). It is worth noting that the other objects described as cool in the chapter are the gin rickeys Tom serves at lunch; just as Gatsby stands correctly accused of bootlegging throughout the novel, so we observe here his tight affiliation with the movies. In *Trimalchio*, Fitzgerald's penultimate draft of *Gatsby*, the author goes further, suggesting an equivalence between Gatsby and the cinema. At the very start of their cataclysmic showdown, Tom belligerently inquires of Gatsby, "All this 'old sport' business. Where'd you pick that up?" to which Daisy replies, "Now see here, Tom .... If you're going to be rude and unpleasant I'm not going to stay here a minute, do you understand? I'm going to walk right out of here and go to—and go to a movie."[71] Although her response can be read merely as a means of snuffing Tom's aggression, it is in fact neither a throwaway remark nor a weak attempt to stop the fight. Rather, it is a threat. Which is to say, Daisy threatens to leave Tom and go where it is cool: to the movies: to Gatsby.

As the embodiment of the Hollywood style, Gatsby is emphatically unreal, as Nick indicates when he writes that his friend is "just the sort of Jay Gatsby that a seventeen-year-old boy would be likely to invent," the product of "reveries" that "were a satisfactory hint of the unreality of reality" (*GG* 96, 97). Appropriately, Gatsby is only truly in his element at his parties, events at which the reality of unreality appears (as do many film people on the list of Gatsby's guests, "all connected with the movies in one way or another" (*GG* 62)). More revealing still, the inversion of reality and unreality occurs in the context of movies. During the second of the party scenes, Gatsby points out guests with whom the tantalized Daisy and supercilious Tom might be familiar: "'Perhaps you know that lady,' Gatsby indicated a gorgeous, scarcely human orchid of a woman who sat in state under a white-plum tree. Tom and Daisy stared, with that peculiarly unreal feeling that accompanies the recognition of a hitherto ghostly celebrity of the movies" (*GG* 104–105). In one sense, the movie star as projected, as merely the photochemical registration of reflected light, is ghostly because insubstantial. However, at the very instant that the movie star becomes flesh, the moment itself becomes "unreal"—ghostlike—as though the entire scene had become a filmic projection and only the star, the synecdoche for the movies, were real. At the parties—which are, like film productions, highly organized, highly capitalized aesthetic events— Gatsby's fundamental affinity with the movies, in the form of a shared reality in unreality, emerges.[72]

It might seem implausible to construe Gatsby as not only born-filmic but, more narrowly, as a creature of Hollywood's Formulated imagination. On a cursory glance, it's not unreasonable to think, as John M. Kenny did, that "the Great Gatsby wasn't great at all—just a sordid, cheap little crook."[73] However, Gatsby's unsavory behavior, his association with the gangster Meyer Wolfsheim and his unstinting pursuit of another man's wife, is incidental to his "Platonic conception of himself" (*GG* 98). This idealization is one explanation for the character's lack of specificity, of which Fitzgerald's editor Maxwell Perkins complained, and which the literary critic Lawrence Buell has more recently noted: "we never see him in a workplace. His business acumen remains as mysterious as that of Henry James's millionaires."[74] By contrast, Tom's vividness—Fitzgerald told Perkins, "I suppose he's the best character I've ever done—I think he and the brother in 'Salt' & Hurstwood in 'Sister Carrie' are the three best characters in American fiction in the last twenty years, perhaps and perhaps not"—coincides with his badness.[75] His incorrect citation of Goddard's "The Rise of the Colored Empires" (he means the racist pseudoscientist Lothrop Stoddard's *The Rising Tide of Color against White Supremacy* [1920]), his pithily described violence against his lover Myrtle Wilson at their apartment in Washington Heights, his repeated "sprees" of infidelity: virtually all of his sharply delineated actions and beliefs testify to his corruption. Jordan Baker, cheater at amateur golf, and Daisy, smasher of things and creatures, are scarcely better. This sordidness is precisely the kind of material that the MPPDA wanted to bar from the screen. Boozing, lying, cheating (at golf; on spouses); vehicular homicide, murder, suicide: such scandalous activity openly defies the dictates of the Formula and flouts M. C. Levee's prognostication of literature's accommodation of moral strictures. By including all of this in his novel, Fitzgerald marks his work as beyond the screen's compass, and, by extension, beyond its protagonist's too.

For Gatsby cannot exist under such an amoral regime. Crucially, he is the only person "exempt from [Nick's] reaction" against the "riotous excursions with privileged glimpses into the human heart" committed by those whom the narrator wanted to see "in uniform and at a sort of moral attention forever" (*GG* 2). In Gatsby's mind, "of course you can!" relive the past and reclaim the love that has passed you by; in Gatsby's mind, there can only be one true love in a life. Gatsby visibly shatters when Daisy admits her dual affections:

> "Oh, you want too much!" she cried to Gatsby. "I love you now—isn't that enough? I can't help what's past." She began to sob helplessly. "I did love him once—but I loved you too."
> Gatsby's eyes opened and closed.
> "You loved me *too*?" he repeated. (*GG* 132)

Gatsby's moral universe cannot tolerate this existential bigamy, but *Gatsby*'s amoral universe presents this situation positivistically as the way things are. The opposition between romantic protagonist and realistic novel extends, as Buell argues, to the belief in untroubled upward mobility, a triumphalist narrative that would have appealed to Pollyannaish production companies as a representation of the wishful thinking of the average American but that proved a flight of fancy in the 1920s. "To the extent that the dream was seen as a lost illusion of yesteryear," Buell writes, "adherence to it was apt to seem regressive, and those still fixated on it, like the protagonists of *Gatsby* and *American Tragedy*, suspiciously like Oscar Wilde's Dorian Gray, bonded to obsolete self-idealizations that destroy them."[76]

Self-idealization may be the motor of Gatsby's demise, but it's not the agent of his undoing. Without coming into conflict with a world in which Tom Buchanans make the rules (or are at least exempt from them), Gatsby would persist and even thrive. Yet the novel self-consciously resists this straightforward, Horatio Alger "self-made man" narrative. The protagonist's death is, in this sense, preordained by the novel's sophistication. Where *Merton of the Movies* and *Gentlemen Prefer Blondes* incorporate their leads into the film industry, signaling those books' ultimately unproblematic pursuit of transmedial possibility, *The Great Gatsby* hews closer to *Manhattan Transfer*'s disappointment of Jimmy Herf, killing its eponymous hero and the movie narrative he represents in a bid for literary prestige. However, by positioning this "regular Belasco" at the core of the novel, Fitzgerald infected his book with a "picture germ," an act that at once made the book appetizing to the industry and ensured that the author would find the eventual adaptation distasteful.

The 1926 FPL adaptation didn't fail to disappoint Fitzgerald. In 1927, while writing a Constance Talmadge vehicle called *Lipstick* for United Artists during his first stint in Los Angeles, Scott and Zelda sat through the Herbert Brenon-directed film until they couldn't stomach it; Zelda told their daughter Frances Scott "Scottie" Fitzgerald, "It's ROTTEN and awful and terrible."[77] From the trailer, the only surviving film evidence of this regrettably lost film, it's difficult to see why. Kenny proved especially prescient in his review of the novel, as the trailer features bathing suit-clad flappers diving into Gatsby's swimming pool and more young women rushing up and down a long spiral staircase in the foyer of Gatsby's mansion. These portrayals of a devil-may-care frenzy of fun amidst opulent sets ably capture the decadent glamor of Fitzgerald's party scenes and confirms the belief that those moments in the text were born-filmic.

It should be noted, too, that this trailer perfectly represents the studio system's, and especially Paramount's, reigning idea of translation between media.[78] The two opening shots of the trailer feature an image of the novel, including Fitzgerald's full name and an ersatz version of the famous art-deco cover art, over which text is projected. The first shot offers standard credits—producer, title, stars, source text author, screenwriter, adapter, and studio—but the second presents Paramount's sales pitch and thus its desired interpretive frame. Against the backdrop of the novel, first the phrase "a record-selling novel" appears, followed by "A theatre-packing play," then "Now a marvelous picture," and finally, in large cursive, "The Great Gatsby." That second shot makes a deft sleight-of-hand conflation that reveals Paramount's thinking about quality. The studio seems to argue that the success of the story in one mode paved the way for success in another, but the terms of that progression magically change in the third instance; where Paramount touts the novel's and the play's financial successes ("record-selling"; "theatre-packing"), it finally claims aesthetic success for the film ("a marvelous picture"). Part of this decision is purely practical—as a preselling device, trailers almost definitionally cannot know the popularity of the film—but it is also predictive and even assertive. In a perfect illustration of the industry's desire to convert cultural into economic capital, Paramount baldly posits an equivalence between monetary and aesthetic value, and thus by claiming the film's quality, it attempts to guarantee the movie's popularity in line with the book and play versions. The trailer would suggest, then, an exceptional alignment of Fitzgerald's aesthetic sensibility and Paramount's will to value (Figure 1.3).

What went so wrong, then, that the Fitzgeralds would call the film "ROTTEN?" Answering this question requires taking recourse to

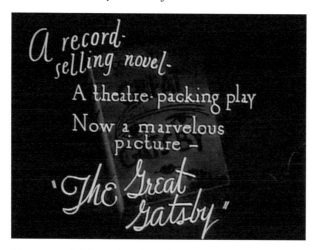

Figure 1.3 The transmedial flow of intellectual property neatly depicted in the trailer for *The Great Gatsby* (Herbert Brenon, Paramount, 1926)

contemporary reviews found in trade journals, fan magazines, and newspapers. Constructing an account of the film entails creating a kind of composite sketch by comparing multiple contemporary accounts, which can then serve as the basis for a comparison with the novel.

Abel Green of *Variety* thought the film "serviceable," but in delineating its virtues and failings he echoes Vance's medium specificity argument: "The picture is no reflection on the original novel, an excellent volume, which, because of its literary form, permits a more faithful adherence to reality than the movies." However, when Green writes of the capabilities and limitations of "the movies," he refers less to the medium as such than to contemporary Hollywood filmmaking conventions. Indeed, this claim is a kind of apology for a more pointed speculation about Paramount's production that he made earlier in the review: "The vacillating shades and touches [of the film] make one wonder whether Brenon (or his scenarist) had not started out to alter the original Scott Fitzgerald story for screen purposes and was confronted with contractual obligations to the author, or other circumstances that prohibited such liberties. This is but a theory, since Fitzgerald is sufficiently established to command such terms if he so elected."[79] As we have seen, Fitzgerald, eager to score a big payday, readily assented to Ober's reported offer for the screen rights to *Gatsby*, and no evidence in the extant correspondence suggests anything like the bargaining power Green imagines. The "vacillating shades and touches" can more likely be attributed, then, to the production's imperfect reconciliation of source text material and the restrictions of mid-1920s Hollywood's narrative and moral protocols and its technological limitations. The critic for *Motion Picture Magazine* made this point explicitly:

> Herbert Brenon has gone about misinterpreting F. Scott Fitzgerald's novel to the very best of his ability.
>
> There is, it seems, a stratum of life that the movies cannot approach with any real understanding, and this must be it. All the characters have been remolded into their movie counterparts, and the thing has become a conventional and not too deftly presented tale of a man who has the misfortune to love a woman outside his sphere, and of his futile attempts to raise himself to a level from which she would at least be accessible.[80]

Implicit in this analysis and more evident in other reviews is that not only are there conventional characters in Hollywood movies, but there exists a conventional worldview as well. This worldview, shaped most recently by the Hays Office's Formula, would, in theory, diametrically oppose the one presented by Nick Carraway. This difference would create the conditions for a major transformation in narrative form from the novel to the film. If Gatsby's tragedy in the novel derives from his fundamental dissonance with the world he inhabits—as a true believer in a cynical world—then to preserve that particular sense of tragedy in a domain characterized by moral rectitude, Gatsby would have to be figured more straightforwardly as a reprobate.

However, the available reviews indicate that rather than abiding fully by the dictates of the Formula or adhering to the precedent of Fitzgerald's novel, the film wavered between the two, resulting in a "baffling story that seems to lack a good many of the essentials of real movie material."[81] Green's sense of the film's "vacillating shades and touches" is thus confirmed. This inconsistency appears to apply both to the movie as a whole and to Gatsby in particular. Some reviews caution that the story itself is "none-too-pleasant" or "by no means" suitable for children under fifteen years old and thus an evident deviation from the MPPDA's mores.[82] This deviation is centered, according to *Photoplay*, in Gatsby himself: "Fitzgerald's novel, with its unscrupulous hero, violates some pet screen traditions. It's unusual entertainment."[83] Yet the film seems to have stopped short of the novel's bitter pessimism, as reviews indicate that Gatsby's violations of the law are violations of the moral order, and his punishment is both merited and the effective cause of the recuperation of Tom and Daisy's marriage (the *Boston Daily Globe*: "Discovering that her lover is a bootlegger, who may go to jail any day for his practices, means the death of Daisy's love and her reunion with her husband.").[84] The morality of the Hollywood film is thereby preserved. Gatsby, a gangster in the final analysis, breaks the law and must be punished by losing the girl and eventually his life; his punishment resolves the marital dilemma. Hence, *Picture-Play Magazine* could incredulously report, "*Daisy* somehow sees happiness ahead with her profligate husband."[85]

In keeping with the Formula's imperatives and in spite of narrative coherence, Gatsby's decision to assume responsibility for Myrtle's death becomes an act of martyrdom, a bid for redemption—rather than an act consistent with his pure faith in his love for Daisy, and by extension, his faith in his ability to relive the past. Taking the blame for Daisy's vehicular homicide thus becomes an instance of what the *Hartford Courant* calls Gatsby's "heroic qualities," which recuperate his character *post mortem*. When the *Courant* contends that the "lonely funeral" will "bring tears to the eyes of the most hardened moviegoer," the presumed pathos derives from the audience's belief that Gatsby, though flawed, wasn't such a bad guy after all: not from, as in the novel, the death of romantic (with big and little "r") ideals.[86] It seems that Brenon and Paramount could not have *Gatsby* ruminate, as Fitzgerald does, on the demise of the "capacity for wonder" (*GG* 180)—that capacity being the *sine qua non* of the Hollywood cinema—and so the stakes of Gatsby's love and death are profoundly reduced, resulting in a "story [that] doesn't seem weighty enough for the footage it consumes."[87] In finally conforming to the needs of the industry—following, however inconsistently, the dicta of the Hays Office and affirming Hollywood's modus operandi of enchantment through entertainment—Brenon and Paramount sap *Gatsby* of its strength.

The case of *The Great Gatsby* thus presents the novel-film translation problematic in its fullest form. On the one hand, in his novel, Fitzgerald negotiated between the transmedial possibility of his prose and his high-literary aspirations; this conflict contributes to the friction between the novel's protagonist (romantic; born-filmic) and the encompassing narrative in which he exists (realist; anti-Hollywood). Through Gatsby's death, the novel claims its literariness; indeed, the narrative emphasizes its writtenness by presenting Nick, the cynical narrator, not merely as the teller but explicitly as the author of Gatsby's tale. On the other hand, in the film, we find Brenon/Paramount faced with a different dilemma—that of adaptation—characterized by the tension between the impulse toward fidelity to the source text and the counterimpulse to follow Hollywood's conventions. The antinomy here, because it manifests in vacillation between the positions as opposed to a clash (as in the novel), results not in a sustained frisson but rather in confusion.

Unnaturalist Transformation

And yet it is a fourth novel published in 1925, American literature's *annus mirabilis*, that constitutes the pathetic and bathetic extreme of the transmedial economy. In 1926, after Theodore Dreiser's *An American Tragedy* achieved bestseller status and was adapted to the stage, Paramount purchased its screen rights for a then-record sum of $90,000, in spite of well-founded fears that the story would run afoul of the Formula (it's worth noting that *Motion Picture Magazine* announced the sale in the same paragraph that it noted the company's acquisition of *Gentlemen Prefer Blondes*).[88] Like Fitzgerald, Dreiser found himself torn between competing impulses toward and against Hollywood. Mandy Merck has painstakingly detailed Dreiser's *Tragedy*-era contact with the film industry, beginning in 1919 when he accompanied his aspiring actress lover (and second cousin) Helen Richardson to Hollywood. There, Dreiser's behavior and attitude toward film production could only be described as self-contradictory: on the one hand, he unsuccessfully pitched scenarios and treatments to FPL and the actress Mary Pickford; on the other, he contributed exposés on the maltreatment of women in Hollywood to *McCall*'s and *Shadowland*.[89] Condemning the cultural mythology that produces Gatsbys and Clyde Griffiths, Dreiser makes his criticism of the dreams of stardom and distinction produced by Hollywood blunt in *American Tragedy* by having the agent of Roberta Alden's death be not Clyde but instead the camera swinging from his neck. Roberta, "stunned, horror-struck, unintelligible with pain and fear," becomes a terribly literal instantiation of an object of concern for the middlebrow moralist, the movie-struck girl likely to become swept up in a fantasy of cinematic glamor.[90]

But, nonetheless, like *Gatsby*, *American Tragedy* is at the same time infected by a strain of the picture germ; Kate Marshall puts it best when she notes that the novel "had been imagining itself as its own adaptation all along."[91] For, like a negative image of a pearl-clutching MPPDA officer, Dreiser's novel is titillated by and desirous of that which it censures: the movies and the American culture they made. *American Tragedy*'s overheated but conflicted transmedial imagination manifests in those vivid moments when the novel castigates image-making most severely. Dreiser describes the venal careerism of District Attorney Mason and the sad publicity "of the crime sensation of the first magnitude" in language similar to that which Fitzgerald used to picture Gatsby's parties[92]:

> And Clyde, as well as Belknap and Jephson, now gazing at them and wondering what the impression of Mason's opening charge was likely to be.

> For a more dynamic and electric prosecutor under these particular circumstances was not to be found. This was his opportunity. Were not the eyes of all the citizens of the United States upon him? He believed so. It was as if some one had suddenly exclaimed: "Lights! Camera!"[93]

In light of these pessimistic lines, whatever action Paramount ultimately took would only disappoint the author.

The saga of *Tragedy*'s adaptation—a five-year ordeal that included an unused script written by the Soviet director Sergei Eisenstein in 1930—and Dreiser's inflamed response have become legendary, standing out even amidst the rich tradition of authors grieving Hollywood's transmogrification of their work. Based on Paramount's promise to produce the movie "exactly as it is written," Dreiser sued the company for breach of contract after seeing Josef von Sternberg's 1931 film. His loss at court only concentrated the vitriol he would express in a screed titled "The Real Sins of Hollywood," which makes a muddle of the perceived aesthetic, ethical, and legal offenses committed by Paramount:

> For when I tried, in the Supreme Court in New York, last July, to restrain Paramount from showing the movie of my book, An American Tragedy [sic], on the ground that by not creating the inevitability of circumstance influencing Clyde, a not evil-hearted boy, they had reduced the psychology of my book so as to make it a cheap murder mystery, I lost the case....
>
> The basis of my attack is that the picture corporations, with their monopoly, owe a certain percentage of their enormous profits to the artistic development of the film. For assuming the correctness of [the studios'] interpretation of the mass mind, should not a genuine effort be made now and then to portray a masterpiece of literature, or present a gifted actor or actress in some such fashion as to widen the appeal of masterpiece or artist, or both?[94]

Clearly, Dreiser objected to Paramount's decision to eschew the biological and social determinism that deprives *An American Tragedy*'s characters of their personal agency, a decision the author should have anticipated given that "character-centered ... causality is the armature of the classical story."[95] Indeed, it is perhaps because Dreiser had already known what Paramount would do that he hoped Erich von Stroheim would direct the adaptation; in 1924, Stroheim had completed his infamous *Greed*, a faithful adaptation of Frank Norris's naturalist classic *McTeague* (1899).[96]

"The Real Sins of Hollywood" is especially interesting, however, because Dreiser figures himself and his abused fellow writers as characters in a naturalist novel much like the ones he wrote and even more like Norris's

The Octopus: A Story of California (1901). As Walter Benn Michaels has argued, for the naturalists, Norris chief among them, "all fiction is corporate fiction." Naturalism "not only imagines a world of 'entities' competing with men but imagines that men, properly understood, already have been reduced to the things ('brutes,' 'machines') they are competing with," and therefore "are not agents at all."[97] Thus, in *The Octopus*, Shelgrim, the President of the Pacific and Southwest Railroad, tells the poet Presley, "you are dealing with forces, young man, when you speak of Wheat and the Railroad, not with men," and that man is merely a minor force among them.[98] Nonhuman agency, discomfiting for the would-be epic poet, is an unproblematic state of affairs for the company president, who, instead of striving to be the head of the cephalopod, is content to be a well-remunerated cog in the "gigantic engine" of "nature."[99]

There is an obvious but important difference, though, between the railroad that overawes Presley and the movie studio that confounded Dreiser: one controls the distribution of wheat while the other controls the production, distribution, and exhibition of audiovisual stories.[100] And if the railroad can be said to announce its power with the inarticulate steam whistles and gnashing gears of its trains, the studio communicates in a consistent, identifiable, and differentiable language of pictures.[101]

It would be to the latter kind of corporation that authors the world over would flock as screenwriters, eager to lay claim to the easy money doled out by what came to be called, after the famously irreverent head of Paramount's recruiting efforts, "The Herman J. Mankiewicz Fresh Air Fund for Writers."[102] Literary scholars have long noted the lack of individual authorship in—to say nothing of credit given for—the writing of screenplays; these scholars typically refer to the activity of screenwriting by the term "collaboration."[103] But that word, with its connotations of willful engagement, whether convivial or conflicted (and setting aside its baleful political connotations), doesn't quite capture the nature of the writers' relationships, nor does it account for the role played by the "person" that actually authored the pictures. Once in Hollywood, writers would not only work within variously organized hierarchies but also come into contact and often conflict with the designs of corporate authors: fleshless, bloodless persons with expressive capacity and brands to maintain. In other words, within the studio system, writers "were moved" by a peculiar variation of what Alfred Kazin, in diagnosing the Depression-era resurgence of literary naturalism, called "an unconscious conflict between their desire to reorganize society and their struggles to survive in it."[104] Following Lisa Siraganian's elucidation of American modernism's "genetic connection" to naturalism in its persistent investigations of corporate agency, intention, and speech, we can now turn to consider the literary consequences of writers' experiences within and against MGM, Paramount's successor as the industry's standard-bearer, which, with its trademark leonine roar, developed the most powerful and distinctive voice in Hollywood.

CHAPTER 2

MGM Modernism

>...the light came on revealing a Dutch lady in blue satin sitting at a harpsichord—sitting, Jeremy reflected, at the very heart of an equation, in a world where beauty and logic, painting and analytical geometry, had become one. With what intention? To express, symbolically, what truths about the nature of things? Again, that was the question. Where art was concerned, Jeremy said to himself, that was always the question.
> —Aldous Huxley, *After Many a Summer Dies the Swan*, 1939[1]

Ironically, Dreiser praised a film, *Greed*, that von Stroheim had disowned, but that irony likely didn't escape the studio executives who responded to "The Real Sins of Hollywood." Amidst the digest of rejoinders published the following week in *Liberty*, one is especially germane:

> And here it is also clear that what is needed more and more is a new type of executive now arising in Hollywood—one who shall be the governing force from the time a story is selected until it is exhibited; one who shall give direction to author, player, and director. Such men will make mistakes, but no greater than the composite blunders now frequently released on fifteen thousand screens. Irving Thalberg of Metro-Goldwyn-Mayer is regarded as the first of a new type of motion-picture executive.[2]

It was Thalberg who wrangled von Stroheim and oversaw the editing of the film from 462 minutes to 140 (from absurd to merely long), and it would be Thalberg who, as vice president in charge of production, would do more than anyone to maintain the company's image.[3]

That image was of unparalleled importance. For if Hollywood's 1920s belonged to Paramount and its enormous properties, the largest theater chain in the country and a similarly grand collection of intellectual property, its 1930s were MGM's, the superlative studio with an inimitable brand identity. After a short period during which the movie business believed it was Depression-proof—three or so years, it turned out, of magical thinking—recreation spending plummeted and the overhead costs of Paramount's real estate holdings became an albatross. The studio found itself bankrupt in late 1932. MGM, meanwhile, was responsible for 75 percent of the industry's profits during the decade.[4] Concluding its famous 1932 profile of the company, *Fortune* magazine noted the other studios' grudging assent to MGM's supremacy: "M-G-M's rivals would doubtless dearly love to cut M-G-M's throat; they are effectively restrained by the fact that they would cut off their noses if they did so. So long as M-G-M makes the best pictures in the U.S., it is valuable to its competitors by filling their theatres better than they can do it with their own product."[5] No picture captured MGM's "common denominator of goodness" better than *Grand Hotel* (Edmund Goulding, 1932), a still of which appeared in *Fortune*'s paean. The overhead shot displaying Cedric Gibbons's art deco design and an array of well-dressed actors that might have included John Barrymore, Lionel Barrymore, Joan Crawford, Greta Garbo, and Wallace Beery is the epitome of MGM's *Ars Gratia Artis* sensibility, conjuring in a single image the studio's galaxy of stars and aura of glamor. If the semiporous and constantly shifting industry had "the character of a hotel lobby," as Leo Rosten, Hollywood's first sociologist, observed, then that lobby should, from the studio's perspective, be presided over by Leo the Lion.[6]

Tycoons, Limited

The phrase "the whole equation of pictures"—words that have featured prominently in the retelling of Hollywood's history over the past four decades—appears in the fourth paragraph of the first and only completed chapter of *The Love of the Last Tycoon: A Western* (1941), F. Scott Fitzgerald's final planned novel.[7]

> You can take Hollywood for granted like I did, or you can dismiss it with the contempt we reserve for what we don't understand. It can be understood too, but only dimly and in flashes. Not half a dozen men have ever been able to keep the whole equation of pictures in their heads.[8]

In the pretense of the fiction, these words are written by Cecelia Brady, the daughter of the producer Pat Brady (modeled on Louis B. Mayer), in admiration of the Thalbergian producer Monroe Stahr. For a novelist as committed to the manipulation of point of view as Fitzgerald was, the gap between author and character becomes a space where concepts find their aesthetic expression. Cecelia's thoughts come first, thoughts that are not only self-consciously literary—"At the worst," she writes in the idiom of Gothic fiction, "I accepted Hollywood with the resignation of a ghost assigned to a haunted house"—but well-schooled (*LT* 3). Like Fitzgerald's one-time screenwriting partner Budd Schulberg, son of the producer B.P., Cecelia had been sent east to college to attain the sophistication that the prior generation by and large lacked, but that Stahr, like Thalberg, seemed to possess by nature.

Cecelia's adoration of Stahr is inseparable from the literary education she had received at Bennington College, where her English teachers "hated [Hollywood] way down deep as a threat to their existence" (*LT* 3). Fitzgerald chose Bennington with care. Unlike the more established Vassar (where his daughter, Scottie, studied) and the rest of the Seven Sisters, Bennington, a progressive women's college founded in 1932, catered to student interests and featured instruction in contemporary literature by active novelists, poets, and critics. Whereas the literary historian at, say, Wellesley might condescend to the movies without fearing them, Cecelia's teachers speak from the same professional position and in the same idiom as Fitzgerald himself, when, in the midst of his crack-up, he saw the novel threatened by the glittering gross power of the movies.[9]

Fitzgerald wised up enough to assign his own melodramatic reification of the two media to Cecelia's anxious instructors. She seems, however, to have learned something from those teachers, who might look on her with a perverse pride as she describes Stahr in language reminiscent of T.S. Eliot's, whose work they taught in introductory courses, and whom Fitzgerald had praised in a letter to Scottie weeks before he died. *Fortune* famously compared Thalberg's mind to a camera, the fundamental tool of the industry, as if to suggest that the producer thought in the images the world wanted to see. If Cecelia's "whole equation" evokes the business rather than the technology of pictures, her mathematical metaphor also bears a striking resemblance to Eliot's vision of the poet in "Tradition and the Individual Talent." Her Stahr is like the writer who "learns in time" that "the mind of his own country" is "much more important than his own private mind," but Cecelia's hero manages rather than makes. His mind isn't a piece of filiated platinum catalyzing a reaction in contact with the oxygen of feeling and the sulfuric acid of literary history. Rather, it is an "equation of pictures," of what makes a movie work (a "picture") and what makes the immense, incomprehensible industry run ("pictures" as synecdoche for system).[10] A portrait of the artist as a frail young producer: Cecelia has figured her Stahr as an arch-modernist, a man who has escaped his personality so successfully as to have absorbed the system whole and yet remain inimitably himself. "He darted in and out of the role of 'one of the boys' with dexterity," the bewitched young Brady concludes, "but on the whole I should say he wasn't one of them" (*LT* 15).

There is, however, another turn of the screw to be observed in *The Last Tycoon*'s formulation of Stahr's genius, one that reveals the producer's strength as a manager but, at the same time, his flawed belief in his ability to fully embody the corporate artist. Although Fitzgerald died before he could reconcile Cecelia's observations with those of his omniscient narrator, in those moments that Cecelia couldn't see, Fitzgerald presented Stahr as a kind of anti-Henry James, at least as Eliot understood him. Despite Fitzgerald's avowed sympathy with the left-liberal sentiments of the Popular Front, he assured *Collier's* editor Frank Littauer that *The Last Tycoon* would be "a novel—not even faintly of the propaganda type"; in making this promise, Fitzgerald aligns himself with Eliot's account of James, he of the "mind so fine that no idea could violate it." In effect, Fitzgerald confirmed Eliot's praise of *The Great Gatsby* from fifteen years earlier, when the poet-critic called the novel "the first step that American fiction has taken since Henry James."[11] Despite his sophistication and elegance, Monroe Stahr is the antithesis of such an artist, because he is driven by what his model Thalberg called "the single idea."

While *Fortune* thought that "Ideas are the seeds of motion picture productions" and that "Ideas permeate the studio structure and the Thalberg day," Thalberg himself believed, as he told Loew's president Nicholas Schenck amidst his 1933 power struggle with Mayer, "someone must do the job I have done in the past…. It has been proven that the successful lots are those dominated by a single idea."[12] The difference between "ideas" and "idea" is decisive. For *Fortune*, ideas are tantamount to currency, the basis of "huge salaries"; for Thalberg, the single idea resembles a studio's animating spirit, the basis of artistic expression. Where Thalberg proved to be an unparalleled steward of MGM's idea, Stahr fatally identifies himself as coincident with the corporate author. This is the kernel of Stahr's demise. According to Fitzgerald's lover Sheila Graham, the writer oriented his proposed conclusion to *The Last Tycoon* around his sense that "L.B. Mayer was out to wrest control of Metro from and/or ruin Irving Thalberg," but Stahr metaphorically falls before Pat Brady has the chance to put out his light.[13] What makes this western a tragedy, rather, is Stahr's own self-defeating, hubristic desire to be the studio's idea incarnate.

When Fitzgerald decided to set his novel "during the four or five months in the year 1935," he again chose meaningfully. By then, Mayer had deposed Thalberg, demoting him from his job as MGM's central producer; the Boy Wonder became a unit producer alongside Harry Rapf, David Selznick, Hunt Stromberg, and Walter Wanger. The resulting wedge between Thalberg and MGM's corporate persona manifested almost immediately onscreen. If *Grand Hotel* presented Thalberg's MGM as a stylish lobby through which stars come and go, *Bombshell* (Victor Fleming, 1933), a backstudio picture of the following year, more straightforwardly presents the studio as the gravity forming the stars into a galaxy. Where Selznick's backstudio picture *What Price Hollywood?* (George Cukor, RKO, 1932) presents a sober, avuncular, and powerful producer (Gregory Ratoff) who helps resuscitate his star's career, and Howard Hawks's theater-based screwball *Twentieth Century* (Columbia, 1934) features a brilliant, manipulative director (Lionel Barrymore) who subordinates his star (Carole Lombard) to his needs, *Bombshell* gives pride of place and a controlling function to a typically anonymous figure, the publicity agent. That agent, who controls communication between the studio's constituents and between the studio and the broader public, perfectly instantiates a studio's structural power, which, according to Jerome Christensen, is "embedded, ordered, expansive, and indirect" and exercised by "those corporate actors who ... have an 'ability to determine the context within which decisions are made by affecting the consequences of one alternative over another.'"[14] It is for this reason that the character's name is Space Hanlon. Though embodied in the form of the fast-talking Lee Tracy, the character is little more than a positive image of negative space, the background against which Lola Burns (Jean Harlow)—mercurial, charismatic, beautiful—can shine. Produced by Stromberg, formerly one of "Irving's boys," *Bombshell*, one of the few 1933 pictures deemed successful by Thalberg himself, testifies to the studio's ongoing viability even after the man himself has declined in power.

Thalberg was a victim of circumstance—his ill health left him vulnerable to Mayer's reorganization. Stahr, on the other hand, was the agent of his own undoing, an undoing foretold in his flashes of doubt in his ability to transcend his own humanity and speak on behalf of the studio. As the "oracle," "Stahr must be right always, not most of the time, but always— or the structure would melt down like gradual butter" (*LT* 56); as a man, Stahr knows this perfection is a sham and that pursuing it is a fool's errand: "Sometimes you have to have will when you don't feel it at all.... You have to say 'It's got to be like this—no other way'—even if you're not sure. A dozen times a week that happens to me. Situations where there is no real reason for anything. You pretend there is" (*LT* 122). Unsettled by his love interest Kathleen's hasty wedding to another man, Stahr overestimates himself while verbally sparring with Arthur Brimmer, an organizer for the Screen Writers Guild, making his limitation all the clearer:

> "First we let half a dozen Russians study the plant," said Stahr. "As a model plant, you understand. And then they break up the unity that makes it a model plant."
> "The unity?" Brimmer repeated. "Do you mean what's known as company spirit?"
> "Oh no, not that," said Stahr impatiently. "It seems to be *me* you're after." (*LT* 121)

Fatally, Stahr fails to see that the labor activist does not want to handicap him, but rather the organization for which he works. In other words, he doesn't recognize that no matter how powerful he had been as the studio's principal producer, Stahr never was the principle of the studio's coherence. In his inability to distinguish himself from and subordinate himself to the studio, Stahr becomes functionally identical to the writers who, like "children[,] … can't keep their minds on their own work" (*LT* 121). Before he dies in a plane crash (Fitzgerald's planned-but-never-executed conclusion) and before he commits moral suicide by planning the murder of Pat Brady, Stahr loses his composure and sense of his proper role. In other words, he experiences a crack-up, making him, amazingly, like Fitzgerald and thus like his "necessary evil," the mere writer. The at once shocking and expected equation of Stahr not with his ideal author, the studio, but with his actual author, Fitzgerald, has negated and replaced Cecelia's romantic equation in the novel's provisional end.

By surreptitiously unbalancing Cecelia's "whole equation of pictures" in *The Love of the Last Tycoon*, Fitzgerald had begun to figure an ironic, pathetic form of the "codified, numeric signs" that Seo Hee Im sees as characteristic of late modernists who, "learning from high modernist failures … plundered empirical experience rather than literary history, replicating logical solutions that had been practically deployed to make the unruly world navigable."[15] Such navigation becomes impossible for Stahr precisely because he fails to realize that he is not equal to his studio. He thus appears as the elegant counterpart to Aldous Huxley's illogical, mock-Hearstian magnate Jo Stoyte of *After Many a Summer Dies the Swan* (1939), who discovers that attaining eternal life—becoming corporation-like—comes at the cost of sinking to a level of vulgarity below even Hollywood's. More surprisingly, both resemble William Faulkner's own tycoon, Thomas Sutpen of *Absalom, Absalom!* (1936), who cannot reconcile the racial contradiction in the Design that compels him, resulting in a life story that, for one of the novel's many narrators, is at bottom a "debtor's farce."[16] The surprise subsides, however, when we consider that writing for MGM was the crucial experience they all shared. The particular version of late modernism that Faulkner, Fitzgerald, and Huxley practiced can therefore be profitably understood as instances of what I'll call MGM Modernism.

While screenwriters often chafed against their lack of control over their work regardless of the studio they worked for, the nature and treatment of their efforts—where they were allowed to write, who and how many people they worked with, and in what arrangement—varied by employer. According to Richard Fine, MGM's "Thalberg system," in which numerous writers might work on the same project without knowing it, proved especially alienating.[17] Some writers, such as John Lee Mahin and Frances Marion, thrived at the studio by ventriloquizing MGM's voice. Mahin, who wrote *Bombshell*, fit in ideally at the conservative studio, founding the studio-supported Screen Playwrights organization to weaken support for the leftist Writers Guild and eventually testifying before the House Committee on Un-American Activities as a friendly witness. Marion, who praised the way Thalberg "gave us the feeling that we were one mind concentrating on a gigantic project," industriously crafted compelling plots that appealed to his desired female audience.[18] She collaborated with Herman Mankiewicz on *Dinner at Eight* (1933), David O. Selznick's first picture at MGM and one modeled explicitly on Thalberg's *Grand Hotel*, which, like *Bombshell*, expressed MGM's claim to strength after the Thalberg era had passed.[19]

A star-studded comedy-drama, *Dinner at Eight* emphasized the studio's self-regard that *Grand Hotel* had left tastefully implicit. The film's titular meal is hosted by Millicent Jordan (Billie Burke), the wife of legacy shipping magnate Oliver (Lionel Barrymore), in honor of Lord and Lady Ferncliffe, the wealthiest family in England. Mrs. Jordan intends for her table's centerpiece to be an aspic British Lion, an edible effigy of MGM's Leo, and although the Jordan family's butler drops and ruins the lion off-camera, the loss ultimately doesn't matter because the Ferncliffes decline their invitation at the last moment.[20] Because the movie, like the play, concludes just before dinner is served, what matters most is the party's planning. As noted in Chapter 1, the party was already a common figure for film production by the mid-1920s; here, the multistranded hubbub emphasizes the studio's star power and sophistication. Dan Packard (Wallace Beery), an unseemly midwestern parvenu given a mustache like the Nebraskan Darryl Zanuck's, then production chief at rival Warners, arranges to buy Jordan's business out from under him, an effort spoiled by Packard's wife Kitty (Jean Harlow), who wants to attend the dinner and cavort with her social betters. Meanwhile, Oliver, believing he's lost his business, suffers an attack of coronary thrombosis, only to be assured of Milly's love and support. *Dinner at Eight* concludes with Jordan maintaining his business as well as his good name and moral integrity and Kitty finding her way into the tony dining room: assurance that MGM would maintain its reputation for classing up stars like Harlow even after the shake-up that brought in Selznick and put Mayer more firmly in charge of the studio he cofounded.

Unlike Mahin and Marion, Fitzgerald, Huxley, and Faulkner struggled for expression, acknowledgment, and agency within the studio and sought their symbolic revenge in their fictions. Instead of portraying the composition of a complex and fragmented work by a heroic individual, as a meta-*Waste Land* might, Fitzgerald delivered the conflicting and opaque machinations behind the production of unified works; his celebration of the tragic tycoon depends on an implicit equation with himself, as Stahr drifts further from identification with the studio and closer, unbeknownst to himself, to the screenwriter, his "necessary evil." Almost contemporaneously, Huxley crafted a counterfactual to Fitzgerald's scenario in *After Many a Summer Dies the Swan*, portraying plutocrat Jo Stoyte's comeuppance for his wrongheaded desire to live forever in a hodgepodge of philosophical dialogue and gothic melodrama that, like the book's grotesque Beverly Pantheon cemetery, makes no attempt to cohere.

Stoyte, modeled on William Randolph Hearst, seeks immortality in various ways: by pursuing a sexual relationship with a young starlet (Virginia Maunciple, a version of Marion Davies); by running a sick ward for indigent children and thereby vampirically subsisting on their gratefulness and youth; by paying an enlightened intellectual (Mr. Propter) to maintain beautiful gardens on his sprawling San Simeon-like estate; by commissioning a fussy British Romanticist (Jeremy Pordage) to catalogue the antiques and archives he collects; and, ultimately, by tasking a Levantine doctor named Obispo to discover a scientific path to eternal life. As Propter, the novel's clear voice of reason (*propter*: "because of"), explains, "the experience of eternity" requires "the transcendence of personality, the extension of consciousness beyond the limits of ego," but Stoyte has no personality to transcend (*AMS* 135–36). He is, in effect, an outrageous anti-Thalberg who hopes to buy eternal life by housing representatives of beauty and logic on the same property and hoping that an equation between them will spontaneously develop.

Befitting his bleak film industry satire, however, Huxley reserves his fullest scorn for the entity that best captures Stoyte's ideal of a non-human, infinitely persistent agent capable of aesthetic expression. When Pordage first arrives in Los Angeles, he is taken to visit Beverly Pantheon, a "personality cemetery" inspired by Forest Lawn cemetery in Glendale (*AMS* 12). "Personality cemetery" is meant in two senses. The first, and more obvious, is that it's where egos go after they die. Containing garish monuments and replicas of fine art as companions for fallen movie stars as well as the would-be famous, the Beverly Pantheon allegorizes Hollywood's absorption of the world's artworks, alienating them from their original contexts and subordinating them to the movies. Transformed into kitsch, the works become ineffective guarantors of immortality. But the Pantheon is also a cemetery with a personality, one of Stoyte's best investments and one which operates independently of and often in spite of its owner. Charlie Habakkuk, who presides over the institution, bemoans his boss's inability to understand the business and ignorance of Habakkuk's contribution: "The ingratitude of people! The stupidity.... Who was it that had made the place what it was: the uniquest cemetery in the world? Absolutely the uniquest? (Charlie slapped himself in the chest.) And who made all the money? Jo Stoyte. And what had *he* done to make the place a success? Absolutely nothing at all" (*AMS* 234). That Stoyte could so easily be a figure for Louis B. Mayer and Habakkuk a figure for Thalberg is important not because it supports the already evidently clear allegory of a film studio, but because Huxley presents the cemetery-studio as the perverse almost-solution to Stoyte's dilemma: "so nearly right; but so enormously wrong!" as Propter would say (*AMS* 162).[21] Beverly Pantheon exists outside of Stoyte and Habakkuk and will endure beyond them, but with an existence that is still egomaniacal and vulgar. The personality cemetery is, therefore, the corporate equivalent of Stoyte's art collection, as Pordage conceives it: "It's as though one were walking in the mind of a lunatic.... Or rather, an idiot.... This is a no-track mind. No-track because infinity-track. It's the mind of an idiot of genius" (*AMS* 174). That paradox would be unimaginable if it weren't the experience of writing for MGM. As *The Last Tycoon*'s screenwriter Boxley (modeled on Huxley) laments, "it's a sort of conspiracy. Those two hacks you've teamed me with listen to what I say but they spoil it—they seem to have a vocabulary of about a hundred words" (*LT* 31). Beverly Pantheon will, like the studio, persist, but it will do so monstrously, appallingly, stupidly, a monument to the decline of the Western tradition to entropic stasis.

Decline takes on a bizarrely literal form in the novel's self-consciously Gothic conclusion. In the Hauberk manuscripts that Pordage has been organizing, Dr. Obispo discovers that the key to bodily immortality can be found in the "intestinal flora," the corpora, of carp. Obispo correctly but crassly treats the human body as a corporation of organisms, referring to Stoyte and others like him as "gut-sacks" (*AMS* 157). But as with the personality cemetery of the Beverly Pantheon, eternal existence comes at the cost of a counter-evolution, with the human regressing to a "foetal ape that's had time to grow up" (*AMS* 353). The creatures Obispo finds in a cellar on Hauberk's English estate are not only physically repulsive but, like the Pantheon, profoundly crude, responsible for "obscene *graffiti*" and "the guttural distortions of almost forgotten obscenities" (*AMS* 355). Though trepidatious, Stoyte nonetheless reconciles himself with that future: "once you get over the first shock—well, [those creatures] look like they were having a pretty good time" (*AMS* 356). If Monroe Stahr's failure to be the studio is the unarticulated basis of Fitzgerald's tragedy, the impending devolution of Jo Stoyte to the hairy, gibbering equivalent of a corporation provides the punchline to Huxley's farce.

As versions of Hollywood fiction written late in the MGM '30s, and in line with their authors' respective sensibilities, Fitzgerald's and Huxley's novels more or less explicitly reflected on and sought a kind of symbolic revenge against the corporate author. A half a decade earlier and in his preferred regional idiom, their fellow MGM alumnus William Faulkner wove similar concerns into the fabric of *Absalom, Absalom!*: a naturalist attention to unwilled action combined with a modernist investment in the nature of narrative and authorship, conceived in the shadow of the premier corporate artist. Faulkner's ambition in and for that novel is legible in every tortuous, profligate sentence, each attempt to "say it all ... between one Cap and one period." That attempt is perhaps most readily grasped in the absurd reduction of the novel's narrative of Thomas Sutpen offered by the Canadian Shrevlin McCannon, Quentin Compson's Harvard roommate: "So he just wanted a grandson.... That was all he was after. Jesus, the South is fine, isn't it."[22] The novel's root simplicity, its attempt to attribute the grandeur and dignity of Greek tragedy to the American South, combines with and complements its "involved, formless 'style'" to place the author himself on the plane of Shakespeare, Keats, and Joyce.[23] *Absalom*'s plot— Sutpen's doomed Stoytian desire to persist indefinitely—was new for Faulkner, as was the style by which he expressed it. The narrative method comprising "embellishment, revision, and reweaving," which, according to Warwick Wadlington, is "now often thought of as essentially Faulknerian," originated in *Pylon* (1935) and *Absalom*.²⁴ Between 1933 and 1936, Faulkner became "Faulkner," realizing his own personal design as he was crafting Sutpen's failure to accomplish his own; he incorporated Yoknapatawpha County, naming himself "sole owner & proprietor" on the map he drew of his own little fabulous postal stamp in *Absalom*, while working for MGM, Universal, and Twentieth Century-Fox, the last of which, under Zanuck, employed a screenwriting system the nearest in design to MGM's.²⁵

In what follows, I will argue that Faulkner internalized and reworked his experiences of corporate agency at these studios and, in the process, devised new characters and plots in the style that would become his signature. Sutpen's Hundred, *Absalom's* personified plantation, with its unwilful factotums and metaphysical bookkeepers, emerges as the novel's true agent, the prime mover from which the narrative seems to originate. It is an agent that speaks, paradoxically but appropriately enough, in an inaudible but visible voice of proliferating punctuation. Therefore, the formal feature that concerns me most here is not the "endless sentences" but, in a sense, their opposite: the parentheses, numbering in the hundreds, which interrupt the smooth flow of a speaker's narration and usurp that speaker's prerogative as the authoritative teller of the story. Those parentheticals, instances of what Stephen M. Ross calls elements of "textual voice," index a controlling, coordinating agent responsible for the novel's normalizing Overvoice, which "envelops the discourse, taking up all subsidiary voices[, … and] becomes an entity unto itself."²⁶ In synthesizing Joseph Urgo's claim that *Absalom* comprises an allegory of screenwriting with Christensen's theory of corporate authorship, I read that voice as deriving from Sutpen's Hundred.²⁷ Thus, the dilated sentence that would become Faulkner's trademark emerged amidst and in dialectical relation with the milieu of corporate expression that the studios, especially MGM, maintained. I therefore hear Faulkner among a chorus of contemporaries, like C. L. R. James and Thurman Arnold, who situated modern business enterprise in a long trajectory of economic history. In 1938, James specifically described the sugar plantation in the West Indies as a "modern system" of production with large-scale agriculture, factory processing, and international distribution, while Arnold identified the fundamental similarity between an American belief in corporate personality and the "reverence and support of great ecclesiastical organizations in the Middle Ages."²⁸ In Sutpen's Hundred, Faulkner in effect synthesized these two notions: the plantation as a vertically integrated organization, and the corporation as a privileged person. This was a lesson, the rest of this chapter suggests, he learned from Leo's roar (Figure 2.1).²⁹

Figure 2.1 MGM advertising its corporate voice (*Variety*, April 14, 1930).
Source: Courtesy of MGM/PhotoFest.

Faulkner's Corporate Voice

Faulkner always seemed to carry part of California back to Mississippi with him.

—Tom Dardis, *Some Time in the Sun*, 1976[30]

(California would be fine, that far away; convenient, proof inherent in the sheer distance, the necessity to accept and believe)

—William Faulkner, *Absalom, Absalom!*, 1936[31]

In an interview for the *Paris Review* in 1956, Jean Stein asked Faulkner, by this point a Nobel laureate, "would you comment on that legendary Hollywood experience you were involved in?" Anyone familiar with

Faulkner's sometime work as a screenwriter would find that question vexing. As Tom Dardis and others have noted, there exist enough tales about his time at MGM, Universal, Twentieth Century-Fox, and Warner Brothers over more than a decade of work to fill a minor volume. Would he recall the time he told Sam Marx, the story editor at MGM, that he preferred to work on Mickey Mouse pictures instead of the Wallace Beery wrestling picture *Flesh* (John Ford, 1932), before proceeding to wander around Death Valley for a couple of weeks? Or the time when, on a dove hunt, he asked Clark Gable what he did for a living?[32] Or the conversations with Howard Hawks about how to make sense of Raymond Chandler's *The Big Sleep*?

The yarn he would spin for Stein—of his firing by Marx in May of 1933 from the set of "Louisiana Lou"—indicates more than the unsurprising sharpness of the author's observations of his working conditions. Faulkner's anecdote about the bungled affair at once demonstrates how closely his vision of MGM aligns with the studio's vision of itself, and how this experience helped create the artist he is now known to be. For it was during his time at MGM that Faulkner came to understand Hollywood's power to usurp the South's prerogative to tell its own stories.

A year before he wrote *Pylon* and less than a year before he formulated the narrative core of *Absalom*, Faulkner found himself in Grand Isle, one hundred miles from New Orleans, on the set of "Louisiana Lou," directed, at least for the time being, by Tod Browning.[33] In Faulkner's telling, the production, an adaptation of Lea David Freeman's "Ruby" (a play itself partially about a well-to-do writer's move to the bayou to find literary inspiration), becomes a tragicomic mock-saga of MGM's appropriation of regionalism and a subtle allegory of the studio's corporate power. After incorrectly suggesting that the film never got made (the picture was eventually released as *Lazy River* in 1934), he told Stein what MGM did manage to complete:

> But they did build a shrimp village—a long platform on piles in the water with sheds built on it—something like a wharf. The studio could have bought dozens of them for forty or fifty dollars apiece. Instead, they built their own, a false one. That is, a platform with a single wall on it, so that when you opened the door and stepped through it, you stepped right off onto the ocean itself. As they built it, on the first day, the Cajun fisherman paddled up in his narrow, tricky pirogue made out of a hollow log. He would sit in it all day long in the broiling sun watching the strange white folks building this strange imitation platform. The next day he was back in the pirogue with his whole family, his wife nursing the baby, the other children, and the mother-in-law, all to sit all that day in the broiling sun to

watch this foolish and incomprehensible activity. I was in New Orleans two or three years later and heard that the Cajun people were still coming in for miles to look at that imitation shrimp platform which a lot of white people had rushed in and built and then abandoned.[34]

Although he implicitly identifies here with the bemused and bewildered Cajuns, Faulkner no doubt understood why MGM built those piers. While he could shake his head at the "false" platform for failing to meet a standard of authenticity, Faulkner surely knew that, for MGM, that standard matters only insofar as it bespeaks production value, what *Fortune* described as the studio's "common denominator of goodness." As he pokes fun, Faulkner slyly captures the studio's vision: the bayou is an extension of the sound stage, and the Cajun, the real inhabitant of the area, is, like the original pier, rendered superfluous, readily replaceable by an extra.

Evidently embellished twenty-three years after the fact, Faulkner's story is nonetheless remarkably consistent with his MGM-era understanding of Hollywood's efforts to remake the United States in its image, efforts that in turn structure the way local populations imagine themselves.[35] Toward the conclusion of *Pylon*, Faulkner presents the industry's romantic stereotyping of regional difference as a raging illness. After pilot Roger Shumann's death, Roger's wife Laverne, her son, and the parachute jumper Jack all travel by train to Myron, Ohio, where Roger's father Dr. Shumann resides. Laverne, poor and pregnant with another child, decides to leave her boy with his grandfather. When the cab stops in front of the doctor's home, Laverne sees

> a kind of cenotaph, penurious and without majesty or dignity, of forlorn and victorious desolation—a bungalow, a tight flimsy mass of stoops and porte-cochères and flat gables and bays not five years old and built in that colored mud-and-chickenwire tradition which California moving picture films have scattered across North America as if the celluloid carried germs, not five years old yet wearing already an air of dilapidation and rot....[36]

The film industry disseminates the epidemic of modernity, as the affordable lower-middle class houses that proliferated in the first decades of the twentieth century are coded as the insubstantial sets on a studio lot. In *Pylon*, modernity, in which spectacle and simulacrum literally become the typical American's domicile, renders the North American a second-class—"colored"—citizen. Moreover, for Dr. Shumann, who lost his "big old place in the country" after mortgaging the property to pay for Roger's aircraft, the move to the California bungalow radically alters his way of thinking (*P* 271). Seven years earlier, Dr. Shumann "was different";

when Laverne confessed that she "did not know whether or not Roger was the father," he averred that the boy would be Roger's son if the couple willed it so (*P* 272). After the move to the bungalow, however, this Romantic self-determination is swallowed up by the logic of contract: "Let us understand one another," he tells her in the idiom of bargaining:

> You leave him here of your own free will; we are to make a home for him until we die: that is understood.... That we give him the home and care and affection which is his right both as a helpless child and as our gra— grand——and that in return for this, you are to make no attempt to see him or communicate with him as long as we live. That is your understanding, your agreement? (*P* 272–273)

Dr. Shumann chokes up, unable to speak in the language of patrimony or will the child to be a grandson. But he can describe the boy as a "helpless child" who has the right to be cared for, or, in other words, who must be assumed as a debt, not unlike the mortgage that forced him out of the country house and into the tight, flimsy mass. Family for Dr. Shumann has become a matter of contractual obligation, a legal-economic structure whose influence on the nature of the self informed turn-of-the-century naturalist fiction. In *Pylon*, that legal-economic structure imposes itself on and shapes the Midwestern mindset through the physical structure of the Hollywood-born homestead.[37]

At his most miffed, confused, and self-pitying, Faulkner described his own relationship to MGM in the same terms of raced self-alienation. He fantasized about the unproblematic and total possession of Yoknapatawpha County while he struggled to make ends meet. In order to support his family, retain the estate of Rowan Oak, and avoid the indignity of the bungalow, Faulkner made his "sojourns downriver" to Los Angeles, and remained psychically downriver even when he did movie work from his home in Oxford, Mississippi. In a September 1932 letter to his friend and agent Ben Wasson, Faulkner complained of his typically impulsive and self-destructive botching of a business situation, in this case, an at-will arrangement with MGM:

> You said something in Memphis about following through all my stories which you handle, into movies, etc. I would like you to do this, myself. But apparently I can do better for myself through Howard Hawks than agents can, and I must approach Hawks through his brother, who is also an agent. I don't think I should have to pay two agents when I do my own shopping for prices. Still, I would like to have you to protect me from myself, but how to do it? I am under no written contract with anyone. *This arrangement is like that of a field hand;* either of us (me or M.G.M.) to call it off without notice, they to pay me by the week, and to pay a bonus on each story.[38]

Faulkner's difficulty in managing his contracts dovetailed with his long-standing confusion regarding his relation to his agents, his conduits to the arcane economic, legal, and social organization of corporate art production. Although he took pride in his ability to negotiate the terms of his work for the studios, he nonetheless recognized his tendency to make hasty decisions, thus leading him to the cusp of the consciousness of his compromised agency. In the same way that California infected Ohio, leading Dr. Shumann to construe family relations according to the logic of contract, Oxford has become an extension of the film industry, and in abjuring contract altogether, the (white) author, crafting in fiction the Big Ideas of man's endurance, becomes his opposite, the (Black) field hand who neither controls the method nor owns the product of his labor. Offensive as this is, given the notoriously bad treatment African Americans received in Los Angeles in the pre-Civil Rights era—Langston Hughes was affronted by assignments to voice Black characters in stereotypical speech; Chester Himes was fired by Warners, with CEO Jack notoriously saying, "I don't want no n*****s on this lot"—Faulkner's self-conception was not uncommon among white writers for the major studios.[39] In the wake of wage cuts at MGM and elsewhere following President Roosevelt's bank holiday, labor organization efforts ramped up in Hollywood; Lester Cole, who helped found the Screen Writers Guild in 1933, found that the upper echelon of the industry conceived of writers as "the n*****s of the studio system."[40] The insult would have been especially acutely felt within the byzantine structure of the Thalberg screenwriting system.

The functioning of that system manifested explicitly in Faulkner's *Paris Review* anecdote about his time on the set of "Louisiana Lou," where he personified MGM in the figure of the anonymous continuity writer, whose job is to write the detailed sequence of shots that serves as the blueprint of the film.[41] "I arrived at Mr. Browning's hotel about six p.m. and reported to him," Faulkner explained to Stein.

> A party was going on. He told me to get a good night's sleep and be ready for an early start in the morning. I asked him about the story. He said, "Oh, yes. Go to room so-and-so. That's the continuity writer. He'll tell you what the story is."
>
> I went to the room as directed. The continuity writer was sitting in there alone. I told him who I was and asked him about the story. He said, "When you have written the dialogue I'll let you see the story." I went back to Browning's room and told him what had happened. "Go back," he said, "and tell that so-and-so—. Never mind, you get a good night's sleep so we can get an early start in the morning...."

> One evening on our return I had barely entered my room when the telephone rang. It was Browning. He told me to come to his room at once. I did so. He had a telegram. It said: "Faulkner is fired. MGM Studio." "Don't worry," Browning said. "I'll call that so-and-so up this minute and not only make him put you back on the payroll but send you a written apology." There was a knock on the door. It was a page with another telegram. This one said: "Browning is fired. MGM Studio." So I came back home. I presume Browning went somewhere too. *I imagine that continuity writer is still sitting in a room somewhere with his weekly salary check clutched tightly in his hand.*[42]

As though parodying himself, Faulkner here perverts his inveterate interest in the great theme of human endurance in the face of overwhelming adversity. Neither Browning nor Faulkner sees the film's production through to the end, but, at least in Faulkner's imagination, the continuity writer, motivated not by an investment in the production itself but by the paycheck, remains on the job. Consonant with Huxley's sardonic allegory of the monstrously stupid corporation, the continuity writer's longevity on the job matches the ongoing life of the studio. Shrewdly declining to name the writer, Faulkner identifies a category rather than any individual; where Browning and Faulkner can be fired and thereby separated from the corporation, the continuity writer, as a necessary function, exists as long as MGM or film production does. Like publicity agent Space Hanlon of *Bombshell*, the continuity writer consummately embodies MGM's structural power because, by demanding that shots be made a certain way so that they can be pieced together into a seamless, spatially and temporally consistent narrative, he represents the constraints on every laborer on the film set from the below-the-line workers up through the director. In this way, Faulkner echoes Fitzgerald's keen but undeveloped observation of the relationship between Thalberg's disdain for writers and his development of MGM's classical style: "he liked them, but to some extent he saw them as a necessary evil.... He developed the process of having the author working behind another, practically his invention; his ideas about continuity, how the links of the chain should be very closely knit rather than merely linked" (*LT* 139). But Faulkner also cagily turns MGM's power against the studio, reappropriating its appropriationist farrago in the bayou to burnish his own legend for the *Paris Review*.

This reappropriation, I want to argue, is a tactic Faulkner devised two decades earlier at the moment when he became the legendary "Faulkner," when he formulated his signature style in *Pylon* and *Absalom*. The germ of the California moving-picture film that settled in the Ohio of *Pylon* similarly infected Sutpen's Hundred, imbuing the plantation with the characteristics of the studio. The Hundred emerges from virgin land (substitute swamp for the Southern California desert) by the effort of an immigrant to the region (poor Scotch-English for Jew), although it seems to build itself (*AA* 203); is separated from the site of financial transactions (Jefferson: New York City); and, after a transitional period of labor and capital investment, begins to produce (cotton: narrative film) so frighteningly successfully that competitors wonder if there is some kind of legal or literal hocus-pocus afoot (*AA* 56–57), but which in any case ends up working like a self-sustaining dynamo (*AA* 57). It is in this respect that Faulkner remains true to his original conception of *Absalom*, but he particularizes and refines the naturalist "outrag[ing of] the land" that he described in a letter to publisher Harrison Smith by emphasizing the quasi-incorporated land of Sutpen's Hundred, the physical and symbolic center of which, like a gated studio lot, is the mansion.[43] Hence the importance of the mansion's architect, who, like Faulkner, was kidnapped from another domain (Haiti: Oxford) and brought in to participate in a larger corporate project despite an at-best equivocal belief in the project's merits. The architect (like Fitzgerald's Monroe Stahr, Huxley's Charlie Habakkuk, or Faulkner himself) may act against the wishes of Thomas Sutpen (Pat Brady, Jo Stoyte, or Louis B. Mayer), but in doing so, he contributes to the success of Sutpen's Hundred (Brady's studio, Beverly Pantheon cemetery, or MGM):

> [H]e was a good architect; Quentin knew the house, twelve miles from Jefferson, in its grove of cedar and oak, seventy-five years after it was finished. And not only an architect, as General Compson said, but an artist since only an artist could have borne those two years in order to build a house which he doubtless not only expected but firmly intended never to see again. Not, General Compson said, the hardship to sense and the outrage to sensibility of the two years' sojourn, but Sutpen: that only an artist could have borne Sutpen's ruthlessness and hurry and still manage to curb the dream of grim and castlelike magnificence at which Sutpen obviously aimed, since the place as Sutpen planned it would have been almost as large as Jefferson itself at the time; that the little grim harried foreigner had singlehanded given battle to and vanquished Sutpen's fierce and overweening vanity or desire for magnificence or for vindication or whatever it was ... and so created of Sutpen's very defeat the victory which, in conquering, Sutpen himself would have failed to gain.[44] (*AA* 28–29)

Similarly, in the novel's fourth chapter, Sutpen's daughter Judith describes a process of collaborative creation where the final product differs from any of the collaborators' intentions. Crucially, Judith chooses a metaphor for corporate aesthetic production to describe the condition of life itself:

> You get born and you try this and you don't know why only you keep on trying it and you are born at the same time with a lot of other people, all mixed up with them, like trying to, having to, move your arms and legs with strings only the same strings are hitched to all other arms and legs and the others all trying and they don't know why either except that the strings are all in one another's way like five or six people all trying to make a rug on the same loom only each one wants to weave his own pattern into the rug; and it cant matter, you know that, or the Ones that set up the loom would have arranged things a little better, and yet it must matter because you keep on trying or have to keep on trying. (*AA* 100–101)

Judith laments the inevitable inscrutable muddle that results when, in the terms of her textile metaphor, the threads that connect the uncoordinated simultaneous efforts of marionette-artisans tangle, preventing them from weaving their own figures into the carpet. However, this mutually undermining conflict results in only apparent chaos; an intended pattern does exist ("it must matter"), but, like one of the half-dozen screenwriters Thalberg would have working on a project at any given time, that intention exceeds the awareness of any individual. That design, in short, belongs to the Ones that Judith cannot name, the Ones who provide the infrastructure and the impetus—here, the loom and the fact of being—for the project. The Greeks, or Mr. Compson, would call the Ones gods, or Fate, or Fortune. *Fortune*, however, would call the Ones corporations.

The crisis of agency Judith describes pervades the Sutpen family in the form of their "perverse automotivation" (*AA* 181), a perversity manifesting not only in the hetero- and homoerotic fantasies of incest and miscegenation among Judith, Henry Sutpen, and Charles Bon, but more generally and prosaically in the uncultured strangeness of Thomas Sutpen's efforts. Ironically, Quentin calls this Sutpen's "innocence":

> All of a sudden he discovered, not what he wanted to do but what he just had to do, had to do it whether he wanted to or not, because if he did not do it he knew that he could never live with himself for the rest of his life…. And that at the very moment he discovered what it was, he found out that this was the last thing in the world he was equipped to do because he not only had not known that he would have to do this, he did not even know that it existed to be wanted, to need to be done, until he was almost fourteen years old. (*AA* 178–79)

That innocence corresponds, initially, to a want of knowledge, a consequence of class position and family history; as the offspring of poor white mountainfolk from what would become West Virginia, "he never even heard of, never imagined, a place, a land divided neatly up and actually owned by men who did nothing but ride over it on fine horses or sit in fine clothes on the galleries of big houses while other people worked for them" (*AA* 179). In addition to defining the bounds of his conception of possibility, his innocence establishes the conditions of Sutpen's experience of space and time as well. Like his grandson Charles Etienne Saint-Valery Bon, who suffers alternating periods of stagnation like "a broken cinema film" and "furious and incomprehensible and apparently reasonless moving, progression" (*AA* 167), the young Thomas's move to the Pettibone plantation in the Tidewater region of Virginia happens as if by a force of nature, experienced less as a discrete "period" than as an "attenuation from a kind of furious inertness and patient immobility" (*AA* 181).[45] This innocence survives "intact" after Pettibone's Black butler turns him away from the front door of the big house, an experience that Sutpen registers as an "explosion—a bright glare that vanished and left nothing, no ashes nor refuse: just a limitless flat plain with the severe shape of his intact innocence, rising from it like a monument" (*AA* 192). Sutpen's great humiliation triggers a recognition of his innocence as the Design—described, strangely but significantly, in terms of modernist artwork. After the Design bursts into being, Sutpen becomes aware that his body moves without his control; in looking for a place to think about the traumatic racial encounter with the butler, "he did not tell himself where to go: … his body, his feet, just went there" (*AA* 188). In *Light in August* (1932), Faulkner had described the young Joe Christmas, smitten with youthful lust, pursuing the object of his desire in similar terms, "without plan or design, almost without volition, as if his feet ordered his action and not his head."[46] However, Sutpen ultimately resembles Christmas less than he does Roger Shumann and Laverne of *Pylon*, whose compulsions to act—in his case, to fly a plane; in hers, to fornicate—derive from the very nature of their inhuman being, aptly described by the narrating reporter in mechanistic terms: "they aint human. It aint adultery; you cant anymore imagine two of them making love than you can two of them aeroplanes back in the corner of the hangar, coupled" (*P* 204).

While the Design reduces the ever-innocent Sutpen to an automaton, it at the same time seems to invest Sutpen's Hundred with the qualities of personhood. General Compson proposes that the big house on the plantation has a "sentience, a personality and character acquired not from the people who breathe or have breathed in them" (*AA* 67); after the Hundred burns down, Quentin thinks that the structure burned "with a smell of desolation and decay as if the wood of which it was built were flesh" (*AA* 293). For this reason, Faulkner scholars have noted the Hundred's Gothic elements, comparing it, for instance, to Edgar Allan Poe's House of Usher. Since the emergence of the genre in the late eighteenth century, writers have employed the Gothic mode, and specifically its grand, decaying structures, as material instantiations of the friction between economic regimes. For Horace Walpole, the titular Castle of Otranto's "supernatural phenomena are emanations of a providential law of inheritance" that, to an increasingly bourgeois late-eighteenth century readership, seemed a spooky hangover of a feudal economy; almost a century later, Nathaniel Hawthorne's House of Seven Gables indexed anxieties about property rights amidst the burgeoning market economy in the United States.[47] In this vein, Sutpen's Hundred can be interpreted, following Richard Godden's analysis, in light of the recent transformation of the South's sharecropping economy by the Agricultural Adjustment Act of 1933.[48] But that New Deal program's instigation of a "Second Reconstruction" cannot account for the most distinctive aspect of Sutpen's Hundred, its capacity for speech. Unsurprisingly, Rosa Coldfield, the self-nominated poet laureate of Jefferson, puts the finest point on the nature of the Hundred's expression. As a young girl, Rosa "[tried] to make [herself] blend with the dark wood and become invisible, like a chameleon, listening to the living spirit, presence, of that house, since some of Ellen's life and breath had now gone into it as well as his [i.e. Sutpen's], breathing away in a long neutral sound of victory and despair, of triumph and terror too" (*AA* 19).[49] In being animated by Sutpen's and Judith's funds of spirit, and yet in being an expressive entity unto itself, the Hundred appears uncannily like a Hollywood studio with a particular house style.[50]

What makes the Hundred more like a studio than any other kind of corporation is its distinct narrative "voice" that everywhere suffuses the text. To hear the Hundred's "long and neutral" sound, Rosa must disappear into the structure of the big house, much as her voice "vanishes" into the story as she tells it (*AA* 4). But because the Hundred's voice is "long" like the "intervals" of the narrative stream—it stretches from one end of the novel to the other—and "neutral"—as though it were uninflected and without a recognizable human grain—it goes unheard. Even Rosa, the most sensitive of Jeffersonians, can only "hear" the voice of the house as ventriloquized through its inhabitants, as when she tries to view Charles Bon's corpse: "It said one word: 'Clytie,' like that, that cold, that still: not Judith but the house itself speaking again, though it was Judith's voice" (*AA* 114). The unadulterated voice of Sutpen's Hundred resonates at a frequency beyond the audible range of any character in this most profusely spoken novel.

It can, however, be "heard" in the curiously consistent voices of Rosa, Jason Compson, Quentin, and Shreve, the novel's four ostensibly distinct narrators. They speak not harmoniously—a word that would imply that discrete voices could be made out—but rather homogenously, in voices that sound astonishingly alike and seem to dissolve into the narrative itself. This merging, detectable throughout the novel, reaches a sublime apex in Chapter 8, as Quentin and Shreve join in a "happy marriage of speaking and hearing" (*AA* 253). Stephen M. Ross calls this monophony the style of *Absalom*'s Overvoice, a voice that "seems excessively motivated, overdetermined in the Freudian sense, as if emanating from sources indefinable yet intensely felt."[51] The intensity of the controlling Overvoice finds its analogue in the intensity of Sutpen's controlling Design. If the closest the novel gets to a material manifestation of that Design is the Hundred, and if the Hundred speaks in an inaudible but perceptible "voice," we might consider the Overvoice as the supersonic trace of the Hundred's effort.

This conjecture, however outlandish, has the virtue of clarifying the parallel between, on the one hand, the inversion, conflation, and ultimate dissolution of the novel's diegetic levels, and, on the other, the convergence of the narrative's voices and persons. Although Quentin is, from the start of the novel, a "commonwealth" containing the voices of his Southern heritage, these voices ultimately overwhelm him (*AA* 7). As Quentin and Shreve reconstruct Sutpen's story from the confines of their Harvard dorm, each remarks that the other sounds like Quentin's father, creating the impression that the pair speaks as a single entity. Quentin and Shreve then seem to join with Henry Sutpen and Charles Bon, respectively:

> Shreve ceased. That is, for all the two of them, Shreve and Quentin, knew he had stopped, since for all the two of them knew he had never begun, since it did not matter (and possibly neither of them conscious of the distinction) which one had been doing the talking. So that now it was not two but four of them riding the two horses through the dark over the frozen December ruts of that Christmas eve: four of them and then just two—Charles-Shreve and Quentin-Henry, the two of them both believing that Henry was thinking *He* (meaning his father) *has destroyed us all*, not for one moment thinking *He* (meaning Bon) *must have known or at least suspected this all the time; that's why he has acted as he has, why he did not answer my letters last summer nor write to Judith, why he has never asked her to marry him*.... (*AA* 267, italics in the original)

The parentheticals here attempt to disambiguate the referents of pronouns, a gesture that is subtly ironic because earlier, another parenthetical remark emerged without an evident source, revealing, in a stunning metaleptic inversion, that the novel is in fact a kind of literary Klein bottle. The Quentin-Shreve frame narrative is in fact encompassed by Thomas Sutpen, the figure at its ostensible center, and stable references become all but impossible to determine:

> That was why it did not matter to either of them which one did the talking, since it was not the talking alone which did it, performed and accomplished the overpassing [to love], but some happy marriage of speaking and hearing wherein each before the demand, the requirement, forgave condoned and forgot the faulting of the other—faultings both in the creating of this shade [i.e. Sutpen] whom they discussed *(rather, existed in)*, and in the hearing and sifting and discarding the false and conserving what seemed true, or fit the preconceived—in order to overpass to love, where there might be paradox and inconsistency but nothing fault nor false. (*AA* 253, my emphasis)

One way out of this paradox is to "overpass" it and suppose that Quentin and Shreve do not occupy the furthest exterior frame of the narrative. Because the stream of the story exists outside of them, they are subject to the novel's general logic of dissolution, too: along with the dissolving of narrative levels, the characters dissolve in the narrative stream such that each exists within the others.

That this narrative logic becomes visible in the form of a brief parenthetical is fitting, because while the Hundred's voice is inaudible, it can be detected in what Ross calls "textual voice," Faulkner's manipulation of typography and other material qualities of print.[52] *Absalom* is overfull with punctuation of various kinds, but the most artfully and expressively used is the parenthesis.[53] The neutral voice of Sutpen's Hundred can be "heard" on nearly every page in the form of the profuse parentheticals in the text (594 by Fred Randel's count of the 1936 Random House edition; 638 in my own count of Noel Polk's 1986 corrected edition), which are not only numerous but also, on occasion, multiply nested and, in one case, stretched across nearly thirty pages. These parentheticals become more frequent and extravagant, moreover, as voices and persons merge more completely in Chapters 7 and 8, as though an external agent coordinates the speakers' efforts.[54] It is in this respect that *Absalom*'s form most resembles that of *Ulysses*. As Hugh Kenner explained long ago, Joyce developed a text-internal consciousness that the critic called "The Arranger" to position typographical incursions and compile the impressions, styles, and puzzles that populate the novel.[55] But whether personal, parodic, or typographical, Joyce's voices remain distinctive, while in *Absalom*, they bend to an overarching idea. If Wadlington is right that Faulkner became "Faulkner" while writing *Absalom*, he did so not only by absorbing the European moderns but also by attuning his inner ear to MGM's voice.

While exposure to corporate expression may have been crucial to the development of Faulkner's style and the narrative design of *Absalom*, he wasn't especially grateful for MGM's exploitation. And it was the studio that ended up calling off the "field hand" relationship, with MGM producing only one of his screenplays (*Today We Live* [Howard Hawks, 1933], adapted from Faulkner's short story "Turnabout").[56] For the writer struggling in semi-obscurity who badly needed the money, a revenge befitting a classical tragedy was in order: the corporate studio's self-sustaining, phantasmatic existence must be snuffed out. Faulkner wreaked that vengeance in his destruction of Sutpen and his Hundred, the novel's final dissolution. Like a proper tragedy, their downfall appears as a form of hamartia with a Thalbergian twist. "I was faced with condoning a fact which had been foisted upon me without my knowledge during the building toward my design, which meant the absolute negation of the design," Sutpen tells General Jason Compson, Quentin's grandfather, explaining the heretofore unknown and invisible taint of Black blood in his French-Creole wife's lineage. The threat to the Design is, of course, none other than the fact of the miscegenation that renders Charles Bon an illegitimate heir and unacceptable husband for Judith.

> I am now faced with a second necessity to choose, the curious factor of which is not … that the necessity of a new choice should have arisen, but that either choice which I might make, either course which I might choose, leads to the same result: either I destroy my design with my own hand, which will happen if I am forced to play my last trump card, or do nothing, let matters take the course which I know they will take and see my design complete itself quite normally and naturally and successfully to the public eye, yet to my own in such fashion as to be a mockery and a betrayal of that little boy who approached that door fifty years ago and was turned away, for whose vindication the whole plan was conceived and carried forward to the moment of this choice, this second choice devolving out of that first one which in its turn was forced on me as the result of an agreement, an arrangement which I had entered in good faith, concealing nothing, while the other party or parties to it concealed from me the one very factor which would destroy the entire plan and design which I had been working toward, concealed so well that it was not until after the child was born that I discovered that this factor existed. (*AA* 220)

Nothing more needs to be said about this as the quintessential horror of American racial ideology. The manner of Sutpen's presentation, however, requires unpacking in two respects. First, not only does the Design function autonomously of Sutpen ("complete itself quite normally"), but it is also flawed, if not inherently, then at least from the start. And that flaw is related to, if not founded upon, the logic and rhetoric of contractual obligation ("an arrangement which I had entered in good faith"): the same logic and rhetoric that indexed the bucolic Midwest's corruption by celluloid-borne modernity in *Pylon*.

Sutpen's automotivation, which renders him more a machine than a man and less of a person than the plantation that takes his name, corresponds to his powerlessness before a notional entity—the Design—conceived in legal terms. And that legalism becomes the explicit downfall of the Design itself in the form of Eulalia Bon's lawyer and business manager. An invention of Quentin and Shreve's—"Sure," Shreve offers, "that's who it would be: the lawyer, that lawyer with his private mad female millionaire to farm" (*AA* 241)—the nameless character has long proved a bugbear to interpretation of the novel. When Faulkner was asked about the character at the University of Virginia two decades later, he claimed to barely remember it; Eric Sundquist suggests that the inexplicable lawyer is an emblem for the excessiveness and confusion of the novel as a whole:

> Because it is the burden of Quentin and Shreve to save from wasted effort the previous struggles of Rosa and Mr. Compson to bring Sutpen's story into coherent focus, the lawyer's role, knitting together a series of unlikely incidents, is necessarily perilous and seemingly fortuitous. But the crisis this produces in Faulkner's own design perfectly matches, and by analogy forces to an agonizing pitch, the reciprocal relationships of Bon and Henry, Shreve and Quentin. More than anything, perhaps, it grows out of the novel's expressed need to suggest, to intimate, to wrest from all doubt while leaving all doubts in place, a motive for Bon's actions that is more than simple revenge.[57]

Far from improbable, though, this malevolent, anonymous lawyer, unknown in Faulkner's fiction before his first sojourn downriver to Culver City, is in fact necessary: he is the epitome of the structural power of a corporation: the embodiment of the Design.

According to Jay Watson, Faulkner's typical lawyer figure is a great practitioner of oration and rhetoric as well as a "lawyer-citizen ... animated by an ethic of service and typically aligned, for better or worse, with communal values."[58] In his post-MGM fiction, however, we find legal functionaries who violate this characterization. In *Pylon*, Colonel Feinman, the benefactor of the New Valois airfield and a lawyer by trade, ensures pilot Roger Shumann's demise by flouting the American Aeronautical Association's safety regulations. Under the guise of philanthropy and public mindedness, Feinman, a Jew on the city's sewage board, attempts to bolster his prestige like a film executive or one of the "flesh peddler" agents like Myron Selznick, whom Faulkner left in order to make his own deals "with no interference from any Jew in California."[59] (It is not for nothing that the Colonel's airspace and -field are littered by glittering waste described in a peculiarly Hollywoodish idiom: the "celluloid" "tinseldung of stars" [*P* 176, 184].) Feinman manages to achieve his ends with the aid of an unctuous male secretary whose ambiguous gender and ethnicity emphasize his anonymity: "he spoke … with a kind of silken insolence, like the pampered intelligent hateridden eunuchmountebank of an eastern despot" (*P* 196). Efficacy and anonymity are therefore split between two figures that work in tandem to effect *Pylon*'s unhappy end. The show business agent, as embodied by the amalgamation of Feinman and his secretary, allows Shumann to violate state bureaucratic law and thereby enables his fatal flight. Likewise, Ira Ewing of "Golden Land" (1935), Faulkner's only story explicitly about Los Angeles, benefits from the aid of an anonymous, smooth-talking male secretary. The secretary helps real estate magnate Ewing arrange with a local newspaper a contract for a 30 percent share of circulation profits in exchange for helping expose his daughter's career-threatening sexual transgression. Ewing trades the intrinsic love he has for his daughter, which has evidently been devalued by his alcoholism, avarice, and the generally corrupting influence of California, for points on the gross. For Ewing, investments in family are just that: measurable and exchangeable for money.

The Ewing mentality reaches its apotheosis in Eulalia Bon's counselor, as "all the lawyer wanted was just the money" that he intends to extract from Sutpen (*AA* 248). In this respect, as well as in his anonymity, he resembles no figure more than Faulkner's continuity writer, check clutched tightly in hand, who outlasts both screenwriter and director on MGM's ersatz bayou pier. Following from his overwhelming cupidity, Eulalia's lawyer makes no distinction between money and emotion, explicitly equating these seemingly incommensurate notions of value. Unlike the whole equation of pictures, known only to Monroe Stahr and a handful of others tycoons, this equivalence of money and emotion is, as Leo Rosten explains, fundamental to life in Hollywood, where "actors and writers and directors … live in a world of emotional rather than numerical symbols."[60] In the "secret drawer in the secret safe and the secret paper in it," Quentin and Shreve imagine that the lawyer keeps a ledger recording Sutpen's actions, whereabouts, and finances along with the "*Emotional val.*" he receives from his children.

> Today he finished robbing a drunken Indian of a hundred miles of virgin land, val 25,000. At 2:31 today came up out of swamp with final plank for house. val in conj. with land 40,000. 7:52 p.m. today married. Bigamy threat val. minus nil. Unless quick buyer. Not probable. Doubtless conjoined with wife same day. Say 1 year ... Son. Intrinsic val. possible though not probable forced sale of house & land plus val. Crop minus child's one quarter. Emotional val. Plus 100% times nil. Plus val. crop. Say 10 years, one or more children. Intrinsic val. forced sale house & improved land plus liquid assets minus children's share. Emotional val. 100% times increase yearly for each child plus intrinsic val. plus liquid assets plus working acquired credit.... (*AA* 241)

Watson rightly asserts that the lawyer "directly or indirectly brings about the complete ruin of everything around him in his lust for power and wealth"; as such, he is the most efficacious character in the novel, a more perfect mechanism than even the infernal Sutpen himself, at once the purest instantiation of Sutpen's Design and the guarantor of its failure.[61] Because the lawyer is a necessary fiction devised by Quentin and Shreve to make sense of the fall of the house of Sutpen, and because Quentin and Shreve are themselves conduits through which that story flows, the lawyer's insidious behavior amounts to the Design's self-immolation.

If MGM reduced Faulkner to (in his view) a field hand, the author got his payback at the novel's end. There, the Overvoice—the Design's corporate voice—is reduced to the long, neutral, semantically empty howling of Sutpen's sole surviving relative, his great-grandson Jim Bond. Bond, as the Compson family's groom Luster explains, is "a lawyer word," making him the counterpart of the confabulated attorney (*AA* 174). In *The Sound and the Fury*, Luster cares for Benjy, Faulkner's more famous inarticulate Jeffersonian. There, Faulkner used Benjy's moaning as an ironic counterpoint to the high modernist stream of consciousness, a repurposing of Joycean technique to represent the cognitively disabled Compson's perception and experience of time.[62] But in *Absalom*, as I've attempted to show, capturing multiple human consciousnesses isn't the novel's central formal problem. All characters are versions of the perversely automotivated mechanisms that act under the sway of the Design, and Faulkner devised a new technique, the typographically marked Overvoice, to address the new problem of corporate aesthetic expression. By proposing, as Shreve does in 1910, that "in time the Jim Bonds are going to conquer the western hemisphere," Faulkner gets the last laugh on MGM and the other studios that by 1936 had inherited the earth (*AA* 302). Although "(Hollywood ... is no longer in Hollywood but is stippled by a billion feet of burning colored gas across the face of the American earth)," as he would write in *The*

Wild Palms (1939) in the now-typically Faulknerian parenthetical, that gas is ultimately nothing more than the miasma of capital—as meaningless as the bonds that finance it.[63]

***

Faulkner wasn't alone in developing his fictional voice against the backdrop of the studio system. However, his, Fitzgerald's, and Huxley's experiences writing for MGM varied significantly from those of less-fortunate writers like James M. Cain, who essentially set the terms by which critics have understood the Depression-era Hollywood novel after failing at Paramount and Columbia. In his essay "Paradise" (February 1933), Cain played the role of pioneer-informant for the eastern readers of *The American Mercury*, and in the process, theorized the sensibility and style that characterized *The Postman Always Rings Twice* (1933), the novel he was soon to publish. "If you are like myself before I came here, you have formed, from Sunkist ads, newsreels, movie magazines, railroad folders, and so on, a somewhat false picture of [Southern California], and you will have to get rid of this before you can understand what I am trying to say." What follows is a bravura exercise in negation, which Cain accomplishes by incessantly repeating his directive "Wash out." Wash out the smell of flowers, the color from a girl's cheeks, the sights of palm trees that don't match the landscape, "movie palazzos" that have all the "lifelessness of movie sets," and "[a]bove all, wash out the cool green that seems to be the main feature of all illustrations got out by railroads. Wash that out and keep it out." In the space of half a page, Cain clears away the pop culture image of the region and, in doing so, erases all trace of human existence. It is on this foundation of the "gray, sunbaked tan" land where "the naked earth shows through everything that grows on it" that Cain proceeds to add the often-remarked architectural travesties that give the place its color. But Cain then obliterates even these, suggesting that when the watercolor painting that has been constructed in the mind's eye is taken out into the "noonday sun ... all that is left is the gray, sunbaked tan that you started with. Well, that is Southern California."[64]

Doing away with local color and detail wasn't Cain's original literary inclination. Beginning with the satirical dialogues he started writing for the *Mercury* in 1925, Cain made hay of American dialects; his first short stories, "Pastorale" (1928) and "The Taking of Montfaucon" (1929), emphasized each narrator's social and intellectual position at the level of syntax and diction. Although he retained the first-person perspective in *Postman*, Cain traded the "eastern" for the "western roughneck" and formulated the voice of "the boy who is just as elemental inside as his eastern colleague, but who has been to high school, who completes his sentences, and uses reasonably good grammar."[65] Frank Chambers sounds like an American everyman, or, better, no-man; put simply, his voice is as arid, clear, and brutal as the California desert. But if that voice matches the petty criminal's rootlessness, it harmonizes too with the sound of Cain's critical journalism. Cain biographer Roy Hoopes seems to be right when he notes that, after being fired by the studios and spending his days driving aimlessly around Southern California, "Cain made the decision to tell *his* story."[66] After washing out at Columbia, Cain embraced the vocal equivalent of the washed-out desert, the bleak environmental correlative of the stylistic and existential poverty of *Postman*. And like him, other early writers of what has come to be called California noir—Todhunter Ballard, author of hardboiled *Black Mask* stories featuring studio "troubleshooter" Bill Lennox, and Horace McCoy (*They Shoot Horses, Don't They?* [1935])— also found their style and subject matter after being turned away by the studios.[67] That McCoy claimed to have started his novel without knowledge of Cain's only emphasizes the fact that authors' experiences of the industry inflected their approaches to ostensibly common subjects: Huxley and McCoy may have each rued the absurdity of Southern California, but they conceived of that absurdity differently according to their respective attitudes toward Hollywood, an attitude conditioned by MGM in the one case, precarious employment in the other.

According to the critical consensus, the "sunshine or noir" antinomy manifests most intensely at the end of the decade.[68] The year 1939 was, the story goes, the best of times for the industry and the worst of times for the industry's immiserated novelists. On the one hand, the studios distributed an unparalleled roster of movies, spearheaded by the commercial and critical success of *Gone with the Wind* and rounded out by *Gunga Din*, *Ninotchka*, *Stagecoach*, *The Wizard of Oz*, and *Wuthering Heights*, among many others; on the other, Random House published Nathanael West's *The Day of the Locust*, a novel whose "negative sublimity" owed to the writer's toil for Republic Pictures, the most prominent producer on Poverty Row.[69] That tale of two Hollywoods, though broadly correct and useful as a heuristic, in fact obscures the extent to which the industry understood itself to be in serious trouble. One reason why the notion of a cool, controlled Classical Hollywood style might strike one as miraculous (or unbelievable) is that life in the movie colony was in no way governed by the canons of decorum, invisibility, and self-effacement. In a sense, the possibility of collapse—of a star's career, of a studio's fortunes, of the industry's maintenance of its economic interests against the demands of censorious third parties and the threat of antitrust proceedings—was the engine of the studio system. Put bluntly by Universal's Maurice Bergman a decade later in the lead-up to the *Paramount* decision, "crisis is the backbone of our industry."[70]

But even for an industry in a constant state of tumult, the late 1930s were not, as Catherine Jurca put it, "crisis as usual." Not only did the industry suffer a downturn in receipts following the 1937 recession; not only did it fret over the looming threat of antitrust action (which would be only partially settled by the consent decrees of 1940) and stand accused of harboring Communists, an allegation that would prompt investigations by the House Committee on Un-American Activities beginning in 1940. It also felt the novel concerns of internecine strife resulting from a failure of public relations. For Jurca, Harry Brandt's famous "box office poison" salvo, which maligned numerous (mostly female) stars, brought into view theater owners' beliefs that the studios had lost touch with their audience's desires, a fatal condition for an industry dependent on satisfying the whims of a capricious public. To address these problems, the studios devised the Motion Pictures' Greatest Year campaign, "the first really cooperative venture in cinema history," which "sought to present the film industry as a 'big and serious business,' run by thoughtful and industrious executives who employed talented, hardworking artists and skilled technicians."[71] Writing in 1939, Margaret Farrand Thorp, a literary critic and student of Hollywood folklore, summed up the studio system's position thus: "The movies must come of age in America but they may prefer to do it by a method of their own, unlike that suggested by any of their reformers."[72]

Thorp was right in every respect save for her subjunctive mood.

CHAPTER 3

The Motion Picture Industry's Coming of Age

A history of the movies should not be a documentary film but a melodrama.
—Margaret Farrand Thorp, *America Goes to the Movies*, 1939[1]

The Motion Pictures' Greatest Year campaign was but one of many efforts Hollywood undertook to convince itself, its fans, and its critics of its maturation as an industry and social presence, a narrative that contributed to and promoted the related discourse of the American cinema's development as an art. These efforts took two forms. On the one hand, the studios became newly willing to produce pictures on political themes, such as Walter Wanger's Spanish Civil War film *Blockade* (William Dieterle, 1938) and Warners' *Confessions of a Nazi Spy* (Anatole Litvak, 1939). On the other hand, they committed to touting the industry's development by commemorating the Golden Jubilee of the invention of the Kinetoscope (1889–1939) and by participating in the progress narratives purveyed by the Museum of Modern Art in New York.[2] By early 1936, Paramount, Loew's, Twentieth Century-Fox, Warner Bros., and Universal finally agreed to contribute materials to Iris Barry's Film Department at MoMA, which would be distributed to college campuses for film study and included in the travelling programs "A Short Survey of American Film, 1895–1932" and "Some Memorable American Films, 1896–1934."[3] In late 1937, Barry opened the exhibit "The Making of a Contemporary Film" featuring David O. Selznick's *The Adventures of Tom Sawyer* (Norman Taurog, 1938), a Technicolor production that attested to the industry's technological progress as well as to the good sense of Film Department president John Hay Whitney, who held stakes in both Technicolor and Selznick-International Pictures. In at least these two respects, MoMA acted shrewdly in choosing the American literary classic of youth to celebrate the American film industry's maturity.[4] The Academy of Motion Picture Arts and Sciences voted to honor Barry's work at the

1938 Awards ceremony, explicitly acknowledging the museum's role in "for the first time making available to the public the means of studying the historical and aesthetic development of the motion picture as one of the major arts."⁵ The industry's investment in MoMA's archive yielded dividends in the form of Lewis Jacobs's *The Rise of the American Film* (1939), the first major history published since Terry Ramsaye's *A Million and One Nights* (1926) and Benjamin Hampton's *A History of the Movies* (1931). In the section titled "Maturity," Jacobs observed that Hollywood reached its "commercial zenith" during the decade following the transition to sound. "Further developments are not in the line of expansion," he concluded, "so much as in that of refinement." If, as Barry wrote in her preface to Jacobs's book, "'The Rise of the American Film' is really a romance[,] … the colorful tale of as typical a group of Americans as one could hope to hear of … drawn into a new kind of creative expression suited to the machine age," the writing of that romance depended on Hollywood's surprising relationship with the museum.⁶ The industry exploited that relationship yet more vigorously during the 1939 Golden Jubilee. *The Movies March On!*, produced by Time, Inc. and distributed by RKO, publicized MoMA's "living encyclopedia" while narrating the progress of the movies from W.K.L. Dickson's minute-long *May Irwin Kiss* (1896) to Edwin S. Porter's *The Great Train Robbery* (1903) to John Ford's adaptation of John Steinbeck's *The Grapes of Wrath* (Twentieth Century-Fox, 1940), an instant classic of an instant classic.⁷

Even sociologist Leo Rosten's demystification of the "Hollywood legend," *Hollywood: The Movie Colony, The Movie Makers* (1941), ultimately reaffirmed the maturation plot, albeit in a backhanded way. For Rosten, who was advised in his writing by Walter Wanger, among others, "Hollywood"—the industry itself as well as its ingenue stars, boy genius producers, and first-generation millionaires—was "young." But if "it [was] too young, too new, and too uncertain," its persistent adolescence worked to the industry's advantage, for Hollywood's apparent immaturity, manifesting in the pervasive narcissism and self-display of a romantic youthfulness, was the basis of its growth. The industry's "feverish, self-interested quality" looked either like the "case of children, or … psychotics," but in reality, "Hollywood [was] sane": its apparent arrested development was a productive pathology, the response of "creative—hence temperamental— personalities" to a business whose "objective conditions … are hazardous." Hollywood is exceptional only in being a more intense version of any major American city, because "in the movie colony, as in the content of the movies themselves, romantic individualism, the most compelling idea in American history, has reached the apogee of its glory." Although Rosten joined Jacobs in observing a zenith, he saw the next age not as an equilibrium but as a decline. Having reached the end of its "lush and profligate phase," Hollywood in 1941 should anticipate, he felt, a "descent" of salaries, an amputation of excess spending, and "violent unemployment [that] will run a scythe through the ranks of the movie makers."[8] According to Rosten, what had looked like the industry's budding was in fact a full flowering, with decay on the horizon.

The combination of the industry's constitutive self-involvement, its mounting concern with public relations, and its strategic emphasis on its historical development gave rise, in the late 1930s, to a significant transformation of the backstudio picture associated principally with Selznick's *A Star is Born* (1937).[9] Preceded by the Paramount programmer *Hollywood Boulevard* (Robert Florey, 1936), about a faded star's sale of his salacious memoirs to a fan magazine, *A Star is Born* prompted A-picture responses from Warner Bros. (*Boy Meets Girl* [Lloyd Bacon, 1938]) and Twentieth Century-Fox (*Hollywood Cavalcade* [Irving Cummings, 1939]). Taken together, these movies signaled the emergence of what could be called the *historical* backstudio film, a variant of the broader 1930s trend of prestige historical epics and biopics.[10] While all Hollywood movies, as Jerome Christensen has argued, are expressions of studio intentions, the backstudio picture, by virtue of its subject matter, offers a particularly vivid depiction of a studio's strategies, if not necessarily of its practices. (When the *New York Times* film critic Frank Nugent coined the term "back-studio" he compared the genre to a burlesque dance, but one where the dancer "builds illusion even as she strips it away.")[11] For the makers of prestige historical backstudio pictures, the common strategy seems to have been two-fold: to join the industry's general public relations effort, albeit to varying degrees of success, while at the same time taking different approaches to the issue of Hollywood history, in accordance with and promoting each studio's identity.[12]

For Selznick, whose father Lewis produced films during the silent era, Hollywood's history was personal history, and *A Star is Born*'s mixture of poignancy and optimism derives from the son's competing desires to both honor the forgotten and tout industrial progress. According to the historian J. E. Smyth, the melodramatic recreation of actor John Gilbert's downfall and death epitomized, for Selznick, the industry's lack of historical awareness and its tendency to embrace the new, sexy, and saleable at the expense of the old: the forgotten pioneer, the faded star, the bygone era, all of which the producer knew intimately from the collapse of his father's career in 1923 and his friend Clara Bow's premature retirement in 1933 (among many other quickly forgotten Hollywood personages).[13] However, in *A Star is Born*, Selznick counterbalanced the melodramatics of personal memory with the core values of Hollywood cinema: stardom, spectacle, and technology. The Technicolor picture describes plucky young Vicki Lester's (Janet Gaynor) rise to stardom thanks to the tutelage and love of Norman Maine (Fredric March), a veteran star in alcoholic decline. In one sense, Vicki's rise from Midwestern hopeful to bit player to major star follows the standard trajectory of boosterish Hollywood fiction like *Merton of the Movies*, but Selznick believed that he was telling a different kind of story. For him, *A Star is Born* was both a passion project and a crusade; the producer hoped "to disprove what [he] had long believed had been a tradition until this time, that pictures about Hollywood could not succeed." Previous failures at the box office had resulted, in Selznick's view, from failures to tell the truth about the industry: "I believed that the whole world was interested in Hollywood and that the trouble with most films about Hollywood was that they gave a false picture, that they burlesqued it, or they oversimplified it, but that they were not true reflections of what happened in Hollywood."[14]

Amidst fears of box office poison and in concert with the industry's burgeoning interest in its narrative of development, *A Star is Born* can be understood as naturalizing and justifying the studio system's pharmakon: stardom as both Hollywood's poison and its remedy. Falling star Maine, having been poisoned by alcohol, has become unsaleable; his personal and professional dissolutions are not only clear references to Hollywood's history of scandal but are also, more specifically, nods to the Production Code Administration's post-1934 purging of unsavory behavior from the screen. A flawed man, Maine is a bad star, which makes his death sad but necessary. For even if he were to live, his star persona had already burnt out, portending box office demise and the social death that accompanies irrelevance in a company town. In committing suicide, Maine acknowledges that his dipsomania threatens his wife's spectacular career, but that acknowledgment is motivated by a fall off the wagon precipitated by a savage tongue-lashing from the publicity man, Libby (Lionel Stander). Less a jubilant fast-talker like *Bombshell*'s Space Hanlon than a Warneresque tough guy, a cynical man of the people, Libby greets the newly sober actor at the Santa Anita Racetrack clubhouse bar: "Why it's Mr. America of yesteryear.... I suppose you'll be here all the time, now that you've retired from the hurly-burly of the silver screen." But what really pushes Norman over the edge is realizing that, from the industry's perspective, Norman never *was* more than his box office take: "Friends, my eye!" Libby sneers.

"I got you out of your jams because it was my job – not because I was your 'friend.' I don't like you. I never did like you. Nothing made me happier than to see all those cute little pranks of yours catch up with you and land you on your celebrated face."[15]

Vicki, meanwhile, is the antidote to Norman's poison. Even as a widow, she is a stalwart wife, introducing herself to her fans at movie's end as Mrs. Norman Maine. Vivacious and virtuous, she is Selznick's vision of Hollywood's star burning bright, yet the virtue that matters most in the movie is not Vicki's fidelity to Norman but rather to her studio and to the movies more generally. Honoring her contract with Oliver Niles (Adolph Menjou), which the ever-gracious producer had permitted her to break, is identical to conserving the metaphysical "bargain" she made, according to her pioneer-spirited Granny, when she decided to pursue her dream. And by embodying "sincerity and naturalness," the characteristics that convince producer Niles to sign her, Vicki also accommodates the late-Depression audience's exhaustion with the "glamour girls" who would populate Harry Brandt's "box office poison" notice the following year.[16] *A Star is Born* thus attempted to accomplish the same goal that the "Motion Pictures' Greatest Year" campaign would soon pursue: "not just to get the public to love the film industry like a favorite star," as Jurca puts it, "but to persuade it to embrace the making of commercial entertainment as a significant, stable, and indispensable enterprise."[17] It did so, in one reviewer's words, by "[r]efuting two rockbound theories of picture-making: that Technicolor must only occur in costume dramas, and that stories about Hollywood are poison at the box-office."[18]

Where Selznick emphasized the link between stardom and technology within Hollywood's prestige spectacle tradition—a path he would follow two years later with *Gone with the Wind*—Warners, the pugnacious "studio of genres," took the opposite tack with *Boy Meets Girl*, a black-and-white movie that, as its name suggests, was invested in story type over stardom.[19] If for Selznick Hollywood history is personal history, for Warners, it's the history of genre. An adaptation of a play by Bella and Samuel Spewack, *Boy Meets Girl* presents the hijinks of J.C. Benson (O'Brien) and Robert Law (Cagney), two extravagantly playful screenwriters modeled on Ben Hecht and Charles MacArthur, a team as famous for their success in Hollywood as for their disdain for it. The movie takes its title from the formula Benson and Law comically repeat throughout: a cut-rate classical narrative structure of "boy meets girl—boy loses girl—boy gets girl." That structure not only describes the scripts that Benson and Law write but also the movie they're in. Susie (Marie Wilson), a commissary waitress, meets Rodney Boven (Bruce Lester), an unsuccessful British extra, but the two are separated when Susie gives birth to a boy, mysteriously conceived, named Happy. By way of Benson and Law's chicanery, Happy becomes the studio's biggest star in such pictures as the epic western *Golden Nuggets* until he contracts measles. Susie and Rodney are reunited when Susie's out-of-wedlock pregnancy is explained away (Happy's deceased father was a bigamist), and Rodney is revealed to be the son of a lord.

Jurca argues that *Boy Meets Girl*, which Warners oddly included in the Motion Pictures' Greatest Year campaign, savaged the industry when it couldn't afford the bad look; the film's combination of in-jokes and disparagement of small-town audiences inflamed the public relations crisis that MPGY had hoped to ameliorate.[20] In a sense, the movie backfired by capturing the studio's ethos too clearly. *Boy Meets Girl*'s iconoclasm targeted the pretentious and bloated aspects of Hollywood against which Warners positioned itself: the know-nothing producer (C. Eliot Friday, played by Ralph Bellamy) who claims to admire Proust; the frustrated author (Law) who would write a great realist novel—"I've got the beginning all planned: two rats in a sewer"—if only he could get away from his $1,500 a week; the poorly managed studio that, unlike Warners, found itself on the brink of financial collapse; and the posturing of other back-studio stories (Law: "Imagine the headlines! A star is born!" Benson: "Law, that's a great title … too bad it's been used"). Conversely, the movie celebrates the virtues of genre: where the Spewacks' play features Benson and Law ruefully hoisted with their own petards as Susie and Rodney leave them without a job, the adaptation ends with producer Friday discovering that his wife is pregnant and the screenwriting team reiterating their "boy meets girl" formula with a new child star, another golden nugget, born in-house. Instead of a shopworn cliché, "boy meets girl" emerges as the timeless precious ore refined and turned out in Burbank.

Though Warners could, in 1938, assert its identity as the studio of genres, it could only do so in large part because of the talent and efforts of Darryl F. Zanuck, who was vice president in charge of production until 1933, when he left to start Twentieth Century Pictures with Joseph Schenck. Twentieth Century merged with the much larger Fox studios in 1935, becoming the final Big Five studio to form; by 1938, Twentieth Century-Fox established its house style, a combination of Zanuck's Warners-style topicality, genre sensibility, and penchant for biopics and the Fox studio's emphasis on Americana.[21] *Hollywood Cavalcade* helped solidify Fox's persona by reconceiving the development of the studio system from 1913 to 1927—from the shift of the locus of production from the East Coast to California through the transition to sound—as the prologue to Zanuck's reign over Hollywood. While the movie follows the rise, fall, and redemption of a D.W. Griffith-Mickey Neilan-Mack Sennett amalgam named Mike Connors (Don Ameche), it takes its inspiration from the arc of Zanuck's career: from Sennett-style pie-gags (Zanuck wrote for the producer) to the Bathing Beauties (Zanuck's wife Virginia was one) to the canine stardom of Rin Tin Tin (Zanuck's big coup at Warners) to the epochal shift signaled by *The Jazz Singer* (Alan Crosland, Warners, 1927).[22] Warners may have been able to take the credit for Zanuck's work in revolutionizing the industry, but, *Hollywood Cavalcade* indicates, those successes are relics of a prior era. The movie concludes with Connors, entranced by *The Jazz Singer*, realizing that his egomania and his inability to single-handedly control increasingly elaborate and expensive productions have undermined his career. Al Jolson's Kol Nidre, sung at the start of Yom Kippur, the Day of Atonement (an evident allegory for the transition between epochs, per Michael Rogin's influential account) elicits a secular epiphany in Connors, spurring him to help his former star Molly Adair (Alice Faye) and his erstwhile producer Dave Spingold (J. Edward Bromberg) prepare sound sequences for their movie *Common Clay*.[23] Both the movie and the trio succeed according to the Fox style: the concurrent celebration of individual talent and subordination of ego to common purpose, all of which amounts to an American democratic ideal and a classical balance. Like *Common Clay*, which, though not the first to speak in synchronized sound, would use the technology to serve the purpose of the prestige realist production—to do for talking, Connors says, what *The Jazz Singer* did for singing—*Hollywood Cavalcade* used cutting-edge Technicolor to offer a more historically grounded, less melodramatic vision of the industry's past than Selznick did. In *Cavalcade*'s final shot of the three friends and top talents, dressed in their formalwear after the premiere at Grauman's Egyptian Theatre, Spingold looks out over Hollywood and offers the final word: "It used to be a kind of game, the movies. Now look at it: a city. As far as the eye can see. Filled with people who make the entertainment for all the peoples of the world." And that new city of the present, *Cavalcade* suggests, belonged to the era of Twentieth Century.

Varieties of Historical Experience in the Hollywood Novel

> Graustark on the Pacific has its own code, its own policies, its own people. There are rulers and commoners, courtesans, jesters, scribes and prophets.
>
> —Frank Nugent and Douglas Churchill, *Graustark*, 1938[24]

At roughly the same time that Edmund Wilson composed his classic study *The Boys in the Back Room: Notes on California Novelists* (1941), a young Budd Schulberg, fresh out of Dartmouth, published an omnibus review of eight novels under the title "Literature of the Film: The Hollywood Novel."[25] The difference in titles is telling. Wilson approached the fiction of writers of the west, including James M. Cain, Horace McCoy, William Saroyan, and John Steinbeck, from a regionalist perspective, blaming the literature's limitations on a land whose cultural center, San Francisco, "was arrested in its natural development by the earthquake of 1906," and was challenged by the "anti-cultural amusement-producing" desert of Los Angeles.[26] Schulberg, by contrast, thought Hollywood deserved to be taken seriously as a place, community, and industry. He was nonetheless sympathetic to Wilson's position because, Schulberg claimed, "there were not sufficient novels about Hollywood serious and penetrating enough even to bear discussion until the late Thirties."[27]

But in Schulberg's estimation, "the time was ripening for writers … to treat [Hollywood] in a new way, more searchingly, more critically, more courageously: realistically," and his assessment was borne out by a cluster of new fictions, all published in 1938–1939, that struck him as elevations of the genre. He argued that none of these, however, was fully successful:

> The definitive Hollywood novel would understand how Hollywood can be unique and at the same time the counterpart of any industrial center in America. It will concern itself not only with the glamour girls, directors, executives and freaks which have figured prominently so far, but with a cross-section of the thousands of men and women who have become the cogs in a powerful, monopolized industry—cutters, makeup men, sound experts, grips, juicers, stenographers, agents, the undiscovered hopefuls and broken-down ex-famous, the creators who work themselves to death and the fabulous phonies, the Producers' Association, the Hays' [sic] Office, the Funerals, the Colony Club, the unions, the Trocadero, the Dies Investigation—the whole industrious, crazy set-up which turns out many of the greatest moving pictures in the world and most of the worst, and which is really an exaggerated, speeded-up, glamourised reproduction of our social system.[28]

Schulberg surely imagined his own contribution, the forthcoming *What Makes Sammy Run?* (1941), as the fulfilment of the Hollywood novel's promise. An exposé of Hollywood treachery told through fabulous phony Sammy Glick's rise from lean-and-hungry Lower East Side Manhattan office boy to lean-and-hungry producer, *What Makes Sammy Run?* was so unflattering that the author's father, the former Paramount producer B.P., told him, "you'll never work in this town again."[29] The basis of the *really* real portrayal of the conniving Glick, as Schulberg tacitly acknowledged, was the studio system's own discourse of maturation. "The time was ripening," he wrote in his review, because Hollywood "had been undergoing a peaceful but none the less drastic revolution these past ten years": the industry itself had ripened.[30] In other words, the emerging historical sense in the backstudio picture paralleled a similar development in Hollywood fiction of the moment, a turn that manifested in and united novels written by authors across the political spectrum during a moment of intense fractiousness. All of these works, in their own ways, conceived the genre's exhaustion as an opportunity for renovation: a version of modernism, if we consider a genre to be a kind of medium.[31]

Unsurprisingly, *That Flannigan Girl* (1939), a novel by the politically conservative former star Patsy Ruth Miller, aligned most neatly with the industry's historical self-imagination. Unlike Norman Maine and other superannuated stars in Hollywood cautionary tales, Miller flourished in her post-acting life. Moreover, she remained of, if not exactly in, Hollywood. Miller published *That Flannigan Girl* two years after marrying John Lee Mahin, who, as we have seen, thrived within MGM's machinery and promoted the studio union, The Screen Playwrights, against the left-wing Screen Writers Guild.[32] Miller shared her husband's convictions. In her memoir *My Hollywood, When Both of Us Were Young* (which approves of both the wholesome entertainment value of studio-era movies and the internment of Japanese Americans in California), Miller concurred with her husband's belief that Hollywood writers' leftist causes ruined F. Scott Fitzgerald's career:

> Poor Scott had been tossed into this whirlpool of Liberalism, and without a political credo to cling to, was drowning in it. He had never espoused causes, nor been very interested in politics; as a writer, Humanity had meant little to him, the Individual everything. His work was condemned to total oblivion, they said, and he believed them. He denounced hmself [sic] even more harshly than his judges, accusing his work of being trivial and superficial.[33]

Befitting Miller's conservative politics, the important history of *That Flannigan Girl* is the history of an Individual: heroine Denise Arden's memories of her acting career since her salad days as the Midwestern émigrée Dora Flannigan. *That Flannigan Girl* resembles the romantic, industry-affirmative narrative template of *A Star is Born*, in line with the privileged insider position that Miller, Mahin, and Selznick had in common.

However, unlike Selznick's movie, whose "realism" consisted in the sober recollection of a star's death from dipsomania, *That Flannigan Girl*'s comes from its frank depiction of Arden's dissatisfaction with the utter conventionality of supposedly unique stardom. Throughout the novel, Arden observes, with a mix of horror, chagrin, and boredom, the life cycle of celebrity: Wallace Reid, a real-world 1920s star who died from complications arising from a morphine addiction, is incorporated into the fiction as a benefactor who recommends her for her first screentest; the fictional Mary Ryan suffers in "that private hell reserved for forgotten actresses."[34] Indeed, as her assistant Jonesy knows well and explains in a lecture, Arden's exhaustion—what her lover Adam calls being "haunted by the ghosts of Hollywood" (*TFG* 129)—is itself a hackneyed trope: "You've talked yourself into believing that you're nothing but a poor movie star, admired and envied by thousands, and loved by none. Oh, yes ... I know all the catchphrases" (*TFG* 163). Arden has, in sum, mistaken the achievement of stardom for personal growth; her realization of that error occurs when she recalls how, at the start of her career, she affected a flapper stance and quoted Dorothy Parker: "Twelve years ... twelve years. And here I am, doing the same thing I was doing then" (*TFG* 185). In Miller's view, parroting the words of the outspoken Hollywood leftist in the late 1930s is the equivalent of prioritizing one's career above all else: each results in a personal mire, a disillusionment without a salutary replacement belief.

In the novel, that replacement is the romantic individualism that, for Rosten, had reached its apogee in the movie colony, and which Miller rendered in the form of literary techniques borrowed from the Modernists that she simplified and deployed in the service of heterosexual melodrama. *That Flannigan Girl* comprises a series of recollections, prompted by Arden's experiences filming on-location in Catalina, that occur as flashbacks: the kind of medium analogy that had been favored by the sophisticated art novel in the 1920s (e.g., *Manhattan Transfer*) and, in the '30s, by the hardboiled "Devil's parody of the movies" (e.g., *They Shoot Horses, Don't They?*).[35] In *That Flannigan Girl*, however, the flashback technique expresses neither high cultural nor proletarian antipathy toward Hollywood and thus appears as an early instance of the narrative structure that would appear in numerous American films in the 1940s.[36] Ultimately, Arden is a synthesis of Emma Woodhouse and Howard Roark, a true talent and fierce individualist whose limitations can be corrected by an appropriate husband. At the novel's conclusion, when Arden is faced with an ultimatum to continue acting or to leave Hollywood with her Mr. Knightley, the allegorically named Adam, she rejects the choice as specious. After she intercepts Adam's eastbound train in Arizona, they gaze into each other's eyes, and she says:

"If we get married at Yuma ... we could fly back tomorrow. I have to be back tomorrow, darling, because I'm in every scene and Dan can't shoot without me."
"Oh Denny," he said. "Oh Denny."
And then it was just as she had imagined it would be. (*TFG* 282)

Miller's libertarian fiction describes the triumph of her protagonist's self-actualization, a priority that will only make for a better film back in Catalina. For Miller, the Hollywood novel, and indeed Hollywood itself, could be revivified, in the promotional language of the novel's dust jacket, by presenting the "characters, the people who live there—as individuals, not dominated by, but dominating their background."[37]

Where Miller saw exhaustion as the result of juvenile idealism, which could be corrected by a robust individuality, writers of the Popular Front—Communists, antifascists, and liberal fellow-travelers—identified the Hollywood novel genre as almost as much of a grind as the exploitative mechanism of the industry itself. By 1938, the subject matter, style, and sensibility of novels such as Cain's *Postman* and McCoy's *They Shoot Horses* had become so legible and commercially viable that they were ripe for pastiche. *You Play the Black and the Red Comes Up* (1938), written by Richard Hallas, aka Eric Knight, the British author of *Lassie Come Home*, tickled Wilson with its pitch-perfect patter: "it is indicative of the degree to which this kind of writing has finally become formularized that it should have been possible for a visiting Englishman to tell this story in the Hemingway-Cain vernacular almost without a slip."[38] Writers of the left leaned into the ossified genre conventions, devising distorted forms of the Hollywood novel to intensify their longstanding criticism of the industry's depredations. These "narratives of breakdown," as Walter Wells rightly called them, take on broken-down forms and have been consistently judged as failures by the criteria of the well-made novel.[39] Indeed, Wells's analysis of John O'Hara's *Hope of Heaven* (1938), a novel that Wilson "could not fathom at all," can only be improved by acknowledging that the novel's ostensible aesthetic failure is the corollary of its story of confusion and disappointment.[40] Those very qualities are, in fact, invoked in the novel's first sentence, where narrator Jim Malloy can barely commit to telling his story: "Maybe I am not the man to tell this story, but if I don't tell it no one else will, so here goes."[41] If *Hope of Heaven* comprises a "pastiche of aesthetic objectives," it wasn't, appropriately, alone: the worn-out befuddlement that characterizes many novels of the moment captures an attitude toward moviemaking that the studios were anxious to correct. Not for nothing does *Hope of Heaven* conclude with Malloy saying,

"I guess we are all washed up": the novels of this vintage aren't just fed up with Hollywood, but also with the ways of criticizing it.[42] From this vantage, Aldous Huxley's *After Many a Summer Dies the Swan* (1939), the self-consciously inelegant evolutionary biology-gothic discussed in Chapter 2 in the context of corporate authorship, is an MGM-inflected instance of the broader tendency to diagnose and perhaps thereby reanimate moribund Hollywood fiction.[43]

The kinds of badness these novels display, I suggest, are similar enough to suggest deliberateness: perversions with a point. It would make sense to regard these works as relatives of the "ghetto pastoral," an indecorous form that, according to Michael Denning, privileges allegory over realism, the latter being a set of conventions "tied historically to social power." Thus, McCoy appears to Denning as a "poet [laureate] of the culture industry's 'extras.'"[44] In his second novel, *I Should Have Stayed Home* (1938), McCoy self-consciously travestied Hollywood novel-writing in the figure of minor character Johnny Hill, a former Universal publicity agent. "That side of Hollywood's never been told," he tells Ralph Carston and Mona Matthews, the two down-at-heel bit-player protagonists.

> All you ever read about Hollywood is the waitress who gets a test and turns out to be a big shot. Like *A Star is Born*.... That was *a* true story, but not *the* true story, if you know what I mean....
> The true story of this town concerns people like you....
> You're symbolic of the twenty thousand extras in Hollywood. Understand, I don't think I've got any special talent for novel-writing—not as much as the novelists have who've been out here. It's only that I think they've missed a good net. Hilton could have written it, Hammett, Hecht, Fowler—although he tried once with Mack Sennett and muffed it—and of course the old master, Dr. Hemingway, who could have done it better than anybody, but who's too goddam busy saving Spanish democracy to worry about a boy and girl in Hollywood. The trouble with those writers is they move to Malibu beach and into mansions at Bel-Air ... and get to see the wrong side of it.[45]

According to Hill, to craft "*the* true story" of Hollywood, the tale of those thousands of hopefuls, has-beens, and others on the borders of the industry, an author must occupy a position in the studio system homologous to those of her subjects. However, Hill chooses to slum it, making him more like a Los Angeles-based Jacob Riis than an artist forced out of the industry like McCoy himself.

Put differently, Hill's proposed transmutation of poverty tourism into proletarian fiction suggests that the techniques that studio washouts developed to capture life on the studio system periphery had become shopworn.

By most accounts, ranging from Schulberg's and Edmund Wilson's to those of contemporary critics such as David Fine, *I Should Have Stayed Home* is a worse novel than (the extraordinary) *They Shoot Horses, Don't They?*, largely because McCoy offers nothing new to the form. That is, critics have been unable or unwilling to see the morass of cliché, and the cliché's strategic revelation in the figure of Hill, as providing the novel's bleak foundation. *I Should Have Stayed Home* recapitulates but does not attempt to transcend the tedium and exhaustion its principal characters feel. That Ralph and Mona are indeed "symbolic," as Hill asserts, is the basis of the novel's poignant irony: not even the characters' pains are their own. By virtue of the double depersonalization of the Hollywood extra—the actor's typical distinction between person and persona is here compounded in the extra, whose role is predicated on emptiness and interchangeability—Ralph and Mona confront, to different degrees, the exquisite misery of seeing, however partially, that they are minor characters in their own existence.[46] Mona trades the demeaning life of the unwanted extra for a statistically more common, and thus potentially less significant, life as the wife of a farmer in the San Joaquin valley, the marriage arranged by letters exchanged through *Lonesome Hearts* magazine. (The reference to Nathanael West's *Miss Lonelyhearts* should be noted.) Ralph, however, remains bewitched by stardom and stays in Hollywood to the bitter end, even as, in the grip of longing for his youth in bucolic Georgia, he wonders whether he should indeed have stayed home.

McCoy's final, brutal irony, however, is that Ralph misses an American South of swimming holes and Jim Crow that everyone else in his destitute Hollywood community regards contemptuously. That irony becomes almost unbearable in the implicit equation of Ralph's childhood home and a Hollywood he never knew, when, near the novel's end, McCoy, breaking from his hardboiled patter, allows Ralph a moment of romantic reverie:

> That night I discovered the park at De Longpre and Cherokee. I was walking around the streets in the neighborhood, Fountain and Livingston and Cahuenga, because they were dark and lonely, looking at the small houses, telling myself that these were where Swanson and Pickford and Chaplin and Arbuckle and the others used to live in the good old days, when making movies was fun and not a business, walking around thinking of those old days and what a shame it was they had to pass, feeling a personal loss that was still very warm and nostalgic, like a visit to a graveyard where your grandfather and grandmother and all your relatives are buried. You don't feel that you are a stranger even though you have never visited the graveyard before because the tombstones represent something and somebody you have known a long, long time, and loved, and it was like that now.[47]

Varieties of Historical Experience in the Hollywood Novel 97

By likening his "very warm and nostalgic" feeling for the bygone industry to that which he would experience at his deceased family's graves, Ralph unknowingly reveals the extent to which his worldview has been warped by the success-narrative fantasy bribes purveyed by fan magazines and backstudio movies. But the full pathos of this passage depends on McCoy's manipulation of the development narrative the industry had begun to push at that time. Ralph's blissful unawareness of the dark side of the industry's 1920s testifies to the triumph of the publicity departments that the would-be novelist Hill loathes. Although supposedly awakened to the poverty of his wish, Ralph's yearning for a Hollywood past that was "fun"—as opposed to "business"—faithfully reproduces Hollywood's latest story about itself. He has thus achieved no real insight at all. Whereas McCoy's characters in *They Shoot Horses* could leave the existential nightmare of the circular marathon dance by way of a mercy killing, Ralph's more insidious cycle of longing for ideal pasts offers no such escape: "I hadn't stayed home, I was here, on the famous boulevard, in Hollywood, where miracles happen, and maybe today, maybe the next minute some director would pick me out passing by...."[48] For him, it's banalities all the way down.

If *I Should Have Stayed Home* most clearly exemplifies a modernist approach to the Hollywood novel's formula—a tired genre fit to tired people—Cedric Belfrage's *Promised Land: Notes for a History* (1938) made the most explicitly political claim for film industry fiction's historical turn. Belfrage, a Hollywood correspondent for the London *Daily Express* and a close friend of screenwriter and eventual Hollywood Ten member Lester Cole, would, by Denning's classification, be the extra-poet's poet, the unsung writer of Hollywood's peripheral leftist novelists. Appropriately enough, Belfrage's novel seems to be considered the least pleasing fiction of the era. David Fine describes the novel, "if it can even be called one," as "lack[ing] any dramatic coherence," in which "characters play minor roles, the roles of extras, to the real drama of the promise gone awry."[49] Written while the Federal Writers' Project's *American Guide Series* was in preparation and local interest in Southern California's history intensified, *Promised Land* presents a semifictional account of the region. The novel begins in the second half of the nineteenth century with the settlement of the Owens Valley and Harvey Henderson Wilcox's founding of Hollywood as a temperance community near Los Angeles, and carries on through the California water wars of the 1920s and the labor organizing of the 1930s.[50] This history is narrated through the mostly unhappy lives of three generations of the fictional Laurie family: uncle Si, who settles on the Owens River and dies when the St. Francisquino Dam bursts; Ed, a laconic, henpecked man who loves growing citrus but converts his groves into real estate lots under his wife Evangeline's (Ma's) orders, and either dies with Si or merely runs away to escape his life; Ma, a member of the Women's Christian Temperance Union and a proponent of divine capitalism, whose land assets make her a millionaire until the market crash wipes her out; Clark, Ed and Ma's son, who becomes a narcissistic but long-suffering extra after returning from service in World War I and is ultimately radicalized by the left; and Don, Si's grandson, an intelligent, sensitive, but increasingly cynical man who becomes a journalist and Hollywood correspondent, and whose castoff girlfriend Ellen ends up in love with Clark.

Film production doesn't appear in *Promised Land* until 1911, about one-quarter of the way in, and in the form of a recondite English literary joke: the industry arrives in Southern California in the form of a cameraman wearing a "cap back-to-front" much as Humphry Clinker belatedly appears rear-first in the eighteenth-century novel that bears his name.[51] By self-consciously countering and de-emphasizing the industry's prevailing historiographical sensibility, most clearly articulated in *Hollywood Cavalcade*'s account of the *fiat lux* beginnings of the industry in 1913, and by rendering that jibe in the form of a backward-looking gag, *Promised Land* reveals itself to be formally inventive in ways critics have declined to acknowledge. The novel takes pains to mark its inventiveness, as Ed, an amateur historian, scrapbooks articles from the city's newspapers that ironically comment on the small-town hypocrisy and governmental mendacity that Ma fails to comprehend. Those clippings are but one instance of a welter of discursive forms, including, for example, an "Entr'acte" that features Don's journalism (a metacritical debunking of hyperbolic judgments of Hollywood, for or against) and a concluding epistolary exchange between Don and Clark. These discursive forms mark, by contrast, the flat characterization elsewhere in the novel as Belfrage's self-conscious choice to render history in a naturalistic, Marxian mode. *Promised Land* looks from this vantage like a miniaturized, simplified version of *The Big Money* (1936), Dos Passos's "Hollywood novel," as Denning calls it, whose exteriorized "objective" characterizations are offset by the array of Camera Eye, Newsreel, and Biography entries.[52] Like *The Big Money*, which traces the refinement of post–World War I American enterprise from the production of airplane motors to the production of spin by public relations executives, *Promised Land* depicts the rapid dematerialization of capital in Hollywood, from the land and water used to grow citrus to the "piece of paper" that allows for the "miracle" of real estate speculation to the moving picture "shadows" upon which the "miracle" of stardom depends (*PL* 200–201).

However, *Promised Land* would be better understood as a corrective to *The Big Money*, whose author's ostensible impartiality had struck Popular Front writers as an abdication of responsibility. Five months before Granville Hicks described, in a *New Masses* review, the recently disillusioned Dos Passos's objectivity as a "refus[al] to think his way through to clear convictions," Belfrage presented an argument against Olympian detachment in a talk titled "Politics Catches Up to the Writer" at a "recent Hollywood symposium."[53] Speaking to a portion of "perhaps the biggest nest of writers in the world," Belfrage warned against a pernicious intellectualism he called "super-liberalism":

> super-liberalism … is liberalism taken to the point where it becomes a definite, positive creed—the belief that everybody is more wrong than right: not only tories and communists, but liberals too, with what [journalist Vernon Bartlett] calls 'their strange blending of bloodlessness and sentimentality.' Liberalism is a fence for escapologists to sit on, but this super-liberalism, this determined resistance to the idea of anything being true at all, is a platform.

For Belfrage, this endless parsing and weighing of positions amounts to a de facto quiescent acceptance of fascism.[54] Where Dos Passos's detachment persists to the end of *The Big Money*—Hicks regrets that the novelist made "the strongest personal note in the book a futilitarian elegy for Sacco and Vanzetti"—Belfrage concludes his novel by jettisoning ironic, flattening distance in favor of the personal exchange between Don and Clark on the subjects of love for Ellen and faith in socialism, thereby clearly indicating the equivalence of the personal and the political.[55] Don, who left Ellen in the lurch and assumed that she pined for him while Clark provided emotional and material support, is as wrong about love as he is about politics. Arguing against a Hollywood united front of workers in order to maintain the "special category" of the artist, Don the super-liberal sides on the question of labor organization, by default, with Sam Wiseglass, a sleazy studio head who populates his parties with prostitutes (*PL* 297).[56] Clark responds less eloquently than his journalist cousin but more persuasively: "You've seen things that have put you in a bit of a fog about what's to be done…. Words and theories aren't important because we've all got the same sense of smell. You must see there's no sitting on the fence now. There aren't even two sides to be on, there's just one" (*PL* 348). This final letter's last words, however, belong to Ellen, who informs Don that she's carrying Clark's child. Unlike Dos Passos's Margo Dowling, the affectless, pragmatic, sterile actress whose star continues to rise at *The Big Money*'s conclusion, Ellen bids Don "Salud!," committed to putting the industry's exploitative past behind her and daring to hope for happy Hollywood labor beginning with her baby's birth (*PL* 349).

Decline of the West?

Nathanael West's *The Day of the Locust* emerged from within this set of conditions: the industry's anxious assertion of its maturity, and a historical turn in the Hollywood novel by which writers reinvigorated the form and expressed political positions. For West, a connoisseur of cliché, the genre's conventions, of which he was well aware, would have been catnip. West advised Random House marketers to distinguish *The Day of the Locust* from earlier industry fictions like *Boy Meets Girl*, *Once in a Lifetime* (Moss Hart and George S. Kaufman, 1930), and *Queer People* (Carroll and Garrett Graham, 1930): "[because] it has a real and even 'serious' theme, and ... its purpose is not to compete with the novels I listed, but others on a much higher plane."[57] The reader's mistake, easily made, would be to assume that West reached that higher plane by denying the protocols established by those earlier works rather than by employing them in discomfiting ways.

By the time West wrote *Locust*, he was accustomed to being misunderstood. Believing that Liveright had inadequately marketed *Miss Lonelyhearts* (1933) by presenting it as a pulp, West determined that the novel "sat hard between two stools," failing among brows of every height. That sense of betweenness extended to the critical establishment, who, he thought, saw him between the stools of the "radical press" and the "literature boys": a purveyor of "private and unfunny jokes."[58] West, perhaps unbeknownst to himself, proposed that the reason for this general sentiment was his inability to write about the "big things," a phrase he couldn't help but place in quotation marks, ironizing but never quite obliterating the sincerity of his aesthetic, moral, and political beliefs.[59] The fear that his reflexive joking would be taken as insulting even by his fellow travelers led West to excise from *Locust* his representations of antifascism. To Malcolm Cowley, West wrote, "I tried to describe a meeting of the Anti-Nazi League, but it didn't fit and I had to substitute a whorehouse and a dirty film. The terrible sincere struggle of the League came out comic when I touched it and even libelous."[60] Proceeding from sentiments like this, many readers of West have understood *Locust* as an enactment of the critical theory developed by the Frankfurt School, seeing the novel as a diagnosis of Hollywood as a culture industry nightmare: a "Sargasso of the imagination" and "dream dump." Rather than controvert the noted affinities between West and Theodor Adorno and Walter Benjamin, I want to suggest that what scholars have lauded is in fact a standard feature of the historical Hollywood novel that emerged in the late 1930s.

To see what sets *Locust* apart from that field, to perceive its politics and ingenious, all-edged satire more clearly, requires a different approach to West's scare-quoting. Those quotation marks, I argue, reveal his understanding of his readers', and especially his critics', expectations: seriousness of subject matter and seriousness of treatment. West, in other words, both internalized and ironized the expectations of critics, making those expectations, and the critics themselves, the subject of a joke, one that is private to the extent that those critics fail to see themselves as dupes, and unfunny to those unable to laugh at themselves.[61] Consider the ostensible throwaway comment that protagonist Tod Hackett overhears at the screenwriter Claude Estee's cocktail party early in the novel: "Guys like that come out here, make a lot of money, grouse all the time about the place, flop on their assignments, then go back East and tell dialect stories about producers they never met."[62] The canny anonymous writer pithily attacks not only the failed screenwriter's sour grapes but also a literary market willing to accept writing, however spurious, that confirmed the preconceptions and satisfied the stylistic preferences of the East Coast literati (the same preconceptions and style that lead McCoy's Johnny Hill from Universal's publicity department to seek out the indigent extras of *I Should Have Stayed Home*). Literature is a "racket" no different from the ones the producers run, with cultural capital substituting for economic (*DL* 71).[63]

Such insight escapes Tod. But just as surely, it has escaped many of West's readers, and their blindness here corresponds to their willingness to attribute Tod's observations to West and even to consider Tod the novel's narrator. According to Wilson, the first to proffer such a view, Tod is "a young Yale man who, as an educated and healthy human being, is supposed to provide a normal point of view from which the deformities of Hollywood may be criticized." However, Tod becomes tragically corrupted by Hollywood, that morass where he "find[s] himself swirling around in the same aimless eddies as the others" (hence, for Wilson, the novel's "lack of a center," a problem mimetic of the movie colony itself).[64] *The Day of the Locust*, however, treats the idea of healthy Yale male normalcy satirically: Tod was never fit to serve as the novel's intellectual, moral, or characterological center of gravity. Rather, West's contribution to American modernist inscrutability takes the form of an occult antibildungsroman that flattered but ought to have shattered the literati's pretensions. Perhaps because it came at their expense, the novel's most private joke is one the critics didn't see. Getting the last laugh by reconciling his pursuit of literary autonomy with his antifascist politics, West makes Tod the figure through which a vision of Hollywood fails to cohere. And, as we will see, he does so by using a form both privileged by transatlantic literary modernists and appropriate to the heightened historical consciousness of the late-1930s studio system: the bildungsroman, and more specifically, the künstlerroman, the narrative of artistic development.

Since the early 1930s if not before, West had been interested in the modernist bildungsroman, which, as Gregory Castle has explained, turned away from the French and English "socially pragmatic" narrative of development within and integration into a commercial, bureaucratic system. By prioritizing the artist who rejects normative social scripts and prioritizes aesthetic self-cultivation and individual expression, the modernist künstlerroman returned to the German Enlightenment origins of the form, which narrated the aesthetico-spiritual development of a youth.[65] However, in keeping with his pessimistic sensibility, West treats the artist-bildung as merely another unsatisfying script: in *Miss Lonelyhearts* (1933), Shrike, the satanic editor, mocks the title character by reeling off numerous solutions to despair, including aesthetic self-cultivation, but dismisses them all as dead ends.[66] The genre nonetheless remained on West's mind. The following year, he applied for a Guggenheim fellowship to write "an autobiographical novel" inspired by Joyce's *A Portrait of the Artist as a Young Man*, Henry Adams's *The Education of Henry Adams*, and Pierre Drieu la Rochelle's *Le Jeune Européen* that would "tell the story of a young man of my generation; that which graduated from college just before the boom and became thirty years old during the Depression. I want to show the difference between it and the one that came before; the famous 'lost generation.'"[67] The reference to Drieu la Rochelle, who had recently embraced fascism and would go on to support the collaborationist Vichy government, suggests that one of the differences that most struck West was the emergence of authoritarianism.[68] That observation figured prominently in *A Cool Million* (1934), in which he demonstrated the compatibility of US nationalism and fascism and thereby, in part, parodied the archetypal rags-to-riches American bildung narrative. That novel "came out," he told Random House editor Saxe Commins, "when no one in the country except a few Jeremiahs like myself took seriously the possibility of a Fascist America."[69]

The Day of the Locust's Tod Hackett is the culmination of West's decade-long refinement of the modernist bildung form, a perhaps too-subtle and privately funny expression of antifascist commitments. Confessing to Wilson his inability to take on the expected serious themes and subjects of the "schools" (again self-scare-quoted), West wrote, "I forget the broad sweep, the big canvas, the shot-gun adjectives, the important people, the significant ideas, the lessons to be taught, the epic Thomas Wolfe, the realistic James Farrell."[70] The choice of authors here isn't coincidental. The recently deceased Wolfe published his second autobiographical coming-of-age novel *Of Time and the River* four years earlier, in 1935, the same year that Farrell finished the final novel in his *Studs Lonigan* trilogy (which depicted the development of a working Irish-Catholic from Chicago) at the Hotel Brevoort in Manhattan, where he shared pages with West.[71] West's invocation of the "canvas" here sheds light on the method he would use in his novel: if he couldn't write about important matters in his own voice, he could ironically represent the limitations of serious grandiosity in the voice of another.

In Tod, West found his artist-vector: a stunted youth whose ostensible education occurs before the novel begins and who makes no artistic, intellectual, or romantic progress over the course of the brief fiction's limited time frame. *Locust*'s great formal debt to Joyce's *Portrait* is its version of what Hugh Kenner called the Uncle Charles Principle, a persistently ironic free indirect discourse. When we read that "'The Burning of Los Angeles,' a picture [Tod] was soon to paint, definitely proved he had talent," we hear the unmistakable assurance of Ivy League aristocracy even as the evidence of such a talent remains unascertainable; Tod never produces anything more than a series of derivative studies for a set of lithographs, which are themselves studies for the canvas (*DL* 60).[72] West figures Tod's apprenticeship as simultaneously over (as evidenced by his bachelor's degree) and continually on the horizon. Analogously, "The Burning of Los Angeles's" allegory of breakdown, which Tod takes as a sophisticated artistic and intellectual position, is itself a cliché, a thought already thought, whose realization is never reached. *Locust* should therefore be considered a particularly acidic and self-conscious instance of the tales of unseasonable youth that, in Jed Esty's account of the modernist bildungsroman, emblematize the ways that the supranational forces of imperialism and global capitalism warp the logic of development within the nation-state.[73] In short, Tod's artistic capacity, however credentialed by New Haven, remains in doubt throughout the novel.

Against the backdrop of vulgar and meretricious Hollywood movies, Tod's numerous, ostensibly Yale-certified references to the history of art suggest a beautiful mind ill-fitted to his surroundings but capable, in a genteel turn on Federal Art Project public-mindedness, of sublimating intellectual and aesthetic poverty into works of beauty. However, his understanding of the artistic lineage to which he feels he belongs comprises what, in other domains, would amount to cocktail party chatter: "He would never again do a fat red barn, old stone wall or sturdy Nantucket fisherman ... despite his race, training, and heritage, neither Winslow Homer nor Thomas Ryder could be his masters and he turned to Goya and Daumier" (*DL* 60). Missing from this breezy description of Tod's forbears is any mention of an actual painting; the American symbolist painter Albert Pinkham Ryder is misnamed, perhaps confused with the eighteenth-century engraver.[74] This joke, like so many in the novel, has its precedent in other Hollywood fictions. For instance, C. Elliott Friday, the asinine producer in the Spewacks' *Boy Meets Girl*, doesn't know the difference between a trumpet and trombone, but has no trouble sounding off on the merits of novelists: "Mind you, not that I think Kipling is a great writer. A storyteller, yes. But greatness? Give me Proust anytime."[75] This is the verbal punchline to a joke established in the playscript's opening stage directions, which describe the contents of his desk—"a copy of 'Swann's Way' (leaves uncut)"—and décor of his smaller private study—"This room contains MR. FRIDAY'S Commencement Day photograph (Harvard '19)."[76] That Friday would be so evidently an object of derision depends not only on the obvious hypocrisy of his judgments but also on the fact that he is a man of business, not art.

Like Tod, the aesthetically bankrupt Friday appears as the risible epitome of the US's stunted development, a condition described in 1915 by Van Wyck Brooks in his essay *America's Coming-of-Age*. In this essay on the limitations of unintegrated national culture, characterized by the opposition between the highbrow and the low, between idealism and commercialism, Brooks identifies the Harvard man, and the Yale, Princeton, and other men that followed the paradigm, as one divided against himself, for whom ideals are a mere abstraction ("a world in itself") set off from "practice" (which "has become simply a world of dollars").[77] What distinguishes the producer Friday and the studio hack Tod is a world of dollars in another sense; on his thirty-a-week salary, Tod would sit squarely at the bottom of the art department hierarchy at National Films. The combination of his poverty and training suggests a romantic sacrifice for his art, the Depression-era equivalent of the Lost Generation's flight to Paris. Nonetheless he, like Friday, bears an unflattering resemblance to Jay Gatsby, whose uncut volumes give superficial credence to his status as a vaunted Oxford man instead of a "mister nobody from nowhere," as true-blue Yalie Tom Buchanan discovers him to be. Fitzgerald's bitter joke, of course, was that the terminally immature Tom, "one of the most powerful ends that ever played football in New Haven" who was "forever seeking ... the dramatic turbulence of some irrecoverable football game" and who cannot correctly remember the name of racist pseudoscientist Lothrop Stoddard or the title of his white supremacist tract, is no less an intellectual fraud than the parvenu he disdains (*GG* 6). West exaggerates that joke in Tod, who will, however belatedly, fulfill his destiny as a nativist Ivy Leaguer and Hollywood employee—and who, like Patsy Ruth Miller and her Harvard-educated spouse, will embrace the industry's middlebrow aesthetics and conservative politics.[78]

Tod and Friday's phoniness participates in a tradition of criticizing the way college affiliation substitutes for character (Friday's ignorance stands out against the two rambunctious and more intelligent but undereducated screenwriters: neither Ben Hecht nor Charles MacArthur, the models for Benson and Law, graduated from college). Fitzgerald was only the most famous to cast aspersion on "that most limited of all specialists, the 'well-rounded man'"; Thomas Wolfe even more dismissively described the most successful campus figure, "'the all-round man'" (scare-quoted derisively) as "some industrious hack who had shown a satisfactory mediocrity in all directions."[79] By the 1920s, the "well-rounded man" had become the desideratum of elite schools, an admissions committee shibboleth distinguishing WASP gentlemen from unpleasantly ethnic and scholarly, therefore one-sided, students.[80] During the socially conscious 1930s, derision of the idea intensified. Journalist John Tunis, surveying his peers in the Harvard class of 1911 in *Was College Worth While?* (1936), answered his question in the negative: "that lamp of learning tended by the ancient Greeks, blown white and high in the medieval universities and handed down to us in a direct line through Paris, Oxford, and Cambridge, has at last produced a group of men whose chief ambitions, if their record tells the truth, is [*sic*] to vote the Republican ticket, to keep out of the breadline, and to break 100 at golf."[81] The Jewish West, who in the 1920s gained admission to Tufts University and Brown under false pretenses, would have delighted in this assessment of elite eastern college "character." If he ever read it, he no doubt would have enjoyed the poet and novelist Conrad Aiken's review of Tunis's book in *The New Republic*, a magazine to which West contributed. Aiken apologized for his cohort by revising the geometric metaphor of character and yoking it to the middle-aged Harvard man's position in a world moving inexorably toward war:

> As "education," in the strict academic sense of the word, it was poorish ... it was too easy to get the equivalent of a "pass" degree, and by adroitly avoiding subjects for which we had no taste or aptitude we tended to become one-sided. One-sided, but not specialized. We took it easy, got a smattering of delightful things in a delightful lazy way—even now we're pretty weak on spelling—but we became philosophers. And in a world too much committed to action we submit that a little quietism might be a good thing.[82]

For Aiken, the well-rounded man lost whatever edge he had in the safe confines of Harvard Yard. His propensity to speculate, fostered by his removal from the affairs of the world, is indistinguishable from the de facto quietism of Belfrage's super-liberal.

In this context, the meaning of West's early description of Tod's character comes squarely into view:

> If the scout had met Tod, he probably wouldn't have sent him to Hollywood to learn set and costume designing. His large sprawling body, his slow blue eyes and sloppy grin made him seem completely without talent, almost doltish in fact.
>
> Yes, despite his appearance, he was really a very complicated young man with a whole set of personalities, one inside the other like a nest of Chinese boxes. (*DL* 60)

Tod is a travesty of well-roundedness: an infinite regress of single sides, he appears as a comic synthesis of Aiken's one-dimensional loafer and Belfrage's super-liberal sublimated out of real-world existence. His flight to Hollywood, like the "uterine flight" of Homer Simpson at the novel's end, is the unknowing movement from one institutional alma mater to another (*DL* 171). Tod is thus made to seem like an overgrown fetus, the antithesis of Earle Shoop, the cowboy-extra whose "two-dimensional face" Faye Greener, Tod's object of lust and disdain, thinks is "criminally handsome": the caricatural quintessence of adult masculinity (*DL* 109). Aiken's diagnosis of the Harvard man's quietism helps explain the novel's almost total avoidance of world politics. Through Tod, West was able to avoid a blasphemous representation of antifascism by rendering his protagonist's lack of political interest laughable instead. Moreover, Tod's Ivy League-trained disinterest in world affairs is regressive and reactionary. An anonymous Yale student of the Class of 1937 (to which Tod might have belonged) told Tunis "What is becoming more and more evident day by day is that when undergraduates sit talking ... they may be discussing next year's football captain, but more likely they are discussing the justice of Mussolini's attack on Ethiopia. The limits of New Haven are no longer synonymous with the limits of the undergraduate's mind."[83]

Tod's stuntedness therefore has an atavistic quality; he is so metaphorically young as to be prepolitical. In this regard, Tod is an extreme extension of Wolfe's Eugene Gant, who desires, at the end of *Look Homeward, Angel*, to go to Harvard and to return to the womb, and who, in the pungent phrasing of Leslie Fiedler, "strives to change and die ... but remains a great, panting, blubbering hulk of an adolescent, who can age but not grow up."[84] But more proximately, Tod fits neatly among those to whom he condescends, the elite movie colony denizens of Rosten's "Hollywood legend," like gossip columnist Louella Parsons, who "in the week in which Mussolini raped Albania ... began one of her extraordinary columns: 'The deadly dullness of the past week was lifted today when Darryl Zanuck announced he had bought all rights to *The Bluebird* for Shirley Temple.'"[85]

Tod thus bears a surprising likeness to Faye, the novel's overtly stereotypical child of Hollywood, whose "egglike self-sufficiency"—a figure of the movie colony's youthful, narcissistic self-involvement—Tod sadistically wishes to crush (*DL* 107). Jonathan Veitch and Rita Barnard, among others, have shrewdly observed the way that Hollywood pablum comprises Faye's dreams, a situation that exemplifies the degrading influence the movies have had on the psychic life of the American populace.[86] But Tod's musings about National Film's backlot are equally shoddy, even if their sources are less evident. For all the name-dropping in *Locust*, the novel positively identifies just two works of art, each suggesting Tod to be as fatally deceived as he imagines Faye to be.

> He left the road and climbed across the spine of the hill to look down on the other side. From there he could see a ten-acre field of cockleburs spotted with clumps of sunflowers and wild gum. In the center of the field was a gigantic pile of sets, flats and props. While he watched, a ten-ton truck added another load to it. This was the final dumping ground. He thought of Janvier's "Sargasso Sea." Just as that imaginary body of water was a history of civilization in the form of a marine junkyard, the studio lot was one in the form of a dream dump. A Sargasso of the imagination! (*DL* 132)

Some of West's most careful readers have, based on glancing references to Salvator Rosa, Francesco Guardi, and Monsu Desiderio, assumed that Janvier's "Sargasso Sea" belongs to Tod's class of "Decay and Mystery" paintings, presumably because of the French flavor of the name and the Renaissance-era Portuguese provenance of Sargasso Sea.[87] However, Thomas Janvier was in fact a Philadelphia-born turn-of-the-twentieth-century fiction writer, and *In the Sargasso Sea* (1898) is an American version of the kind of imperial adventure story that Joseph Conrad was then in the process of dismantling.[88] West's analogy between the popular art forms of successive empires—the adventure novel of England; the Hollywood movie of the United States—comes at Tod's expense. Although Tod believes himself to be above and apart from the trash of mass culture, physically positioning himself on a promontory as a self-styled surveyor in the cast of Caspar David Friedrich's wanderer, he maintains a perspective conditioned by the young adult dime novel. If "A Sargasso of the imagination!" at first reads as a eureka moment, that discovery of Hollywood's insidiousness is, as this chapter has demonstrated repeatedly, no discovery at all but rather a stock feature of the late-1930s Hollywood novel. Tod recapitulates the language and thus worldview of the very mass culture he disdains; in his moment of ostensible intellectual triumph over these bogus reproductions of history, he reveals himself to be just another self-important, self-deceived dupe of the culture industry.

Further teasing his readers' regard for his protagonist's intellectual merit, West lifts Tod's surrealist insight almost directly from *America's Coming-of-Age*, which had recently been reprinted in Brooks's *Three Essays on America* (1934):

> America is like a vast Sargasso Sea—a prodigious welter of unconscious life, swept by ground-swells of half-conscious emotion. All manner of lively things are drifting in it, phosphorescent, gayly colored, gathered into knots and clotted masses, gelatinous, unformed, flimsy, tangled, rising and falling, floating and merging, here an immense distended belly, there a tiny rudimentary brain (the gross devouring the fine)—everywhere an unchecked, uncharted, unorganized vitality like that of the first chaos.[89]

Tod's unacknowledged citation of Brooks covertly suggests his own limitations, not as an aesthete—West himself practiced a form of Dadaist appropriation throughout his career—but as an incipient political being.[90] For here Tod lifts ideas from an author who, in publishing *The Flowering of New England* (1934), had committed, at least in the eyes of contemporary American leftist writers, two Westian sins: of being a nationalist and a middlebrow.[91] The reaction against Brooks would come to a head in 1941, when Dwight Macdonald called him "our leading mouthpiece for totalitarian cultural values" and accused him of developing a homegrown Kulturbolschewismus, the Nazi policy against decadent art.[92] Typically ahead of his time, West anticipates the *Partisan Review*'s criticism in the way he formulates Tod's pseudo-profundity. In the bluff exclamation "the Sargasso of the imagination!" Tod reveals that he need not paint fat red barns in the style of Winslow Homer to be a cultural nationalist, so long as the studios remain the wellspring of American national culture; the styles of Goya and Daumier fit well enough in science fiction and horror movies such as *Son of Frankenstein* (Rowland V. Lee, Universal, 1939), a movie art-directed by the Yale-trained painter Jack Otterson, son of erstwhile Paramount president John Otterson, a former Naval lieutenant and president of the Winchester Repeating Arms Company.[93]

Tod's inchoate reactionary politics come into clearer view as he leaves the Sargasso of the imagination and happens upon the filming of the climactic titular sequence of *Waterloo*. Inflected by the painter's mock-Olympian consciousness, the narrator presents a set of bathetic juxtapositions between the historical events and National Film's production.

> The desperate and intrepid Prince was in an especially bad spot. Tod heard him cry hoarsely above the din of battle, *shouting to the Hollande-Belgians, "Nassau! Brunswick! Never retreat!"* Nevertheless, the retreat began. Hill, too, fell back. *The French killed General Picton with a ball through the head* and he returned to his dressing room. *Alten was put to the sword* and also retired. The colors of the Lunenberg battalion, borne by a *prince of the family of Deux-Ponts*, were captured by a famous child star in the uniform of a *Parisian drummer boy*. *The Scotch Grays were destroyed and went to change into another uniform. Ponsonby's heavy dragoons were also cut to ribbons.*[94] (*DL* 133–34, my emphasis)

Where before Tod had conflated the imagery of young adult fiction with the ideology of cultural nationalism, here, again covertly, he plagiarizes Isabel F. Hapgood's translation of *Les Misérables*, a book he used to sketch *Waterloo*'s costumes. That theft is then reformulated through a perspective informed by Oswald Spengler's theory of world history in *The Decline of the West*. In his ill-fated Guggenheim application of 1934, West had indicated that the penultimate fifth chapter of his proposed künstlerroman—after the experience of "college in New England" (Chapter Three) and "Business and the objectives involved" (Chapter Four)—would feature "The ideas of Spengler and Valéry."[95] And in *A Cool Million*, Valéry and Spengler are extolled by Israel Satinpenny, the antimodernist, Harvard-educated Native American. West's interest in sending up Spengler comes to fruition here as Tod, watching *Waterloo*, smugly performs an analogical interpretation of the course of civilizations.[96] For Spengler, Napoleon was a profound historical actor, the equivalent of Alexander, whose inevitable demise marked Western culture's turn to Civilization, the "fulfilment and finale of a culture."[97] The farcical parallel of Waterloo and *Waterloo* thus attributes to Tod a belief common enough among cultural mandarins: that Hollywood epitomized the dregs of the West. But more importantly, by the time of Nathanael West's writing, American intellectuals had already begun to associate Spengler with Nazism; reviewing a new Spengler volume in 1932, Lewis Mumford wrote, "Spengler and Hitler, living in Munich, have more in common than their place of residence." In this light, Tod's analysis implicitly but unmistakably signals the fascist politics congealing in him.[98]

Thus, Tod's greatest affinity is not with re-enwombed Homer or old-beyond-her-years Faye, but with Adore Loomis, the would-be child-star, who "[bows] stiffly with his heels together" (the way they "do it in Europe," as Adore's mother approvingly says) (*DL* 139). In Adore, one sees a premonition of Gary Cooper, the only real-life male actor mentioned in the novel and one whom the historian Carey McWilliams had accused of play-acting as a fascist.[99] In 1935, Cooper formed the Hollywood Hussars, a paramilitary organization which, according to cocreator Arthur Guy Empey, was "armed to the teeth and ready to gallop on horseback within an hour to cope with any emergency menacing the safety of the community, fights or strikes, floods or earthquakes, wars, Japanese 'invasions,' communistic 'revolutions,' or whatnot." Although the Hussars, like Adore, principally enjoyed the performance of a heroic masculinity, the group was motivated, as Cooper told the *Motion Picture Herald*, by an earnest Americanism.[100] If not an out-and-out fascist, the nativist Cooper, one of the top-grossing male stars of the late '30s, modeled himself offscreen as the ideal American, an image consistent with the screen persona that Frank Capra, an admirer of Franco and Mussolini and opponent of Roosevelt, crafted for him in *Mr. Deeds Goes to Town* (Columbia, 1936).

It is fitting, therefore, that Tod's long-delayed coming of age occurs during the novel's concluding melee, when a movie premier—"Yeah. Somebody hollered, 'Here comes Gary Cooper,' and then wham!"—coincides with the mob-lynching of Homer after he stomps Adore to death (*DL* 183). While Tod loses his distance from the living world and, with it, his ability to engage in lazy Spenglerian speculation, the novel here asserts its most telling homology. By naming the theater at which the premier occurs "Kahn's Persian Palace," West occludes from Tod's vision the two Grauman theaters that provide its model. The more famous hand-printed Chinese Theatre, featured in *A Star is a Born*, succeeded the original Egyptian Theatre that appeared in *Hollywood Cavalcade*. The latter theater offers insight into the novel's title by translating Tod's elitist distaste for the midwestern Americans "who come to California to die," the "cream" of "America's madmen," into the mythological register of the Old

Testament (*DL* 118). "The Day of the Locust" is the novel's final as well as its first gag, one that spared no one, especially the critics who would take the mythological analogy seriously. For to believe that the rioters are the titular insects, as Tod does, is to see people as a plague and to align oneself with Pharaoh and the slavers, the great tyrannical villains of the Book of Exodus.

In the novel's final sentence, Tod finally awakens to his preference for authoritarianism as he apes the siren of the police car that whisks him from the riot:

> He was carried through the exit to the back street and lifted into a police car. The siren began to scream and at first he thought he was making the noise himself. He felt his lips with his hands. They were clamped tight. He knew then it was the siren. For some reason this made him laugh and he began to imitate the siren as loud as he could. (*DL* 185)

Perhaps because of the persistent felt need to characterize the relationship between the forms of the elite art-novel and the Hollywood film—is *The Day of the Locust* a modernist attack on popular culture or a proto-postmodernist deconstruction of those categories?—many of West's critics have focused on Tod's scream at the expense of his laughter. But where the scream emphasizes Tod's capacity for imitation, artistic and otherwise, the laughter suggests his final, belated recognition that his naiveté has been the joke all along. Earlier, while musing on Faye's cruel sexuality, Tod "managed to laugh at his language, but it wasn't a real laugh and nothing was destroyed by it" (*DL* 68); the purely formal, insincere laughter offered only incomplete insulation of his super-liberal pose. Here, however, the laugh is ostensibly real (he can find no reason for it), and it ostensibly destroys something. That something may merely be his sanity—the "some reason" is really no reason—but the novel seems to deny that reading in the willfulness suggested by Tod's imitation.[101] More likely, then, that which is destroyed is Tod's youth along with his Yale-trained aloofness. His laughter recognizes all of that as pretense.

If the purpose of the bildungsroman is to narrate the process by which the young are integrated into society, in *The Day of the Locust* we find a horrifying quintessence of the genre: in his replication of the mechanical siren, Tod embraces the ideal of order purveyed by the classical Hollywood style and protected by the police.[102] For West, the antifascist aesthete always sitting hard between two stools, the real nightmare of *The Day of the Locust* isn't, in the end, the nightmare of history from which a subaltern like the Irish Stephen Dedalus tries to awaken or a formless present in decentered

Los Angeles; it is instead the terror of a future to which Tod, and the industry establishment of which he is a budding microcosm, aspire. The ludicrous but logical extension of this Westian horror—a world and a modernist literature made in Hollywood's image amidst the global cataclysm of the Second World War—was, appropriately enough, already in development.

CHAPTER 4

Global Hollywood
Parker Tyler and Malcolm Lowry,
between Myth and System

Writing in Code

Roughly half a year after *The Day of the Locust* narrated the studio system's maturation as the apocalyptic smashing of Hollywood's "egglike self-sufficiency" on the hard realities of national and international conflict, a young Malcolm Lowry picked up where West left off. In December 1939, freshly settled in British Columbia after a stay in Los Angeles in which he failed to find work as a screenwriter but succeeded in courting Margerie Bonner, a former actress, Lowry published an essay titled "Hollywood and the War" in the Vancouver *Daily Province*.

Written three months after the Molotov-Ribbentrop Pact of August 1939 shocked the Hollywood Anti-Nazi League along with the rest of the world, "Hollywood and the War" opens with these ominous lines: "Somewhere in Hollywood, a soldier leaned against a radio. Round his head was a blood-stained bandage. In his muddy uniform, he seemed rigid with listening." Any reader questioning why a wounded soldier would be in Los Angeles soon receives the following answer: "This man, an extra, despite his unlikelihood, was real. So was what he heard from Warsaw. His look, as of one who sees into hell but doesn't believe it, was real too."[1] Thus the initial meaning of the blood-soaked soldier learning of the Nazi invasion of Poland shatters, and in invoking the extra, Lowry introduces a favorite concept of his, the muddied distinction between reality and unreality. This interest of Lowry's dovetails with the 1930s troping of unreality—of Hollywood as unreal—in the vein of T. S. Eliot's *The Waste Land*. As an actor, the extra is obviously not the soldier he pretends to be; the soldier, then, is unreal. In a more fundamental sense, as a man, he is very much real, like the fighting in Poland that he hears over the radio. A complicated circumstance emerges: a real man, acting as a soldier, listens to an unbelievable, seemingly illusory broadcast of a real event. The fundamental reality of a man processing a news event is thus doubly mediated, by technology on the one hand and by the film industry's practices on the other: two forms of mediation that converge in the mechanically reproduced narrative form of Hollywood cinema. "Hollywood the Unreal," Lowry's epithet for the movie colony, conflates the historical with the fictional, and the ancient with the modern, into a metaphysically homogenized and temporally compressed zone of illusion. Meanwhile, world war, which had seemed far-fetched only a year earlier in 1938 has become, in 1939, no laughing matter. Lowry temporarily distinguishes between the realm of Hollywood illusion and the war's shock of reality, which affected not only the industry's logistics but also the personal lives of European filmmakers who had fled the continent or returned to fight. However, he again destabilizes his distinction by returning to the twin mediations of technology and industrial practice:

> The broadcasting stations, N.B.C. and C.B.S., kept their loudspeakers going day and night with bulletins, news, speeches, eliminating or breaking into their normal programmes with an even more maddening regularity than their advertisements....
>
> And all this, together with the static, the interference from foreign stations, the confusion of tongues, produced a pandemonium as indescribable as the advance of a mechanized army itself, so that finally one was forced to wonder whether or not our extra, or anyone else in Hollywood listening to the radio, was convinced that the war was real at all. Did it not seem, perhaps, on the contrary, an ultimate UNreality?[2]

The crackling Babel of the radio combines with the insulated universe of the movie colony to put the invasion of Poland into doubt.

In Lowry's view, the industry's representation of the world constitutes an ironic but powerful and convincing counternarrative to contemporary events. The "confusion," he writes, "was self-extending to other Hollywood confusions, past and present," a remarkable but obscure formulation that seems to suggest a purpose to Hollywood's mediated conflations of fiction and reality. Lowry takes *The Last Command* (Joseph von Sternberg, Paramount, 1928) as exemplary of the industry's prescience as well as its self-involvement, its sense of its own importance, and its desire to remake the world in its image. The writer, as numerous commenters have demonstrated, was a devotee of the German cinema of the 1920s, but here as throughout his career, Lowry presents foreign films and filmmakers, however interesting to him on their own terms, as part of a narrative of Hollywood global hegemony.[3] As Lowry notes, *The Last Command* features Emil Jannings, "that very German German" playing the Grand Duke Sergius Alexander, a Tsarist general who, after improbably escaping execution with the help of his Bolshevik spy-lover, becomes a Hollywood extra. Lowry does not explain the reference but suggests that the coincidence of the actor's actual and fictive nationalities ironically foretells by a decade the newly established Russo-German alliance. That Jannings's character declines in stature to become a minor player in Hollywood further strikes Lowry, it seems, as representative of the way the industry uses the events of the world to tell a story ultimately about itself. Hollywood becomes, contradictorily, both a powerful and an extremely limited, self-obsessed purveyor of global affairs.

"Hollywood and the War" coordinates many of Lowry's literary preoccupations: the porous boundaries between levels of narrative and between reality and fiction; his obsession with mechanisms, engineering, and technology; and the anxious pursuit of elusive meaning. It can thus be read, somewhat counterintuitively, but nonetheless in line with Lowry's own search for abstruse symbolic explanations, as a kind of program statement for his career.[4] But as illuminating as the analysis on offer in the essay is, what Lowry does not adequately explain yields a less evident but equally profound insight into the relation between his writing and American cinema. For Lowry's interpretation of Hollywood's relation to the world itself derives from *The Last Command*, which concludes with Jannings's Sergius Alexander being forced to play a version of himself in a Russian Revolution picture directed by Leo Andreyev (William Powell), a former Bolshevik actor whom Alexander had once humiliated with a whipping. As belated retribution, the director forces Alexander to strike an insubordinate soldier, farcically repeating as a film industry grunt the act he had committed as an aristocrat, an act that has the unintended effect of psychologically transporting Alexander to the battlefield of the previous decade. Losing his sense of the distinction between past and present, reality and fiction, Alexander exhorts his men to victory before bellowing "Long live Russia!" and succumbing to a heart attack. If the authenticity of Alexander's commitment to Russia both perfects the scene and validates him in Andreyev's eyes—"He was more than a great actor—he was a great man"—that aesthetic and ethical resolution follows from an implicit claim of institutional might: the studio managed to recuperate Alexander and to take his life, accomplishing what the revolutionaries could not. Thus, while it trenchantly observes the industry's power to write the history of the world in its own mythical image, "Hollywood and the War" also suggests the force the industry exerted on the author himself. Hollywood's self-extending confusions extended even to Lowry's art, profoundly influencing the construction of his masterpiece *Under the Volcano* (1947).

Why should Hollywood cinema be considered mythic, and why should that myth be considered the meta-ordering system in a novel of epic ambition overstuffed with "a wide range of arcane, occult, mythical, philosophical, religious, and psychological works"?[5] Why, in other words, should it be considered the equivalent to and reformulation of the ordering myths of the high modernists? To answer these questions, we must understand the relation between Hollywood's global reach and its institutionally codified hermeneutics.

To this point, this book has artificially limited the scope of its history of the studio system in order to demonstrate the ways that works of literature have mediated ideas and experiences at multiple scales that range from the individual (writers, actors, directors, producers) to the collective (the studio, the political movement) to the community (the industry, the South) to the nation (the United States of America). But from the moment that the concept of the studio was coined and movie rights were invented, the Hollywood studio system's development occurred within and contributed to a broader transformation in global economic and geopolitical organization. "During this period," the film and media historian Lee Grieveson has observed, "the United States eclipsed a British-dominated liberal world system and inaugurated new forms of economic globalization founded on a compact between state and capital. Media played significant roles in that consequential process."[6] Even as the fledgling industry vied with the French company Pathé for control of the US market, the studios began to imagine their market in global terms, ultimately surpassing European producers after World War I.[7] Carl Laemmle's 1912 decision to rebrand his Independent Motion Pictures Company as Universal was only the baldest evidence of this desired ambit.

During the silent era, the American film industry both abetted and mystified its domination of the world's film markets by way of a quasi-theory that has come to be known as the "universal language" metaphor, whereby the silent movie functioned as a kind of visual Esperanto, available to the understanding of all viewers despite linguistic difference. This mystification emerged both from within the industry and without: most infamously in D. W. Griffith's *Intolerance* (1916), as well as in theorizations of the hieroglyphic quality of the film image by the poet Vachel Lindsay in *The Art of the Moving Picture* (1915) and by *Motion Picture Herald* editor Terry Ramsaye in *A Million and One Nights* (1926), among others. The notion of film as a universal language, as Miriam Hansen has demonstrated, in fact obscured differences in exhibition and reception; Hollywood movies were frequently reedited to appeal to locally specific tastes and were made to accommodate those modifications.[8] Be that as it may, the prevalence of the metaphor suggests that from the moment the American film industry became "Hollywood," it yoked together a business strategy with something like an interpretive theory. The strategy and the theory converged in the perfection of continuity editing, which, in supposedly mimicking humans' evolutionarily developed, biologically established spatiotemporal perception, grounds Bordwell, Staiger, and Thompson's account of Hollywood classicism. However right or wrong silent-era filmmakers, folk theorists, trade journalists, and fans may have been about the movies' universality, that notion nonetheless served as an enabling fiction and point of self-congratulation for the industry.[9]

Nonetheless, two roughly simultaneous developments, one technological, the other cultural, and both institutionally implemented, invalidated the universal language theory, creating the conditions for another hermeneutic principle, always latent, to come to the fore. The first development, the quick conversion to synchronized sound talkies between 1927 and 1930, raised the problem of national language difference; no longer could images, with occasional help from easily-swapped intertitles or other extradiegetic aids, bear the weight of expressing a movie's meaning. Whether the challenge was met by the creation of multiple-language versions (films shot on the same sets with different personnel), or by way of less costly dubbing or subtitling, in either case the ostensibly identical meaning of different iterations of a particular movie could not be maintained.[10] This shifting international orientation coincided with and supplemented the second development, the maturation of the industry's self-censorship protocols. This took the form of the Production Code, which the MPPDA implemented in 1930 and invigorated in 1934. By preempting state and federal censorship and ensuring that American movies respected foreign countries' censorship regimes, the Code represented the MPPDA's attempt to guide the reception of Hollywood movies at every conceivable scale and ensure the largest possible market for its products.

Limiting the range of possible representation paradoxically established the basis of Hollywood movies' openness to interpretation. The MPPDA in effect codified "a particular kind of ambiguity, a textual indeterminacy that shifted the responsibility for determining what the movie's content was away from the producer to the individual spectator."[11] By the dictates of the Code, a cigar really was just a cigar for the naïve viewer (typically, the child in need of moral protection); the sophisticated viewer, on the other hand, was implicitly invited, by virtue of textual underelaboration, to divine the risqué, or the symbolic, or whatever else that could be plausibly denied. Thus, with the transition to sound and the end of the pretense of the universal language, the "commercial aesthetic" and its attendant hermeneutic came to dominate: "In keeping with the ideological assumptions surrounding the circulation of money in the cultures that have produced and consumed Hollywood movies," Richard Maltby explains,

> viewers may reasonably demand to do what they like with the movie they paid to watch.... Within limits, Hollywood movies are constructed to accommodate, rather than predetermine, their audiences' reactions, and this has involved devising systems and codes of representation that permit a range of interpretations and a degree of instability of meaning.[12]

A Hollywood movie could mean whatever a paying viewer wanted so long as it invariably meant "Hollywood," that is, harmless entertainment. If this interpretive openness bears a striking resemblance to later theories of textuality that would characterize the postmodern aesthetic of late capitalism, that's because Hollywood "developed a full-fledged program of globalization well before many other industries," a program based, of course, on commodified images.[13]

In this chapter, I turn to a consideration of the American film industry's global presence, enabled by Hollywood movies' strategic openness to interpretation, during the period when that presence was most vexed: the brief epoch of World War II and its immediate aftermath, from the Anschluss of 1938 to 1947, the year before the *Paramount* antitrust decree. At the height of its power, Hollywood cinema, a symbol of the burgeoning global hegemony of the United States, confronted a world crisis initiated by the Axis powers. The closing of European markets led the studios to emphasize distribution in Latin America, and through the Office of War Information, the US government exercised oversight of the film industry for the first time, utilizing it as a channel of propaganda.

Under these conditions, both Parker Tyler, a queer surrealist poet, film critic, and erstwhile studio reader, and Lowry, a Britain-born but effectively stateless novelist, each conceived Hollywood as something akin to the Grail legend for Eliot or Homer's epics for Joyce.[14] Described by critics as writing on the "fault line" or "threshold" of modernism and postmodernism, each wrote works of grand ambition—Tyler, the long poem *The Granite Butterfly* (1945), a self-conscious inversion of *The Waste Land*; Lowry, the anti-Joycean *Under the Volcano* (1947)—while living in an incipient Cold War-conditioned world characterized by what Leela Gandhi and Deborah L. Nelson call "global interinextricability."[15] Their styles and ideas are bombastic, at turns astonishing and inscrutable; as such, they occupy the leading edge of a group of paradoxically allegorical and encyclopedic works that comprise the critic Matthew Wilkens's "long" 1950s. For Wilkens, the period roughly between 1948 and 1962 constituted a moment of crisis between "the collapse of an older order—namely the systems of industrial capital, durable social hierarchy, restricted democracy, modernist experimentation, and the like—before any adequate new arrangement had emerged to take its place." Wilkens therefore sees works like Ralph Ellison's *Invisible Man* (1952) and William Gaddis's *The Recognitions* (1955) as evidence of a radical break, an era that "told the stories it knew how to tell in the ways it knew how to tell them, hoping in the process to bend both the narratives and their forms toward the more productive alternatives that it couldn't yet articulate." I, on the other hand, find a smoother if no less outlandish meshing of old ways and new in the writings of Tyler and Lowry.[16]

These two writers occupied an uneasy but enlivening position between, on the one hand, the modernist desire to find the mythological undergirding that would shore up the ruins of a fragmented world and, on the other, their attunement to the fact that such coordination was already underway, a consequence of the networking of the world through media technologies, or what Marshall McLuhan would later call the transition from the Gutenberg Galaxy to the global village. Each registered this transition through a strikingly similar engagement with Hollywood cinema, which, by way of its mighty international distribution and self-conceived myth of universal appeal, appeared as a force binding the globe into One World of viewers.[17] Their major works should, I suggest, be considered exemplars of a transformation of what Franco Moretti has called "the modern epic," a small canon of "*world* texts, whose geographical frame of reference is no longer the nation-state, but a broader entity—a continent, or the world-system as a whole."[18] For Moretti, a modern epic like *The Waste Land* employs myth to "tame polyvocality," the linguistic friction that emblematized the unevenly integrated world system. In my view, Tyler and Lowry each found in Hollywood the appropriate myth to accomplish a similar end. For them, however, the problem was not the polyvocality of their Great War-era predecessors, but rather the mass media-enabled cacophony of the Second World War: when, as Lowry wrote in "Hollywood and the War," the "pandemonium" of the Nazi invasion of Poland was exacerbated by the "static, the interference from foreign stations, the confusion of tongues" of an imperfect radio broadcast playing in the movie capital.[19] Tyler and Lowry's uses of Hollywood together appear, symptomatically, as an inflection point between the transcendent ordering principle of the modernists (informed by late–nineteenth- and early–twentieth-century comparative mythology and anthropology), and the Cold War-era preference for the immanent structuring system (emerging from cybernetics, structuralism, and systems theory more generally) that came to characterize demythologized, paranoid postmodernity.[20] As such, *The Granite Butterfly* and *Under the Volcano* appear as exemplary works of late modernism as recently formulated by C. D. Blanton and Seo Hee Im. Although Tyler and Lowry never explicitly attest to their modern epics' indebtedness to Hollywood in the ways that *Ulysses* and *The Waste Land* (by virtue of titling and footnotes, respectively) betray their authors' intentions, this lack of explicitness in fact aligns them with Blanton's late modernist poets, for whom "epic affords the instrument through which to conceive a 'lost totality' without 'actually *naming* the unity' that gives it both force and cryptic coherence."[21] The American film industry, with its global reach and its formulation (as discussed in Chapter 2) as a "whole equation of pictures," constitutes a species of what Im calls the late modernist "empirical logical forms" that replace myths of antiquity as the means of representing a transnational totality.[22]

But—here *Under the Volcano* diverges from *The Granite Butterfly* even as it puts into practice Tyler's conception of the "theoretically endless elasticity" of American movies—unlike the ordering principles of other late modernists, the Hollywood of Lowry's imagination points up the impending collapse of the great divide between high and mass/popular culture. It also indicates the convergence or conflation of the different understandings of ambiguity that each sphere emphasizes. Whether an expression of the artist's mind, as in William Empson's account, or a quality of the work itself, as in the New Critics', in either case, the ambiguities of a poem are held in irreducible suspension and constitute the complex meaning the reader pursues.[23] Commercial art, however, substitutes an array of discrete, differentiable possibilities for the poem's complex meaning; in parallel fashion, it transfers the responsibility for the determination of those discrete meanings to the audience. Where Eliot's "massive edifice of cultural facts," as Marc Manganaro observes, "displays the signature of the compiler," and Joyce ensured his immortality by keeping the scholars guessing at the solutions to his puzzles, Lowry recapitulates the allusiveness, density, and difficulty of his predecessors while renouncing his authority over the meaning of his work.[24] Hovering outside of *Under the Volcano*—in Tyler's criticism, in Lowry's letters, and everywhere else—Hollywood, with its commercial aesthetic, suggests for Lowry a model of interpretive pluralism or, put another way, the triumph of consumer choice. The implicit theoretical problem that Lowry raises—can a work of literature be both meaningful (i.e., authored) and open to any interpretation?—allows us to identify one way that modernism confronted its limits.[25]

"Hollywood's Protean Law" and Other Paradoxes of Parker Tyler's Poetics

> Mr. Tyler ... sets *The Golden Bough* right in the Hollywood Bowl.
> —Marshall McLuhan, *Inside Blake and Hollywood*, 1947[26]

> If Joyce's *Ulysses* could be dubbed an intensive capitalization of a day's culture, every Hollywood studio is to some degree an Alexandria of technical devices and cultural fetishes working on speed-up daily schedules.
> —Parker Tyler, *The Movies as a Fine Art*, 1957[27]

In 1950, the same year that the sociologist David Riesman described the movies as the tutors of character development in a consumption-driven, other-directed society, Tyler defined Hollywood's commercial aesthetic as a kind of religious institution.[28] Hollywood "fulfills the place of a Universal Church," he wrote, summarizing an argument about late-1940s social problem films, "in propagating the sacred image of a basically snobbish democracy: an anti-intellectual, 'nonsectarian,' and socially crass *personability*." In this concluding thought, Tyler reiterates his claim that Hollywood is a perversely democratic institution, open to all who are capable of "mak[ing] the grade," that is, of marketing themselves. Hence Tyler's italicization of "personability." This personability, in the critic's view, takes on a new valence in the immediate postwar, as Hollywood supplemented its longstanding appeal to the American fetish of individuality by developing "race glamour" in dramas of passing such as Fox's Elia Kazan-directed *Gentleman's Agreement* (1947) and *Pinky* (1949). As Tyler understands it, the passing drama's exploitation of the proto-Civil Rights era investment in racial and ethnic identity is nothing so much as an elaboration of the "Hollywood professional myth": the valorization of "personal charms and personal success so ascendant in an era of individual competitiveness and in a society where the dominant moral ideas derive their ideal nature from the ideal aspect of the economy." Tyler effectively identifies the Hollywood cinema as nothing less than the mythological underpinning of the American Century and the spectacular capitalism of incipient postmodernity, a vision of the world to which the country has been "converted … because the existing economy structures have been found inadequate to totally unite a democracy retaining (all sentimentalism to the contrary notwithstanding) serious racial and religious differences."[29]

This conceptualization of Hollywood can be detected earlier in Tyler's books of film criticism, *The Hollywood Hallucination* (1944) and *Magic and Myth of the Movies* (1947), and, in a different form, in his poetry on the American cinema, including his magnum opus, *The Granite Butterfly* (1945). Recognizing its presence across genre and mode renders a picture of Tyler's writing that is rather different from those formulated by scholars in film and literary studies, respectively. Where American cinema scholars Greg Taylor and David Bordwell have focused on Tyler's film and art criticism and have therefore emphasized the writer's indebtedness to surrealism and employment of a camp attitude toward kitsch, the literary critic Sam See views Tyler's literary work, and especially *The Young and Evil* (1933), a novel coauthored with Charles Henri Ford, as an act of queer mythopoeia that torqued the earlier modernists' mythical methods. Yet the two positions are compatible. In the early 1930s, Tyler theorized his relationship to the poetic styles and approaches then practiced. In his introduction to *Modern Things* (1934), a poetry anthology he edited and understood explicitly as a canonizing effort, Tyler described his own style as "turning on the one hand to the metaphysical lucidity of metaphor and on the other to Rimbaudian hallucination," and indebted to "certain technical handlings from Pound, [E. E.] Cummings, and [William Carlos] Williams."[30] *Modern Things* opens with selections from Eliot, Pound, Cummings, Marianne Moore, Williams, Wallace Stevens, and Gertrude Stein; a host of "younger moderns … not yet intrenched in the libraries" including Ford and Louis Zukofsky follow. Tyler concluded that second section with a sampling of his own poetry that begins with "Hollywood Dream Suite." A phantasmagoric meditation in two parts, "Prelude" and "III. Elegy," "Hollywood Dream Suite" starts with an invocation of "laughing noun/Time," the fundamental medium of moving pictures, and ends with an appreciation of an unnamed deceased star of "sham sex" (likely Rudolph Valentino), a "begetter of dream-children/ by constant visibleness." The poem thus introduces the seriousness with which Tyler will treat the cliché of movie stars as gods and goddesses over the coming decades.[31] More importantly, though, it indicates Tyler's sense of his relation to his forbears; in "Hollywood Dream Suite," he can be seen beginning what might be considered his camping of Eliotic modernism, archly transforming the tradition of the "mind of Europe" into the kaleidoscopic Hollywood hallucination in which "we twine being// metaphorical dreams."

Greg Taylor, Parker Tyler's most patient and comprehensive critic, would likely disagree with my assessment. His Tyler condescends to Hollywood and remakes its movies according to his own sophisticated and idiosyncratic sensibility. In a sense, this is evidently the case, but Tyler's critical position in the 1940s should not, I think, be described so unambiguously. After all, his brief author biography in *Magic and Myth of the Movies* reads, "He says he loves the movies, but also hates them."[32] Although he approached the Hollywood cinema archly and never denied its tendency toward banality and badness, Tyler also asserted that any critical interpretation he might offer, regardless of its content, was accommodated in advance by the industry itself, what in *The Hollywood Hallucination* he called Hollywood's "psychologically cubistic" approach and in *Magic and Myth* Hollywood's "protean law." Describing this principle in the latter book, he writes,

> The lack of individual control in movie-making in this country, the absence of respect for the individual work, the premise that a movie is an ingenious fabrication of theoretically endless elasticity—all these positive and negative elements make for lack of form (or art) and specifically encourage the spontaneous growth of popular forms … thus leaving crevices for whatever there be in actor, dialogue writer, cinematic trick shot, or directorial fantasy to creep through and flower. Under such conditions the factor most likely to succeed in Hollywood would unquestionably be the mythic; that is, the basic vestigial patterns surviving in popular imagination and reflecting the unconscious desires and the secret remnants of the primitive belief in magic.[33]

Recognizing the paradox here between the purpose of a totalizing theory (that Hollywood movies ought to be understood as purveyors of myth) and the plurality of interpretations that the movies invite and that his theory entails (a paradox evident in the term "protean law" itself), Tyler acknowledges that his idea cannot be operationalized as a method. In *Magic and Myth of the Movies*, Tyler again riffs on Eliot, who in "The Perfect Critic" presents Aristotle as "an eternal example—not of laws, or even of method, for there is no method except to be very intelligent," by asking "Do I have *a method*?"[34] "Not," he answers, "in the sense that I am selling ideas, nor above all, is mine a method by which one can test the high or low esthetic content of a given movie.… Indirectly, however, I have only been obeying Hollywood's own law of fluidity, of open and ingenious invention."[35]

Tyler was yet more direct when defending *The Hollywood Hallucination* from accusations of a "general 'screwiness' of form," averring that his style was necessitated by his subject and proceeded from the "necessary premise [of] a profound, irrational acceptance of the ritual of movie-going with all its lures of fantasy: a positivism of approach which so-called sophisticated critics have hitherto lacked."[36] Thus, his creative reimagination of the movies—his taxonomy of character archetypes, his arguments about the Hollywood cinema as the "daylight dream" of an advanced capitalist society, his brilliant and idiosyncratic interpretations of such movies as *Double Indemnity* (Billy Wilder, Paramount, 1944) and *Mildred Pierce* (Michael Curtiz, Warners, 1945)—are, in the final analysis, based in and following from Hollywood's own practice.

Tyler's antimethodological method of interpreting Hollywood movies—his production of eccentric analyses accommodated in advance by the studio system's commercial aesthetic—corresponds with his poetics, which Barbara Fialkowski rightly identified as similarly paradoxical. Fialkowski nominates the medium of cinema as the basis of his poetry's contradictory emphases on movement and stillness, change and changelessness, formlessness and form, an assessment supported explicitly by Tyler himself in an unpublished essay on *The Granite Butterfly* titled "Cinematic Effects in a Long Poem."[37] But it would be just as accurate to identify the foundation of his poetics in the industry's protean law. In "Ode to Hollywood" (1940), Tyler not only celebrates Garbo, Valentino, and Chaplin, but also and more importantly, the Olympus where the deities reside:

> We can learn how futile it is in nature
> To imitate the mind, whose perpetual life is
>   Rewinding, and springing, and blurring…
>
> Still, forever from that city of incredibly
> Rapid and beautiful and fragile movement,
>   The kiss in perpetuum mobile![38]

In its ability to capture the erotic flux of the unconscious, giving a provisional, protean form to formlessness—the kiss in perpetuum mobile—Hollywood excels beyond other artificers in rendering the vicissitudes and vagaries of the human mind. The American film industry thus presents a solution to what Tyler saw as the problem of orthodox surrealism. In his essay "Beyond Surrealism" (1935), Tyler rejected André Breton's "anarchic" surrealism as inimical to art, since the practice's "systematic disorganization" contradicts "the fundamental nature of the esthetic, the apprehension of a given system of the universe; the preëminence of a single *point of view*."[39] According to Tyler's theory of the industry as the "Entrepreneur of Anything," while any individual movie is akin to and can be read as a surrealist work—as nonart, because its endless elasticity (formlessness) and lack of a controlling point of view make it better understood in terms of myth—its surreal quality is a purposeful consequence of the studio system's commercial logic. What looks like formlessness at one order (that of the individual movie) is in fact intended, and therefore formed, at a higher one (the operation of Hollywood as a whole). In "Ode to Hollywood," that higher-order form finds a geographical analogue in the way that the American talkies derived their look and sound from the world's filmmaking talent ("Lubitsch brought lightness, the French the mature;/Shakespeare's land gave the arabesque vowel") and efficiently incorporated techniques devised by their ideological antithesis ("Russia the Esperanto iris").[40] Tyler's "city of incredibly/Rapid and beautiful and fragile movement" becomes the model for and source of a poetic strategy that moves rapidly across seemingly incommensurate scales, from the individual psyche to the grandest events of world history. He would put that strategy into effect in *The Granite Butterfly*.

An epic of the poet's psychic, aesthetic, and homoerotic development in nine cantos that William Carlos Williams called "the best poem written by an American since *The Waste Land*," *The Granite Butterfly* comprises three interwoven and densely figured narratives in the modes of verse, drama, and prose monologue.[41] Tyler's fundamental elaboration of his relationship with his parents, formulated in the idioms of Greek myth and psychoanalysis, becomes, at the next figurative level, the rape of a movie actor in front of his wife by "Black Oedipus," an African American intruder into the star's country home with whom, as the figure of a "socially inevitable type of inferiority," the homosexual Tyler identifies.[42] That fable then becomes the occasion for a further fantasy, in which the movie star's wife, prompted by a film scenario that has been presented as a possible job for the movie star, dreams that, amidst the Russian Revolution, Countess Liza Escutanoff looks on as her husband, Count Alexei, is sexually assaulted by an invading serf. In its extraordinary compression and rapid shifting of narrative level, idiom, and mode, *The Granite Butterfly* mimics the condensation and displacement of the Freudian dreamwork, a form that matches the rapid shifting between and merging of violence, desire, and injustice at the levels of psychic, familial, national, and ultimately world history. The superimposition and interpenetration of scales also recalls Eliot's poem, which Tyler took as an inspiration but in which, crucially, he saw a strategy opposite to his own. In his "Author's Note on the Meaning of the Poem," itself a nod to Eliot's pedagogical footnote, Tyler wrote, "the ellipses of this poem are, on the whole, by no means as stark and rapid as those in, for example, *The Waste Land*. But this poem does not require, as does Eliot's, an array of sources to fill out its pattern and render it rationally or easily coherent. All its sources are in the poem itself."[43] This isn't strictly true, as *The Granite Butterfly* refers to Oedipus, naturally, as well as Medusa and Narcissus from the Greek tradition; to Shakespeare's *Romeo and Juliet* and *Hamlet*; and to the styles he touted in *Modern Things*. Nonetheless, Tyler's claim of effectively turning *The Waste Land* inside out, substituting a dense interconnection of internal references for eccentric erudition, suggests a self-conscious inversion of Eliot's mythical method.[44]

That inversion takes the form of the meta-mythical granite butterfly, a figure that contains multiple contradictions: of the inanimate and animate; of hardness and fragility; and of stasis and flux. Paradoxically, though, the granite butterfly was, before the poem began, itself contained, as the poem's epigraph indicates:

> chrysalis of cellophane
> through which time flows
> silhouette of the expanding universe
> torn, untorn
> by space's rush:
> the granite butterfly

For Tyler, *The Granite Butterfly* bore "that fatal *symbolism* in poetry which modern materialism, rationalism, and logical positivism disdain," because it emerged from and in opposition to "the chrysalis of cellophane," *The Hollywood Hallucination*'s material emblem of techno-rationality:

> science's burning eye, while it creates vast abstract structures, tends to show that in relation to the total physical world, with man at its center, such structures might as well be made of cellophane. It is as necessary for science to be humanly modest as it is for art to be humanly pretentious, and Hollywood is art at its most pretentious; and thus, I hint at its necessity.[45]

Though Tyler wrote about the granite butterfly in the language of mysticism and literary criticism—"The poet's soul, formally an abstraction, is well likened to a butterfly.... Yet the butterfly is woven securely as a symbol and as a living image in the integument of this poem"—it is, ultimately, a cryptic figure for the Hollywood cinema, itself born of cellophane enlightenment only to become the "daylight dream," "the mass unconscious" formlessly formed on celluloid.[46] Hence it is Hollywood

The Name

*F*ROM this name take off, this platform of love

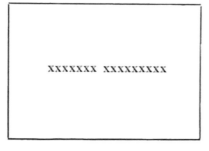

Figure 4.1   The x's replace "Carlyle Blackwell," a silent era star with whom Tyler had fallen in love at age twelve. By redacting Blackwell's name, Tyler accentuated the star's importance to the development of his sexuality, as though the name were too holy to write. The redaction is also a synecdoche of the poem's structuring absence; shaping *The Granite Butterfly* from without is the Hollywood mythology Tyler was in the process of elaborating in *The Hollywood Hallucination* (1944) and *Magic and Myth of the Movies* (1947). Charles Boultenhouse and Michael Fournier suggest that the opening epigraph's "chrysalis of cellophane" refers to the sleeve in which Tyler kept a collage of photographs of Blackwell. *The Granite Butterfly: A Poem in Nine Cantos, A Facsimile of the First Edition, with Supplementary Materials*, eds. Charles Boultenhouse and Michael Fournier (Orono, ME: National Poetry Foundation, 1994), unnumbered photograph insert page 3.

that shapes the poem's fantasies at every level, from the speaker's psyche—the muse he invokes in "Canto Two: The Name" is Carlyle Blackwell, a movie star of the silent era and early object of Tyler's desire, whose name appears redacted within a rectangle of the dimensions of a movie screen—up through the movie star's wife's final dream of the Russian Revolution film (Figure 4.1). And it is Hollywood, "Entrepreneur of Anything" for which "there is nothing which the camera cannot conceive and project on a conveniently empty screen[,] nothing, from journalism to Shakespeare," that provides the model for the poem's omnivorous consumption and regurgitation of modes.[47] If, as Marjorie Perloff has suggested, *The Granite Butterfly* is an "emblem of the transition from modernism to postmodernism," a queer epic that inverted Eliot but did not, in its self-seriousness, reach Frank O'Hara and John Ashbery's "burlesque world of New York poetry," it became so by taking seriously the magic and myth of the American movies.[48]

Under the Hollywood Sign

"If I could only convey the effect of a man who was the very shape and motion of the world's doom," he went on, "But at the same time the living prophecy of its hope!"

"You would need a screen as big as the world to show it on," said the doctor.

—The director Jacques Laruelle and Dr. Arturo Díaz Vigil in Malcolm Lowry, *The 1940 Under the Volcano*[49]

"(and ah, the eerie significance of cinemas in our life…)"
—Ethan Llewelyn in Malcolm Lowry, *October Ferry to Gabriola*[50]

Months after *The Granite Butterfly* fluttered into the world, Malcolm Lowry attempted to convince Jonathan Cape, his eventual editor, to publish *Under the Volcano* despite a negative reader's report regarding the novel's tedium and complexity: in effect, its self-conscious modernism.[51] Intensifying the day-in-the-life form of *Ulysses* and *Mrs. Dalloway* by presenting its protagonist's last living hours, *Under the Volcano* follows Geoffrey Firmin, an Anglo-Indian former British consul to Mexico stationed in Quauhnahuac (the Nahuatl name for what became Cuernavaca). The Consul's alcoholism and broken trust in his unfaithful wife Yvonne have led him to the brink of dissolution, a condition matching the world's in 1938, on the eve of the Second World War. On November 2, the Mexican Day of the Dead, Yvonne, an American former starlet who believed that she had "*outgrown Hollywood*" returns to Quauhnahuac to see Geoffrey and attempts to recuperate their marriage.[52] Hugh, Geoffrey's half-brother who had at some point had an affair with Yvonne, and a journalist ashamed of having avoided the Spanish Civil War, arrives as well, dressed like a cowboy in the manner of Yvonne's erstwhile costar Bill Hodson. The three meet up with Geoffrey's childhood friend, Jacques Laruelle, a French modernist film director who refuses to see the pictures he made in Hollywood and who has also slept with Yvonne. Various ostensible banalities occur until Geoffrey, drunk beyond hope at the Farolito bar in Parián, is first accused of being a Communist spy, is then shot to death by Fascist sympathizers, and is finally tossed into one of the deep ravines that surround the city. This brief summary suggests that nothing terribly exceptional occurs until the novel's tragic conclusion. But that is exactly the point: either nothing in Geoffrey's life is extraordinary, or, packed with symbolic meaning, everything potentially is. Faced with the bleakness of a world on the verge of annihilation, it is for the characters, and for the reader, to decide what exactly counts as meaningful. What is being symbolized at any given moment—"it was symbolic, of what [Geoffrey] could not conceive, but it was deeply symbolic"—and how that symbolism works are questions at the novel's heart (*UTV* 232).

Lowry scholars have long noted the novel's investment in the operation of the symbolic register, connecting it to the author's incorporation of elements of the Cabbala, the Faust legend, and the *Divine Comedy*, among many other sources and systems. In doing so, Lowry established the possibility that such systems warrant connections between apparent symbols and their supposed meanings. But, in their very superfluity, those many ordering principles fail in advance, with none capable of acting as the key to all mythologies. This Faulknerian flaw in design resides in the deep structure of the novel. Toward the conclusion of an earlier draft of *Under the Volcano* completed in 1940, the Consul muses, "Life was a forest of symbols, was it, Baudelaire had said? But it occurred to him, even before the forest, if there were such a thing as 'before,' were not there still symbols? … And the more you tried to comprehend them, confusing what life was, with the necessity for this comprehension, the more they multiplied."[53] If these lines resemble Tyler's claim that Hollywood movies tap into and reformulate persistent mythic meanings while opening themselves up to proliferating interpretations through their "theoretically endless elasticity," that's because the system capable of incorporating the *Volcano*'s many structuring schemes is the studio system.[54] The aptly named Dr. Vigil, a local physician and the Consul's confrère in "the Great Brotherhood of Alcohol," prophetically if obliquely suggests just such an outlandish possibility as he stumbles from multilingual malapropism to inadvertent clairvoyance: "But after much tequila the eclectic systemë is perhaps un poco descompusesto, comprenez, as sometimes in the cine," he tells Geoffrey, likening his hangover to the faulty electricity in Señor Bustamente's cinema (*UTV* 146, 151).

Lowry responded to the skeptical reader's report with an extraordinary description of the novel's intricacy, defending it in terms Tyler would have appreciated. "[... T]he book is written," he wrote in a letter to Cape,

> on numerous planes with provision made, it was my fond hope, for almost every kind of reader, my approach with all humility being opposite, I felt, to that of Mr Joyce, i.e., a simplifying, as far as possible, of what originally suggested itself in far more baffling, complex and esoteric terms, rather than the other way round. The novel can be read simply as a story which you can skip if you want. It can be read as a story you will get more out of if you don't skip. It can be regarded as a kind of symphony, or in another way as a kind of opera—or even a horse opera. It is hot music, a poem, a song, a tragedy, a comedy, a farce, and so forth. It is superficial, profound, entertaining and boring, according to taste. It is a prophecy, a political warning, a cryptogram, a preposterous movie, and a writing on the wall. It can even be regarded as a kind of machine: it works too, believe me, as I have found out.[55]

In the same way that Tyler inverted the form of *The Waste Land*, enclosing the poem within Hollywood's dream logic, Lowry understands himself as Joyce's negative image. Lowry goes beyond Tyler's formal upending of Eliot, however, by implicitly setting Joyce's claim to authorial control (suggested by Joyce's Homeric parallel and the interpretive schemata he formulated for *Ulysses*) against his own belief that his novel's meaning exists in the minds of his readers. Lowry said perhaps more than he knew in the litany of ways his novel can be read; a horse opera (another name for a Western film), a preposterous movie, a cryptogram, a writing on the wall, and a machine are all terms that can be and indeed have been used to describe the works or the operation of the American movie business.[56]

For the peripatetic Lowry, who "had practically lost all sense of national barriers and had almost come to look on the world as a citizen thereof and its inhabitants as one happy or unhappy family," the internationally distributed American film stood for the industry that united an ambivalent planet.[57] He made the point explicitly in 1950, the same year Tyler called Hollywood a Universal Church. In the preface that he and his wife Margerie wrote for a screenplay adaptation of Fitzgerald's *Tender Is the Night* that they hoped to sell to MGM, they remarked:

> The formative power, for better or worse, of Hollywood on the youth of the world has been colossal: and we never know how much our own character has been moulded by it. And it is the same in Canada. Whether one feels grateful or abusive, most everyone has a stake in it, whether they know it or not. To most people it's the only Sunday school, college, or military to say nothing of sexual training they ever get.[58]

The American film industry usurps the roles of national institutions, binding the world under the Hollywood sign as thoroughly as it shapes individual minds and—it would be fair to add as an unacknowledged and perhaps unrecognized corollary—art. The influence need not be observed in order to have its effect.

Figurations of this unknowing influence appear in Lowry's pre-*Volcano* writing of the 1930s. In his first novel *Ultramarine*, protagonist Dana Hilliot, a pretentious upper-middle-class youth modeled on the author, joins a merchant marine crew on the *Oedipus Tyrannus* and finds himself thoroughly alienated from both the working-class men onboard and the British colonial port city of Hong Kong, where they briefly disembark. Drunk and reeling through the streets with a German sailor named Hans Popplereuter, Hilliot finds himself arrested by the sight of a movie theater marquee:

> We paused, swaying on our heels, before the snowy theatre front. A sailor was reeling round in front of the box office....
> "Olga Tschechowa in *Love's Crucifixion*," spelt out Popplereuter. "Richard Barthelmess in *The Amateur Gentleman*. A smashing drama of the good old days of Merrie England! Next week!"⁵⁹

The two displaced nationals have come upon films ostensibly from their respective home countries. From Germany comes *Liebeshölle* (1928), here titled *Love's Crucifixion*. *The Amateur Gentleman*, however, is the more salient one for the narrative. A bildungsroman set during the Regency era written by Jeffrey Farnol in 1913, *The Amateur Gentleman* was adapted in 1926 by the American company Inspiration Pictures. As Hilliot's revelry becomes increasingly drunk and manic, visions of "*Richard Barthelmess in 'The Amateur Gentleman'*" repeatedly obtrude into his besotted consciousness, an indication of the attraction that a sign of "Merrie England" holds for him. Further, the emphasis on the name of the American actor playing the title character also indicates Hollywood's mediating role in presenting the British fantasy. At Hilliot's lowest moment, when he's most in need of comfort, Hollywood has the power to offer him an image of home (an image, alas, only available "next week," when the *Oedipus Tyrannus* will have left for another port). Similarly, in the unfinished novel *In Ballast to the White Sea*, like *Ultramarine* a semiautobiographical künstlerroman written in 1935–1936, protagonist Sigbjørn Hansen-Tarnmoor sees signs advertising "*Leslie Howard in Outward Bound*."⁶⁰ Based on a play written by the British Sutton Vane, *Outward Bound* was adapted by Warner Brothers in 1930 and starred Howard, a British actor; it begins with three title cards, the last of which reads: "As you sit in this theatre, we cordially beg you to place yourselves in the same position as that first-night audience in London, and see if the deep sincerity of our Vitaphone version of the play impresses you as it has impressed the appreciative theatre audiences of the world." The metaphysical drama, which presents souls unknowingly sailing to the afterlife, obtrudes into Sigbjørn's consciousness as he feels himself "between two worlds" following the suicide of his brother Tor and the "enormous loss of life" that resulted from the crashing of one of his father's ships.[61] What for Warners was an opportunity to tout its artistic and technological prestige becomes the foreknowing narrative of Sigbjørn's existential crisis.[62]

In observing the formal ramifications of Lowry's engagement with the American film industry, I deviate from the standard account of the novelist's relation to cinema. Lowry's florid prose, which often roves among and rapidly shifts in montage fashion between images and voices, has been understood, like so many authors before him, as "cinematic."[63] However, unlike the first-generation modernists (but like Tyler), Lowry had no compunction about making such a claim for himself. To translator Clemens ten Holder, Lowry explained, "the influences that have formed the Volcano are in a profound degree largely German," and "the first twenty minutes of" F.W. Murnau's *Sunrise: A Song of Two Humans* (1927) "have influenced me as much as any book I ever read." Statements of this kind have justifiably led eminent Lowry critics to interpret the novel vis-à-vis the Expressionist cinema of the 1920s. It's not difficult to see why he would find *Sunrise* so affecting. With a fluidly mobile camera, Murnau's film tracks the adultery of a Man with a treacherous Woman from the City, followed by the Man's reconciliation with his Wife. An elemental drama that occurs within the contrasting milieus of the Edenic country and wicked modern metropolis, *Sunrise* has a style and sensibility that resonate deeply with those of the baroque *Volcano*. But Lowry knew well that this most influential movie was made not for Ufa, the studio responsible for most of the other German films he loved, but rather for Fox. "It falls to pieces [after the first twenty minutes] doubtless due to the exigencies of Hollywood," he told ten Holder, but hovering above the blame is the acknowledgment that the movie, at once an allegory of human existence and an artwork that spoke directly to the writer, was at bottom a Hollywood product.[64] Like the Soviet cinema, which Lowry also admired and which came into existence "through a process of Americanization," *Sunrise*, whatever its limitations, would simply not have existed if not for William Fox.[65]

In *Under the Volcano*, Lowry developed the trope he initiated in *Ultramarine* and *In Ballast to the White Sea* in the form of the recurring poster for *Las Manos de Orlac*, the Spanish-language title of MGM's *Mad Love* (1935), the movie playing in the "eclectic systemë" of Señor Bustamente's cine. A movie Lowry called a work of "awe-inspiring badness," *Mad Love* could justly be considered the ridiculous counterpoint to *Sunrise*'s sublimity, capturing all his ambivalence about Hollywood's position in the world. Directed by German emigré Karl Freund, *Mad Love* was adapted from the Austrian film *Orlacs Handë* (Pan-Film, 1924), made by Robert Wiene and starring Conrad Veidt (both of *The Cabinet of Dr. Caligari* [Decla-Bioscop, 1920], a Lowry favorite); that Weimar film was itself an adaptation of *Les Mains d'Orlac*, a French novel of 1920 by Maurice Renard. While the European sources tell a strongly Freudian tale of intrafamilial animus, guilt, repression, and wish fulfillment, the Hollywood reformulation is at turns grisly and goofy. In the latter, Dr. Gogol—Peter Lorre in his first American role—grafts a deceased murderer's hands onto an injured piano player named Stephen Orlac (Colin Clive). The operation somehow transfers the murderer's tendencies, including his knife-throwing ability, to the maimed pianist. Meanwhile, Dr. Gogol develops an off-putting infatuation with Orlac's wife Yvonne (Frances Drake), an actress in Grand Guignol-style productions. (That Yvonne is the name of the Consul's wife, and that no character comments on this, is perhaps the clearest indication that the awe-inspiringly bad movie meant more to the novel than Lowry was willing or able to say.) Gogol's obsession intensifies throughout the film, beginning with his adoration of a wax statue of Yvonne and continuing through his attempts to drive Orlac insane and, ultimately, strangle Yvonne when her love is inexorably beyond his reach. The film concludes abruptly with Orlac rescuing Yvonne by landing a knife in Gogol's back.

Set in Europe, adapted from European predecessors, and starring an international and multiethnic cast comprising the American Drake, the British Clive, the Hungarian Lorre, and the Chinese American Keye Luke, *Mad Love* captures as well as any other movie Hollywood's ability to lay claim to the vast space and cultures of the Earth, compress them, and represent them diegetically. Moreover, despite its adherence to the horror movie conventions established by Universal in the early 1930s, *Mad Love*, as an MGM product, conceives of itself as artistic in line with its *Ars Gratia Artis* motto. Thus, the film refers to various high-cultural formulations of mad love: the myth of Pygmalion and Galatea, the poetry of Robert and Elizabeth Barrett Browning, and—even as it mocks the Freudian theory that *Orlacs Handë* took so seriously—psychoanalysis, the theory of neuroticism and eroticism (Figures 4.2, 4.3, and 4.4).

Figure 4.2   "Galatea … but I am no Pygmalion"
Mad Love (Karl Freund, MGM, 1935)

Figure 4.3   Dr. Gogol recites portions of Elizabeth Barrett Browning's
Sonnets from the Portuguese (out of order):

The face of all the world is changed I think,
Since first I heard the footsteps of thy soul…
"Guess now who holds thee!"—"Death," I said, But, there,
The silver answer rang, "Not Death, but Love."
Mad Love (Karl Freund, MGM, 1935)

Figure 4.4

GOGOL: "After the shock of the wreck came a second shock: your hands were altered by my knife. You could no longer play. As a result, your disturbed mind was ready for any phobia."
ORLAC: "But the knives, the wish to kill?"
GOGOL: "Your case is one of arrested wish fulfilment."
ORLAC: "But why should I wish to throw knives?"
GOGOL: "Perhaps, as a little child, some playmate threw a knife cleverly, you wished you could do it like him. Now that wish was not fulfilled. It festered deep in your subconscious. If you could bring that forgotten memory, whatever it is, into consciousness, you will be cured instantly."
Mad Love (Karl Freund, MGM, 1935)

Film historian Gregory Mank has further identified numerous references in *Mad Love* to contemporary horror films, including *Frankenstein* (James Whale, Universal, 1931), *Freaks* (Tod Browning, MGM, 1932), and *Doctor X* (Michael Curtiz, Warners, 1932), among many others.[66] The movie is therefore knowingly encyclopedic and self-reflexive by virtue of its desire to situate itself within and comment on the body of films to which it belongs, but it conceals its complicated genre-referential and self-referential undergirding beneath an easily understandable (if ludicrous) narrative.[67]

While the *Volcano*'s framing first chapter, set one year in the future on the Day of the Dead, 1939, begins with a literal mapping of the world, it concludes with M. Laruelle's visit to Señor Bustamente's inconsistently powered cine, where the director comes upon a poster advertising *Las Manos de Orlac*. Startled to see that the terrible movie is not only playing again but also playing on the same day a year later, Laruelle asks the proprietor of the cinema whether he had "revived" the "Orlac picture." Bustamente replies, "Compañero, we have not revived it. It has only returned" (*UTV* 27). "Revival" would entail the effort of the owner; "return," alternatively, suggests a power beyond Bustamente's control. In the 1940 *Under the Volcano*, the "bloodthirsty theme [of *Las Manos de Orlac*] was so popular with Mexican audiences the manager had been obliged to put it on at least a half a dozen times at this very cinema in the last few years," and it is Laruelle who muses on this commercial decision's philosophical value, conceiving it as an instance of a Nietzschean "eternal return."[68] In the revised novel, however, the manager has been stripped of his agency and Laruelle has been deprived of the opportunity to speculate on the return's metaphysical implications. Lowry synthesizes Bustamente's mundane imperative and Laruelle's speculation about a transcendent power into a force exerted by Hollywood's powerful international distribution, here conflated with the Day of the Dead, a holiday in which the spirits of the deceased visit their families.

Indigenous Mexican mythology becomes subsumed by the American movie industry at a moment when Hollywood paid closer attention to Latin America than it ever had before, following the closure of European markets and the concomitant rise of the US's desire to establish strong diplomatic relations with its hemispheric neighbors by way of the Office of Inter-American affairs.[69] "The American film is the greatest sales force our country has in foreign lands," Twentieth Century-Fox president Sidney R. Kent said in April 1939, "and it is our hope to increase this prestige in South American countries."[70] Following from the US government's Good Neighborly interest in Latin America, and manifesting most blatantly in the Disney/RKO animated musical *The Three Caballeros* that premiered in Mexico City in December 1944, a vogue for Mexican themes and locales emerged in the 1940s and 1950s. As Jennifer Fay and Justus Nieland have demonstrated, even in the best of these films, such as the 1947 *noir* masterpiece *Out of the Past* (Jacques Tourneur, RKO), Mexico is "unreal": both romanticized and, what amounts to the same thing, Hollywoodified. When doomed protagonist Jeff Bailey (Robert Mitchum) finds his shady boss's runaway girlfriend Kathie Moffat (Jane Greer) in the La Mar Azul cantina, he falls in love with her in a version of Mexico that the movie knowingly invokes as "an imaginary national space of romantic longing." That knowingness manifests concretely in the exterior shots of La Mar Azul, where Bailey passes the hours waiting for Kathie to return: "Set under the neon sign of the 'Cine Pico,' the lovers' ill-fated first meeting in

Mexico is not something just out of the past, but also out of the movies."⁷¹ The unreal nostalgic flashback as well as the scalar dilation and metaleptic movement that Fay and Nieland observe in *Out of the Past*—from the diegetic street furniture of the Cine Pico to the romantic–tragic melodrama of the movie itself to the industry's role in war-era North American diplomacy—occur with remarkable similarity in the opening frame chapter of *Under the Volcano*.

Mad Love is not only the bathetic sign of the novel's deepest, darkest thematic concerns (an idea Lowry asserted), but also, outrageously enough, it is a privileged emblem of the novel's overwhelming investment in rampant signification (an idea the author may have recognized only dimly, if at all). The awe-inspiringly bad film, vampiric of European high culture and thus quintessentially kitsch, predicts the chain of responses Laruelle, the dandified artist-intellectual, produces. Laruelle is distinct from Tyler the camp critic in only vaguely recognizing how his interpretations have been molded in advance:

> Only then it had been Conrad Veidt in "Orlac." Strangely, that particular film had been scarcely better than the present version, a feeble Hollywood product.... But so far as he remembered not even Peter Lorre had been able to salvage it.... Yet what a complicated endless tale it seemed to tell, of tyranny and sanctuary, that poster looming above him now, showing the murderer Orlac! An artist with a murderer's hands; that was the ticket, the hieroglyphic of the time. For really it was Germany itself that, in the gruesome degradation of a bad cartoon, stood over him.—Or was it, by some uncomfortable stretch of the imagination, M. Laruelle himself? (*UTV* 25–26)

After dismissing the film—the zero degree of interpretation—Laruelle reconsiders its allegorical signification in line with the developing discourse of social psychoanalysis. In identifying the image as a "hieroglyphic of the times," Laruelle invokes not only Sir Thomas Browne's *Religio Medici* but also the discourse of cinema as a hieroglyphic language, a variant on the universal language theory.⁷² Here we find a Frenchman at a Mexican cinema decoding an advertisement for a Hollywood film as an allegory of Teutonic aggression, a situation exemplary of the classical studio system's incorporation and ordering of the world system. That Laruelle mistakenly identifies Lorre as Orlac by pairing the actor with Veidt and thus devises a comparison between Lorre's Gogol and Hitler derives, importantly, from Lorre himself. As Lowry wrote in "Hollywood and the War," Lorre claimed to leave for the United States because "Germany was too small for two monsters like Hitler and himself."⁷³ In an uncanny echo of Lowry's unacknowledged debt to *The Last Command* in that essay, Laruelle's clever interpretation is preempted by Hollywood's, a situation that comes closer to the filmmaker's consciousness as he proceeds to self-reflection and sees the movie becoming a sign of his guilt for cuckolding his friend. Laruelle will later aver that he won't watch his own Hollywood films, but he doesn't explain why (*UTV* 212). The ready reason would be that he disdains what the industry did to his art; however, given his anxious response to the poster, it is as likely that Laruelle fears the Hollywood cinema's ability to speak to him and to know him at his core.

As we have seen, for *Under the Volcano*, this ability to operate at every scale, to know how to reach every individual and to encompass the world, is no small matter. The novel is preoccupied by works of art with pretenses to those powers, only to find them lacking. When the Consul inspects the volumes in Laruelle's library in search of a collection of Elizabethan plays that his friend had neglected to return, he observes that the shelves contained "everything"; nonetheless, "in none of these books would one find one's own suffering" (*UTV* 216–217). Similarly, Laruelle's film, *Le Destin de Yvonne Griffaton*, which so impresses Yvonne Firmin as "the best film [she had] ever seen in [her] life" (*UTV* 276), and which moves from Spain and Italy and across the sea to Algiers, Cyprus, and Egypt, is deflated in advance by the Consul, who describes another of the director's movies as "shot in a bathtub" and edited together with "sequences of ruins cut out of old travelogues, and a jungle hoiked out of *In dunkelste Afrika*, and a swan out of the end of some old Corinne Griffith—Sarah Bernhardt" (*UTV* 212). Where the great books fail—*Under the Volcano* leaves behind Mallarmé's dictum "everything in the world exists to end up in a book"—a failed Hollywood movie succeeds. The best film the former actress Yvonne had ever seen, featuring an eponymous character with whom she identifies, achieves through painstaking bricolage what *Mad Love*, a terrible Hollywood movie, accomplishes as a matter of course; that terrible movie moreover features a character of the same name of whom Yvonne is unaware, suggesting that she too is deeply known in advance by the system she disdains. Orlac's bloody hands are capacious enough to hold insight into global catastrophe and individual betrayal at once, and each recurrence of the poster acknowledges those disasters: the defeat of the Republican army in Spain (*UTV* 27); Hugh's tryst with Yvonne (*UTV* 63); the first appearance of the horse that will kill Yvonne at the novel's end (*UTV* 114); the Consul's doomed "great battle … [a]gainst death" (*UTV* 227); and, finally, the moment when the Consul, Hugh, and Yvonne observe a drunken thief ("pelado") handling bloody money pilfered from the body of a murdered Indian, an image, as Lowry explained to Cape, that "symbolize[d] the guilt of mankind" (*UTV* 244).[74]

By this light, Laruelle's self-comforting ruminations on the Mexican countryside on the anniversary of the Consul's death assume an unintended aspect.

> How continually, how startlingly, the landscape changed! Now the fields were full of stones: there was a row of dead trees. An abandoned plough, silhouetted against the sky, raised its arms to heaven in mute supplication; another planet, he reflected again, a strange planet where, if you looked a little further, beyond the Tres Marías, you would find every sort of landscape at once, the Cotswolds, Windermere, New Hampshire, the meadows of the Eure-et-Loire, even the grey dunes of Cheshire, even the Sahara, a planet upon which, in the twinkling of an eye, you could change climates, and, if you cared to think so, in the crossing of a highway, three civilisations; but beautiful, there was no denying its beauty, fatal or cleansing as it happened to be, the beauty of the Earthly Paradise itself. (*UTV* 10)

This "Earthly Paradise," containing in miniature not only the scenery of various European, North American, and African locales but also the sites of societies throughout history, might seem entirely encompassed by Mexico. Yet Laruelle's vision is mediated by one of Hollywood that goes unacknowledged by the director; his description, as represented in free indirect discourse, bears a strong resemblance to Tod Hackett's "Sargasso of the imagination" in *The Day of the Locust*, among so many other depictions of studio spaces before and since.[75] But the most proximate and salient similarity is with Lowry's own writing, specifically in "Hollywood and the War," in which he presents the dream factory confronting reality: "Scene of the Exodus and the Retreat from Mons alike ... Hollywood the Unreal, where Marie Antoinette can see Juliet's tomb from the tumbril, and Waterloo and the Battle of Somme are fought contiguously, had been jolted out of its timeless existence by the actuality of war."[76] Disdainful of Hollywood though he may be, Laruelle's mindset has nonetheless been shaped decisively by the logic of the industry. His vision of Earthly Paradise becomes indistinguishable from his Hell; Eden, the original site of life, a foundational mythical location from which meaning originates, is identical to a studio backlot, the site of contemporary mythmaking. If, as Lowry told publisher Cape, "the allegory [of *Under the Volcano*] is that of the Garden of Eden, the Garden representing the world," that allegory is overwhelmed, at least from Laruelle's brilliant but benighted perspective, by the shaping power of Hollywood.[77] And if, as Lowry claimed, the rest of the novel can be read as a "sort of fantastic movie through M. Laruelle's mind," that fantasy—that is to say, *Under the Volcano* as a whole—is implicitly but profoundly shaped by Hollywood too.[78] It isn't difficult, therefore, to understand why Lowry considered *Under the Volcano* his *Inferno* in *The Voyage that Never Ends*, the massive career-long project he didn't complete. For a writer who conflated art and life as thoroughly as Lowry did, the meaninglessness of a work—a meaninglessness that the Consul fears and that Lowry acknowledges in citing the many ways the novel can be read—is the meaninglessness of a life. And that, it's safe to say, is a true torment.

***

In August 1949, Frank Taylor, a producer at MGM who had formerly been an editor of *Under the Volcano* at Reynal & Hitchcock, sent Malcolm and Margerie Lowry a treatment of Fitzgerald's *Tender Is the Night* written by screenwriter Ben Maddow. The Lowrys became obsessed with the idea of the project and undertook their own script unsolicited by the producer. Given Malcolm's interest in globe-encompassing, world-shaping Hollywood, it's easy to see the novel's appeal as well as the appeal of adapting it for MGM, the studio that produced *Mad Love*. While doomed protagonist Dick Diver, a psychiatrist, worked at the kind of hospital that served as a paradigm case of the "total institution" for the sociologist Erving Goffman, the truly enveloping and conditioning institution, in Fitzgerald's own life, was Hollywood. When Fitzgerald wrote that the glittering, grosser power of the movies would render the novel obsolete, he could well have had in mind the studio that fired him in 1939 and continued to fascinate him until his death two years later, as none glittered more grandly and none profited (if not always grossed) more than MGM. The Lowrys' writing task was thus multiply motivated: they hoped to honor Fitzgerald's underappreciated novel ("a work of a genius of importance") by improving it (a "near failure … not fully realized as a book") as a movie, and, at the same time, they sought to contribute to the uplift of Hollywood's art and thereby defend the industry from the persistent attacks of the literati. To accomplish these goals in the same stroke, the Lowrys employed a tried-and-true formula, purposefully incorporating into the script the interpretive pluralism that Malcolm had employed in *Under the Volcano*: "the film," they promised Taylor, "gains in complexity of interpretation, while being perfectly simple on the surface."[79]

At any earlier moment in the history of the studio system, the success of such a gargantuan effort would have been more farfetched than anything the Consul's drink-addled mind could ever have conjured. A four-hundred-some-page screenplay would without doubt have ended up buried in an MGM file, if not stacked in a "two-ton truck" full of "a million dollars worth of literature" heading to "the incinerator," as former MGM writer Aldous Huxley put it in *Ape and Essence* (1948), an unremittingly bitter novel in the form of a rejected original script.[80] But Lowry had reason to hope because the system was engaged in its own dystopian projections. As Malcolm and Margerie began their adaptation, the industry was all but eulogizing itself, wondering aloud about how it might survive in the wake of the *Paramount* antitrust decision, the House Committee on Un-American Activities investigations, the rise of television, and the decline in box office receipts.

In the "sort of preface" they wrote as a cover letter to Taylor, the Lowrys cite as motivation *Life* magazine's "A Round Table on the Movies," which featured a who's who of American film discussing such issues as artistic quality, the Production Code, and the changing American audience. Of all these luminaries, the Lowrys were most compelled by Joseph L. Mankiewicz, Twentieth Century-Fox's star writer, director, and producer, who with righteous indignation sneered, "if the motion picture audience of America and friends of the film want to help us, they could start the battle in their own bailiwicks." "Being writers ourselves," the Lowrys concluded, "perhaps the best thing we could do was try to write a good film ourselves."[81] Malcolm and Margerie answered Mankiewicz's call because they admired him and his work, rightly observing, in language that would anticipate the later auteur theory, that his "stamp is on everything he does." They erred only in supposing that the filmmaker was "a very large exception in himself."[82]

In the late 1940s, the self-consciously erudite Mankiewicz was in fact at the center of the most profound transformation in the film industry's understanding of and relationship to literature and the idea of literariness since the birth of moving-picture rights. Starting in the immediate postwar period and coincident with the breakup of the studios, writers of both fiction and screenplays began to insist newly on the ownership of the literature they produced. The Screen Writers Guild established the Committee on the Sale of Original Material to negotiate rights to original stories along the lines of works of literature. Where the writer since 1912 maintained the separable subsidiary rights of their copyrighted novel or play, the screenplay had, during the studio era, been owned in its entirety by the hiring studio. James M. Cain, the author of such adapted properties as *Double Indemnity* and *The Postman Always Rings Twice*, had hoped to push this issue of rights ownership even further with the American Authors' Authority (AAA), a copyright clearinghouse that would shift power from corporations to writers and allow the latter to insist on the temporary licensing of copyright instead of outright sale. To Cain, writers of fiction operating under a genteel conception of authorship were a rabble without a clause. The AAA was ultimately scuttled by a jurisdictional conflict between The Authors' League and the Writers Guild because of the former's commitment to a nineteenth-century conception of the gentleman author; as Cain would tell H.L. Mencken in 1947, the Authors' League's "fallacy [lay] in their effort to organize writers rather than properties."[83]

At the same time that writers began to conceive of themselves as corporate bundles of properties, the industry began to investigate the "little" picture geared to a sophisticated adult audience. Noticing the trend of formally self-conscious, stylized pictures, Manny Farber claimed "Movies Aren't Movies Anymore"; Margaret Farrand Thorp suggested that the movies were more like novels than ever before. That is, as authors came to behave like corporations, coinciding with the trend of stars, directors, and producers incorporating themselves as production companies, Hollywood pictures tended toward literariness in form and content. The convergence of a conflict over rights to original stories, the push for First Amendment protection of moving pictures, the autochthonous development of an idea of film authorship, and a trend toward increasing sophistication in Hollywood movies: this comprised the legal-institutional-conceptual basis of what midcentury critics like Dwight Macdonald disparaged as midcult but which recent scholars have preferred to understand as the democratization or mainstreaming of modernism.[84] These transformations—the proliferation of modernism and the feared dissolution of the studio system—will occupy this study through to its conclusion.

CHAPTER 5

The Scenes of an Ending
Adaptation, Originality, and the New Authorship of Hollywood Pictures

> Until their 1948 business and political jitters, the big movie companies ... were most aggressive in seeking publisher-promotion of movie-selected manuscripts. When they have regained their liberty to spend and to speak, they may be expected to press for this again.
> —William Miller, *The Book Industry*, 1949[1]

This study began by observing a pair of phenomena that coincided with and were promoted by the extension of copyright protection to moving pictures in 1912. On one hand, the rise of the feature film and decline of the Motion Picture Patents Company engendered competition among film companies for exclusive source materials, a phenomenon that, I argued, contributed to the emergence of the modern idea of the "studio." On the other hand, the invention of motion picture rights altered the economic incentives and formal possibilities of fiction writing. Despite the many real and imagined crises that the American film industry faced from that moment on, the system's reliance on presold materials to "feed the maw of exhibition" remained relatively constant, as did writers' ability to anticipate the sale of their subsidiary rights.[2] Ever since, in exchange for substantial monetary compensation, the fiction writer has sacrificed their right to control the adaptation of their narrative, a circumstance understood to be risible or tragic depending on the artist's particular view of the situation.

The studios' shared attitude toward the adaptation of source material can be usefully understood as an index of the system's stability. Whatever each company's particular preferences, the studio system, since the creation of the Hays Office, by and large succeeded in keeping the screen clear of material directly critical of itself. Following from the same motivation that gave rise to the Production Code, the studios consistently sanitized the screen of unfavorable depictions of Hollywood and its community; indeed, as Justin Gautreau notes, in the wake of controversy surrounding

Hollywood Boulevard (1936), Fred Beetson, secretary of the Production Code Administration, reminded Joseph Breen of the need to steer clear of "immoral activity 'in and around Hollywood.'"³ This unwritten rule comes into clearest focus when studios considered for adaptation source materials written by industry scribes with an axe to grind. Some books, like Carroll and Garrett Graham's *Queer People* (1930) and Jane Allen's *I Lost My Girlish Laughter* (1938), were suppressed by a concerted effort among the studios. In the case of the Grahams' novel, Howard Hughes intended to adapt the sensationalist, antisemitic novel as one of his first forays into production, only to find that no studio would lend him the talent he needed to staff the picture. *I Lost My Girlish Laughter*, cowritten under a pseudonym by Silvia Schulman Lardner, David O. Selznick's erstwhile secretary, pilloried the producer's behavior during the long production of *Gone with the Wind*, leading Selznick's father-in-law Louis B. Mayer to buy the property and thus prevent it from further insulting his family.⁴

A perhaps more common strategy, one pursued when attractive source materials contained isolated moments of animosity toward the industry, was to scrub the negative commentary and redirect the animating energy into the movie's subtext. Edna Ferber and George S. Kaufman's *Stage Door* (1936), a play about Depression-era Broadway hopefuls struggling against dissolution, furnishes a famous instance of this approach. *Stage Door* becomes a caustic commentary on the imbrication of pseudo-politics and debased artistry in Hollywood film when the talentless but beautiful actress Jean Maitland returns from the movie capital to her former boarding house to promote a Popular Front play financed by "Papa" Adolph Gretzl, a clear travesty of Papa Adolph Zukor. In a sendup of the crassness and poor taste of fan magazines, a photographer for *Screenland* magazine attempts to depict Jean's struggling former friends in Dorothea Lange-style portraits in order to promote Jean's "Humble Beginnings in the Footlight Club."⁵ When Katharine Hepburn played the lead role of Terry Randall in Gregory La Cava's loose adaptation the following year—so loose that Kaufman quipped it should have been called "Screen Door"—the character, like the movie more generally, bore no trace of disdain for the industry.⁶ Indeed, the conclusion to RKO's *Stage Door* (1937) plots the same course as its contemporary *A Star is Born*, with the suicide of the sensitive understudy Kaye Hamilton (Andrea Leeds) inaugurating the ascent of Randall, the new, true star. All movie business mockery falls by the wayside, paving the way for Hepburn to momentarily revitalize her career and for the film to garner four Academy Award nominations.

RKO's sanitation project resulted in perhaps the clearest case of intra-Academy recognition, but it was far from the only or even the greatest of such successes; that distinction belongs to *All About Eve* (Joseph L. Mankiewicz, Fox, 1950), the principal subject of this chapter's final section.

Between *Stage Door* and *All About Eve* came the industry's war boom, a moment when, even as they reduced production amidst ration restrictions, the studios continued to splurge on literary properties, "believ[ing] they had money and prestige to gain from books 'famoused up' in advance by trade sellers."[7] During that time, the majors took greater risks in their depiction of sex and violence, but attacking the industry onscreen remained a firm taboo. Ironically, the crime melodramas and psychological thrillers that would soon be called films noirs, often adapted from lurid fictions by disaffected, usually left-leaning screenwriters, whitewashed the source materials' intraindustry criticism. Take Vera Caspary's *Laura* (1943), a murder mystery comprising a wide array of voices and narrative modes: Waldo Lydecker's dandyish, pedantic essay; Mark McPherson's police report; Laura Hunt's disillusioned romance. Common to all, however, is a distaste for and distrust of Hollywood and its products. In his 1944 adaptation for Fox, Otto Preminger kept all of the novel's implications of sexual perversity, including Lydecker's clearly marked latent homosexuality and Shelby Carpenter's gigolo lifestyle. He even added McPherson's quasi-necrophilic fantasy about the supposedly deceased Laura. But the film tellingly omitted the novel's backstory of the woman who died in Laura's stead: "There were stacks of movie magazines in the room. Pages had been turned down and paragraphs marked. You could tell Diane had dreamed of Hollywood. Less beautiful girls had become stars, married stars, and owned swimming pools."[8] Likewise, *Murder, My Sweet* (RKO, 1944), Edward Dmytryk's adaptation of Raymond Chandler's *Farewell, My Lovely* (1940), retains minor villain Lindsay Marriott's queerness but changes his artistic occupation from failed screen actor—"He would photograph like Isadora Duncan," Chandler's Marlowe muses—to failed sculptor.[9] James M. Cain's *The Postman Always Rings Twice* (1933), the "red meat" tale considered unadaptable since MGM purchased its rights in 1934, finally found its way to the screen in bowdlerized form in 1946.[10] In Cain's original, femme fatale Cora Papadakis (née Smith) finds herself in an existential wasteland twenty miles outside of Los Angeles after winning a screen test at an Iowa beauty contest. The test "was all right in the face," she tells Frank Chambers, her partner in crime. But "when I began to talk, up there on the screen, they knew me for what I was, and so did I. A cheap Des Moines trollop, that has as much chance in pictures as a monkey has.

Not as much. A monkey, anyway, can make you laugh. All I did was make you sick."[11] Hollywood's economically and sexually exploitative practices are the efficient causes of Cora's misery, but that cause is shunted into the subtext of the adaptation. In place of bitter musings on screen tests and monkeys, all Lana Turner's Cora says is "You don't know the half of it."

Given the studios' history of scrubbing away the pervasive anti-industry sentiment in perverse source texts, the jaundiced view of Hollywood in Nicholas Ray's adaptation of *In a Lonely Place* (Santana-Columbia, 1950) seems remarkable. Although set in Los Angeles, Dorothy Hughes's 1947 novel of the same name pushes the movie business to the margins of its plot. There, antihero Dixon "Dix" Steele pretends to be a novelist ("I write books, Lady. When I try to break into screen work, it will be because I need the money.") as he pursues a career of sexual assault and murder, while the object of his desire, Laurel Gray, has played some bit parts in pictures.[12] By contrast, Ray's bleak vision of paranoia in the HUAC-era film colony, which has long been understood as a hallmark of the studio system in crisis, registers the increasingly unmanageable conflict between personal vision and philistinism in Hollywood at midcentury. In the movie, genius screenwriter Dix's (Humphrey Bogart) reluctant agreement to adapt the hokey bestseller *Althea Bruce* initiates a chain of events that results in the demise of his personal life and perhaps professional life as well.[13] His fateful decision to invite hat-check girl Mildred Atkinson (Martha Stewart) to his apartment to explain the novel's plot to him late one evening establishes him as a plausible suspect in her murder. The pall this casts over Dix, combined with his own overdetermined tendency toward emotional coolness and violence, scuttles his engagement to Laurel (Gloria Grahame), who attempts to run away to New York and is nearly strangled by the enraged writer. Arch and brutal Dix presents a ready double for director Ray, soon to become a darling of the *Cahiers du Cinéma* writers who found in him a model auteur, capable of expressing a personal vision within the confines of a restrictive industry. For Ray, as for Dix, the masscult schlock that *Althea Bruce* epitomizes poses something like an existential threat that must be resisted or at least remade according to the artist's sensibility.

Counterintuitively but just as accurately, Dix's attitude toward the novel corresponds to that of decision-makers at the major studios who, in 1948, had come to find high-priced novels increasingly deadly to their operation. But *In a Lonely Place* was made by a different kind of executive: Bogart himself, who, instead of rejecting an expensive presold property, paid $40,000 for the rights to Hughes's novel after forming Santana

Productions that year, and who manipulated the source text to assail the very system that made him a star.[14] For Bogart, starting his own production company presented both financial and artistic benefits: a reduced effective tax rate on the one hand and greater artistic freedom on the other. *In a Lonely Place*'s iconoclastic sensibility followed from its iconoclastic production by a small independent. Santana mocked the industry's old way of treating books, and by extension the studio system's customs more generally, by having its own way with Hughes's; *Althea Bruce* ruins Dix's artistic life, while *In a Lonely Place* provided the opportunity for Bogart to live and make movies as he wanted, in this case a film whose tragedy is initiated precisely by expensive source material. Not for nothing did the filmmakers name Mildred Atkinson's murderer Henry Kesler, the woman's wealthy beau who still lives with his parents and takes the coward's way out by killing himself. Only a movie produced without regard for the system's norms of taste and decorum could give its villain-McGuffin the name of its associate producer and so brazenly attack the executives that the classical style assiduously hid from view.[15] Santana's adaptation strategy—star becomes producer; director becomes auteur; novel becomes industry-damning independent film—effectively counters the studio system's standard operating procedure of the previous two decades.

In a Lonely Place emblematizes the most profound transformation in Hollywood's relation to "literature" since 1912. Just as the studio system's origins can be usefully mapped vis-à-vis literature—conceived broadly as an act of writing, an artform, and as commodifiable intellectual property—so can its self-conceived dissolution. In the wake of the *Paramount* antitrust decree, amidst the looming threat of the HUAC investigations and a cooling postwar economy, and at the start of television's ascendance as the principal form of entertainment in the United States, best sellers like *Althea Bruce* were considered dangerous investments, and both high-caliber literary agents and the trade publication of record saw that danger as a sign of the end of an era.

In 1939, the year they touted as a zenith, the studios relied heavily on source material, with more than a third of all total movies (186 out of 527) deriving from novels and short stories.[16] Such a ratio at that level of output ensured that fiction writers with "one eye cocked on the movie lots," as Fitzgerald was disparagingly described, could anticipate a lucrative sale of movie rights. But a decade later, with feature film releases significantly below their 1930s level—361 features were released by domestic producers in 1949—Donald Friede, the literary agent and cofounder of the publishing company Covici-Friede, mourned the passing of a good, stable thing:

those days—when any best-seller was an almost certain picture sale and when any book stood an excellent chance of becoming a best-seller, when anybody who had written a book was automatically considered a potential screen-writer, when any picture, no matter how trite and dull, was a certain money-maker and a quarter of a million dollars was not considered too high a price to pay a star to act it—those days will probably never come back.[17]

Variety concurred, though more belligerently than the wistful Friede. "Brushoff 'Brainy' Bestsellers," reads a page-five headline on August 17, 1949. "There was a day, up to a half-dozen years ago, when few books that even got close to the bestseller category didn't get snapped up for pictures." From *Variety*'s perspective, writers bore some responsibility for the changing state of affairs. "Used to be that plenty of authors could be counted on to sit down and write action and adventure and romance.... Now the writer of fiction who wants to be called sophisticated, smart and modern—rather than corny—sets down more of how people think than what they do."[18] The "now" here betrays nothing so much as the trade paper's myopia and amnesia; as we saw in Chapter 1, the distinction between represented action and represented cogitation constituted the basis of fiction-writing strategies for transmedia-minded writers beginning in the 1910s. What *had* changed was the willingness of filmmakers to join the chorus of sophisticated writers who attacked the industry in public, a shift that suggests the weakening of the system's ability to maintain its norms. "Within the trade," the producer John Houseman observed in 1950, "sentiments are now openly expressed which, three years ago, would have been regarded as rank heresy."[19] The system's faltering capacity for self-regulation correlated with deformations of the classical aesthetic, the form characterized by protagonist-driven narratives optimized for maximal enjoyment by an undifferentiated mass audience. This resulted not only in the "mannerist flicker" that Manny Farber diagnosed in 1952 but also, as importantly, in the movies' inability to maintain a comfortable distance between story and backstory, as previously verboten criticism of Hollywood made its way into pictures.[20]

In the flush years pre-*Paramount*, the studios saw their bibliophilia projected most perfectly onscreen in John Stahl's lavish Technicolor melodrama *Leave Her to Heaven*, adapted from a Ben Ames Williams novel for which Darryl Zanuck paid $100,000 in 1944.[21] *Leave Her to Heaven* follows Richard Harlan (Cornel Wilde), a tall, handsome, unfailingly charming and preternaturally loyal writer of popular novels, through the vicissitudes of his fraught marriage to obsessive psychopath Ellen Berent (Gene Tierney). Ironically, Richard has no idea that he has been living in a fiction contrived by Ellen, who cares nothing for his literary career and who seeks exclusive possession of her husband. Unbeknownst to Richard, Ellen allowed his brother to drown while swimming in the lake behind their New England cabin (a clear nod to the climax of Dreiser's *An American Tragedy*) and later threw herself down a flight of stairs to abort their unborn son. Only after Ellen betrays herself as an enemy of literature as well as of those who claim Richard's attention—after observing that Richard had dedicated his new novel to her younger sister Ruth (Jeanne Crain), who helped him revise it, she commits suicide and frames Ruth for murder—does Richard come to recognize his love for literate Ruth. On trial, Richard describes Ellen's acts and exonerates Ruth, but in the process, he reveals himself to have been an accessory to his wife's past crimes and is sentenced to two years in prison. The movie, like the novel, nonetheless ends joyfully. Flashing back to the present after those two years away, Richard and Ruth, writer and editor, row slowly away on the same placid lake, an implausibly happy ending made even happier by the movie's $5.5 million in domestic rentals. *Leave Her to Heaven* was the most successful of Fox's touted crop of bestseller adaptations of 1945 and the second-most lucrative movie of the year behind *The Bells of St. Mary's* (Leo McCarey, RKO).[22]

By contrast, on the off chance that writers of action, adventure, and romance saw themselves on screen five years later, they found unflattering portrayals like that of the homicidal Stephen Byrne in *House by the River*, directed by Fritz Lang for the newly formed independent Fidelity Pictures (1950). A modestly budgeted, highly stylized film about a psychologically unstable writer, *House by the River* strikingly resembles *In a Lonely Place*, while its thoroughgoing negation of *Leave Her to Heaven* speaks to the speed with which the industry turned against source literature. Like Santana's production, Fidelity's was adapted from a twentieth-century fiction, A.P. Herbert's 1921 novel *The House by the River*. Lang did more than merely drop the definite article from the title of his adaptation; like Ray, he departed from his source in a manner that can be seen as a swipe at the contemporary adaptation economy. Where Herbert's villain Stephen is a successful poet, "the treasure of England," Lang's is a struggling fiction writer who becomes a bestselling author after the news of his maid's murder is reported but before he is acknowledged as her killer.[23] In 1945, audiences had every reason to believe that Richard Harlan and Ruth Berent would row the unrippled surface of Deer Lake in perpetuity, an easy metaphor for a life with beloved children and successful books; the roiling river of Lang's film, on the other hand, functions like the

Figure 5.1 "Mr. James Joyce ... Now where would you put him?"
"Would you mind repeating that question?"
The Third Man (Carol Reed, London Films, 1949)

unconscious from which repressed and undesirable entities—dead bodies and failed narratives—return. "My manuscripts are like the tide out there," Stephen tells a servant at the movie's start, well before he attempts to kiss his maid, accidentally strangles her, and dumps her body in the current. "They always come back."

A decade earlier, *Variety* might have expected that its assessment "it is mighty hard to transpose a 'stream of consciousness' to the screen" would remain only in print or in intra-industry gossip, but in 1950, the trade paper heard an echo of itself in Carol Reed's *The Third Man* (London Films, 1949), released by Selznick in February of that year. There, Holly Martins (Joseph Cotten), a writer of popular stories, is mistaken for a writer of literary fiction of the same name and is invited to speak to a group interested in modern American fiction. Faced with the question "Do you believe, Mr. Martins, in the stream of consciousness?" he barely attempts a response. A writer like Martins—of Zane Grey-like Westerns, the kind of book that had passed so easily to the screen over the previous thirty years—would, in the late 1940s, be as confused and disappointed by the prospects of selling his motion picture rights as he would be by *The Third Man*'s Dutch angles, low-key lighting, and on-location shooting (Figure 5.1).[24]

The pivot away from presold properties was accompanied by two complementary movements toward more reliable sources of narrative, a shift that would raise concern among the Screen Writers Guild and set the terms for the studio system's new austerity campaign. Smaller studios (Columbia, Goldwyn, Universal) closed their story departments completely while larger ones reduced them substantially, outsourcing that work to agents. Instead of scouring the best-seller list for the Next Big Thing, the studios looked inward, combing their vaults for reissues and, in the process, behaving like book publishers who had long understood the value of their back catalogues.[25] The turn to the library also took the form of resuscitating properties that had been bought and shelved as well as old movies that could be successfully updated and remade. If, in the early years of the studio system, producers looked for the "picture germ" in fictional works, now, according to *Variety*'s medics in April 1948, they were "afflicted by the remake germ, an economical ailment painful to writers. About one-fifth of the total number of films currently in work are warmed-over oldies, for which the original authors get nothing."[26] Columbia, which eliminated its story department in 1947, projected this development onscreen in the form of *The Dark Past* (Rudolph Maté, 1948), a pop-Freudian crime film in which a psychology professor (Lee J. Cobb) analyzes a criminal (William Holden) who has broken into the professor's home and has held hostage his wife, son, and three friends that comprise a love triangle: a financier, his wife, and her novelist lover. A remake of Charles Vidor's *Blind Alley* (1939), *The Dark Past* exemplifies the studio's turn to its library; Columbia's turn away from new literature comprises the movie's B-plot. There, the novelist Owen Talbot (Stephen Dunne) reveals himself to be a feckless playboy whom the financier's wife forsakes for her man of action. Indeed, everyone, criminals and captors both, deem "Romeo" unworthy of their attention. While Hollywood would never truly abandon popular fiction and would, in fact, redouble its pursuit of presold properties in its turn to the "big picture" in the mid-1950s, this late 1940s discovery of the many values of a replete library of intellectual property would profoundly alter the industry's modus operandi, beginning with the studios' licensing of pre-1948 films for broadcast on television. The multimedia, multichannel narrative events of our present day—the universes and multiverses, the reboots, the resuscitated franchises—are direct descendants of this mid-century development.[27]

    At the same time, the studios began to prioritize original stories conceived first for the screen because, unlike novels and plays, originals were owned entirely by the studios and were therefore exploitable in any subsidiary form in perpetuity. The Writers Guild attempted to rectify this issue beginning in 1945 with the formation of the Committee on the Sale of Original Material, but it wouldn't alter the norm until 1951, when the studios consented to a new Minimum Basic Agreement (MBA). Under that new MBA, writers hired to work on their original stories were able to negotiate separate consideration for book-publication, dramatic, and radio rights; they also "won equality with producer and director on screen and advertising credits."[28] Two years later, the Writers Guild finally managed to negotiate "the first provision that a writer is eligible for separated rights when the writer writes an original story or teleplay, even if the work is a work for hire."[29] The late-1940s shocks to the system thus encouraged the studios to prioritize originality and, at the same time, ennobled the writer, now an owner of a property as opposed to a mere wage laborer.

The Guild's push for ownership of subsidiary rights to original material engendered theoretical speculation about film authorship fifteen years in advance of Andrew Sarris's 1962 importation of *Cahiers du Cinéma*'s auteur theory. In May 1947, Joseph L. Mankiewicz published a review essay-cum-polemic in *The Screen Writer*, the Guild's monthly magazine, under the strident title "Film Author! Film Author!" Elaborating Jean Benoît-Lévy's "casual" coinage *film auteur* in *The Art of the Motion Picture* (1946), the self-consciously literary Mankiewicz insisted on the necessary relation between screenwriting and directing and the ideal consolidation of both roles in a single figure: "Writing and directing moving pictures ... are—and should be—the two components of an hyphenated identity."[30] However, where the *Cahiers* critics and Sarris would celebrate individual expression against a restrictive milieu in the tradition of the Romantic genius, Mankiewicz had an altogether more practical purpose in mind.[31] "It must be admitted," he admonished his colleagues, "that there are in Hollywood right now many producers of courage, taste and perception—many more, again, than it is comfortable to admit. *They will buy good original screen material, they are desperate for good original screen material.*"[32] In line with practitioner-theorists dating back to the early 1910s, Mankiewicz concerned himself less with personal vision than with the mastery of craft. More competent writing would, he argued, result in more attractive original properties and more authority yielded to the filmmaker. In the following issue of *The Screen Writer,* several veteran writers good-naturedly took Mankiewicz to task for either too much idealism (Philip Dunne: "It is only natural that these gentlemen prefer to risk the stockholders' cash ... on established novels, serials and plays") or not enough (Allen Rivkin: "I'm afraid ... that John and Joe didn't go far enough in with their argument. A 'film author' can learn his craft as solidly as a surgeon allegedly learns his, but when a surgeon does his final sewing-up, it is not likely that the head of the hospital will reserve the right to do more cutting").[33] More important than any individual response, though, was the fact that a notion of a filmmaker's authorship was emerging out of the Guild's emphasis on original materials, and, with that, a notion of the Hollywood film as a kind of literature would follow.

Of the several writer-directors that Mankiewicz commended—Robert Rossen, John Huston, Dore Schary, Preston Sturges, and Norman Krasna, among others—the successful writing team of Charles Brackett and Billy Wilder formulated the most explicit and extraordinary claims for originality and film authorship in *Sunset Boulevard* (Paramount, 1950), the original story that would end their partnership. Like *In a Lonely Place*, *Sunset Boulevard* asserts its makers' authorship and authorial independence by way of a twin attack on studio system attitudes toward adaptation and on the norms of the classical style. Though Norma Desmond, the delusional star of yesteryear, attempts to assemble a version of a pre-*Paramount* studio in her decaying Dickensian mansion, her atavism is complicated by the fact that she not only attempts to play the teenage Salomé but also to write the titular princess's story for the screen. Norma's tragedy derives from her Gatsby-like yearning for an irrecoverable halcyon past, but also, more acutely, from the fact that that past hardly existed at all (in that regard, she is less like Gatsby than Ralph Carston, the fatally bewitched extra, at the end of Horace McCoy's *I Should Have Stayed Home*). Female stars only rarely transcended the division of labor and exerted the force of their personalities on both sides of the camera. An important exception was Alla Nazimova, who after splitting from Metro in 1921, founded her own production company and went on to produce, star in, write (under pseudonym Peter M. Winters), and direct (under the name of her husband Charles Bryant) her adaptation of Oscar Wilde's *Salomé* (1922). *Salomé* bombed and ruined Nazimova, forcing her to transform her legendary mansion into a hotel, the Garden of Allah, that she would eventually sell and, at the end of her life, inhabit as a tenant. Even before she loses her grip on "the dream [that] enveloped her," as Joe puts it at the film's conclusion, Norma's decision to follow in Nazimova's footsteps and undertake this vexed adaptation of a play that was itself barred from the English stage for four decades—and in a similarly overlarge pleasure palace, no less—foretells her mental and material dispossession no less surely than her gigolo's postmortem narration indicates his own doom.[34]

Norma is neither here nor there, neither the "lovely little girl of seventeen" that Cecil B. DeMille calls her, nor the self-consciously mature and canny contemporary hyphenate that Ida Lupino became. In fact, *Sunset Boulevard* presents Norma as a kind of anti-Lupino. Where the

1940s star achieved independence by writing original scripts on contemporary social issues for her own company, The Filmakers, Norma is uncannily in step, despite her almost total separation from the world, with the studio system's burgeoning interest in source materials out of copyright and in narratives of the distant past. The actress astutely identifies DeMille as the ideal person to direct her picture. Not only had he directed her to stardom in the 1920s, but he had also returned to the biblical tales that had brought him his greatest fame in the form of that other Judeo-Christian narrative of treacherous female decapitation, *Samson and Delilah* (the production of which is recreated in *Sunset Boulevard*). *Samson and Delilah* would go on to be the highest grossing film of 1950 and would christen a decade and a half of blockbuster epics of antiquity, rearguard attempts by the Hollywood establishment to project a studio system at full strength.[35] It is as though Norma, despite distinguishing herself from "all this new Hollywood trash," has unconsciously registered its ways in an attempt to turn back time, making the pathos of her impossible struggle yet more acute.

Desmond's and DeMille's biblical adaptations are two sides of the same conservative coin, neither of which, from the position of Wilder and Brackett's original, is amenable to the work of a forward-looking Hollywood. *Sunset Boulevard*'s more profound tragedy, therefore, is Joe's inability to complete "Untitled Love Story," an original screenplay based on his unproduced story "Dark Windows," which he had been writing with Betty Schaefer (Nancy Olson). The professional and romantic relationships Joe develops with Betty are in every way opposite to the unsatisfying and unsavory ones he has with Norma; these contrasts parallel the differing attitudes Brackett and Wilder would have had toward "Untitled Love Story" and "Salomé." Fittingly, the most prominent phrase legible on the script's first page is a dreary invocation of "dusty confiscated property," an apt description of just the kind of retread Joe and Betty and, extratextually, Brackett and Wilder sought to avoid (Figure 5.2). In his only gallant act, Joe sends Nancy away to marry assistant director Artie Green (Jack Webb); it will be up to them to complete the love story and give a name to their effort. Indeed, between the backward-looking Norma and DeMille and the future-oriented Betty and Artie are Joe and his antithesis, the writer-director Wilder. Joe's inability to place an original story at Paramount results in his tenure as a kept man paid in kind for services as a script doctor on an unsold screenplay, a worse deal than even the most exploitative studio contract. The metaphorical deaths Dix Steele experiences during the denouement of *In a Lonely Place* are, for Joe, brought to a

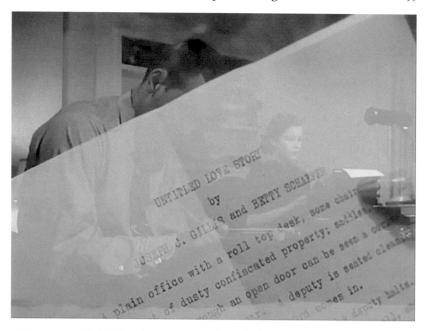

Figure 5.2 *Untitled Love Story*, an original tragedy by Joe Gillis and Betty Schaefer. *Sunset Boulevard* (Billy Wilder, Paramount, 1950)

ludicrous extreme as they are literalized from the start of *Sunset Boulevard*: "You see, the body of a young man was found floating in the pool of her mansion, with two shots in his back and one in his stomach. Nobody important, really. Just a movie writer with a couple of 'B' pictures to his credit. The poor dope. He always wanted a pool."[36] Joe's sorry state serves as Wilder's opportunity to announce his own success in pursuing originality at the studio system's expense, which he does in the form of Joe's voiceover from beyond the grave, the outrageous exaggeration of the 1940s vogue for flashback frame narratives. Wilder could pull off this impish thumb in the eye of classical conventions in large part by keeping the production "top secret," something more easily accomplished at Paramount, known for its hands-off approach, than at any other studio.[37]

That the writer-director conceived *Sunset Boulevard* as an apocalyptic tragicomedy of the studio system and a baroque salvo at classical norms is confirmed explicitly just before Norma descends her staircase and calls for Mr. DeMille's close-up in the film's devastating final shot. In order for that shot to achieve its full gravity—in order for it to achieve a sense of Norma Desmond's absolute descent into a world of pure fantasy, the

Figure 5.3   Paramount picturing its own demise. *Sunset Boulevard* (Billy Wilder, Paramount, 1950)

movies come to life—the heretofore extra-diegetic camera conflates with one of the newsreel cameras that have been waiting to report on the sad, sordid affair. Where do those cameras come from? The film tells us in a brief exterior shot, when the crew truck rolls up to Norma's mansion. That truck briefly but clearly reads "PARAMOUNT PICTURES INC": the name of the vertically integrated corporation that, when the movie was released, no longer existed (Figure 5.3). On January 1, 1950, Paramount Pictures, Inc. was split into the production-distribution company Paramount Pictures Corporation and United Paramount Theatres, as mandated by the Justice Department's consent decree. Under Wilder's direction, the cameras of Paramount Pictures, Inc., a company on the verge of corporate dissolution, are made to capture Norma's full mental dissolution as she walks directly toward one of them. As the shot concludes in a slow dissolve, a watery overlay obscures Norma, a reminder of Joe's impossible narration at the movie's start but also a manifestation of the dual disintegrations affecting Norma and Paramount. It's no wonder that the Production Code Administration report on the film called the original story's ending unhappy, and no wonder, too, that after seeing the film,

Louis B. Mayer, for twenty years the figurehead of the system, would accost the writer-director: "You bastard! You have disgraced the industry that made and fed you! You should be tarred and feathered and run out of Hollywood!" In the verbal equivalent of his frame-breaking attack on the decorum of the classical Hollywood aesthetic, Wilder simply replied, "Fuck you."[38]

All About Everything

> When it comes to subjecting the artist to pressure, the history of art shows that art flourishes under pressure. Titian's art flourished under pressure. The pressures in our business or in radio or in television only serve to create better programs.
> —Dore Schary, vice president in charge of production, MGM, 1952[39]

> He can never be a great artist, who is grossly illiterate.
> —Sir Joshua Reynolds, *Discourses on Art*, 1778[40]

In their respective assaults on source literature and the classical style, *In a Lonely Place* and *Sunset Boulevard* emblematize what Margaret Farrand Thorp immediately understood as a newfound affinity between the Hollywood film and the novel: "It is not to the theater," she wrote in "The Motion Picture and the Novel" (1951), "but to the novel that we must turn when we wish to find analogies useful to the development of the film." Thorp saw great significance in the fact that none of the writing award winners at the Oscars that year—*Sunset Boulevard* for best original screenplay, *Panic in the Streets* (Elia Kazan, Fox, 1950) for best story, and *All About Eve* for best screenplay—had been adapted from Broadway plays but were rather "three stories created for the screen."[41] In fact, *All About Eve*, unlike the other two, had been adapted from a previously published source.[42] However, Thorp's misunderstanding felicitously indicates how *Eve* engages the problems of authorship and originality as expressed through adaptation.

A backstage production associated with *Sunset Boulevard* and *In a Lonely Place* since its release in October 1950, *Eve* presents a different and far more complex solution to these problems.[43] Although *Eve* does not overtly thematize adaptation and originality as Wilder's and Ray's films do, those concerns structure the film from without. Indeed, writer-director Joseph L. Mankiewicz seems to have conceived his work as a kind of adaptation in reverse. In late 1950, around the time *Eve* premiered, Mankiewicz agreed to release the movie's screenplay in book form, becoming the first ever such publication undertaken by Bennett Cerf at Random House. Mankiewicz and Random House both understood the novelty of their effort, a novelty based in the elevation of a previously subliterary form. Cerf told Mankiewicz, "I am glad you're excited about having the script published. I am just as pleased as you are. It remains to be seen whether a script in book form can be sold, but of one thing you may be certain: we are going to make it a fine looking book and we are going to do our darndest to put it over."[44] It would be difficult to identify a more succinct demonstration of the emergence of a transmedial midcult than *All About Eve*'s path from magazine fiction to lauded literary screenplay to published book.

Unlike *In a Lonely Place* and *Sunset Boulevard*, which openly flouted the studio system's conventions, *All About Eve* had been conceived as a blue-chip property for its blue-chip writer-director by one of the most powerful studios of the moment. Twentieth Century-Fox, the major studio most committed to its story department amidst the late-1940s contraction, purchased Mary Orr's short story "The Wisdom of Eve" in 1949 for Mankiewicz, who had just completed *A Letter to Three Wives*, the movie that would garner him his first writer-director double Oscar. At that time, Fox was positioning itself as the industry's premier studio and the one best suited to guide it through its most recent crises. It did so by way of a Janus-faced approach. On the one hand, Fox had the most atavistic corporate organization, employing the central-producer structure, helmed by Darryl Zanuck, that MGM used in the halcyon days of the Thalberg era. By 1950, Zanuck would be called a "One-Man Studio" and crowned king of Hollywood by *Time* (Figure 5.4). He ruled his demesne according to the studio system's principle of appealing to an undifferentiated mass audience—the dream of universality described in Chapter 4—modified to accommodate the postwar interest in social problems. By way of such highly regarded, commercially successful movies as *Gentleman's Agreement* (Elia Kazan, 1947), *The Snake Pit* (Anatole Litvak, 1948), and *Pinky* (Elia Kazan, 1949), Zanuck found the "subject matter that can appeal to the intellectual and yet not alienate the masses."[45]

As a study of the theatrical community at a moment of high stress, *All About Eve* can be profitably understood as a Zanuck social problem film. Leo Rosten suggested that, with "the most literate film of the year," Mankiewicz "put the seal of personal monopoly on an entire area of dramatic materials—the field of social commentary," where the society in question is one especially close to the industry's own.[46] *Eve* is ostensibly all about Margo Channing (Bette Davis), a forty-year-old prima donna

Figure 5.4   Darryl F. Zanuck on the cover of *Time* magazine, June 12, 1950. The caption reads "Does it pay to make good pictures?"
Source: Courtesy of Time/Photofest

who, in her latest role, plays a Scarlet O'Hara-like ingenue in a *Gone with the Wind*-style Southern epic. A decade younger than Norma Desmond, Margo is nonetheless aging out of the roles upon which she had made her name. Her concerns about her show business mortality and the broader existential crisis those concerns instigate intensify upon the arrival into her life of the titular Eve Harrington (Anne Baxter). Eve first appears as a callow fan but is, in reality, a savvy hopeful actress who ingratiates her way into Margo's coterie and then into the individual lives of its members: Margo's fiancé, the director Bill Sampson (Gary Merrill), the playwright Lloyd Richards (Hugh Marlowe), and Lloyd's wife Karen (Celeste Holm). Eve achieves what she sets out for, sniping Margo's role in Lloyd's play *Footsteps on the Ceiling* and winning the Sarah Siddons Award, a fictional prize on the level of a Best Actress Tony or Oscar. However, her actions fail to bring her happiness, and the film concludes with her departure for Hollywood in pursuit of more fame.

Sam Staggs suggests that *Eve* is only "technically about Broadway rather than Hollywood," but it is that technical difference that makes all the difference, what separates *Eve* from its backstudio siblings.[47] *In a Lonely Place* and *Sunset Boulevard* are, as backstudio pictures, both excessive and obvious (though not excessively obvious, the slogan Bordwell, Staiger, and Thompson coined to describe the classical style).[48] There is no need, really, to *interpret* either movie's position toward the system; having wrested authorship from the studios, the makers of each expressed their positions unambiguously. But by preserving the thinnest of all distinctions—substituting the backstage for the backstudio—*Eve* maintains the separation between story and backstory and thus the necessary condition for allegorical transformation.[49] Because of the close conceptual proximity of the Broadway stage and Hollywood film, fans and critics alike have sought the real-world referents for the players: is Bette Davis playing Margo Channing as Tallulah Bankhead? Is George Sanders's "venomous fishwife" critic Addison DeWitt modeled on George Jean Nathan?[50] However, the coding and questioning are precisely the point; DeWitt is emphatically not Hedda Hopper, who appears as herself in Wilder's film. In the classical style, all such correspondence is only plausible, never definitive, and therefore open not only to a range of interpretations but also, as J.D. Connor has argued, a range of authorial expressions.[51]

Mankiewicz had already begun to use the classical style for his own purposes from the moment he achieved hyphenate status with *Dragonwyck* (1946), a movie released shortly before he published "Film Author!" In *Dragonwyck*, antebellum Hudson Valley tenant farmers assert their independence from their patroon Nicholas Van Ryn (Vincent Price), who operates the eponymous estate on the outmoded and inappropriate model of a Dutch barony. Here, Mankiewicz leveraged Fox's penchant for studio allegory to attack creative tyranny and valorize independence.[52] Ownership of land inflates Van Ryn's sense of self to god-like proportions; in the movie's most harrowing moment, he tells his wife Miranda (Gene Tierney), "No one that gives life takes it without purpose. Why do you suppose you are here, Miranda, by the Lord's will or by mine? What you are is a reflection of what I want you to be; you live the life that I gave you." Van Ryn is, however, evidently under the sway of a delusion of poietic grandeur fueled by an opium addiction. He has confused ownership for creation; he cannot be the maker of his wife because, as a pseudo-feudal lord, he makes nothing at all. Taking place predominantly on the Fourth of July, *Dragonwyck* emphasizes the un-Americanness of just such an arrangement, an accusation that, in the early days of the Cold War, would have been especially damning and would have been well in keeping with Zanuck's patriotic liberalism. The movie's overt Americanism conceals Mankiewicz's more local, more personal position. In his drug-fueled dissipation and self-delusion, Van Ryn resembles no character more than Norman Maine, Selznick's figuration of box office poison in *A Star is Born*. But in the ascending writer-director's view of postwar Hollywood, what's sick is the idea of the studio-as-fiefdom, with the hard material reality of the studios' real estate ownership as the cause of its own illness.

In other words, Mankiewicz found in *Dragonwyck* the allegorical means by which to express his disdain for the theater chains upon which the studio system was based and for the exhibitors who exercised an outsize influence on the kind and quality of pictures that could be produced. Mankiewicz would dispense with metaphor three years later when, in May 1949, just after requesting the purchase of "The Wisdom of Eve" and fresh off the rousing success of *A Letter to Three Wives*, he launched his equivalent of Harry Brandt's "Box Office Poison" salvo (the exhibitor's attack on unbankable stars discussed in Chapter 3). In *Life*'s "A Round Table on the Movies," a follow-up to Eric Hodge's article "What's Wrong With the Movies?" Mankiewicz offered his diagnosis in no uncertain terms:

> When Mr. [Alistair] Cooke speaks of the publisher who publishes books he knows will not succeed, that publisher is not owned by the book shops. We're different. Are we selling to an audience or do we make pictures for theaters? There's a hell of a difference. The theaters are one of the things I would like to explore as an aspect of the entire movie structure. *Who controls the movies?* Here at this table are people who *make* movies. We would like to make good movies. I do not think that the cost of making movies is too high. But isn't it true that a real-estate operator whose chief concern should be taking gum off carpets and checking adolescent love-making in the balcony—isn't it true that this man is in control?[53]

Predictably, the attack occasioned heated response from exhibitors around the country, who wrote scathing letters to the *Motion Picture Herald* denouncing the director. In his August 16th response, Mankiewicz doubled down on his literary aspirations for the movies:

> Certainly, no one should expect [Fred Zinnemann's] 'The Search,' for example, to be as profitable as a 'Belvedere' [i.e. *Mr. Belvedere Goes to College*], for example. Just as in the theatre a revival of 'Hamlet' will not outgross 'South Pacific,' and Thomas Mann will not outsell Erle Stanley

Gardner in the bookshops. But given an equitable share of what the audience paid to see 'The Search' let us say, terms equal to the worst in theatre—the producers of that film could have shown a modest but encouraging profit. Encouraging in the all-important sense of encouraging them to make other films like it—to the all-important end that the American Motion Picture will attain an ever-broadening audience of many tastes and interests, that it will regain not only the respect but the custom of a vast, varied and discriminating world audience.[54]

What had been sublimated into allegory in *Dragonwyck* was here broadcast by the writer-director in plain English: better pictures aimed at specialized audiences—more literary pictures—would save the industry from itself.

In retrospect, Mankiewicz's assault on exhibitors can be understood as a flashpoint for Twentieth Century-Fox's bid for leadership of the industry. According to *Variety*, Spyros Skouras, a theater operator before assuming the presidency of Fox, "spank[ed] Manky" for his breach of decorum by telling *Variety*, "If it were not for exhibitors … Mankiewicz would find himself out of a job."[55] Skouras had private reasons for dressing down his increasingly powerful writer-director. That July, Fox released Mankiewicz's *House of Strangers*, a family melodrama based on the Gianninis, the founders of Bank of America. Skouras construed the heavily accented Italian clan as a jab at his own Greek family, and Mankiewicz thought that the perceived offense led Skouras to throttle the distribution of his movie.[56] At the same moment that the conflict between writer-director and studio president broke the surface tension of the screen and erupted into public view, some sixty representatives from various film industry constituencies convened at the Drake Hotel in Chicago to devise an industry-wide public relations strategy. There, with the Mankiewicz-exhibitor conflict clearly in mind, Motion Picture Association of America (MPAA) president Eric Johnston cautioned against "reckless and irresponsible statements from within our own ranks which may get publicity for their authors."[57] At this meeting, the idea of a slogan on par with 1938's "Motion Pictures' Greatest Year" was first proposed, with nominees including "Movies are Your Best Buy," "Hollywood is Clicking," "The Movies—A Three-Hour Holiday," and "The Movies—A Family Holiday."[58] Responsibility for the slogan and for the public relations push would ultimately fall to Skouras, whose studio employed the inflammatory Mankiewicz and reaped the benefits of the writer-director's successes. By March 1950, the month Mankiewicz completed *Eve*'s screenplay and took up his directorial duties, Fox undertook the public relations campaign under the slogan "Movies are Better than Ever," thereby assuming the mantle that MGM had worn for the previous two decades and that Paramount bore before that. In April, Skouras issued a "Guarantee of Performance," a promise that "motion pictures are still incomparable, entertainment-wise."[59]

Both the self-nominated industry leadership and the commitment to "performance" were, in keeping with Fox's paradoxical progressive traditionalism, instantiated in Zanuck's decision to replace an injured Claudette Colbert with Bette Davis to play Margo Channing. If any actress personified the studio system at the height of its power, it was Davis. In addition to being a seven-time nominee and two-time Best Actress Oscar winner before her popularity began to decline in the immediate postwar period, Davis had been elected president of the Academy of Motion Picture Arts and Sciences in 1941, making her the first woman to earn that honor. By selecting Davis, who had, after seventeen years, broken off her unhappy relationship with Warners, Fox found its answer to *Sunset Boulevard*'s Gloria Swanson. But where Wilder's Swanson, the great star of the Paramount '20s, embodied in Norma Desmond the idea that the studio and the studio system weren't much worth returning to, Davis, the grandest star of the studio era, would capture Fox's desire to maintain the order of the past while at the same time embracing a future of freelance careers for stars and greater artistic autonomy for writer-directors like Mankiewicz.

Befitting the pervasive sense of the project as an inflection point in the trajectories of Davis, Mankiewicz, Fox, and the industry as a whole, *Eve* most clearly acknowledges its reflexivity at its narrative midpoint, when the friendships and partnerships that constitute Margo's personal and professional lives nearly disintegrate. And because *Eve*, like its backstudio brethren, is even more specifically an occasion to reflect on the nature of expressive authority in a transitional Hollywood, this threatened disintegration occurs in the form of a dispute over the authorship of a collaborative production. After Margo takes offense at Lloyd's decision to cast Eve as her understudy in *Aged in Wood*, the two translate their personal animosity into conflicting bids for the control of the play's meaning:

> LLOYD: I shall never understand the weird process by which a body with a voice suddenly fancies itself as a mind! Just when exactly does an actress decide they're *her* words she's saying and *her* thoughts she's expressing?
> MARGO: Usually at the point that she's got to rewrite and re-think them to keep the audience from leaving the theater![60]

Mankiewicz would cagily confirm Lloyd as his mouthpiece in his foreword to the published screenplay. There, he asserted his claim to the production by denying actors' intelligence and, more specifically, their "literacy": "One of the most common misconceptions about a filmscript," he wrote in his typical fustian style, "is an apprehension that it is a highly technical blueprint made up of incomprehensible symbols, graphs and charts—and that the dialogue is rather casually made up by the actors as they go along. It is true that some actors, under a delusion of literacy, try to tamper with written words."[61] That quarrel between Lloyd and Margo over who gets to determine the meanings of words encrypted a dispute between writer-director and studio over who gets to control the rights to a work. Though Random House would attribute the screenplay to Mankiewicz on its title page, the copyright of that book, like all subsidiary rights to adapted works made under contract, belonged to Fox. Years later, when reflecting on *Applause* (1970), the Broadway adaptation of *Eve*, Mankiewicz put his thinking on the matter bluntly:

> I wrote and directed *All About Eve* as a salaried employee, a "gun for hire," as it were. As studio contracts were then written, whether you were Bill Faulkner, Bob Sherwood, Joe Blow, or Joe Mankiewicz, every conceivable right to what you created—in every conceivable medium, past, present or yet to be invented (my writing contracts as far back as 1932 refer by name to television rights!)—was, in every conceivable aspect, turned over to the studio. As if the studio were, in fact, the creator.[62]

Fox did, in fact, consider itself the creator of *All About Eve*, presenting the movie as the cinematic articulation of the looking-back-to-move-forward strategy encapsulated in its "Movies are Better than Ever" mantra. With *Eve*, Fox sought to justify why the movies still mattered by focusing on what makes the movies the movies. And to explain what makes the movies the movies, Fox looked back to what it shares with its former rival, the theater. Three years before its February 1953 commitment to differentiating cinema from television through the spectacular experience of widescreen Cinemascope, color, and surround sound—a decision that, according to John Belton, returned the movies to the fairground—Fox attempted to reconfigure the audience's theatrical experience through a novel exhibition format for *Eve* it called "scheduled performance."[63] Fox would, in effect, make good on Skouras's Guarantee of Performance by literalizing the slogan in a trial run at the Roxy in New York. Prior to Skouras's experiment, movies at the Roxy, like many other theaters, had been shown on a continuous basis: a program would play more or less nonstop, and viewers could arrive whenever they wanted and stay until they wanted to leave. While a similar format had been used when exhibiting superspecials in the roadshow format as far back as the 1910s, with *Eve* Fox attempted to normalize the format according to the terms of its Broadway-themed picture. A definition of "scheduled performance" was included in newspaper advertisements along with the following pitch:

> Now, for the first time in history, in a theatre with a continuous policy and at no advance in prices—a program of Scheduled Performances has been devised, to make it possible for you to see "All About Eve" from the beginning—just as we saw it. Tickets may be purchased in advance. A seat will be assured for all, and no one will be seated after the start of any of the four daily performances. This guarantees you the fullest enjoyment when you see the most provocative picture of the year—"All About Eve."
>
> We believe this bold departure will win your complete support. We are confident you will agree that it is a new and exhilarating experience in movie-going. (Figure 5.5)[64]

Figure 5.5 Twentieth Century-Fox's Advertisement of "Scheduled Performances" of *All About Eve* (*Boxoffice*, October 7, 1950)

Fox turned backward to the exhibition practices of the cinema's past competitor, the "theatre," in order to distinguish film from its new rival, television. In this new exhibition model, film would be raised to a certain level of seriousness by Fox's insistence that the movie be seen in order, from beginning to end, fundamentally distinct from the grind of continuous exhibition and the flow of broadcast TV.[65] Audiences weren't ready for the innovation, and after a week of confusion, Fox nixed the scheduled performance model; it wouldn't become the standard exhibition format until a decade later when Alfred Hitchcock refused to let patrons see his *Psycho* (Shamley-Paramount, 1960) after it started.[66] Nonetheless, by embedding *All About Eve*, a narrative of the theater, within an exhibition campaign modeled on the theater, Fox made clear the movie's purpose: to demonstrate that movies were indeed better than ever, in part by asserting their continuity with the past. Fox would have *All About Eve* be not only an exemplary Fox picture but an exemplary Hollywood movie more generally, the epitome of the form's affordances in contradistinction to those of television. In other words, Fox would figure *Eve* as an instantiation of the virtue of the classical style—and, at the same time, as both a story about the threat posed by television and an argument about how to weather that threat.

Those allegories share a common emblem in the form of Sir Joshua Reynolds's portrait *Sarah Siddons as the Tragic Muse* (1784), the painting that provided the model for the award bestowed by the Sarah Siddons Society to Eve at the movie's start and upon which the camera lingers before the fadeout that marks *Eve*'s midpoint (Figure 5.6). As a plot device, the portrait subtly but trenchantly points up Margo's existential crisis. Painted when the actress portrayed Lady Macbeth at age twenty-eight, Mrs. Siddons presents a marked contrast to the forty-year-old Margo. Moreover, *Sarah Siddons* speaks clearly to Mankiewicz's fascination with eighteenth-century theater and should be understood as his attempt at an authorial signature; two years later, the writer-director would leave Hollywood for New York to write plays. *Sarah Siddons*'s pride of place in *Eve* participates in the culmination of a decade-long trend of utilizing portraits as narrative pivots and signs of intellectual sophistication. In some cases, like Preminger's *Laura* and other movies retroactively considered noir, the framed portraits served as the material analogues to frame narratives and, at a further degree of abstraction, the emblems of a heightened formal self-consciousness amounting to an intensifying pressure exerted on the classical style. As David Bordwell has keenly observed, portraiture accompanied assertions of authorship as early as 1945, when director Albert Lewin "signed" his initials in a shot in his adaptation of *The Picture*

Figure 5.6 *Sarah Siddons as the Tragic Muse* (Sir Joshua Reynolds, 1784). *All About Eve* (Joseph L. Mankiewicz, Fox, 1950)

of Dorian Gray (MGM) in a location corresponding to Basil Hallward's autograph on the eponymous portrait.[67] Both *Sunset Boulevard* and *In a Lonely Place* exaggerate this tendency in the form, respectively, of the multitude of press images of a young Norma that surround and overwhelm Desmond and the canvases of Vincent Van Gogh, Pierre-Auguste Renoir, and Diego Rivera that appear prominently in Laurel's apartment just before Dix attacks her (Figures 5.7 and 5.8).[68]

But where Wilder violates decorum with his baroque décor and Ray and Bogart signal their affinity with modern artists against the classical ideal, *Sarah Siddons as the Tragic Muse* indicates the synchronization of Mankiewicz's and Fox's commitments to the system's stylistic norms against their total dissolution. *Sarah Siddons* has been understood as the "ne plus ultra of Reynolds's artistic endeavors" in a career defined by an investment in the Academic neoclassicist tradition in opposition to the burgeoning cult of Romantic genius. Though in his aesthetic-philosophical *Discourses on Art* he failed to reconcile the antinomies of neoclassical and

Figure 5.7   Norma and the profusion of portraits.
Sunset Boulevard (Billy Wilder, Paramount, 1950)

Figure 5.8   Laurel's Modernist portraits and *In a Lonely Place*'s anticlassicism.
In a Lonely Place (Nicholas Ray, Santana/Columbia, 1950)

proto-Romantic ideas—General Nature and Custom, universal standard and contingent experience—Reynolds achieved a symbolic resolution in the balancing of "realism and the imagination" in his synthesis of portraiture and history painting, an argument in circulation since E. H. Gombrich presented it in 1942.[69] Reynolds and his paintings therefore stand as allegories of Academic painting's own fraught position in the forward movement of the history of art. The analogy between academic painting and the studio system might have been more readily available to Mankiewicz, the Columbia-graduate "arrogant bastard," than to Zanuck, whose formal education ended in his early teens, but it would have appealed equally, with each in favor of solid craftsmanship and common criteria of judgment and opposed to the idiosyncrasies and vicissitudes of Genius.[70]

As much as *Sarah Siddons* signals *Eve*'s rearguard classicism, it also more specifically identifies the movie's story of contested medium transition. Reynolds's portrait is itself a medium allegory—"Tragedy personified" as William Hazlitt put it—and thus speaks directly to the industry's deepest concerns about its medium's ongoing viability.[71] *Eve* insists on its analogical relation to Reynolds's portrait and, therefore, on its own conception of its principal characters as medium allegories. Halfway up her staircase, fed up with Eve and the threat the latter poses to her career, Margo holds court for thirteen seconds against a portrait that looks astonishingly like her, large enough to capture her entire body, regally seated and rendered in neoclassical style (Figure 5.9). In the following reverse shot and on numerous occasions after, Eve is framed against her own smaller, impressionistic likeness (Figure 5.10).[72] If Sarah Siddons personifies the theater, as the movie suggests, then Margo and Eve themselves represent different media. Given the film's narrative of contested succession and the industry's collective handwringing over what to do about television, it makes sense to read Margo as the cinema and Eve as TV (compare yet again with Norma Desmond's literalism: "I am big. It's the pictures that got small.").[73] In Hollywood films a handful of years hence, television, the low-quality usurper, would play itself as the poor substitute for familial and romantic love in Douglas Sirk's *All That Heaven Allows* (Universal, 1955) or as the staticky sign of intergenerational miscommunication in the Stark household in Ray's *Rebel Without a Cause* (Warners, 1955). Here, however, it is Eve who wheedles her way into Margo's dressing room, her theatrical family's home away from home. Diminutive Eve makes herself yet smaller as she first narrates her confabulated hard-luck war widow story, a tale that would not have been out of place in the radio soap operas that were just beginning to appear on television. Positioned in the center

Figure 5.9   Margo, framed. *All About Eve* (Joseph L. Mankiewicz, Fox, 1950)

Figure 5.10   Eve, framed. *All About Eve* (Joseph L. Mankiewicz, Fox, 1950)

All About Everything 171

Figure 5.11   All about TV. *All About Eve* (Joseph L. Mankiewicz, Fox, 1950)

of the frame and the focal point of each person's look, Eve performs the role of the electronic hearth, the glowing bulb above her serving as the metonymic tube (Figure 5.11).[74]

The allegory of contested medium succession encompasses more than a simple comparison of frame dimensions, for what mattered to Fox was not the medium of film in itself but rather its specific uses, especially its ability to reach audiences and have audiences, in turn, reach back. During Fox's turn to Cinemascope in 1953, Zanuck articulated a crucial distinction between the models of passive entertainment, implicitly epitomized by television, and the new desideratum of active recreation: "Entertainment is something others provide for you, while recreation is something you provide in some measure for yourself—something in which you participate."[75] That sense of the necessity and pleasure of active mutual engagement against the atomizing idiot box manifests not only in *Eve*'s invitation to interpret the movie but also in the figuration of Eve's invasion of Margo's coterie, which, as a group of theatrical professionals and friends, condenses and concretizes multiple forms of communion: family, production unit, audience. If, as the studios feared, television was an antihearth, fragmenting the American public into millions of homebound entertainment-sated monads, Eve fits her allegorical image perfectly, dividing that family unit into its component parts, appealing to the basest egotistical needs of each, and thereby threatening destruction to all.[76] To Margo, Eve is an obsequious flatterer; to Karen, a good-natured kid in need of a break; to Lloyd, a talented starlet and possible mistress. As such, she fits Houseman's apocalyptic description of the new medium in "Battle over Television": "Television is not just the latest and most miraculous of ... media. It is a synthesis of them all. It is radio with eyes; it is the press without the travail of printing; it is movies without the physical limitations of mechanical reproduction and projection."[77] Eve manages to turn writer and star against each other, such that domestic strife invades work life just after *Sarah Siddons* fades to black.

All About Eve does not, however, follow its source story in allowing its titular antiheroine to divide and conquer the family-cum-production unit-cum-audience. As in Mary Orr's "The Wisdom of Eve," and in keeping with the studios' newfound willingness to portray itself in a less-than-positive light, Eve heads off to Hollywood, making the allegorical medium conquest all but literal. But Eve goes west alone, unable to persuade Lloyd to leave Karen and come with her. The writer's integrity—his faith in and responsibility to his wife, his star, and his craft—means everything from the perspective of Mankiewicz, just as his participation in and self-subordination to the professional family means everything to Fox. Indeed, Eve, as a common enemy, ultimately galvanizes the reintegration of the group, a comedy of remarriage served family-style. At dinner with Bill, Karen, and Lloyd, Margo explains that her personal satisfaction rests on two interlocking conditions: having her theatrical family—here explicitly conceived as a stable audience that listens to her ("You know why I forgive Eve? She left good behind. The four of us together") and understands her ("Never try to outguess Margo," says Bill)—and choosing the roles that are right for her. The suddenly content and even magnanimous actress renounces her claim to the role of Cora in *Footsteps on the Ceiling*, ceding it to Eve: "Lloyd," she apologetically says,

> I don't want to play Cora.... It isn't the part. It's a great part. And a fine play. But not for me anymore—not a foursquare, upright, downright, forthright married lady.... I've finally got a life to live! I don't have to play parts I'm too old for—just because I've got nothing to do with my nights![78]

The statement is one we ought to expect from Fox's figuration of the cinema. Both a stable audience and the limitation of performances to the best ones are exactly what *Variety* saw in Fox's "scheduled performance" exhibition plan: a house full of viewers ready to actively engage with the film and the beginning of the end of the double bill. Though Skouras himself took a pragmatic approach to the double bill, telling *Variety* that he could not kill it with one stroke—"'While I am against double features from every angle,' he declared, 'there are too many outside factors present in each situation for us to attempt to change them at one time'"—Fox could express its unadulterated wish through the mouth of Bette Davis, its stand-in for the industry.[79] Margo, it barely needs to be said, needs only one Bill to live well. James Savage thus proved preternaturally insightful when, in his *Chicago Tribune* column of November 10, 1950, he identified Bill, the director who had left Broadway for an Elia Kazan-like spell with Fox and Zanuck, as the artist-prophet who delivers the theory underpinning the movie's solution to the film industry's television problem:

> Our current adventures in televiewing bring to mind the line from the film 'All About Eve': 'Wherever there's magic and make-believe and an audience—there's theater.' Put the emphasis on the word 'audience.' … That's the vacuum in video entertainment. No living room is large enough to spill over with the crowd excitement that makes the 'magic and make-believe' in front of the footlights and screen equal to that behind them.[80]

Savage decoded Fox's sense that Hollywood's future success rested on collective spectatorship, and, more specifically, on "crowd excitement": the audience's active participation in its own recreation. Margo achieves a calm stability upon discovering her new role and her new criterion of success, but Eve receives no satisfaction from her Sarah Siddons award. She is, in fact, unsatisfiable, as she craves not an audience but applause, not flesh-and-blood fans but an abstract affirmation of success, the sonic equivalent of Nielsen ratings.[81] Eve will move restlessly on to Hollywood, as television already has, but the industry may yet survive, now and into the future, if it will follow Fox's lead.

Eve ends on this note of embattled persistence beyond the immediate crises of 1950 in one of the most awe-inspiring concluding images produced during the studio era. When Eve retires to her hotel room after winning her award, she is met by a young woman, the president of her Brooklyn high school's Eve Harrington Club. Profoundly self-conscious allegoricity reaches yet another level of intensity and insistence: just as Gertrude Slescynski megalomaniacally named herself Eve—both the first woman and the dark end of days—so does this Phoebe (Barbara Bates) take the Greek word for sun, a star so bright it blots out all others. After Eve heads to bed, Phoebe reverentially carries the Sarah Siddons trophy to the room's triptych mirror; the resulting portrait pushes the classical style as far as it can go, exactly to the point, according to Margaret Farrand Thorp, where it has begun to become a literary symbol.[82] Phoebe is framed against her image just as Margo and Eve were; the image, however, has achieved an extraordinary cubistic density, as virtuosic a visual display as Orson Welles's mirror shots in *Citizen Kane* (RKO, 1941) or *The Lady from Shanghai* (Mercury-Columbia, 1947). In the media allegory of the film, Phoebe represents the inevitable but as-yet-unimagined next challenge to the dominant media regime. Fox had no way of knowing about the particular transformations in distribution and exhibition that would come in the next seventy-five years (e.g., streaming), but the theoretical possibility of such developments was predicted by the logic of subsidiary rights that would, from this point forward, comprise an important source of revenue. That possibility is embedded in this final proliferation of Phoebes.

However, the most proximate and salient contrast is, of course, with *Sunset Boulevard*. Norma's address to Paramount's newsreel camera and to those wonderful people out there in the dark violates the classical proscription against looking the lens in the eye; the subsequent watery dissolve amounts to an obliteration of the classical style (Figure 5.12). But in *Eve*,

Figure 5.12   Classicism dissolved. *Sunset Boulevard* (Billy Wilder, Paramount, 1950)

All About Everything   175

Figure 5.13   Classicism preserved at its limit.
All About Eve (Joseph L. Mankiewicz, Fox, 1950)

none of Phoebe's gazes ever crosses the plane of the screen perpendicularly; the fourth wall remains secure; the frame binds and supports the ramifying reflections (Figure 5.13). In this final image, photographed on the eve of the studio system's dissolution, *Eve* shows how the increasingly centripetal dispersion of power and authority in the industry might be coordinated, contained, and expressed in the preferred classical style while also pushing it to the brink: how, on the verge of fragmentation, the movies could be made different—sophisticated; protected speech; literary—while also remaining what they had always been.

***

If *Eve* constituted Fox's defense of Hollywood, the industry seemed to answer the call to arms; it was anointed the triumphant picture of 1950 with an unmatched fourteen Academy Award nominations, including Best Screenplay and Best Director awards for Mankiewicz and Best Picture for Zanuck. Notably, *Eve* bested the thirteen earned by *Gone with the Wind*, the historical epic whose massive popular success and consensus Academy

SOURCE MATERIAL OF FEATURE-LENGTH PICTURES APPROVED BY PRODUCTION CODE ADMINISTRATION 1935-1956*

Year	Original Screen Stories		Stage Plays		Novels		Biographies		Short Stories		Source Unknown		Miscellaneous†	
	Number	Per Cent	Number	Per Cent	Number	Per Cent	Number	Per Cent	Number	Per Cent	Number	Per Cent	Number	Per Cent
1935**	244	47.0	41	7.9	142	27.4	3	.6	37	7.1	28	5.4	24	4.6
1936**	371	67.8	38	7.0	92	16.8	2	.4	39	7.1	....	....	5	.9
1937	391	64.3	39	6.4	102	16.8	12	2.0	46	7.6	11	1.8	7	1.1
1938	316	58.0	30	5.5	140	25.7	2	.4	54	9.9	....	....	3	.5
1939	329	56.3	34	5.8	127	21.8	17	2.9	59	10.1	10	1.7	8	1.4
1940	323	61.8	51	9.8	109	20.8	8	1.5	21	4.0	....	....	11	2.1
1941	358	63.0	57	10.0	58	10.2	4	.7	82	14.5	5	.9	4	.7
1942	401	73.4	31	5.7	57	10.4	7	1.3	29	5.3	8	1.5	13	2.4
1943	312	74.8	23	5.5	42	10.0	2	.5	6	1.4	16	3.9	16	3.9
1944	321	72.6	28	6.3	48	10.9	2	.5	10	2.3	9	2.0	24	5.4
1945	251	64.5	26	6.7	59	15.2	....	....	10	2.6	2	.5	41	10.5
1946	259	60.9	22	5.2	65	15.3	1	.2	10	2.4	5	1.2	63	14.8
1947	233	57.7	17	4.2	87	21.5	....	....	5	1.2	10	2.5	52	12.9
1948	244	56.1	26	6.0	76	17.5	2	.4	23	5.3	10	2.3	54	12.4
1949	285	68.0	18	4.3	76	18.1	4	1.0	16	3.8	....	....	20	4.8
1950	315	73.4	18	4.2	67	15.6	3	.7	10	2.4	....	....	16	3.7
1951	291	67.3	25	5.8	70	16.2	2	.5	25	5.8	....	....	19	4.4
1952	246	66.9	17	4.6	64	17.4	....	....	21	5.7	....	....	20	5.4
1953	227	64.1	19	5.4	72	20.3	3	.9	17	4.8	....	....	16	4.5
1954	177	58.4	11	3.7	61	20.1	1	.3	12	4.0	....	....	41	13.5
1955	158	51.8	23	7.5	73	24.0	4	1.3	28	9.2	....	....	19	6.2
1956	172	51.0	20	5.9	71	21.1	8	2.4	39	11.6	....	....	27	8.0
1935-56	6224	62.9	614	6.2	1758	17.8	87	.9	599	6.0	114	1.1	503	5.1

* Does not include pictures reissued.
** Data for this year includes pictures approved in Hollywood only.
† Including such sources as comic strips, radio and television programs, non-fiction, travelogues, poems, etc.

Figure 5.14 The spike in original screen stories that began in 1949 subsided by 1953. "Source Material of Feature-Length Pictures Approved by Production Code Administration," *1956 Annual Report*, Motion Picture Association of America, Inc, 17 (Margaret Herrick Library, Academy of Motion Pictures Arts and Sciences https://digitalcollections.oscars.org/digital/collection/p15759coll11/id/11758)

recognition consecrated 1939 as the year of Hollywood's full industrial and artistic maturation.

And yet the solution *Eve* offered—of a brilliant balancing of the competing intentions of studio, director, and star—soon began to look untenable. After five years of skittishness (1949–1953), the industry began to turn back to literary source materials. In 1956, original screenplays comprised 51 percent of total feature films produced, the lowest such share since 1935, with novels and short stories picking up most of the slack (Figure 5.14).[83] This transformation can be seen as a symptom of the industry's changing constitution, with agents like MCA's Lew Wasserman achieving greater power as packagers of talent and story material, as well as its shifting strategy toward television. As Eric Johnston noted in his annual report for the MPAA that year, Hollywood had fully embraced the "big picture," a "term," he explained, that "has been used to describe pictures, not only big in terms of budget, length, scope and number of stars, but pictures that the industry believes will gain big audiences."[84] With fewer movies of greater budgets being produced, with block booking and blind selling outlawed by the *Paramount* decree, and hence with more at risk in each production than ever before, the reliability of the presold property became yet more important. Only a decade after William Miller wrote the dreary assessment that serves as this chapter's epigraph, critic Arthur Knight could say in *The Saturday Review*, "Best-selling novels, hit plays, for a time successful television shows—all of these have become grist for the movie mills, far more in demand than ever before."[85]

For Knight, writing in *The Saturday Review* in 1959, the demand for source literature mattered more than ever, but not differently, at least not yet. "In the past, the best-selling novels and hit plays were purchased, then conscientiously transformed into acceptable movie material—acceptable, that is, to the Production Code, the Legion of Decency, and the various censorship boards that graced the nation." But the Supreme Court's 1952 decision in *Joseph Burstyn, Inc. v. Wilson* (also known as the *Miracle* case, after the controversial Roberto Rossellini film) extended First Amendment protection to movies and overturned the ideological foundation of the studio system. As a result, Hollywood filmmakers finally had the opportunity to meet critics' demands for sophisticated, "frank" pictures. In Knight's view, if conservative producers insisted on only using their newfound freedom to titillate audiences with sensationalist subject matter and "interpolated four- and five-letter words," they would miss their chance to make literary films and would instead persist in a vain attempt to realize the "dream of the undifferentiated mass audience"—the impossible dream of a bygone era.[86] Not until the official replacement of the Production Code by the ratings system in 1967 and the concomitant emergence of the so-called "Hollywood Renaissance" would Knight find the US equivalent of the adventurous filmmaking in France, Sweden, and England he sought. That a reconstituted, conglomerate-based studio system—what J.D. Connor has called "neoclassical Hollywood"—would follow shortly thereafter would prove, however, that the real dreamers of that particular golden dream were critics like Knight.

CHAPTER 6

Conclusion
Read Anything Good Lately?

Historians and theorists often demur from identifying an end to the era of "Classical Hollywood" or "the studio system," and offer apologias when they do; like eras, books, in order to be books, must end.[1] With apologies, then: the year 1952 marks an inflection point in the intertwined histories of Hollywood filmmaking and American literature that this book has tracked, and is therefore an appropriate moment at which to conclude.

That year saw a decisive decline in the total output of the American film industry, understood in terms of films approved by the Production Code Administration during the ten years spanning 1947 and 1956. Between 1952 and 1956, the PCA approved an average of 327 features per year, down roughly 23 percent from an average of 424 between 1947 and 1951.[2] But the numbers only tell part of the story. It was also the year of the *Miracle* decision, which recognized movies as forms of expression as opposed to mere commodities—that is, in a basic sense, as literary. At the same time, writers used the American cinema to push literature in new directions that would more readily align with the trends of the half-century to come.

In 1952, Lillian Ross completed *Picture*, the first book-length making-of narrative ever written and a prototype of participant-observer longform journalism that would characterize the works of the "New Journalism." *Picture* tracks the aspirations, conflicts, frustrations, and failures in the production of John Huston's adaptation of Stephen Crane's *The Red Badge of Courage* for MGM. Huston, a self-styled rebel and writer-producer like Billy Wilder and Joseph L. Mankiewicz who planned an atmospheric film modeled on the Civil War photography of Mathew Brady, ran afoul of MGM cofounder Louis B. Mayer, who saw the picture as a surefire flop and attempted to stymie it. Dore Schary, recently installed as vice president in charge of production after Loew's president Nicholas Schenck had instructed Mayer to "find another Thalberg," butted heads with the studio's founder.[3] Schenck ultimately sided with Schary over Mayer; MGM forged ahead with the production; Huston's vision was ultimately corrupted; Schary was humbled by the film's commercial failure; and Mayer was effectively forced out of the studio that bore his name.

Ross famously told *New Yorker* editor William Shawn, who commissioned the articles on which the book was based, that her reportage would be novelistic. By allowing Hollywood fact to appear to be even stranger than preceding Hollywood fictions, Ross would demonstrate the viability of a form to be taken up by Truman Capote, Joan Didion, Norman Mailer, and Hunter Thompson, among many more. *Picture* in fact emerged from one of the readiest symbols of a studio system in transition—the end of Mayer's reign over the studio that led the industry for much of the sound era—and employed a next-generation naturalism aligned at once with Crane's source novel, Huston's visual pastiche, and the works of Faulkner, Fitzgerald, and Huxley, the writers of MGM modernism. Almost twenty years after Faulkner found *Absalom, Absalom!*'s voice in the echoing virtual corridors of MGM's corporate apparatus, Ross perfected her form in the heart of the Loew's "octopus" at 1540 Broadway in Manhattan, thousands of miles from Los Angeles and hundreds of feet above the ground in Schenck's office.

> [Producer Gottfried] Reinhardt's and Huston's struggle to make a great picture, Mayer's opposition, Schary's support, the sideline operations of a dozen vice-presidents, the labor and craftsmanship of the cast and technical crew, the efforts of Huston's aides to help him get his concept of the Stephen Crane novel on film, the long series of artistic problems and compromises, the reactions of the preview audiences—all these seemed to compose themselves into some sort of *design*, but a few pieces were still missing. I felt that somewhere upstairs I might find them.[4]

Occupying the same "small and modest" office for thirty years, and stoically accepting a slightly lesser salary than the histrionic and prideful Mayer, Schenck resembles Faulkner's anonymous, malevolent figures of corporate power: the continuity writer in Faulkner's "legendary" anecdote of MGM's 1933 production of "Louisiana Lou" and Eulalia Bon's lawyer in *Absalom*. Schenck is at his most successful, Ross indicates, when he dissolves entirely into the company's organizational "design"—the term Faulkner used to describe the obsession driving Thomas Sutpen—and inhabits its ledgers. As Ross explains, those ledgers contain an entry for *The Red Badge of Courage*, which was, as she has elaborated over scores of pages, a cataclysm for Mayer and a lesson for Schary. For Loew's and Schenck, however, the movie is Production No. 1512, a mere 6 percent of the $26,243,848.61 spent on completed but unreleased productions: a picture worthy of "only slight attention in … Schenck's annual report to the stockholders of Loew's Inc., for the fiscal year ending August 3, 1951."[5] What Ross discovered, then, is that the "design" she sought belonged to Loew's, the corporation, not Schenck, the head executive. Schenck capably manages Loew's because, as Howard Dietz, MGM's director of publicity, explains in praise of his boss, "there are no rules for choosing what you're going to make…. *You know what to choose only by growing up in the fabric of the business.*"[6] Likely unbeknownst to himself, Dietz channels Faulkner's Judith Sutpen, who proposed that the metaphysical carpet of life was designed by the "Ones": the beings that *Fortune* magazine would call corporations, MGM supreme among them. Ross thus renovated Fitzgerald's and Huxley's neo-naturalism by letting the studio executives' fantasies speak for themselves. If the New Journalism and nonfiction novel were instances of a general postmodern doubt in the distinction between fact and fiction, they emerged, in part, from depictions of what Malcolm Lowry called Hollywood the Unreal.[7]

Ross was far from the only writer to have Faulkner on her mind at midcentury. Shortly after he ceased writing for Warner Bros. on his three-hundred dollar-a-week contract, Faulkner witnessed a rapid revaluation of his career, beginning with Malcolm Cowley's *The Portable Faulkner* (1946) and culminating in the 1949 Nobel Prize for Literature. Naturally, the literate media clamored for the work of the newly august man of letters. Faulkner's *Intruder in the Dust* (1948) proved irresistible to MGM; chosen by Southern director Clarence Brown and shot on location in Faulkner's hometown of Oxford, Mississippi, the racial conflict murder mystery comprised an ideal marriage of Schary's gritty liberalism and the studio's prestige fetish. To a young Ralph Ellison, in the midst of writing his seminal *Invisible Man* (1952), the adaptation of *Intruder in the Dust* (1949) was exemplary of the shifting status of Black people in the collective American mind between *The Birth of a Nation* (D. W. Griffith, 1915) and the social problem films of the late 1940s. The MGM film features prominently in Ellison's essay "The Shadow and the Act" (1949), an insightful early instance of criticism that examines the social and political ramifications of racial representation in artworks, a mode of analysis that would become central to cultural studies in the latter half of the twentieth century. However, in identifying "the enormous myth-making potential of the film form," and in taking as his central case study the translation of Faulkner's Yoknapatawpha myth into the mythical form of Hollywood cinema, Ellison, like Parker Tyler, looks backward to the practices of the modernists as well.[8] When he later observes his debt to Joyce and Eliot, who "made [him] conscious of the literary value of [his] folk inheritance," Ellison indicates his deep affinity with his late modernist peers, not only in finding new use for the mythical method, but, more specifically, in seeing the movies as a folk form as fundamental as the "spirituals ... blues, jazz and folktales" he names.[9]

Hence the importance of the unnamed Invisible Man's two initial negations in the eponymous novel's second sentence: "No, I am not a spook like those who haunted Edgar Allan Poe; nor am I one of your Hollywood-movie ectoplasms."[10] That is, he is neither a Gothic antebellum nightmare, like the treacherous South Sea Islanders of *The Narrative of Arthur Gordon Pym of Nantucket* (1838), nor any of the unnamed racist stereotypes that take phantasmatic form on the screen, like the African villagers in *Trader Horn* (W.S. Van Dyke, MGM, 1931) that Bigger Thomas sees early in Richard Wright's *Native Son* (1940). The Invisible Man rejects the idea that he is, as Ellison put it in "The Shadow and the Act," one of the "negative images [that] constitute justifications for all those acts, legal, emotional, economic and political, which we label Jim Crow."[11] But at the same time that he denies that he is a mere image, a stereotype upon which a racist state policy is based, he also refuses a name, the hallmark of individuation in the long history of the novel.[12] Neither flattened image nor named character, Ellison's Invisible Man would be more aptly described, using the author's own vocabulary, as a "mythic hero." And if one defining feature of Joyce's modernist mythic hero was his parallel with the protagonist of an ancient epic, Ellison's late-modernist version has his correspondence in American movies. Despite his protestation to the contrary, the Invisible Man resembles the antihero of H. G. Wells's novel and James Whale's adaptation of *The Invisible Man* (Universal, 1933) perhaps more than he recognizes. For in the novel's final pages, the Invisible Man finds himself a "disembodied voice," alienated from himself and hunted by an angry mob like Whale's villain.[13] Like Lowry, who in *Under the Volcano* figured the *Mad Love* poster's image of an artist with a murderer's hands as a "hieroglyphic of the times," Ellison found in the Universal horror genre a comic and only semi-ironic emblem for his own late-modern epic of a Black man in search of an identity consonant with his humanity.

As Ross's *Picture* and Ellison's *Invisible Man* went to press in 1952, James Baldwin was completing his own meditation on Black identity, his semi-autobiographical first novel *Go Tell It on the Mountain* (1953). If Ellison's novel can be taken as an end of one lineage, as Matthew Wilkens posits in his discussion of the "long 1950s," Baldwin's might be understood as the start of another, the "portraits of the artist" that would become a "signature genre" of American fiction after World War II.[14] Here, Baldwin presents a portrait of the artist as a young moviegoer. Though the film that fourteen-year-old John Grimes sees on his fateful birthday goes unnamed, Baldwin scholars agree that it is *Of Human Bondage* (John Cromwell, RKO, 1934), starring Bette Davis. The film enraptures Grimes, troubling the Christianity he learned from his father, and Davis is his Satan: "he wanted to be like her, only more powerful, more thorough, and more cruel; to make those around him, all who hurt him, suffer as she made the student suffer, and laugh in their faces when they asked pity for their pain."[15] That devilish identification is, however, halted and replaced by a more complex response comprising an aesthetic experience and a moral judgment:

> Nevertheless, when she came to die, which she did eventually, looking more grotesque than ever, as she deserved, his thoughts were abruptly arrested, and he was chilled by the expression on her face…. Had the thought not been so blasphemous, he would have thought that it was the Lord who led him into this theater to show him an example of the wages of sin.[16]

For the young Grimes (and for the young Baldwin, as he would later explain in *The Devil Finds Work* [1976]), Davis's face is an epiphany in the Joycean sense, a moment of clarity gleaned from the "vulgarity" of everyday life.[17] What's clear to Grimes is the choice available to him, between a life of piety leading to paradise or of worldly pleasure leading to damnation. But epiphanies in Joyce are ironic, and so too is Baldwin's here: the alternatives emerge preconditioned by the idiom and worldview of the church, which warp Grimes's vision at the moment the church's teachings ostensibly clarify it.[18] John Grimes presumably will not come to see the very framing of the alternatives as specious until after the novel concludes, as Baldwin did when he grew disillusioned with the "gimmick" of organized religion and chose a life as an artist.[19]

Grimes's epiphanic moviegoing experience thus serves, extra-diegetically, as a statement of Baldwin's own artistic self-fashioning. Written in the wake of Baldwin's famous criticism of Wright's *Native Son* as a "rejection of life," *Go Tell It on the Mountain* offers in the young Grimes's encounter with Davis an implicit rejoinder to Bigger Thomas's angry, literally onanistic moviegoing.[20] *Go Tell It on the Mountain* treats seeing Hollywood movies not only as a real experience (what, in *The Moviegoer* [1961], Walker Percy would wryly describe as the only existentially certifying experience), but also as a formative experience from which the sensibility of the artist emerges. When Hollywood moviegoing, the common experience of a plural world, comes to be understood as the basis of serious literature, modernism becomes, in a sense, for everyone. It ceases to be restricted: ceases, in a crucial sense, to be Modernism.

And it becomes, depending on your view, the postmodernism that Lowry and Tyler anticipated, or the democratization and institutionalization of modernism that Mark McGurl sees as the great achievement of university-based creative writing programs. Baldwin didn't attend college or teach in an MFA program; in the self-mythology presented in *Go Tell It on the Mountain* and revisited in *The Devil Finds Work*, he learned to be an artist in the movie theater, among other places, under the sway of and in reaction to the universal tutor Hollywood.[21] In other words, he was not trained to write his "autopoetic" story of artistic becoming as so many of his successors were. In writing workshops, such reflexivity became "routine," resulting in a preference for the "portraits of the artist" genre.[22] If the creative writing seminar trained a penchant for the kind of künstlerroman that Nathanael West pilloried in *The Day of the Locust*, it also gave rise to the campus novel, a form that emerged from a shift in writers' employment prospects in the second half of the twentieth century and shared West's sardonic sense of humor, as Leslie Fiedler noted long ago. "The College Novel," Fiedler wrote,

> resembles the War novel of the Twenties, and especially the Hollywood novel of the Thirties: that other product of the American writer's dream of finding a job not wholly at odds with what he is driven to do, whether it pays or not. The encounter between such a dream and the reality to which its dreamer awakes is bound to eventuate in a catastrophe at once comic and horrible, a pratfall from which the comedian does not rise again.[23]

As the studio system collapsed—as the number of films produced plummeted and opportunities for subsidiary rights sales followed in kind; as story and screenwriting departments shrank or closed entirely—writers looked elsewhere, and especially to the university, for stable work.

Also published in 1952, *The Groves of Academe*, which Mary McCarthy wrote after her stint teaching at Bard College, features the great Buck Mulliganesque Joyce scholar Henry "Hen" Mulcahey, who emblematizes the transition from the Hollywood novel to the campus novel that Fiedler observed. Hen's mind is shaped as much by Hollywood as by his Jesuit training (a fact that would dismay him, were he aware of it). The tragicomedy of *Groves* properly begins with Hen's discovery that the "sentimental appeal" of his wife's fragile health might persuade the Jocelyn College administrators to reverse their decision to not renew his teaching contract. Hen convinces himself of the gravity of his wife's illness while meditating on a warning a doctor may or may not have given him: "'I will not answer for the consequences'—his thought grimly fastened on this phrase, which he had heard in so many movies that he could not recall whether it had actually been pronounced to him by one of the family's many physicians or whether it was simply the gist, the hard core of what they had kept telling him."[24] If, as Michael Trask argues, *The Groves of Academe* exemplifies the academic novel's consistent thematization of make-believe, Hen's hypothetical exploitation of his wife's infirmity here indexes Hollywood fiction as the antecedent of the campus novel's pervasive sense of unreality.[25] As it had earlier hovered over Gatsby's parties, animated Sutpen's Hundred, and infused horror in Jacques Laruelle's Day of the Dead, the spirit of the studio system, now a ghostly afterimage, haunts the program era's signature genre.

***

But since, in 1952, the movies officially earned their right to speak, it's only fair to give the movies themselves the chance to speak this book's last words.

While the debacle of *The Red Badge of Courage* unfolded, MGM had in production two historical backstudio pictures, each of which offered a different view of how the studio might persist in the post-*Paramount* world. The more famous one, *Singin' in the Rain* (Gene Kelly and Stanley Donen, 1952), was produced by Arthur Freed's profitable musicals unit. As Ross reports, the company chose to screen this movie at the stockholders' meeting of 1952, and it's easy to see why it did. Set in 1928–1929, amidst the transition to sound cinema and before the major fallout of the stock market crash, *Singin' in the Rain* is, as everyone knows, a story about Don Lockwood (Gene Kelly), a successful silent film actor, who helps Kathy Selden (Debbie Reynolds), an aspiring actress, merge her image and her voice to become a star of musicals. The resolution saves Don, who finds renewed purpose in his life and work as a star himself (he no longer is and believes himself to be a mere "shadow on film," as Kathy mocked his silent-era "dumbshow") and rescues Monumental Studios from an obsolescence figured as MGM's nightmare: control by the outmoded but contractually powerful silent-era star Lina Lamont (Jean Hagen).

In line with MGM's ethos and aesthetic throughout the era of the studio system, *Singin' in the Rain* prioritizes the glamor and sparkle of its stars. Yet more fundamentally, the musical prioritizes the voice of the corporation and should therefore be understood as a successor to *Bombshell*, the backstudio comedy that explained the persistence of the MGM Idea after the end of Irving Thalberg's oversight in 1933. For just as Lola Burns's platinum blonde luster shone brightly against publicity man Space

Hanlon and was controlled by the corporate voice he channeled, in *Singin' in the Rain* Don and Kathy are able to constellate thanks to the gravity of Cosmo Brown (Donald O'Connor), Lockwood's music man. Crucially, Cosmo has the understanding of sound required by the talkies, an understanding that manifests in singing, tapdancing, piano playing, and, most importantly, expressing the right Idea. It is Cosmo who, after the failure of *The Duelling Cavalier*'s preview and Don's dark night of the soul, discovers the necessary separability of voice and body in sync-sound film that allows Kathy to substitute for Lina Lamont and ultimately replace her; and it is Cosmo who proposes reconfiguring *The Duelling Cavalier* as the self-reflexive musical *The Dancing Cavalier*. There is simply no "Good Morning" for Don, Kathy, or Monumental Studios without the sound thinking of Cosmo, just as there is, according to *Singin' in the Rain*, no success for MGM without its own music man, Arthur Freed.

Where *Singin' in the Rain* is a Technicolor confection that celebrates making 'em laugh through song and dance—the highest value of a Hollywood movie, as Cosmo teaches Don in the film and Freed taught Ross amidst the *Red Badge of Courage* debacle—*The Bad and the Beautiful* is a black-and-white melodrama originated by *Citizen Kane* producer and Hollywood liberal John Houseman, newly arrived at MGM thanks to Schary. Houseman, director Vincente Minnelli, and writer Charles Schnee transformed *The Bad and the Beautiful*'s source material, a short story about a talented and conniving Broadway producer, in order to differentiate the movie from *All About Eve* and capitalize on the recent cycle of critical backstudio revelations that included *In a Lonely Place* and *Sunset Boulevard*. *The Bad and the Beautiful* tells the history of powerful, charismatic, uncompromising, and ultimately doomed Jonathan Shields (Kirk Douglas), a second-generation Hollywood producer intent on resuscitating his father's studio. Jonathan's voice is never heard in the movie's narrative present; his rise and fall are described by director Fred Amiel (Barry Sullivan), star Georgia Lorrison (Lana Turner), and writer James Lee Bartlow (Dick Powell), former friends and associates who found themselves enthralled and manipulated by Jonathan. Because of its sensational stories of personal betrayal in the industry, MGM's lawyers took great care to ensure that no character resembled any real-life personage too closely. Jonathan, the "genius boy" obsessed with his father's failure who finds himself exiled from his namesake studio, draws from three of MGM's major personalities: most obviously Selznick, but also Thalberg, the original boy genius, and Mayer (as well as Orson Welles and Val Lewton).

However, because Minnelli and Schnee meticulously blended their originals, the characters effectively become mythic archetypes of Hollywood personalities even as their actions and behaviors remain vivid. Likewise, the moments recollected by Fred, Georgia, and James Lee evoke quite specific associations in the career of MGM even as they refer to major moments in industry history. Unlike *Singin' in the Rain*, which emerged from MGM's desire to exploit Freed and Nacio Herb Brown's catalogue of songs and therefore literally derives its Hollywood history from Freed's creative history, *The Bad and the Beautiful* tells its history of Hollywood as a literary history. Jonathan's rise to prominence in 1934, his industry dominance in 1945, and his failure resulting in self-exile to France in 1949 all center on cases of ostensibly impossible adaptation. In his ability to wrangle even the most recalcitrant—the most prestigious—source texts onto the screen and turn them to a profit, he is the ideal producer, the vision of an MGM man at the height of the classical era. When he falls, it is because he does not adapt himself to Hollywood's new reality, a reality in which the pictures themselves have become literary.

Itching for bigger projects after the breakout success of B horror picture *The Doom of the Cat Men*, Fred presents Jonathan with his "baby," the script for an adaptation of *The Far Away Mountain* (a novel that exists only in the fiction of the film). Jonathan calls it a "great book" but one that "three studios tried to lick … and couldn't." Jonathan and Fred don't indicate why it's great or why it's unadaptable, nor do they explain how they ultimately lick it, credit for which Jonathan steals. All of the forces militating against adaptation during the studio era therefore come into play (Figure 6.1). The title, reminiscent of Thomas Mann's *The Magic Mountain* (1924), conjures a sense of literary prestige and narrative complexity. Its content, a story of a revolution in an unnamed Latin American country, suggests the kind of political narrative inimical to conservative MGM's modus operandi in the mid-1930s. Commenting on the studio's lack of interest in Faulkner's final completed screenplay, the untitled "Mythical Latin-American Kingdom Story," story editor Sam Marx explained, "Back in my day they stayed away from revolution stories, Central American in particular."[26] And 1934 is, of course, the beginning of Joseph Breen's tenure at the Production Code Administration, indicating that *The Far Away Mountain*'s difficulties might be moral as well as formal, a possibility obliquely suggested by a screentest featuring the beginning of a seduction scene. According to MGM's production files, *The Far Away Mountain* had originally been called "Blood Money," a title that evokes the category of unadaptable "red meat" pulp tales, exemplified by James M. Cain's *The*

Figure 6.1 "*The Far Away Mountain* … three studios tried to lick it and failed." *The Bad and the Beautiful* (Vincente Minnelli, MGM, 1952)

Postman Always Rings Twice.²⁷ As we saw in Chapter 5, after buying the rights to *Postman* in 1934, MGM's proposed script finally cleared the PCA a decade later, with Lana Turner starring as Cora Papadakis in her first major dramatic role.

Production of *Postman* began in 1945, the same year that, in the fictional world of *The Bad and the Beautiful*, Jonathan, at his late-World War II peak in power, decides to turn Georgia, a Hollywood washout, into a star. Jonathan assumes his role as Pygmalion when coaching Georgia, who has been cast in a bit part in an untitled crime melodrama, to behave as the type of femme fatale that Cora Papadakis epitomizes. Appropriately, Georgia starts on her path with a smoldering delivery of her one line— "Read anything good lately?"—while framed against a rack of paperbacks, a novel by Ben Hecht, the greatest screenwriter of the era, just behind her (Figure 6.2). Jonathan's desire to "make a star out of someone this town tossed on the ash heap"—to prove that he could make a star from nothing, just as Cosmo Brown and Don Lockwood could turn Lina Lamont back into nothing—coincides with his ability to bring a book destined for the gutter to the screen.

Conclusion: Read Anything Good Lately?

Figure 6.2 "Read anything good lately?"
The Bad and the Beautiful (Vincente Minnelli, MGM, 1952)

Jonathan ultimately fails, however, for the same reason that Lina fails: he thinks he's bigger than his studio. As Schenck's deposing of Mayer made clear, no man, not even a namesake, can be a corporation. But where Lina's fatal flaw is her lack of talent, Jonathan's is his loss of contact with reality, which the fictional director Von Ellstein would call his lack of "humility." In that regard, he is as much *The Last Tycoon*'s Monroe Stahr as he is Lina Lamont. In 1949, Jonathan assumes that he could direct as well as produce and cowrite the script for *Proud Land*, an adaptation of James Lee's historical novel of Virginia, which, in its epic sweep and Civil War setting, bears more than a passing resemblance to Selznick and MGM's *Gone with the Wind*, up to that point both the most profitable film of all time and the film with the most Academy Award nominations (in the world of *The Bad and the Beautiful*, *All About Eve* was but a gleam in Fox's eye). Ten years earlier, in 1939, Selznick could exercise nearly the same degree of control over the adaptation of Margaret Mitchell's novel and set the industry standard for the blockbuster. In contrast, in 1949, the year of economization, the studios turned away from expensive literary properties; it was the year of MGM's *Battleground*, which, according to Jerome Christensen, was the decisive picture of Dore Schary's early years as head of production at the studio. Based on an original story by Robert Pirosh and produced well under budget, *Battleground* demonstrated Schary's ability to reverse the studio's fortunes by updating what Christensen calls "the trope of social adjustment that was the studio's distinctive device of the 1930s."[28] Jonathan fails precisely because of his inability to adjust to MGM's vision of the post-*Paramount* world. Just as Dix Steele's career is killed by *Althea Bruce*, so Jonathan is undone by the kind of novel that studios were then refusing to buy. If Jonathan is to make his comeback, an open question at the movie's end, more adjustments, literary and otherwise, would be necessary.

If we're willing to accept that *The Bad and the Beautiful* tells MGM's version of the literary history of the studio system, we might then wonder what it's leaving out. Certain remarkable coincidences indicate one such omission. The fictional author James Lee Bartlow, writer of the South-set novel *Proud Land* and so, ostensibly, a Faulkner type, nonetheless bears a striking resemblance to the real-life author Ross Lockridge, Jr., like James Lee a Harvard- and Sorbonne-educated professor who took a fateful trip to Hollywood in the late 1940s after his novel *Raintree County* (1948) won MGM's semiannual novel award (Figure 6.3). A 1,000-page novel set in a fictional municipality in Indiana, *Raintree County* was Lockridge's self-conscious attempt to write the Great American Novel and give shape to nothing less than the myth of America. Like *Ulysses* and *Mrs. Dalloway*, which inspired Lockridge, and the contemporary *Under the Volcano*, to which it was compared, *Raintree County* occurs on a single day, Independence Day 1892. Flashing back across the nineteenth century by way of the memories and dreams of an everyman hero, John Wickliff Shawnessy, the novel draws on Freud and Frazer and follows the form of *Intolerance* and *Citizen Kane*; its harrowing depictions of the siege of Chattanooga and the burning of Atlanta evoke *Gone with the Wind* and look forward to Jonathan's adaptation of *Proud Land*.[29] To the Joyce scholar William York Tindall, *Raintree County* was nearly a dream alternative to an impoverished middlebrow literature, a work that "succeeded in narrowing, if not entirely closing, the space that has separated the general reader from the many-leveled novel. Adapting Joyce and Woolf, [Lockridge] served a wider audience without the loss of value that might be supposed." For Tindall, *Raintree County* was a vision of what American modernism might become in an era of liberal consensus.[30] But to my eye, it looks like the culmination of the forty-year trajectory this book has traced. *Raintree County*, even more evidently than *Under the Volcano*, attempted to bring into harmony the high modernism Lockridge loved and the studio system's vernacular modernism.

Figure 6.3 James Lee Bartlow, author of *Proud Land*. *The Bad and the Beautiful* (Vincente Minnelli, MGM, 1952).

That dream synthesis would not, however, come to fruition. MGM wouldn't deliver the award if the novel wasn't selected for the Book of the Month Club, and Book of the Month wouldn't choose *Raintree County* unless Lockridge cut 50,000 words—portions in a stream-of-consciousness style—from a novel he spent seven years writing. Thus began Lockridge's fraught negotiations with MGM, Book of the Month, and his publisher Houghton Mifflin, a conflict that sapped his health and led him to vacation with his wife in Los Angeles. There, Lockridge met with MGM representatives in Culver City; although his interactions were initially pleasant, his mental health declined rapidly, leading him to cancel his meeting with *The Postman Always Rings Twice* producer Carey Wilson and return early to Bloomington. Three months later, on March 6, 1948, exhausted and depressed following unsympathetic reviews, Lockridge took his own life. Seven months after that, MGM, whose exorbitant spending and large overhead costs had become especially onerous in the postwar downturn, announced plans to sell the rights to Lockridge's novel, along with 242 other stories and 135 plays by other authors, in the hope of raising a million dollars.[31]

It would be excessively melodramatic—more melodramatic than any Minnelli—to say that MGM killed Ross Lockridge, Jr. It would be much fairer to say that in his effort to make his book palatable to the studio— to write with the movies in mind, as so many authors had since 1912— Lockridge overstressed his health as he compromised his artistic conscience. And it would be only somewhat fanciful to say that, circulating within the unconscious of the studio's library of properties and reconfigured in the daylight dreamwork of *The Bad and the Beautiful*, there existed within MGM a literary history it would rather forget.

Notes

Introduction

1 William Empson, *Seven Types of Ambiguity* (New York: New Directions, 1947 [1930]), 47.
2 Here, I hazard a conflation of two distinct meanings of "institution": of social forms governed by rules and norms (e.g., the "family, religion, state" that underpin Stephen Greenblatt's work in *Renaissance Self-Fashioning*); and of what institutional economists call an "organization," that is, agents (e.g., firms) that operate with respect to the conventions of broader institutions. The story of one influential strand of post-Marxian literary criticism and theory over the past thirty years has been the gradual shift in emphasis from the former sense to the latter by way of the American uptake of Pierre Bourdieu's sociology. The landmark study of the latter kind, Mark McGurl's *The Program Era: Postwar Fiction and the Rise of Creative Writing*, in fact manages a synthesis of the two approaches by incorporating insights from Niklas Luhmann's systems theory. For a useful overview of treatments of the "New Institutionalisms" in modernist studies, see Robert Higney, *Institutional Character: Collectivity, Individuality, and the Modernist Novel* (Charlottesville: University of Virginia Press, 2022), 49.
3 Interestingly, these first uses of "studio system" (at least as they are available through publications collected by the Media History Digital Library) appear in Epes Winthrop Sargent's advice to writers of scenarios. See Epes Winthrop Sargent, "The Scenario Writer," *Moving Picture World*, December 23, 1911: 981; Epes Winthrop Sargent, "The Scenario Writer," *Moving Picture World*, March 2, 1912: 765. For an early use of the contemporary sense of "studio system," see Edwin Schallert, "This Question of Extravagance," *Picture-Play Magazine*, May 1924:

> It wasn't that there was any sudden and disastrous suspension of work, except possibly at one or two studios, for the most part popular actors went right ahead getting jobs. It was rather that the successes of the year, which had been purchased for such a huge outlay, left the pessimistic sentiment behind them that the producers had overtaxed themselves financially. *Any number of knowing authorities can, in fact, be found who blast and condemn what they call the studio system*, and also take a violent whack at what they say is squandered for settings and stars. While they do not discount the public demand for better pictures, they express emphatic doubts as to whether

    any of the bigger productions can make money, because there are so many of them. (48, my emphasis)
 4 Thomas Schatz, *The Genius of the System: Hollywood Filmmaking in the Studio Era* (New York: Metropolitan, 1996 [1988]); Douglas Gomery, *The Hollywood Studio System: A History* (London: BFI Publishing, 2005).
 5 David Bordwell, Janet Staiger, and Kristin Thompson, *The Classical Hollywood Cinema* (New York: Columbia University Press, 1985), 4.
 6 John Thornton Caldwell, *Production Culture: Industrial Reflexivity and Critical Practice in Film and Television* (Durham, NC and London: Duke University Press, 2008), 111.
 7 For instance, Mann writes in her study of the rise of independent filmmaking between 1947 and 1960 that Caldwell's "methodology can be usefully adapted to the increasingly 'knowing' participation of independent filmmakers in the proto-postmodern New Hollywood." Denise Mann, *Hollywood Independents: The Postwar Talent Takeover* (Minneapolis: University of Minnesota Press, 2008), 24. Jurca's *Hollywood 1938*, a study of the industry's first major public relations campaign, is in line with the Caldwell approach insofar as it reads films themselves as expressions of studio intentions. Jurca does not cite Caldwell but does cite Christensen; this indicates that the reconciliation of Caldwell and Christensen was already underway before Connor's essential synthesis in *The Studios after the Studios: Neoclassical Hollywood (1970–2010)* (Palo Alto, CA: Stanford University Press, 2014).
 8 I owe this insight, and many others, to conversations with J.D. Connor.
 9 Jerome Christensen, *Lord Byron's Strength: Romantic Writing and Commercial Society* (Baltimore and London: Johns Hopkins University Press, 1993), xvii.
10 Christensen, *Lord Byron*, xvii; Christensen, *America's Corporate Art*, 158, 160.
11 J.D. Connor, *Studios after the Studios*, 11.
12 Christensen, *America's Corporate Art*, 7.
13 Empson, *Seven Types of Ambiguity*, 46.
14 Christensen, *America's Corporate Art*, 14. Interestingly, Christensen implicitly formulated his theory of the corporate author as both an evolution and an inversion of his theory of the literary career. Where the critic observes an abstracted virtual career from the literary artifacts produced by the biographical Byron in the "'overshading' of character onto poet, poet onto poem, poem onto reader, time after time," he infers the existence of a corporate author from the meaningful movies they underwrite and brand with their logos (Christensen, *Lord Byron*, xx).
15 Jerome Christensen, *Practicing Enlightenment: Hume and the Formation of a Literary Career* (Madison, WI: University of Wisconsin Press, 1987), 5.
16 Christensen, *America's Corporate Art*, 14.
17 Christensen is clearest on the equation of corporate personality and corporate strategy in "Studio Authorship, Corporate Art," *Auteurs and Authorship: A Film Reader*, ed. Barry Keith Grant (Malden, MA and Oxford: Blackwell Publishing, 2008), 167–179, especially 176: "[Kenneth R.] Andrews' corporate executive is an *actor* who interprets a set of decisions as establishing the

character of the organization, which he impersonates in order to make a decision that will accomplish corporate objectives and do so as if the corporation, not he, were the author of that strategy."

18 Michael Szalay, *New Deal Modernism: American Literature and the Invention of the Welfare State* (Durham, NC: Duke University Press, 2000), 233–244; Donal Harris, *On Company Time: American Modernism in the Big Magazines* (New York: Columbia University Press, 2016), 107–150; and Lisa Siraganian, *Modernism and the Meaning of Corporate Persons* (New York and Oxford, UK: Oxford University Press, 2021). On the corporation's presence in the mind of America in the early twentieth century, see Roland Marchand, *Creating the Corporate Soul: The Rise of Public Relations and Corporate Imagery in American Big Business* (Berkeley and Los Angeles: University of California Press, 1998).

19 Siraganian, *Corporate Persons*, 34.

20 Mark Goble, *Beautiful Circuits: Modernism and the Mediated Life* (New York: Columbia University Press, 2010), 10.

21 Steven G. Kellman, "The Cinematic Novel: Tracking a Concept," *Modern Fiction Studies* 33, no. 3 (Autumn 1987): 467–477.

22 Miriam Hansen, "Vernacular Modernism: Tracking Cinema on a Global Scale," *World Cinemas, Transnational Perspectives*, eds. Nataša Durovicová and Kathleen Newman (New York and Oxford, UK: Routledge, 2010), 295. When they have taken up Hansen's theory, scholars of literary modernism have done so in order to indicate Hollywood film's role in creating the twentieth century's "new sensory culture" or the American cinema's visual inventiveness and narrative complexity. What they have neglected is Hansen's critique of Hollywood as an institution. See, among others, Genevieve Abravanel, *Americanizing Britain: The Rise of Modernism in the Age of the Entertainment Empire* (New York and Oxford, UK: Oxford University Press, 2013), 89; Foltz, *Novel After Film*, 237n59; Laura Frost, *The Problem with Pleasure: Modernism and Its Discontents* (New York: Columbia University Press, 2013), 27; and Brooks Hefner, *The Word on the Streets: The American Language of Vernacular Modernism* (Charlottesville, VA: University of Virginia Press, 2017), 88. For an important exception, albeit one in which the ramifications of Hansen's argument are touched on only briefly, see Patrick Jagoda, "Hollywood and the American Novel," *The Oxford History of the Novel in English: Volume 6: The American Novel 1870–1940*, eds. Priscilla Wald and Michael A. Elliot (New York: Oxford University Press, 2014), 501–516.

23 Miriam Hansen, "The Mass Production of the Senses: Classical Cinema as Vernacular Modernism," *Modernism/modernity* 6, no. 2 (April 1999): 68.

24 Siraganian, *Corporate Persons*, 34. This understudied strand of 1930s neo-naturalism supplements work undertaken on what Jeff Allred has called "documentary modernism." Though he doesn't put it in quite these terms (he prefers "proto-modernist"), Allred sees a similar transformation of a naturalist form, in his case the photojournalism inaugurated by Jacob Riis's *How the Other Half Lives* (1890). Where, for Allred, Riis recorded injustice while affirming the authority of the more fortunate half, "the modernist

documentary book represents social others in ways that arrest or interrupt, rather than confirm, dominant ideologies." Jeff Allred, *American Modernism and Depression Documentary* (Oxford, UK and New York: Oxford University Press, 2010), 12, 7.

25 Clayton R. Koppes, "Regulating the Screen: The Office of War Information and the Production Code Administration," in Thomas Schatz, *Boom and Bust: American Cinema in the 1940s* (Berkeley and Los Angeles: University of California Press, 1999 [1997]), 262.
26 *A King in New York / A Woman of Paris* (2 Disc Special Edition), Warner Home Video. Sarah Gleeson-White expresses a similar wonder at the lack of attention to Barton and Loos's Camille in the introduction *to Silent Film and the Formations of US Literary Culture: Literature in Motion* (Oxford, UK and New York: Oxford University Press, 2024).
27 Bruce Kellner, *The Last Dandy, Ralph Barton: American Artist, 1891–1931* (Columbia, MO and London, UK: University of Missouri Press, 1991), 152.
28 Though filmed predominantly in Barton's home studio, the movie also contains footage shot in Central Park, Paris, and Salzburg. Frederick James Smith, "What the Amateurs are Doing," *Photoplay*, April 1927, 127. *Photoplay* spared no hyperbole in extolling the greatness of Barton's *Camille*: "Ralph Barton, the well-known caricaturist who has contributed frequently to PHOTOPLAY, is just completing a burlesque version of 'Camille' with the most remarkable cast ever gathered for an amateur film play."
29 Barton's entreaties to Pringle were decidedly less urbane than the one he sent to Mencken:
> GLAD YOU ARE BRINGING UP THE BOYS PROPERLY BUT WHAT ABOUT ME I AM POSTPONING SUICIDE TILL I GET ANSWER TO MY WIRE TELL HENRY I AS PERFECT TYPE RESERVE JOE CANNON ROLE TO MYSELF BUT DESPERATELY NEED CHERUBIM FOR GREATER RELIGIOUS TABLEAU AT END OF PICTURE BEST LOVE TO YOU AND FAMILY
> RALPH

Ralph Barton, telegram to Aileen Pringle, November 9, 1926, Aileen Pringle Collection, Beinecke Library, Yale University, Box 1, Folder 2.
30 For a full account of the players in Barton and Loos's *Camille*, see Kellner, *The Last Dandy*, 251–252.
31 Susan Hegeman, "Taking *Blondes* Seriously," *American Literary History* 7, no. 3 (Autumn 1995): 525.
32 Anita Loos, *Gentlemen Prefer Blondes: The Illuminating Diary of a Professional Lady* (New York: Penguin, 1998 [1925]), 17. Future citations as (*GPB* pp).
33 Anita Loos, "Biography of the Book," in *Gentlemen Prefer Blondes: The Illuminating Diary of a Professional Lady* (New York: Penguin, 1998 [1963]), xxxvii.
34 Anita Loos, *But Gentlemen Marry Brunettes* (New York: Penguin, 1998 [1928]), 138.
35 See, for instance, Laura Marcus, *The Tenth Muse* (Oxford, UK and New York: Oxford University Press, 2007).

1 Paramount Pictures and Transmedial Possibility

1. William Lord Wright, "Hints for Scenario Writers," *Picture-Play Magazine*, July 1919, 74, emphasis in the original.
2. John Dos Passos, *Manhattan Transfer* (Boston: Houghton Mifflin, 2000 [1925]), 262–263.
3. *The Story of the Famous Players-Lasky Corporation: Paramount-Artcraft Motion Pictures* (New York: Famous Players-Lasky Corporation, 1919), 5.
4. "Accused of Hushing Movie Men's Revels," *New York Times*, July 12, 1921, 13; Mark Lynn Anderson, "The Historian Is Paramount," *Film History* 26, no. 2 (2014): 9–10. My sincere thanks to Mark for helping firm up the historical specificity of Dos Passos's references to the organization.
5. "The Famous Players-Lasky Corporation to Proceed with Big Times Square Project," *New York Times*, March 8, 1925, S6; Douglas Gomery, "What Was Adolph Zukor Doing in 1927?" *Film History* 17, nos. 2–3 (2005): 205.
6. *The Story of the Famous Players-Lasky Corporation*, 11.
7. F. Scott Fitzgerald, *As Ever, Scott Fitz—: Letters between F. Scott Fitzgerald and His Literary Agent Harold Ober, 1919–1940*, ed. Matthew J. Bruccoli (Philadelphia: Lippincott, 1972), 66.
8. Simone Murray, *The Adaptation Industry: The Cultural Economy of Contemporary Literary Adaptation* (New York and Oxford, UK: Routledge, 2012).
9. "Cinema of attraction" and "cinema of narrative integration" appear frequently in Gunning's work on early cinema. See, for instance, Tom Gunning, *D. W. Griffith and the Origins of American Narrative Film: The Early Years at Biograph* (Urbana and Chicago: University of Illinois Press, 1991).
10. Peter Decherney, *Hollywood's Copyright Wars: From Edison to the Internet* (New York: Columbia University Press, 2012), 54–57.
11. Ibid.
12. Charlie Keil and Shelley Stamp, eds, *American Cinema's Transitional Era: Audiences, Institutions, Practices* (Berkeley: University of California Press, 2004), 2. All of the developments listed here appear in Keil and Stamp's introduction save for the adaptation of literary classics, which is addressed by Roberta E. Pearson in her essay "The Menace of the Movies: Cinema's Challenge to the Theater in the Transitional Period," 315–321, and at greater length in William Uricchio and Roberta E. Pearson, *Reframing Culture: The Case of the Vitagraph Quality Films* (Princeton, NJ: Princeton University Press, 1993).
13. W. Stephen Bush, "Factory or Studio," *Moving Picture World*, September 21, 1912, 1153. Note that the quotations are unattributed in the original.
14. For more on Harrison's criticism, see Jordan Brower and Josh Glick, "The Art and Craft of the Screen: Louis Reeves Harrison and the *Moving Picture World*," *Historical Journal of Film, Radio, and Television* 33, no. 4 (December 2013): 533–551.
15. Catherine Kerr, "Incorporating the Star: The Intersection of Business and Aesthetic Strategies in Early American Film," *Business History Review* 64, no. 3 (Autumn 1990): 387.

16 Janet Staiger, "'Tame' Authors and the Corporate Laboratory: Stories, Writers, and Scenarios in Hollywood," *Quarterly Review of Film Studies* 8, no. 4 (1983): 33–45.
17 For instance, in *West of Eden*, a comprehensive study of forty eastern writers' experience in film production, Richard Fine devotes only scant attention to the issue of subsidiary rights ownership (33–34) and to "screenrights" in particular (68–69). For a brief but informative discussion of subsidiary rights, see James L. West III, *American Authors and the Literary Marketplace since 1900* (Philadelphia: University of Pennsylvania Press, 1988).
18 ["Introductory Editorial"], *Bulletin*, April 1913, 1–2.
19 Arthur C. Train, "Ownership of Moving-Picture Rights," *Bulletin*, June 1913, 8–10.
20 "Dramatic and Moving Picture Rights: Recent Decision by Judge Hand," *Bulletin*, March 1914, 13–14.
21 "Assignments of Copyright," *Bulletin*, March 1915, 9.
22 Jeffrey Sconce, qtd. in Richard Maltby, "To Prevent the Prevalent Type of Book: Censorship and Adaptation in Hollywood, 1924–1934," *American Quarterly* 44, no. 4 (December 1992): 557. Jean-Louis Jeannelle conceives of adaptability similarly in "Adaptability: Literature and Cinema Redux," *Studies in French Cinema* 16, no. 2 (May 2016): 95–105.
23 Murray traces these calls but finds that none has resulted in the political-economic analysis she advocates. See Murray, *The Adaptation Industry*, 1–24, 192n1. For a compelling analysis of adaptation during the studio era as it is constrained by economic and institutional prerogatives, see Patrick Faubert, "'Perfect Picture Material': *Anthony Adverse* and the Future of Adaptation Theory," *Adaptation* 4, no. 2 (2010): 180–198.
24 Jay David Bolter and Richard Grusin, *Remediation: Understanding New Media* (Cambridge, MA and London: The MIT Press, 1999).
25 I do not mean to suggest that media act on their own, autonomous of their social development and deployment. Rather, I follow Bolter and Grusin, who write "When we write something like 'digital media are challenging the status of television and film,' we are asking readers to treat this as shorthand. A longer, and less felicitous, version would be that 'the individuals, groups, and institutions that create and use digital media treat these media as improved forms of television and film'" (78).
26 Bolter and Grusin, *Remediation*, 45.
27 It is worth considering whether motion picture rights could be said to engender transmedial possibility given the prior existence of theatrical adaptations of fiction. The Copyright Act of 1870 established dramatic rights as licensable, but only after the International Copyright Act of 1891 did US publishers support domestic fiction strongly enough to make these potential rights a valuable commodities. As theater historian Glenn Loney explains, because producers were required to share profits with both the novelists upon whose work the plays were based as well as with the playwrights, theatrical adaptation was limited to the most successful fiction, by figures such as

Mark Twain and William Dean Howells. With the emergence of the "best seller," however, the pace of dramatic adaptation increased markedly: between 1900 and 1906, "no less than seventy-one novels were adapted for the New York theatres." Loney doubts, though, that authors tailored their fiction to potential dramatic adaptation; he surmises that the best seller and the popular play converged at the "public taste for melodramatic romance and local color stories," resulting in "the same inane simplicity of plot, character, and thought." Moreover, it is unlikely that dramatic adaptation was ever common enough to register in the mind of the fiction writer. During the period studied by Loney, roughly ten novels were translated into New York stage productions each year. By comparison, out of 585 dramatic films (i.e., not including "educationals and short comedies") produced in 1918 that were included in the National Board of Review's *A Garden of American Motion Pictures*, a publication detailing films deemed appropriate by the organization, 190 were adapted from source material in other media. Of those adaptations, 121 came from "Modern novels [i.e., not classics] and magazine stories," 59 from "stage plays or operas," 4 from "poems," and 17 from "Other literature, classic or unquestionably standard." The next edition of *A Garden* found that the percentage of total adaptations was even greater in 1919: where 32 percent of films in 1918 were adaptations (190 of 585), the number climbed to 36 percent (139 of 382) in the last three quarters of 1919. The legitimate stage therefore required far less narrative material than the film industry at the moment of the feature film's ascendancy. Because the quantity of adaptation from page to stage during its height differs by an order of magnitude from the quantity of adaptation from both fiction and drama to the silent screen, it makes sense to treat them as different phenomena with correspondingly different effects on the form of source material. See Glenn Loney, "The Heyday of the Dramatized Novel," *Educational Theatre Journal* 9, no. 3 (1957): 196, 197, 199; "The Sources of Motion Picture Stories," *Moving Picture World*, June 7, 1919,: 1501; "Sources of Motion Pictures," *Bulletin*, June 1920, 11–12.

28 Decherney, *Hollywood's Copyright Wars*, 5.
29 "Eminent Authors Pictures Formed," *Moving Picture World*, June 7, 1919, 1469.
30 "Sixteen Noted Authors Writing Original Stories for Paramount," *Exhibitors' Herald*, June 4, 1921, 82.
31 Louis Pizzitola, *Hearst over Hollywood: Power, Passion, and Propaganda in the Movies* (New York: Columbia University Press, 2002), 190, my emphasis.
32 Whitman Bennett, Letter to Charles Eyton, October 18, 1919, Adolph Zukor Correspondence, Margaret Herrick Library Digital Collections, http://digitalcollections.oscars.org/cdm/ref/collection/p15759coll3/id/118.
33 "Hold Film Rights," *Wid's Daily*, March 2, 1921, 1; "Literary Shop Talk," *The Writer*, May 1921, 69–70.
34 William Prichard Eaton, "The Latest Menace of the Movies," *The North American Review* 212, no. 776 (July 1920): 81–83.

35 Jesse L. Lasky, "What Kind of a 'Menace' Are the Movies?" *The North American Review* 212, no. 776 (July 1920): 89.
36 Ida Donnally Peters, "The Play's the Thing," *The Writer's Monthly* 22, no. 3 (September 1923): 227, 226.
37 Whitman Bennett, "The Artistic Influence of the Motion Picture," *Munsey's*, June 1920, 107.
38 Ibid.
39 Wright, "Hints for Scenario Writers," 74–75, emphasis in the original.
40 "The Gossip Shop," *The Bookman*, December 1920, 378–379.
41 Burton Rascoe, "The Motion Pictures: An Industry, Not an Art," *The Bookman*, November 1921, 193–199.
42 For fascinating case studies of transmedial consideration by authors during the 1940s centered on the representation of African Americans, see Elizabeth Binggeli, "Burbanking Bigger and Bette the Bitch," *African American Review* 40, no. 3 (Fall 2006), 475–492, and Elizabeth Binggeli, "The Unadapted: Warner Bros. Reads Zora Neale Hurston," *Cinema Journal* 48, no. 3 (Spring 2009): 1–15.
43 Fred W. Beetson, Letter to J. Homer Platten, July 21, 1924, MPPDA Digital Archive, Flinders University Library Special Collections MPPDA Record #162. Resolution: 1-1602. Web. 30 October 2014. http://mppda.flinders.edu.au/records/162.
44 "Film Reform to Redeem All Modern Fiction," *Los Angeles Times*, August 24, 1924, B22.
45 Richard Maltby, "'To Prevent the Prevalent Type of Book': Censorship and Adaptation, 1924–1934," *American Quarterly* 44, no. 4 (1992): 561.
46 My model proceeds from the scheme that Mark Eaton proposes in his insightful essay "What Price Hollywood? Modern American Writers and the Movies," who acknowledges his own debt to Edmund Wilson's seminal *The Boys in the Back Room*: "we might envision Hollywood's influence on modern American fiction as occurring in one of three ways: as a conscious or unconscious pressure on literary form; as an influence on literary content; and as a major source of income for writing through selling screen rights to novels and stories as well as through screenwriting contracts" (472). This model moves beyond that of Wilson and Eaton by (1) suggesting the historical specificity of the relation among those three ways, and (2) by indicating that all works produced exist within the matrix of transmedial possibility, which exerts influence on both form and content. Mark Eaton, "What Price Hollywood? Modern American Writers and the Movies," *A Companion to the Modern American Novel, 1900–1950*, ed. John T. Matthews (Oxford, UK: Wiley-Blackwell, 2009), 466–495.
47 George Randolph Chester and Lillian Chester, *On the Lot and Off* (New York: Harper & Brothers, 1924), 102.
48 See, for instance, "MERTON IS REALLY IN THE MOVIES NOW: Star of Stage Success to be Seen on Screen in Original Role," *Los Angeles Times*, June 8, 1924, B13.

49 John Emerson and Anita Loos, *The Whole Town's Talking: A Farce in Three Acts* (London and New York: Samuel French, 1924), 74.
50 Ibid., 78.
51 Susan Hegeman, "Taking Blondes Seriously," *American Literary History* 7, no. 3 (Autumn 1995): 546.
52 "Lorelei Lee on Film," *New York Times*, 18 December 1927, X7, quoted in Bethany Wood, "Gentlemen Prefer Adaptations: Addressing Industry and Gender in Adaptation Studies," *Theater Journal* 66, no. 4 (December 2014), 573. Wood's essay is among the best of the post-2010 spate of articles on Loos following Mark McGurl's discussion of Lorelei's vernacular in *The Novel Art* (These include Laura Frost, "Blondes Have More Fun: Anita Loos and the Language of Silent Cinema," *Modernism/modernity* 17, no. 2 (April 2010), 291–311 and Brooks E. Hefner, "'Any Chance to Be Unrefined': Film Narrative Modes in Anita Loos's Fiction," *PMLA* 125, no. 1 (January 2010): 107–120). Wood carefully details the process of translation of *Blondes* from page to stage to screen, with the Paramount film being considered by critics to be inferior to both prior forms. Wood attributes this failure to an attempt to appease the Hays Office by scrubbing the "sophistication" of the play and the "imagination" of the fictional diary (575). In this regard, Wood's analysis of Paramount's *Blondes* rhymes with my account of the company's *Gatsby* below.
53 Hegeman also sees an unlikely resemblance between Lorelei and Loos in their respective efforts at intellectual self-improvement. Hegeman, "Taking Blondes Seriously," 530.
54 Lewis, "Manhattan at Last!," 361.
55 In the eyes of Michael Gold, his erstwhile colleague at *The New Masses*, Dos Passos failed in just these terms: "[T]he book is a failure, perhaps, for the aloofness of the Harvard aesthete still lays a damp, restraining hand on its humanity. We feel no pity, hatred, or love for these bewildered New Yorkers. They move too fast, like the scenery that flashes by a tourist's train. There is description, but not understanding" (93). Michael Gold, "The Education of John Dos Passos," *The English Journal* 22, no. 2 (February 1933), 87–97. Sartre on Dos Passos is quoted in James Naremore, "Film Noir: The History of an Idea," *Film Quarterly* 49, no. 2 (Winter 1995–1996): 22.
56 Kate Marshall, *Corridor: Media Architectures in American Fiction* (Minneapolis: University of Minnesota Press, 2013), 83.
57 John M. Kenny, Jr., *"The Great Gatsby," F. Scott Fitzgerald: In His Own Time: A Miscellany*, eds. Matthew J. Bruccoli and Jackson R. Bryer (Kent, OH: The Kent State University Press, 1971), 358.
58 Michael North, *Camera Works: Photography and the Twentieth-Century Word* (Oxford, UK and New York, 2005), 128; F. Scott Fitzgerald, *The Great Gatsby* (New York: Scribner, 2013 [1925]), 2. Future citations will be noted parenthetically as (*GG* page number). Jonathan Enfield makes a similar point about *The Beautiful and Damned*, arguing that the internal contradictions of the novel can be traced to the unstable combination of realist and romantic modes. See

Enfield, "'A More Glittering, a Grosser Power': American Film and Fiction, 1915–1941," PhD diss., (University of Chicago, 2005).
59 Robert A. Martin, "Hollywood in Fitzgerald: After Paradise," *The Short Stories of F. Scott Fitzgerald: New Approaches in Criticism*, ed. Jackson R. Bryer (Madison: University of Wisconsin Press, 1982), 129–130.
60 Martin, "Hollywood in Fitzgerald," 132.
61 F. Scott Fitzgerald, *The Beautiful and Damned* (New York: Scribner, 2013), 222.
62 Fitzgerald, *As Ever*, 41, 55; Martin, "Hollywood in Fitzgerald," 132. Although critical sources including Wheeler Winston Dixon's "The Three Film Versions of *The Great Gatsby*: A Vision Deferred" (2003) and Eaton's "What Price Hollywood" (2009) have noted that Fitzgerald received $45,000 for the rights to *The Great Gatsby*, this does not seem right given the terms of Fitzgerald's contract with William A. Brady, the producer of the dramatic adaptation of *The Great Gatsby*, and his bookkeeping records for 1926. According to Matthew J. Bruccoli, Fitzgerald's contract with Brady stipulated that the author would receive one-third of the motion picture rights to the novel, and because Fitzgerald reported receiving $16,666 from the film rights to *Gatsby*, it should be assumed that the rights sold for $50,000 to Famous Players-Lasky (see Fitzgerald, *As Ever*, 79, footnote 2). The discrepancy is perhaps due to the fact that, as Fitzgerald clearly notes in his ledger, he paid a 10-percent commission twice: first from $16,6666.66 to $15,000, and then from $15,000 to $13,500. F. Scott Fitzgerald, Ledger, 1919–1938, Matthew J. & Arlyn Bruccoli Collection of F. Scott Fitzgerald, Irvin Department of Special Collections, University of South Carolina: 60. https://digital.tcl.sc.edu/digital/collection/fitz/id/20.
63 Fitzgerald, *As Ever*, 53, 54, 73.
64 Matthew J. Bruccoli, "The Man of Letters as Professional," *F. Scott Fitzgerald on Authorship*, ed. Matthew J. Bruccoli with Judith S. Baughman (Columbia: University of South Carolina Press, 1996), 11.
65 Fitzgerald, *As Ever*, 68.
66 See Pamela Bourgeois and John Clendenning, "Gatsby, Belasco, and Ethnic Ambiguity," *The F. Scott Fitzgerald Review* 6, no. 1 (2007–2008): 105–120.
67 Cass Warner Sperling and Cork Millner, *Hollywood Be Thy Name* (Rocklin, CA: Prima Publishing, 1994), 76–77.
68 Rebecca Walkowitz, "Comparison Literature," *New Literary History* 40, no. 3 (Summer 2009): 569.
69 F. Scott Fitzgerald, *The Crack-Up*, ed. Edmund Wilson (New York: New Directions, 2009 [1945]), 78.
70 Joss Lutz Marsh, "Fitzgerald, *Gatsby*, and *The Last Tycoon*: the 'American Dream' and the Hollywood Dream Factory," *Literature/Film Quarterly* 20, no. 1 (1992): 5.
71 F. Scott Fitzgerald, *Trimalchio: An Early Version of the Great Gatsby*, ed. James L. West III (Cambridge, UK and New York: Cambridge University Press, 2000), 102.

72 Note that the only other mention of "unreal" also unites Gatsby's house with the movies, with the house projecting light "which fell unreal on the shrubbery and made thin elongating glints upon the roadside wires" (Fitzgerald, *The Great Gatsby*, 81). Fitzgerald would confirm the sense of unreality of the movie life in *The Crack-Up*: "Summoned out to Griffith's studio on Long Island, we trembled in the presence of the familiar faces of *The Birth of a Nation*; later I realized that behind much of the entertainment that the city poured forth into the nation there were only a lot of rather lost and lonely people. The world of the picture actors was like our own in that it was in New York and not of it" (29).
73 Kenny, "The Great Gatsby," 357.
74 Maxwell Perkins to F. Scott Fitzgerald, November 20, 1924, *Dear Scott/Dear Max: The Fitzgerald-Perkins Correspondence*, eds. John Kuehl and Jackson R. Bryer (New York: Scribner, 1971), 83; Lawrence Buell, *The Dream of the Great American Novel* (Cambridge, MA: The Belknap Press of Harvard University Press, 2014), 144. In arguing for the movie quality of Gatsby's lack of specificity, I follow Marsh, who writes, "in *Gatsby*, Fitzgerald had *deliberately* constructed not a protagonist or even a character of fiction subject to the conditions of 'development,' 'roundness,' 'individuality,' and 'interiority,' but a 'star'" ("Fitzgerald, *Gatsby*," 5).
75 F. Scott Fitzgerald to Maxwell Perkins, ca. December 20, 1924, *Dear Scott/Dear Max*, 90.
76 Buell, *The Great American Novel*, 141.
77 Cerasulo, *Authors Out Here*, 24; Sally Cline, *Zelda Fitzgerald: Her Voice in Paradise* (London: John Murray Ltd, 2002), 200.
78 See, for instance, Paramount's advertisements for *Gentlemen Prefer Blondes*, which feature star Ruth Taylor sitting atop the cover of the Boni and Liveright edition of the novel. Bethany Wood, *Adapting Women* (Iowa City: Iowa University Press, 2019), 1–2.
79 Abel Green, "The Great Gatsby," *Variety*, November 24, 1926, 14.
80 E.G., "The Great Gatsby," *Motion Picture Magazine*, February 1927, 61.
81 Marguerite Orndorff, "The Theatrical Field," *The Educational Screen*, January 1927, 39.
82 "A Confidential Guide to Current Releases," *Picture-Play Magazine*, April 1927, 70; "Film Estimates," *The Educational Screen*, January 1927, 36.
83 "Brief Reviews of Current Pictures," *Photoplay*, April 1927, 12.
84 "'Great Gatsby' at Metropolitan," *Boston Daily Globe*, November 16, 1926, 14. The critic for *The Billboard* concurred: "Gatsby tries to win the girl, even tho [*sic*] she is married, but in vain. His life is a complete failure, as he admits. The bullet finishes it, disentangling the mess the Chicago man and his wife made of their lives." "Film: 'The Great Gatsby,'" *The Billboard*, December 4, 1926, 63.
85 "Family Life on Long Island," *Picture-Play Magazine*, March 1927, 64, italics in the original.
86 "'The Great Gatsby' Opens Tonight at Palace Theater," *Hartford Courant*, December 5, 1926, C3.

87 "The Great Gatsby," *Film Daily*, November 28, 1926, 13.
88 Agnes Smith, "Just Among Ourselves," *Motion Picture Magazine*, June 1926, 43.
89 Mandy Merck, *Hollywood's American Tragedies: Dreiser, Eisenstein, Sternberg, Stevens* (Oxford, UK and New York: Berg, 2007), 26.
90 See Shelley Stamp, *Movie-Struck Girls: Women and Motion Picture Culture after the Nickelodeon* (Princeton: Princeton University Press, 2000). In his discussion of the "cinematic realism" of *An American Tragedy*, Jonathan Enfield notes that Dreiser departed from the case on which the novel was based and therefore intentionally figured the camera as a murder weapon. Enfield, "'A True Picture of Facts': Cinematic Realism in Dreiser's *An American Tragedy*," *Arizona Quarterly* 66, no. 3 (Autumn 2010): 56–57.
91 Marshall, *Corridor*, 62.
92 Theodore Dreiser, *An American Tragedy* (New York: Library of America, 2003 [1925]), 662.
93 Dreiser, *An American Tragedy*, 734.
94 Dreiser, "The Real Sins of Hollywood," *Liberty*, June 11, 1932: 6.
95 Bordwell, Staiger, and Thompson, *Classical Hollywood*, 13.
96 Lea Jacobs notes an intensifying naturalist tendency in Hollywood filmmaking after *Greed*; these movies, she goes on to note, were rued by the trades as trouble at the box office: "Yet despite the vitality and importance of this tradition, these films occupied a marginal status within the industry. The trade press, and particularly *Variety*, consistently described them as drab and downbeat and unlikely to appeal to a mass audience. Studio executives also seem to have entertained doubts about their commercial viability. That is why so many of these projects suffered extensive interference." Lea Jacobs, *The Decline of Sentiment* (Berkeley: University of California Press, 2008), 77.
97 Walter Benn Michaels, *The Gold Standard: The Cultural Logic of Naturalism* (Berkeley: University of California Press, 1987), 200–201.
98 Frank Norris, *The Octopus: A Story of California* (New York: Penguin, 1994 [1901]), 576.
99 Ibid., 577.
100 On naturalist fiction and early cinema's common relation to the scientific management of time, see Katherine Fusco, *Silent Film and U.S. Naturalist Literature: Time, Narrative, Modernity* (Oxford, UK and New York: Routledge, 2019 [2016]).
101 On the noises of corporate bodies in *The Octopus*, see Daniel J. Mrozowski, "How to Kill a Corporation: Frank Norris's *The Octopus* and the Embodiment of American Business," *Studies in American Naturalism* 6, no. 2 (Winter 2011): 161–184, esp. 166–170.
102 Fine, *West of Eden*, 64.
103 For instance, with respect to the work of William Faulkner, the main subject of Chapter 2, Joseph Urgo reads the collaborative storytelling of Quentin Compson and Shreve McCannon in *Absalom, Absalom!* as a form of screenwriting. More recently, Robert Jackson has queried Faulkner's strong distinction

between the solitary novelist-artist and the collegial filmmaker by enumerating the author's meaningful relationships with his lover Meta Carpenter and the director Howard Hawks. See Urgo, "*Absalom, Absalom!*: The Movie," *American Literature* 62, no. 1 (March 1990): 56–73; Jackson, "Images of Collaboration: William Faulkner's Motion Picture Communities," *Faulkner and Film: Faulkner and Yoknapatawpha, 2010*, eds. Peter Lurie and Ann J. Abadie (Jackson: University of Mississippi Press, 2014), 26–46.
104 Alfred Kazin, *On Native Grounds: An Interpretation of Modern American Prose Literature* (New York: Reynal and Hitchcock, 1942), 369.

2 MGM Modernism

1 Aldous Huxley, *After Many a Summer Dies the Swan* (Chicago, IL: Elephant Paperbacks, 1993 [1939]), 44. Subsequent citations of this edition will be included parenthetically as (*AMS* page number).
2 Fulton Oursler, "Is Hollywood More Sinned Against Than Sinning?" *Liberty Magazine*, June 18, 1932, 23.
3 Schatz, *Genius of the System*, 34.
4 Ibid., 159; Goble, *Beautiful Circuits*, 94. Douglas Gomery notes that Loew's/MGM only briefly led the industry in profits—Paramount took back its leading position in that arena by 1941—but its reputation was still unrivaled. See Gomery, *The Hollywood Studio System*, 99.
5 "Metro-Goldwyn-Mayer," *Fortune*, December 1932, 122.
6 Leo Rosten, *Hollywood: The Movie Colony, the Movie Makers* (New York: Harcourt, Brace and Company, 1941), 56.
7 See, for example, Schatz, *Genius of the System*, 3–15; Gomery, *The Hollywood Studio System*, 1; David Thomson, *The Whole Equation: A History of Hollywood* (New York: Vintage, 2006); Richard Jewell, *RKO Pictures: A Titan is Born* (Berkeley: University of California Press, 2012), 201–211; J.D. Connor, *Hollywood Math and Aftermath* (New York and London: Bloomsbury Academic, 2018), 1–15; and Mark Lynn Anderson, "The Silent Screen: 1895–1927," *Producing*, ed. Jon Lewis (New Brunswick, NJ: Rutgers University Press, 2016), 35.
8 F. Scott Fitzgerald, *The Love of the Last Tycoon: The Authorized Text*, ed. Matthew J. Bruccoli (New York: Scribner, 2003 [1941]), 3. Subsequent citations of this edition will be included parenthetically as (*LT* page number).
9 Fitzgerald was appalled to learn that his daughter Scottie considered taking a course called "English Prose since 1800" at Vassar: "Anybody that can't read modern English prose by themselves is subnormal—and you know it. I don't care how clever the ... professor is, one can't raise a discussion of modern prose to anything above tea-table level. It is a course for clubwomen who want to continue on from *Rebecca* and Scarlett O'Hara." *The Letters of F. Scott Fitzgerald*, 86–87. For a description of the novelty of Bennington's literature program compared to, for example, Wellesley's, see Thomas P. Brockaway, *Bennington College: In the Beginning* (Bennington, VT: Bennington College Press, 1981), 169–182.

10 T.S. Eliot, "Tradition and the Individual Talent," *The Sacred Wood* (New York: Knopf, 1921), 46. Lisa Siraganian similarly likens Eliot's conception of tradition to a corporate person and sees Fitzgerald's conception of Stahr's relation to his studio as an investigation of corporate personhood. Siraganian, *Corporate Persons*, 34, 95–105.
11 F. Scott Fitzgerald, Letter to Kenneth Littauer, September 29, 1939, qtd. in Matthew J. Bruccoli, preface to *The Love of the Last Tycoon*, xiii; T. S. Eliot, "In Memory," *The Little Review: A Magazine of the Arts* 5, no. 4 (August 1918): 46; Matthew J. Bruccoli, *Some Sort of Epic Grandeur: The Life of F. Scott Fitzgerald* (New York: Carroll & Graf Publishers, 1993 [1981]), 256.
12 Mark A. Vieira, *Irving Thalberg: Boy Wonder to Producer Prince* (Berkeley and Los Angeles: University of California Press, 2010), 229.
13 Bruccoli, preface to *The Last Tycoon*, xvii.
14 Christensen, *America's Corporate Art*, 19; William Roy, qtd. in Christensen, *America's Corporate Art*, 19.
15 Seo Hee Im, "Philip K. Dick, Late Modernism, and the Chinese Logic of American Totality," *Modernism/modernity: M/m Print Plus* 4, no. 3 (November, 2019), https://modernismmodernity.org/articles/im-chinese-logic-american-totality.
16 Seo Hee Im, *The Late Modernist Novel: A Critique of Global Narrative Reason* (Cambridge, UK and New York: Cambridge University Press, 2022), 16.
17 Fine, *West of Eden*, 117.
18 Sam Marx, *A Gaudy Spree: The Literary Life of Hollywood in the 1930s When the West Was Fun* (New York and Toronto: Franklin Watts, 1987), 31; Frances Marion, *Off with Their Heads! A Serio-Comic Tale of Hollywood* (New York: Macmillan Company, 1972), 145. Mahin and Marion were among the seventeen or so of nearly one hundred writers who, according to Howard Emmett Rogers, Mahin's colleague in the Screen Playwrights counter-guild, "wrote 90 percent of the productions" at the studio. As Andrew Collins noted in *The New Masses*, that outsize proportion resulted from the manipulative in-house crediting system, a system that the Guild's plan would eventually replace in their June 1941 contract. Andrew Collins, "Hollywood's Yes-Men Say 'No,'" *The New Masses*, August 31, 1937, 8.
19 Schatz, *Genius of the System*, 163.
20 Christensen, *America's Corporate Art*, 62.
21 For an account of the willful perversity and ugliness of Huxley's later novels and an argument for their relationship with the medium of film, see Foltz, *The Novel after Film*, 167–216.
22 William Faulkner to Malcolm Cowley, early November 1944, *Selected Letters*, ed. Joseph Blotner (New York: Random House, 1977), 185; William Faulkner, *Absalom, Absalom!: The Corrected Text*, ed. Noel Polk (New York: Vintage, 1990 [1986]), 176. Future citations will be included parenthetically as (*AA* page number).
23 Faulkner to Cowley, *Selected Letters*, 185.
24 Warwick Wadlington, *Reading Faulknerian Tragedy* (Ithaca and London: Cornell University Press, 1987), 188.

25 Fine, *West of Eden*, 117. On Faulkner's experiences working under Zanuck, see Sarah Gleeson-White, introduction to *William Faulkner at Twentieth Century-Fox: The Annotated Screenplays*, ed. Sarah Gleeson-White (New York and Oxford, UK: Oxford University Press, 2017), 17, and Stefan Solomon, *William Faulkner in Hollywood: Screenwriting for the Studios* (Athens, GA: University of Georgia Press, 2017), 68–73. Zanuck's role in developing Twentieth Century-Fox's persona is addressed in Chapters 3 and 5 of this book.

26 Stephen M. Ross, *Fiction's Inexhaustible Voice: Speech and Writing in Faulkner* (Athens: University of Georgia Press, 1989), 145–147, 220–221.

27 Solomon correctly observes that "if we were to embrace Christensen's persuasive thesis, then we would have to allow that Faulkner had little control over his material, since it proposes such a high level of commercial influence." However, he does not pursue its implications for the interpretation of Faulkner's fiction and instead recapitulates Urgo's argument. My point is that although Urgo presents a compelling picture of Quentin and Shreve's conversation as like collaboration on a screenplay, his argument does not and indeed cannot account for other salient features of the novel that I study here unless it is supplemented by Christensen's theory. Solomon, *William Faulkner in Hollywood*, 10.

28 C.L.R. James, *The Black Jacobins: Toussaint L'Ouverture and the San Domingo Revolution* (New York: Vintage, 1989 [1938]), 392; Thurman Arnold, *The Folklore of Capitalism* (New Haven: Yale University Press, 1956 [1937]), 185–206. This understanding bears affinities with the concept of "plantation modernity" developed by Amy Clukey. See "Plantation Modernity: *Gone with the Wind* and Irish-Southern Culture," *American Literature* 85, no. 3 (September 2013): 505–530.

29 The Hundred can therefore be understood as what Richard Godden has called a "split sign," a semantic unit that indicates the copresence of two opposing meanings corresponding to incommensurate modes of production: while the plantation emblematizes the Southern feudal plantocracy, the socioeconomic structure that Sutpen seeks to dominate, it also serves as an allegory of its ostensible opposite, the Hollywood studio. For Godden's interpretation of split signs elsewhere in Faulkner's writing, see "*As I Lay Dying*, a Horse, a Fish, Telepathy, and Economics," *William Faulkner in the Media Ecology*, ed. Julian Murphet and Stefan Solomon (Baton Rouge: Louisiana State University Press, 2015), 244.

30 Dardis, *Time in the Sun*, 113.

31 Faulkner, *Absalom, Absalom!*, 244.

32 Joseph Blotner, *Faulkner: A Biography: One Volume Edition* (Jackson: University Press of Mississippi, 2005), 305, 310.

33 "Healy Spotted as Lead in MGM Salvage Job," *The Hollywood Reporter*, January 10, 1934, 6. On Freeman's *Ruby*, see Blotner, *Biography*, 316.

34 William Faulkner, "The Art of Fiction No. 12," interview by Jean Stein, *Paris Review* 12 (Spring 1956), reprinted in *The Paris Review Interviews II*, ed. Philip Gourevitch (New York: Picador, 2007), 41–42.

35 Blotner, *Biography*, 317.
36 William Faulkner, *Pylon: The Corrected Text* (New York: Vintage International, 2011 [1935]), 270. Subsequent citations of this edition will be included parenthetically as (*P* page number).
37 Taking Leopold von Sacher-Masoch's *Venus in Furs* as a point of departure, Michaels theorizes the relation between contract and desire in a market economy: "[I]magining the slave as a buyer and seller, the contract at the same time defeudalizes slavery, replacing a social fact that exists independent of the desires of master or slave with a market agreement that insists on and enacts the priority of those desires." Michaels, *The Gold Standard*, 129.
38 William Faulkner to Ben Wasson, February 12, 1933, *Selected Letters*, 70–71, my emphasis. See also Gleeson-White, introduction to *Faulkner at Fox*, 40.
39 Mike Davis, *City of Quartz: Excavating the Future of Los Angeles* (New York: Vintage, 1992), 42–43.
40 Sheila Schwartz, *Hollywood Writers' Wars: The Hollywood Ten and Their Lawyers, January 1948* (New York: Knopf, 1982), 12.
41 On the continuity writer as a "technical expert" distinct from a story writer on the one hand and the continuity clerk (or, because of gendered hiring practices, the "script girl") responsible for eliminating continuity errors on the other, see Bordwell, Staiger, and Thompson, *Classical Hollywood*, 146, 152–153.
42 Faulkner, "The Art of Fiction," 41, my emphasis.
43 In early 1934, around the time he formulated an idea called "Dark House," "an anecdote" about "a man who outraged the land" that would serve as the kernel of *Absalom, Absalom!*, Faulkner proposed a project that indicated both his familiarity with and distaste for the protocols of corporate art production (Faulkner to Harrison Smith, ca. February 1934, *Selected Letters*, 78–79). In February 1934, he wrote his literary agent Morton Goldman about an idea called "A Child's Garden of Motion Picture Scripts," a miscellany of sorts comprising a "burlesque of the sure-fire movies and plays, or say a burlesque of how the movies would treat standard plays and classic plays and novels, written in a modified form of a movie script." He never wrote "A Child's Garden of Motion Picture Scripts," but, as Peter Lurie suggests, the knowledge and insight that would be required to make this project work found its way into his post-MGM fiction (Faulkner to Morton Goldman, late winter/early spring 1934, *Selected Letters*, 79).
44 Robert Jackson makes a similar point here, comparing Faulkner to the architect and Sutpen to either Irving Thalberg or Darryl Zanuck. Jackson, however, is ultimately interested in the different forms of collaboration in which Faulkner participated; his analysis does not extend to a consideration of corporate authorship. See Jackson, "Images of Collaboration," 26–46.
45 Peter Lurie identifies this moment as a crucial point of entry into the cinematic aspects of Faulkner's writing, linking his literary self-consciousness to his "understanding of the apparatus of film" (Lurie, *Vision's Immanence*, 106–107). Lurie suggestively reads Rosa Coldfield's rhetoric as parodying Hollywood films' invariably Romantic representation of the American

South, but he errs, I think, in construing Mr. Compson's image as a sign of Faulkner's knowledge of film equipment, unless, perhaps, this is a case of a rule being proven by its breakage. For this is a very peculiar way of describing the failure of the cinematic apparatus. Having worked for three studios by this point, and, more generally, having grown up with the moving image, Faulkner would have known that this description of celluloid doesn't comport with reality. If a filmstrip actually breaks, the projector casts solid white light on the screen. Alternatively, if the film itself doesn't break but the projector does, the filmstrip would stick and quickly combust, especially in 1909, the moment of Mr. Compson's narration, when film stock was made of highly flammable nitrocellulose. Faulkner refers to the combustibility of film stock while musing on the insubstantiality and tawdriness of Southern California in the most pyrotechnically Faulknerian sentence in "Golden Land," a short story discussed more fully below. Here, Ira Ewing, a wealthy Beverly Hills real estate broker, drifts into an alcohol-induced reverie of Los Angeles, "that city of almost incalculable wealth whose queerly appropriate fate it is to be erected upon a few spools of a substance whose value is computed in billions and which may be completely destroyed in that second's instant of a careless match between the moment of striking and the moment when the striker might have sprung and stamped it out." William Faulkner, *"Golden Land," Collected Stories of William Faulkner* (New York: Vintage International, 1995 [1935]), 718–719. In the *Absalom* instance, something else is clearly going on.

46 William Faulkner, *Light in August: The Corrected Text* (New York: Vintage International, 1990 [1932]), 177.

47 E. J. Clery, introduction to Hugh Walpole, *The Castle of Otranto* (Oxford, UK and New York: Oxford University Press, 1996), xxx–xxxi; Michaels, *The Gold Standard*, 92. In later twentieth-century fiction, authors would continue to use the gothic mode to work through their positions in the conglomerated multimedia-sphere. See Palmer Rampell, "The Shining and the Media Conglomerate; or, How All Work and No Play Made Jack a Creative Artist in the 1970s," *American Literature* 91, no. 1 (March 2019): 151–182.

48 The Agricultural Adjustment Act was a New Deal program that paid plantation owners to plow under their cotton crops in order to ease the glut on the world market and stabilize falling prices. The federal subsidy changed the relationship between planters and sharecroppers; rather than leasing the land to tenants and thereby giving them a share of the subsidy, owners could instead hire those sharecroppers for a wage and thus reap the entire subsidy for themselves. A "Second Reconstruction" resulted, freeing the previously bound labor. Godden thus reads *Absalom* as a novel about dependency, calling attention to the economic mode rendered archaic at the moment of Faulkner's writing. See Godden, *Fictions of Labor*, 115–119.

49 Later, as an adult, when Clytie, Sutpen's enslaved illegitimate daughter, urges her not to visit the recently killed Charles Bon upstairs at the big house, Rosa thinks it was "*the house itself that said the words,*" and, when Sutpen addresses Clytie, Rosa, and Judith, the homespun Romantic believes that the grandee

explains his plans to accomplish the Design to the "*presence, spirit*" of the Hundred (*AA* 111, 129, italics in the original).

50 For the Gothic implications of the Hundred's voice, see François L. Pitavy, "The Gothicism of *Absalom, Absalom!*: Rosa Coldfield Revisited," *"A Cosmos of My Own": Faulkner and Yoknapatawpha, 1980*, eds. Doreen Fowler and Ann J. Abadie (Jackson: University Press of Mississippi, 1981), 215. The idea of a corporate voice, especially as it manifests in a house style, and its influence on American literature in the 1930s has been addressed usefully by Donal Harris in his study of James Agee's writing during and following his employment by Henry Luce. See Harris, *On Company Time*, especially chapter three, "On the Clock: Rewriting Literary Work at Time Inc."

51 Ross, *Fiction's Inexhaustible Voice*, 221. In his study of the manuscript revisions of *Absalom*, Gerald Langford demonstrates that often what appears as attributed speech in the published novel was third-person narrative in the manuscript version. Gerald Langford, *Faulkner's Revision of Absalom, Absalom!* (Austin and London: UT Press, 1971), 21. More recently, Jeanne Follansbee has read the Overvoice as the aesthetic manifestation of fascism: "*Absalom* also embodies a central contradiction; its narrators reveal Sutpen's violent will-to-power, and the novel demonstrates the reproduction of that will-to-power in the narrators who repeat his story, yet the novel itself repeats a version of the same will-to-power, the same incantatory staging of domination in its own structure." Jeanne Follansbee, "'Sweet Fascism in the Piney Woods': *Absalom, Absalom!* as Fascist Fable", *Modernism/modernity* 18, no. 1 (January 2011): 84.

52 Ross, *Fiction's Inexhaustible Voice*, 145. Alternatively, Sarah Gleeson-White argues that Faulkner's deployment of typography should be considered one of many kinds of auditory experimentation the author undertook following his work for Universal on *Sutter's Gold*. See Sarah Gleeson-White, "Auditory Exposures: Faulkner, Eisenstein, and Film Sound," *PMLA* 128, no. 1 (2013): 87–100. Closer to my theory is Lisa Siraganian's reading of the presence of a corporate agent in the "grammatical, structural absence" at work in Muriel Rukeyser's "The Dam" (*Corporate Persons*, 10).

53 Faulkner famously manipulated orthography and typography from the start of his authorial career, from adding the "u" to his family name to planning to use different colors of ink to signify shifts in temporality in the Benjy section of *The Sound and the Fury* to incorporating a diagram of the beveled clock-shape casket Cash constructs for Addie in *As I Lay Dying*. See Blotner, *Biography*, 244. For a striking graphic representation of Faulkner's punctuation shorn of semantic content, see Adam J. Calhoun, "Punctuation in novels," *Medium*, February 15, 2016. https://medium.com/@neuroecology/punctuation-in-novels-8f316d542ec4.

54 These functions are culled from Randel's typology. For the full list, see Fred Randel, "Parentheses in Faulkner's *Absalom, Absalom!*," *Style* 5, no. 1 (Winter 1971): 70–87.

55 Hugh Kenner, *Ulysses* (Baltimore and London: Johns Hopkins University Press, 1987), 61–71.

56 Bruce Kawin, "Introduction: Faulkner at MGM," *Faulkner's MGM Screenplays*, ed. Bruce Kawin (Knoxville: University of Tennessee Press, 1982), xxxix.
57 Eric Sundquist, *Faulkner: The House Divided* (Baltimore: Johns Hopkins University Press, 1983), 120. Regarding Faulkner's inability to even remember the lawyer in *Absalom* see the following interview in *Faulkner in the University*, eds. Frederick L. Gwynn and Joseph L. Blotner (New York: Vintage, 1965), 77:

> Q. Mr. Faulkner, in *Absalom, Absalom!* when Shreve and Quentin are reconstructing the story for each other, they set up a lawyer who was directing the campaign of Charles's mother to gain revenge against Sutpen. Was there really a lawyer, do you think, or is just a product of their imagination as they reconstructed the story?
> A. I'm sorry, I don't remember that.

58 Jay Watson, *Forensic Fictions: The Lawyer Figure in Faulkner* (Athens and London: University of Georgia Press, 1993), 6. Julian Murphet also observes the link between Feinman and Hollywood, but he instead suggests that the New Valois sewage maven's influence on the airshow and its reportage chimes with the old antisemitic saw that Jews control the media. See Julian Murphet, *Faulkner's Media Romance* (New York and Oxford, UK: Oxford University Press, 2017), 221.
59 Faulkner to Ben Wasson, ca. November 1932, *Selected Letters*, 68.
60 Rosten, *Hollywood*, 91.
61 Watson, *Forensic Fictions*, 38.
62 See Mark McGurl, *The Novel Art: Elevations of American Fiction after Henry James* (Princeton: Princeton University Press, 2001), 132–134.
63 William Faulkner, *The Wild Palms [If I Forget Thee, Jerusalem]* (New York: Vintage, 1995 [1939]), 176.
64 James M. Cain, "Paradise," *American Mercury*, March 1933, 266–267.
65 Roy Hoopes, *Cain: The Biography of James M. Cain* (Carbondale: Southern University of Illinois Press, 1982), 231.
66 Hoopes, *Cain*, 224–225, 231.
67 On McCoy's resentment of being seen as derivative of Cain, see Mark Royden Winchell, *Horace McCoy* (Boise, ID: Boise State University Press, 1982), 9 and Walter Wells, *Tycoons and Locusts*, 14. On Ballard's failure as a screenwriter: James L. Taylor, "Tod Ballard: An Appreciation," in *Hollywood Troubleshooter: W.T. Ballard's Bill Lennox Stories* (Bowling Green, OH: Bowling Green University Press, 1985), 1. On McCoy's experiences as an extra, see Winchell, *Horace McCoy*, 7. Both circumstances are mentioned in Springer, *Hollywood Fictions*, 153, 238.
68 See Davis, *City of Quartz*, 15–98.
69 David Fine, *Imagining Los Angeles*, 162–163; John Parris Springer, *Hollywood Fictions*, 168–169; Otto Friedrich, *City of Nets: A Portrait of Hollywood in the 1940's* (New York: Harper and Row, 1986), 1–29. "Negative sublimity" is Harold Bloom's description of West's *Miss Lonelyhearts*, but it applies equally well (contra Bloom) to *The Day of the Locust*. Harold Bloom, *Miss Lonelyhearts* (New York: Chelsea House, 2005), 1.

70 Maurice Bergman, "Crisis is the Backbone," *Variety*, January 7, 1948, 40.
71 Catherine Jurca, *Hollywood 1938: Motion Pictures' Greatest Year* (Berkeley: University of California Press, 2012), 2, 6, 8.
72 Margaret Farrand Thorp, "A Family Affair," *Delphian Quarterly* 22, no. 2 (April 1939), 38, qtd. in Dana Pollen, "'What Movie Tonight?': Margaret Thorp between the Aesthetics and the Sociology of American Cinema," *Film History* 26, no. 1 (2014): 176.

3 The Motion Picture Industry's Coming of Age

1 Margaret Farrand Thorp, *America at the Movies* (New Haven: Yale University Press, 1939), 216.
2 On the industry's strategic openness to controversial politics, see Richard Maltby, "The Production Code and the Hays Office," in Tino Balio, *Grand Design: Hollywood as a Modern Business Empire, 1930–39* (New York: Scribner, 1993), 68–71.
3 See Robert Sitton, *Lady in the Dark: Iris Barry and the Art of Film* (New York: Columbia University Press, 2014), 203, and Peter Decherney, *Hollywood and the Culture Elite: How the Movies Became Modern* (New York: Columbia University Press, 2005), 101.
4 Sitton, *Lady in the Dark*, 230.
5 Ibid., 246.
6 Lewis Jacobs, *The Rise of the American Film: A Critical History* (New York: Harcourt, Brace and Company, 1939), 432; Iris Barry, preface to Jacobs, *Rise of the American Film*, viii.
7 "Industry to Observe its Golden Jubilee October 1–7," *The Film Daily*, July 12, 1939, 1, 7; "The Movies March On," *March of Time* Vol. 5, Episode 12, 1939, 21min.
8 Rosten, *Hollywood*, 36; 37; 35; 34; 53; 16; 30–31.
9 Frank Nugent, "Another Dance of the Seven Veils: The Screen Reveals its Mysteries to the Public, Yet Manages to Hide Behind the Cloak of Illusion," *New York Times*, October 10, 1937, X5. Critic Ezra Goodman concurred with Nugent in a 1938 assessment: "For many years in its spare moments, the cinema has been taking hasty little peeks at itself in the mirror, but it was not until 1937 that it stopped long enough to get a reasonably full-length view, and—Narcissus-like—became fascinated with itself. The result was *A Star is Born* in which the motion picture took a public screen test and discovered its photogenic and box-office potentialities. The latter quality, particularly, impressed the movie moguls and there was soon forthcoming such introspective efforts as *It Happened in Hollywood, Super Sleuth, Pick a Star, Hollywood Cowboy, Ali Baba Goes to Town*, and *Stand-In*." Ezra Goodman, "The Cinema Becomes Introspective," *World Film News*, March 1938, 28.
10 As Steven Cohan has argued, the historical backstudio pictured would flourish in the 1950s in the form of such films as *Sunset Boulevard* (Billy Wilder, Paramount, 1950) and the second iteration of *A Star is Born* (George Cukor,

Warners, 1954). Steven Cohan, *Hollywood by Hollywood: The Backstudio Picture and the Mystique of Making Movies* (New York and Oxford, UK: Oxford University Press, 2018), 116–129. I follow Cohan in preferring "backstudio picture" to name the genre. On the different forms that Hollywood historical filmmaking took in the 1930s, see J. E. Smyth, *Reconstructing Hollywood: American Historical Cinema from Cimarron to Citizen Kane* (Lexington: The University of Kentucky Press, 2006). For Smyth, the historical backstudio picture's principal forerunner is the Selznick-produced *What Price Hollywood?* (Cukor/RKO, 1932), the original of *A Star is Born*.

11 Scholars following Nugent include Richard Maltby, *Hollywood Cinema: An Introduction*, second edition (Malden, MA: Wiley-Blackwell, 2003), 147; Christopher Ames, *Movies about Movies: Hollywood Reflected* (Lexington: The University of Kentucky Press, 1997), 8; and, Cohan, *Hollywood by Hollywood*. For Christensen's articulation of corporate authorship as studio strategy, see *America's Corporate Art*, 13–21.

12 Cohan, *Hollywood by Hollywood*, 1–9.

13 Smyth, *Reconstructing Hollywood*, 251–253, 266–277.

14 Rudy Behlmer, ed., *Memo from David O. Selznick* (New York: The Viking Press, 1972), 96.

15 William A. Wellman, Jack Conway, David O. Selznick, Robert Carson, Dorothy Parker, Alan Campbell, Ben Hecht, John Lee Mahin, Budd Schulberg, and Adela Rogers St. Johns, *A Star Is Born (1937): Shooting Script* (Alexandria, VA: Alexander Street, 1937), 134–135. https://search.alexanderstreet.com/view/work/bibliographic_entity%7Cbibliographic_details%7C2958504.

16 Cohan, *Hollywood by Hollywood*, 107.

17 Jurca, *Hollywood 1938*, 183.

18 Delight Evans, "Reviews of the Best Pictures," *Screenland*, July 1937, 53.

19 Christensen, *America's Corporate Art*, 4.

20 Jurca, *Hollywood 1938*, 189–190.

21 Peter Lev, *Twentieth Century-Fox: The Zanuck-Skouras Years, 1935–1965* (Austin, TX: University of Texas Press, 2013), 26.

22 Smyth identifies Griffith, Neilan, and Sennett as the bases for the fictional Mike Connors. See *Reconstructing American Historical Cinema*, 287. On the arc of Zanuck's career, see George F. Custen, *Twentieth Century's Fox: Darryl Zanuck and the Culture of Hollywood* (New York: Basic Books, 1997), 53, 66–73, 87, and 92–113.

23 See Michael Rogin, *Blackface, White Noise: Jewish Immigrants in the Hollywood Melting Pot* (Berkeley and Los Angeles: University of California Press, 1996), 45–72.

24 Frank Nugent and Douglas Churchill, "Graustark," *We Saw It Happen: The News behind the News That's Fit to Print*, eds. Hanson W. Baldwin and Shepard Stone (New York: Simon and Schuster, 1939 [1938]), 103.

25 Budd Schulberg, "Literature of the Film: The Hollywood Novel," *Films* 1, no. 2 (Spring 1940): 68–78.

26 Wilson, *Boys in the Back Room*, 59.

27 Schulberg, "Literature of the Film," 72–73.
28 Ibid., 78.
29 Nicholas Beck, *Budd Schulberg: A Bio-bibliography* (Lanham, MA and London: Scarecrow Press, 2001), 18.
30 Schulberg, "Literature of the Film," 72.
31 The idea of genre-as-medium can be found, in different forms, in Stanley Cavell, *Pursuits of Happiness: The Hollywood Comedy of Remarriage* (Cambridge, MA and London: Harvard University Press, 1981), 28–30; J. D. Connor, *Studios after the Studios*, 247–251; and Nicholas Brown, *Autonomy: The Social Ontology of Art under Capitalism* (Durham, NC and London: Duke University Press, 2019), 25–26, 158–177.
32 John Lee Mahin, Todd McCarthy, and Joseph McBride, "Bombshell Days in the Golden Age," *Film Comment* 16, no. 2 (March–April 1980): 65–66.
33 Patsy Ruth Miller, *My Hollywood, When Both of Us Were Young* (Duncan, OK: BearManor Media, 2002 [1988]), 93. See also Richard Brody, "A Brilliant, Unknown Memoir about Classic Hollywood," *The New Yorker*, March 3 2016, www.newyorker.com/culture/richard-brody/a-brilliant-unknown-memoir-about-classic-hollywood.
34 Patsy Ruth Miller, *That Flannigan Girl* (New York: Morrow, 1939), 129. Subsequent citations of this edition will be included parenthetically as (*TFG* page number).
35 Wilson, *Boys in the Back Room*, 14. See also Charles Musser, "The Devil's Parody: Horace McCoy's Appropriation and Refiguration of Two Hollywood Musicals," *A Companion to Literature and Film*, eds. Robert Stam and Alessandra Raengo (Malden, MA and Oxford, UK: Blackwell Publishing, 2004), 229–257.
36 David Bordwell, *Reinventing Hollywood: How 1940s Filmmakers Changed Movie Storytelling* (Chicago: University of Chicago Press, 2017), 71.
37 Miller, *My Hollywood*, 245.
38 Wilson, *Boys in the Back Room*, 12.
39 Wells, *Tycoons and Locusts*, 12. They were commercial failures as well, as *Variety* noted: "no novel located in the film capital has clicked as yet, no matter what the quality or the author's rep, and despite the vast interest in things cinematic." "Another One on Hollywood," *Variety*, June 21, 1939, 52. *Variety* reiterated the point when acknowledging Schulberg's success with *What Makes Sammy Run*: "This type of yarn is a notoriously poor merchandising article in publishing circles." "'Sammy' Tops H'wood Novels," *Variety*, October 1, 1941, 92.
40 Wells, *Tycoons and Locusts*, 47.
41 John O'Hara, *Hope of Heaven, Four Novels of the 1930s* (New York: Library of America, 2018), 433.
42 O'Hara, *Hope of Heaven*, 535.
43 Thus, what Jonathan Foltz sees as the particular way that Aldous Huxley "flagrantly violates the aesthetic precepts of a Jamesian high style, stubbornly telling where he should be showing, and eschewing the involving delicacy,

obliquity, and nuance afforded by free indirect discourse in favor of bluntness" in *After Many a Summer Dies the Swan* is in fact typical of the array of supposedly misfit and outcast fictions produced at the time. See Foltz, *The Novel after Film*, 171.

44 Michael Denning, *The Cultural Front: The Laboring of American Culture in the Twentieth Century* (London and Brooklyn: Verso, 1997), 249, 256.

45 Horace McCoy, *I Should Have Stayed Home* (London and New York: Serpent's Tail, 1996), 74.

46 The problem of the Hollywood extra can thus be understood as a special type of the statistical personhood developed in the social sciences and implemented by the government in the form of the New Deal. See Michael Szalay, *New Deal Modernism* and Richard Maltby, "*Film Noir*: The Politics of the Maladjusted Text," *Journal of American Studies* 18, no. 1 (April 1984): 49–71.

47 McCoy, *I Should Have Stayed Home*, 169.

48 Ibid., 184.

49 Fine, *Imagining Los Angeles*, 76.

50 Belfrage mistakenly identifies Harvey Henderson Wilcox by the first name Horace in *Promised Land*. Cedric Belfrage, *Promised Land: Notes for a History* (London: Victor Gollancz, 1938), 13. Subsequent citations of this edition will be included parenthetically as (*PL* page number). Regarding *Promised Land*'s relation to the writing of Southern California history, it should be noted that Belfrage acknowledges in the novel's prefatory "Thanks" the influence of Edwin Obadiah Palmer's "Hollywoodiana," published in 1938 as *History of Hollywood*. Carey McWilliams, in his much more famous *Southern California Country: An Island on the Land* (1946), cites *Promised Land* without indicating its fictional status. Carey McWilliams, *Southern California Country: An Island on the Land* (Salt Lake City: Gibbs Smith, 1973 [1946]), 332.

51 Belfrage, *Promised Land*, 75.

52 Denning, *The Cultural Front*, 191.

53 Granville Hicks, "The Moods and Tenses of John Dos Passos," *The New Masses*, April 26, 1938, 22.

54 Cedric Belfrage, "Politics Catches up with the Writer," *The New Masses*, December 28, 1937, 6, 8.

55 Hicks, "John Dos Passos," 23.

56 It is revealed in the novel's first epilogue that Ellen was sexually assaulted at an X.Y.Z. Studios junket for traveling salesmen; after she sues, the studio assassinates her character. The details of the incident match the Patricia Douglas case, in which Douglas, an extra lured under false pretenses to a party at Hal Roach's ranch, was raped by David Ross. Ross was never indicted, however, and when Douglas sued Roach, Eddie Mannix, Ross, and others, the studio tied up the case until it was ultimately dismissed. Years later, Mannix claimed "we had her killed." David Stenn, "It Happened One Night At MGM," *Vanity Fair*, April 2003, www.vanityfair.com/news/2003/04/mgm200304.

57 Jay Martin, *Nathanael West: The Art of His Life* (New York: Hayden, 1970), 321–322.

58 Nathanael West to Edmund Wilson, April 6, 1939, *Novels and Other Writings*, ed. Sacvan Bercovitch (New York: Library of America, 1997), 793.
59 In a May 11, 1939 letter to Malcolm Cowley, West described his crisis of faith in terms of his "enormous temptation to forget the bitter, tedious novels and to spend that time on committees which act on hope and faith without a smile," followed by the telling parenthetical "(It was even a struggle this time for me to leave off the quotation marks.)" West, *Novels and Other Writings*, 794–795.
60 Nathanael West to Malcolm Cowley, *Novels and Other Writings*, 795.
61 Casey Shoop is therefore astute when he writes that in *Locust* there is "the scandalous sense that the novel has somehow *enabled* its own misreadings." Casey Shoop, "The California Occult: Nathanael West, Theodor Adorno, and the Representation of Mass Cultural Desire," *Modernism/modernity* 25, no. 2 (April 2018): 313, emphasis in the original.
62 Nathanael West, *Miss Lonelyhearts and the Day of the Locust* (New York: New Directions Books, 2009 [1939]), 70. Subsequent citations of this edition will be included parenthetically as (*DL* page number).
63 West presents this view of art patronage rather explicitly in "The Impostor," an unpublished and undated short story in which a putative artist, Beano Walsh, produces no art but, in stealing a corpse from a morgue, strikes the eccentric pose of an artist, resulting in the renewal of his scholarship awarded by the fictional Oscar Hahn Foundation. See West, *Novels and Other Writings*, 411–424. For an argument about the centrality of the themes of "The Impostor" to West's career, see Jonathan Veitch, *American Superrealism: Nathanael West and the Politics of Representation in the 1930s* (Madison: University of Wisconsin Press, 1997), 23–26.
64 Wilson, *Boys in the Back Room*, 70.
65 Gregory Castle, *Reading the Modernist Bildungsroman* (Gainesville: University of Florida Press), 23.
66 Barnard, *The Culture of Abundance*, 207.
67 Martin, *Nathanael West*, 252.
68 Sarah Shurts, "Continental Collaboration: The Transition from Ultranationalism to Pan-Europeanism by the Interwar French Fascist Right," *French Politics, Culture & Society* 32, no. 3 (Winter 2014): 89. For a fascinating account of Drieu la Rochelle's own use of the bildungsroman form in the service of his fascist politics in *Gilles* (1939), see Chris Bongie, "Between Apocalypse and Narrative: Drieu la Rochelle and the Fascist Novel," *Romanic Review* 84, no. 1 (January 1993): 55–76.
69 West to Saxe Commins, February 14, 1939, *Novels and Other Writings*, 791.
70 West to Commins, *Novels and Other Writings*, 793.
71 Martin, *Nathanael West*, 258.
72 "To a remarkable extent, the modernism made by Americans had a Harvard education." Marcus Klein, *Foreigners: The Making of American Literature, 1900–1940* (Chicago and London: University of Chicago Press, 1981), 8. See also Denning, *The Cultural Front*, 59.

73 Jed Esty, *Unseasonable Youth: Modernism, Colonialism, and the Fiction of Development* (New York and Oxford, UK: Oxford University Press, 2012).
74 See Erika Doss, "Artists in Hollywood: Thomas Hart Benton and Nathanael West Picture America's Dream Dump," *The Space Between* 7 No. 1 (2011): 12.
75 Bella and Samuel Spewack, *Boy Meets Girl*, in *Sixteen Famous American Plays*, eds. Bennett Cerf and Van H. Cartmell (New York: Garden City Publishing Inc., 1941), 542.
76 Spewack and Spewack, *Boy Meets Girl*, 537.
77 Van Wyck Brooks, *America's Coming-of-Age* (New York: B. W. Huebsch, 1915), 24–25.
78 Hegeman, *Patterns of Culture*, 132.
79 Thomas Wolfe, *Look Homeward, Angel* (New York: Scribner, 2006 [1929]), 397.
80 Jerome Karabel, *The Chosen: The Hidden History of Admission and Exclusion at Harvard, Yale, and Princeton* (Boston: Houghton Mifflin, 2005), 205–210 and passim.
81 John R. Tunis, *Was College Worth While?* (New York: Harcourt, Brace and Company, 1937), 233–234.
82 Conrad Aiken, "Was Harvard Worth While?" *The New Republic*, September 30, 1936, 231.
83 Tunis, *Was College Worth While?*, 162.
84 Leslie Fiedler, *Love and Death in the American Novel* (New York: Criterion Books, 1960), 442.
85 Rosten, *Hollywood*, 35.
86 Barnard, *The Culture of Abundance*, 194; Veitch, *American Superrealism*, 115–116.
87 Thomas Strychacz, *Modernism, Mass Culture, and Professionalism* (New York and Cambridge, UK: Cambridge University Press, 1993), 198; Gavriel Moses, *The Nickel Was for the Movies: Film in the Novel from Pirandello to Puig* (Berkeley and Los Angeles: University of California Press, 1995), 196.
88 See Edward H. C. King, "The World Historical Novel: Writing the Periphery," PhD diss., (Yale University, 2017), 27–76.
89 Brooks, *America's Coming-of-Age*, 164.
90 Martin, *Nathanael West*, 51–52.
91 See, for instance, Bernard Smith, "Van Wyck Brooks," *After the Genteel Tradition*, ed. Malcolm Cowley (New York: Norton, 1937 [1936]), 76–78, and F.O. Matthiessen, review of *The Flowering of New England*, *The New England Quarterly* 9 no. 4 (December 1936): 707. See also Hegeman, *Patterns of Culture*, 80.
92 Brooks had attacked the modernist pantheon as a formally self-conscious and thus etiolated "secondary" clique of authors distinct from and inferior to the work of "primary" writers, such as Tolstoy, who were invested in "the progress of humanity." Dwight Macdonald, "Kulturbolschewismus Is Here," *Partisan Review* 8, no. 6 (November–December 1941): 445, 451.
93 "It's Otterson President and Zukor Chairman," *Motion Picture Herald*, June 8, 1935, 14.

94 Compare to the Hapgood translation: "Towards four o'clock the condition of the English army was serious. The Prince of Orange was in command of the centre, Hill of the right wing, Picton of the left wing. The Prince of Orange, desperate and intrepid, shouted to the Hollando-Belgians: 'Nassau! Brunswick! Never retreat!' Hill, having been weakened, had come up to the support of Wellington; Picton was dead. At the very moment when the English had captured from the French the flag of the 105th of the line, the French had killed the English general, Picton, with a bullet through the head. A sergeant of the English Guards, the foremost boxer in England, reputed invulnerable by his companions, had been killed there by a little French drummer-boy. Baring had been dislodged, Alten put to the sword. Many flags had been lost, one from Alten's division, and one from the battalion of Lunenberg, carried by a prince of the house of Deux-Ponts. The Scots Greys no longer existed; Ponsonby's great dragoons had been hacked to pieces." Victor Hugo, *Les Misérables*, trans. Isabel F. Hapgood (London and Glasgow: Collins, 1922 [1862]), 326.
95 Nathanael West, Guggenheim fellowship application, qtd. in Martin, *Nathanael West*, 253.
96 Hegeman, *Patterns of Culture*, 150.
97 Oswald Spengler, *The Decline of the West*, trans. Charles Francis Atkinson, vol. 1 (London: George Allen and Unwin Ltd, 1928), 31.
98 Lewis Mumford, "The Decline of Spengler," *The New Republic*, March 9, 1932, 104. As Martin reports, West at one point used a quotation from Mumford as an epigraph to *Locust*: "From the form of a city, the style of an architecture, and the economic functions and social grouping it shelters and encourages, one can derive most of the essential elements of a civilization." Martin, *Nathanael West*, 309.
99 Carey McWilliams, "Hollywood Plays with Fascism," qtd. in William Solomon, *Literature, Amusement, and Technology*, 140. See also Rosten, *Hollywood*, 139, and Martin, *Nathanael West*, 348.
100 Donald Critchlow, *When Hollywood Was Right* (New York and Cambridge, UK: Cambridge University Press), 36–37; "Hollywood Forms Own Army for Protection in 'Emergencies,'" *Motion Picture Herald*, May 11, 1935, 27.
101 Robin Blyn comes closest to this position but does not register the relation between Tod's two laughs. See Blyn, "Imitating the Siren: West's *The Day of the Locust* and the Subject of Sound," *Literature/Film Quarterly*, 32, no.1 (2004): 51–59.
102 West's decision to end the novel this way came late in his revisions, and that choice matches the shift in his critical focus from the angry, disaffected rabble (reflected by his preliminary title, *The Cheated*) to the reactionary mediocre elite. In his original conclusion, Tod leaves the riot and describes his vision of "The Burning of Los Angeles" to Claude Estee, who attempts to bring Tod down from his prophetic mode: "He admitted that they might be desperate enough to burn a few houses in Hollywood, but said that they were the pick of America's madmen and not at all typical of the country as a whole." West transferred this material to the center of the novel—chapter 14 of 27—and

modified it in ways that emphasize the centrality of Tod's character. In the published novel, Tod conducts this conversation with himself after drunkenly failing to rape Faye in Pinyon Canyon; his abstract speculation about politics and social life are, like aesthetic contemplation, mere diversions from cruder impulses. Importantly, however, West removed a single line that radically changed his formulation of Tod's worldview: "Only the working classes would resist." In *The Day of the Locust*, the distinction between "madmen" and "working classes" never occurs to Tod; instead, he asserts an aestheticized opposition, that of "The Dancers" and "The Starers" who populate his preliminary lithographs, which reduce the people in his world to flattened types. For images of West's manuscript drafts, see Martin, *Nathanael West*, photographic insert 14–15.

4 Global Hollywood

1 C.M.L. (Clarence Malcolm Lowry), "Hollywood and the War," *Daily Province*, December 12, 1939.
2 Ibid.
3 See, for instance, Sherrill Grace, *Regression and Apocalypse: Studies in North American Literary Expressionism* (Toronto: University of Toronto Press, 1989), 163; Miguel Mota and Paul Tiessen, preface to and acknowledgements for *The Cinema of Malcolm Lowry: A Scholarly Edition of Lowry's Tender Is the Night* (Vancouver, British Columbia: University of British Columbia Press, 1990), vii; Paul Tiessen, "Literary Modernism and Cinema: Two Approaches," *Joyce/Lowry: Critical Perspectives* (Lexington: University of Kentucky Press, 1997), 160.
4 Porousness of boundaries between life and art is most explicitly elaborated in "Through the Panama," a densely layered story in *Hear Us O Lord from Heaven Thy Dwelling Place*, in which Lowry's alter-ego Sigbjørn Wilderness imagines that he has become a character in his book-in-progress. On mechanisms and engineering in Lowry, see Michael Wutz, *Enduring Words: Literary Narrative in a Changing Media Ecology* (Tuscaloosa: University of Alabama Press, 2009), 85–132.
5 Patrick McCarthy, *Forest of Symbols: World, Text, and Self in Malcolm Lowry's Fiction* (Athens: University of Georgia Press, 1994), 56. Among many works devoted to Lowry's allusions, David Markson's *Malcolm Lowry's Volcano: Myth, Symbol, Meaning* (1978) and Chris Ackerley and Lawrence J. Clipper's *A Companion to Under the Volcano* (1984) (along with its web-based supplement, *The Malcolm Lowry Project: Under the Volcano*; www.otago.ac.nz/english-linguistics/english/lowry/index.html) are especially helpful.
6 Lee Grieveson, *Cinema and the Wealth of Nations: Media, Capital, and the Liberal World System* (Berkeley and Los Angeles: University of California Press, 2018), 1.

7 On the reasons for Hollywood's supersession of European producers following World War I, including increased costs related to the production and promotion of feature films, see Gerben Bakker, "The Decline and Fall of the European Film Industry: Sunk Costs, Market Size, and Market Structure, 1890–1927," *The Economic History Review* 58, no. 2: 310–351.
8 Hansen, "Mass Production of the Senses," 68.
9 See Miriam Hansen, *Babel and Babylon: Spectatorship in American Silent Film* (Cambridge, MA: Harvard University Press, 1991), especially 76–86 and 173–198.
10 See Ginette Vincendeau, "Hollywood Babel: The Coming of Sound and the Multiple Language Version," in *The Classical Hollywood Reader*, ed. Steve Neale (New York and Oxford, UK: Routledge, 2012), 137–146.
11 Maltby, "The Production Code," 40.
12 Richard Maltby, *Hollywood Cinema*, Second Edition (Malden and Oxford, UK: Blackwell Publishing, 2003), 61, 63. Importantly for the purposes of this study, Ruth Vasey, who first applied the phrase "principle of deniability" to Production Code-era Hollywood's hermeneutic, claims that the strategy emerged in the wake of the industry's concern about the unsuitability of the "prevalent type of book" for adaptation to the screen that gave rise to The Formula in 1924. The industry changed tack with the "Don'ts and Be Carefuls" of 1927, exploiting the differences between sophisticated source text and wholesome adaptation in order to appeal to multiple constituencies while maintaining the fiction of addressing a single undifferentiated audience. A movie that bowdlerized an unfilmable source text could, by virtue of strategic ambiguity, appeal implicitly to the source while remaining morally unimpeachable, "present[ing] at least two stories to at least two audiences at once, maximizing revenues while minimizing offense." Both chronologically and logically, then, Hollywood's commercial aesthetic of ambiguity derived at least in part from the institutional conditions of adaptation that engendered the transmedial possibility described in Chapter 1. Ruth Vasey, *The World According to Hollywood, 1918–1939* (Madison: University of Wisconsin Press, 1997), 106.
13 John Trumpbour, *Selling Hollywood to the World: U.S. and European Struggles for Mastery of the Global Film Industry, 1920–1950* (New York and Cambridge, UK: Cambridge University Press, 2002), 8. On the image and its privileged status in postmodern culture, see Fredric Jameson, *Postmodernism; or, the Cultural Logic of Late Capitalism* (Durham, NC: Duke University Press, 1990), 18: "Appropriately enough, the culture of the simulacrum comes to life in a society where exchange value has been generalized to the point at which the very memory of use value is effaced, a society of which Guy Debord has observed, in an extraordinary phrase, that in it 'the image has become the final form of commodity reification.'"
14 Alexander Howard has recently described Charles Henri Ford in similar terms. Ford was a coauthor, with Tyler, of *The Young and Evil*, and the editor of *View*, for which Tyler worked. See Alexander Howard, *Charles Henri Ford: Between Modernism and Postmodernism* (London and New York: Bloomsbury Academic, 2017).

15 Leela Gandhi and Deborah L. Nelson, "Editors' Introduction," *Critical Inquiry* 40, no. 4 (Summer 2014): 297. In a 1949 essay, Tyler attributed Hollywood's late-1940s naturalism, emerging from social scientific developments and instantiated both in the techniques of "fact fiction" (location shooting, a rhetoric of "social documentation") and in representations of the "individual apt to be overwhelmed by mass formations," to a sense of environment that "has become, in current parlance, 'global.'" Putting a finer point on the imbrication of Hollywood's commercial aesthetic and its global reach, he remarks, "Man is not yet a 'behavioristic animal,' though it would considerably simplify the problems of Hollywood profit-making if the world could be convinced at once that it is." Presumably, Tyler means that if humans can be thoroughly conditioned to purchase whatever the studios produce, their problem of appealing to multiple audiences (or having to appeal at all) all but evaporates. Parker Tyler, "Movie Letter: *Hamlet* and Documentary," *The Kenyon Review* 11, no. 3 (Summer, 1949): 531.

16 Matthew Wilkens, *Revolution: The Event in Postwar Fiction* (Baltimore: Johns Hopkins University Press, 2016), 2, 14.

17 Here I refer to Wendell Willkie's *One World* (1943), a popular liberal internationalist work. On the relation between Willkie's thesis and Hollywood cinema of the mid-1940s, see Richard Maltby, "Film Noir," 49–71.

18 Franco Moretti, *Modern Epic: The World System from Goethe to García Márquez*, trans. Quintin Hoare (London and New York: Verso, 1996), 227, 50, emphasis in the original.

19 On British and Anglophone modernism's relationship to radio, see Peter Kalliney, *Commonwealth of Letters: British Literary Culture and the Emergence of Postcolonial Aesthetics* (New York and Oxford, UK: Oxford University Press, 2013); Daniel Ryan Morse, "An 'Impatient Modernist': Mulk Raj Anand at the BBC," *Modernist Cultures* 10, no. 1 (May 2015): 83–98; and Edward King, "'What Muck & Filth Is Normally Flowing through the Air': The Cultural Politics of Atmosphere in the Work of George Orwell," *Journal of Modern Literature* 41, no. 2 (Winter 2018): 60–76.

20 Michael Bell, on the other hand, prefers the term "ideology" to "system": "over the latter part of the century 'myth' has given way to ideology as the favoured term to denote the implicit structure of a worldview." His analysis has much to recommend it, not least of which is the fact that writers of the midcentury explicitly considered myth's relation to ideology. For instance, in "Ideology and Myth" (1947), Kenneth Burke (a correspondent of Tyler's) argues that ideology is analogous to myth, but in a form appropriate to "a highly developed money economy, with its extreme divisions of labor and a maximum of abstract relationships for which the ideologist seeks to compensate by all the deliberate subterfuges for persuading people to 'identify themselves' with the factions, doctrines, or policies he represents." (Note, however, that Burke will later insist that myth exists before politics.) More famously, Roland Barthes's *Mythologies*, and especially his concluding essay "Myth Today," demystifies myth as ideology. I prefer to emphasize "system," however, because of its

associations with technology on the one hand and bureaucracy on the other. See Michael Bell, *Literature, Modernism and Myth: Belief and Responsibility in the Twentieth Century* (Cambridge, UK: Cambridge University Press, 1997), 226; Kenneth Burke, "Ideology and Myth," *Accent* 7 (Summer 1947): 201. On Barthes's *Mythologies* as a "hinge text" between modernism and postmodernism, see Marianne DeKoven, *Utopia Limited: The Sixties and the Emergence of the Postmodern* (Durham, NC: Duke University Press, 2004), 57–71. On structuralists' debt to theories of communications, cybernetics, and systems, see Mark Greif, *The Age of the Crisis of Man: Thought and Fiction in America, 1933–1973* (Princeton: Princeton University Press, 2015), 298.

21 C. D. Blanton, *Epic Negation: The Dialectical Poetics of Late Modernism* (Oxford, UK and New York: Oxford University Press, 2015), 19.

22 Im, *The Late Modernist Novel*, 10. Also fundamental to my thinking here is Fredric Jameson's notion of late modernism as a moment of artistic practice undertaken by a generation of artists for whom modernist experimentalism had taken on recognizable characteristics. See Fredric Jameson, *A Singular Modernity: Essay on the Ontology of the Present* (London and New York: Verso, 2002), 197–210.

23 *Pace* Jennifer Ashton's claim that the doctrines of the intentional fallacy and the heresy of paraphrase make the New Criticism inimical to interpretation and align the movement with postmodern theorists of the open text. For Ashton, Laura (Riding) Jackson would be the supreme poet-theorist of modernism, who posits the absolute irrelevance of experience to the interpretation of a poem and thus believes that poetry is "a vacuum and therefore nothing." Jackson quoted in Jennifer Ashton, *From Modernism to Postmodernism: American Poetry and Theory in the Twentieth Century* (Cambridge, UK and New York: Cambridge University Press, 2005), 109.

24 Marc Manganaro, *Myth, Rhetoric, and the Voice of Authority: A Critique of Frazer, Eliot, Frye, and Campbell* (New Haven and London: Yale University Press, 1992), 80.

25 Here I follow Ashton's study of modern and postmodern aesthetics, based on Michael Fried's accounts of modernism and literalism.

26 Herbert Marshall McLuhan, "Inside Blake and Hollywood," *The Sewanee Review* 55, no. 4 (October-December 1947): 714.

27 Parker Tyler, "Film Chronicle: The Movies as a Fine Art," *Partisan Review* 24, no. 3 (1957): 424.

28 David Riesman with Nathan Glazer and Reuel Denney, *The Lonely Crowd: A Study of the Changing American Character* (New Haven: Yale University Press, 1960 [1950]), 348–351.

29 Parker Tyler, "Hollywood as a Universal Church," *American Quarterly* 2, no. 2 (Summer 1950): 176, 175, 165. Tyler's identification of the spurious progressiveness of *Gentleman's Agreement* and *Pinky*, both by Twentieth Century-Fox, anticipates Ellen Scott's more recent criticism of the limitations of the studio's representations of African American civil rights issues under Darryl Zanuck. See Ellen Scott, *Cinema Civil Rights: Regulation, Repression, and Race*

in the Classical Hollywood Era (New Brunswick, NJ: Rutgers University Press, 2015), 108–146.
30 Parker Tyler, introduction to *Modern Things* (New York: The Galleon Press, 1934), 7, 12.
31 See, in addition to *The Hollywood Hallucination* and *Magic and Myth of the Movies*, Parker Tyler, "Hollywood in Disguise: Gods and Goddesses Paid to be Alive," *View* 1, no. 2 (October 1940): 1, 6.
32 For instance, Taylor misconstrues Tyler as valorizing himself as the practitioner of "the authentic artistry of the vanguard critic" and as the "exceptional and validly accredited individual" who is "too good for the movie theater." Tyler's full statement in *Magic and Myth* reads:

> One fears that many snooty observers of filmic development are innately soft-boiled and always will be. This cultural gelatinousness is a trait of the listless conservative, whose temper is always roiled by the hint that he can be torn away from Mozart, Shakespeare, and Rembrandt to sully eyesight and hearing with less pure addresses to the two faculties involved. It is the same old, faintly malodorous petty-bourgeois fairy tale: the opera, the ballet, the concert hall. Even the modern aesthete, since his very mental life is based firmly and solely on his esthetinng, takes special satisfaction in remaining cloistered before the blandishments of the cinema entertainment, pastime of *hoi polloi*. I affirm that the only reasons for being too good for the movie theater and for its vibrating messages about the modern psyche are the best in the world, and the best is the exclusive property, at this juncture of planetary time lapse, of the exceptional and validly accredited individual; anticinema grounds therefore fail to constitute an attitude of real significance. (120–121)

Tyler here affirms that the movies are worthy of an artist-critic's attention, and that the movies fall short only in the sense that they are not the products of a single truly exceptional mind (e.g., Mozart, Shakespeare, Rembrandt). Tyler is, then, defending Hollywood movies, if not as works of art, then as objects of interest to the critic; he is not, however, defending his own superior mind.

In general, Taylor (and Bordwell) takes Tyler too much at his retrospective word. The claim that Tyler practiced a form of critical camp derives from Tyler himself in, for instance, his introduction to the revised edition of *The Three Faces of Film* (1967), a collection of essays from the 1950s and 1960s. This version of Tyler differs notably from the Tyler of the mid-1940s. In the last years of the decade into the first years of the next, Tyler took an increasingly hostile stance toward Hollywood cinema and, correspondingly, described his critical persona as a "satirist and disparager of the conscious claims of Hollywood movies" (Tyler, "Movie Letter: Foreign Films and the Main Problem," *The Kenyon Review* 12, no. 1 [Winter 1950]: 187). At the conclusion of a despairing three-part "Movie Letter" in the summer 1951 issue of *The Kenyon Review* (considerably lightened in tone when reprinted in *Three Faces*), Tyler disavowed the writing he had done over the better part of a decade in the appropriate idiom of waking from a dream. "In my ripened stage as a mythographer of the Hollywood product," he writes, "I am suddenly oppressed by the consciousness of what I have written. It brings the faintly overwhelming thought that perhaps too much sadism is involved in my part amidst the great public. Furthermore, facing my seventh year of intensive and unflattering analysis, I have come to feel that my particular game is no longer worth the candle of critical prose—at least, without danger of repetition. Readers should not be surprised, therefore, if in the future my writings are signally void of any notice of American or English movies, barring the very rarest of such phenomena; I mean those which have positive artistic value." Tyler here crafts his own myth of critical rebirth: exit the Hollywood hallucinator; enter the champion of art film. Parker Tyler, "Movie Letter: Three Myths," *The Kenyon Review* 13, no. 3 (Summer 1951): 542.

33 Parker Tyler, preface to *Magic and Myth of the Movies* (New York: Henry Holt and Co, 1947), xiv.
34 T.S. Eliot, "The Perfect Critic," in *The Sacred Wood* (New York: Knopf, 1921), 10.
35 Tyler, preface to *Magic and Myth of the Movies*, xix.
36 Parker Tyler, "Communications: Mr. Tyler's Approach," *The Kenyon Review* 7, no. 4 (Autumn 1945): 689.
37 M. Roy Mason (Parker Tyler), "Cinematic Effects in a Long Poem," in *The Granite Butterfly: A Poem in Nine Cantos, A Facsimile of the First Edition, with Supplementary Materials*, eds. Charles Boultenhouse and Michael Fournier (Orono, ME: National Poetry Foundation, 1994), 82–87.
38 Parker Tyler, "Ode to Hollywood," in *The Will of Eros: Selected Poems 1930–1970* (Los Angeles: Black Sparrow Press, 1972), 29.
39 Parker Tyler, "Beyond Surrealism," *Caravel* 2, no. 3 (1935), 5.
40 Tyler, "Ode to Hollywood," 28.
41 William Carlos Williams, review of *The Granite Butterfly*, in *The Granite Butterfly*, 97. In an insightful review of the National Poetry Foundation's edition, Marjorie Perloff suggests that Williams may have seen in Tyler's version of surrealism a possible alternative to "the seemingly all-encompassing Eliotic mode" of the mid-1940s. Marjorie Perloff, review of *The Granite Butterfly: A Poem in Nine Cantos*, *William Carlos Williams Review*, 22, no. 1 (Spring 1996): 111.
42 Tyler, author's note to *The Granite Butterfly*, 68.
43 Tyler, author's note to *The Granite Butterfly*, 67.
44 This is to say that Tyler all but asserts the continuation of the project of queering modernism he began with Ford in *The Young and Evil*: more evidence of the persuasiveness of Sam See's account. See Sam See, *Queer Natures, Queer Mythologies*, eds. Christopher Looby and Michael North (New York: Fordham University Press, 2020), 194–228.
45 Tyler, *The Hollywood Hallucination*, 240.
46 Tyler, author's note to *The Granite Butterfly*, 71; Tyler, *The Hollywood Hallucination* 237, 238.
47 Tyler, *The Hollywood Hallucination*, 6.
48 Perloff, review of *The Granite Butterfly*, 109. Michael Clune's account of O'Hara's poetics suggests another way in which Tyler might be conceived as a precursor. For Clune, O'Hara's poetics of personal choice derives from a desire to engage directly with the world without recourse to intersubjectivity and hence to sociality: a poetics formulated, that is, on the model of the free

market. Compare Tyler's emphasis on the idiosyncratic interpretation accommodated in advance by Hollywood's commercial logic—not the market as such, but close—with O'Hara's comments on the work of Larry Rivers as described by Clune: "O'Hara's reaction to this work is not to try to ferret out the secret of Rivers' 'private association'; he knows there isn't one. Rather, he treats Rivers' work as an encouragement to form his own instant, contingent 'private associations.'" The difference between the Tyler of the 1940s and O'Hara would be that the former undertakes personal interpretations—the choice made available by an art-commodity—while the latter prefers yet more individual associations, unanchored in reasons. See Michael Clune, *American Literature and the Free Market: 1945–2000* (Cambridge, UK and New York: Cambridge University Press, 2010), 53–76.

49 Malcolm Lowry, *The 1940 Under the Volcano*, eds. Miguel Mota and Paul Tiessen (Ottawa: University of Ottawa Press, 2015), 7.

50 Malcolm Lowry, *October Ferry to Gabriola*, ed. Margerie Lowry (New York and Cleveland: The World Publishing Company, 1970), 26.

51 See Gordon Bowker, *Pursued by Furies: A Life of Malcolm Lowry* (New York: St. Martin's Press, 1995), 350–355.

52 Malcolm Lowry, *Under the Volcano* (New York: Harper Perennial Modern Classics, 2007 [1947]), 274, emphasis in the original. Subsequent citations of this edition will be included parenthetically as (*UTV* page number).

53 Malcolm Lowry, *The 1940 Under the Volcano*, 232. On the importance of this quotation for understanding the relation between the Consul's tragic demise and his incessant acts of interpretation, see McCarthy, *Forest of Symbols*, especially 44–66.

54 Tyler, preface to *Magic and Myth*, xiv.

55 Lowry to Jonathan Cape, January 2, 1946, *Sursum Corda! The Collected Letters of Malcolm Lowry*, ed. Sherrill E. Grace (Toronto and Buffalo: University of Toronto Press, 1997), 1:510.

56 For an analysis of this description from a Deleuzean angle, see Brian Rourke, "Malcolm Lowry's Memory Machine: An Eclectic Systemë," *Journal of Modern Literature* 29, no. 3 (Spring 2006): 19–38.

57 Lowry to Robert Giroux, ca. January 17, 1952, *Sursum Corda!*, ed. Sherrill Grace, vol. 2 (Toronto: University of Toronto Press, 1996), 501. Lowry is therefore unlike other late-modernist British writers like Graham Greene, George Orwell, and Evelyn Waugh who, according to Jed Esty, "take imperial decline to imply national decline." Jed Esty, *A Shrinking Island: Modernism and National Culture in England* (Princeton: Princeton University Press, 2009), 215. On Lowry as a "post-national" writer, see Andrew John Miller, "Under the Nation-State: Modernist Deterritorialization in Malcolm Lowry's *Under the Volcano*," *Twentieth-Century Literature* 50, no. 1 (Spring 2004): 1–17.

58 Malcolm Lowry and Margerie Lowry, "Malcolm and Margerie Lowry: A Few Items Culled from What Started Out to be a Sort of Preface to a Film-Script," ed. Paul Tiessen, *White Pelican* 4, no. 2 (Spring 1974): 7. Miguel Mota and Tiessen note Lowry's "prophetic" tone in their introduction to the *Tender*

Is the Night screenplay. Mota and Tiessen, introduction to *The Cinema of Malcolm Lowry*, 5.

59 Malcolm Lowry, *Ultramarine* (New York: Overlook Press, 2005 [1933]), 103.
60 Malcolm Lowry, *In Ballast to the White Sea: A Scholarly Edition*, ed. Patrick A. McCarthy (Ottawa: University of Ottawa Press, 2014), 77, 78, 166, 167.
61 Lowry, *In Ballast*, 78, 4.
62 The purposefulness of Howard's Englishness becomes clear when contrasted with Lowry's reference to *Outward Bound* later in *In Ballast to the White Sea* and in his final, incomplete novel *October Ferry to Gabriola*, where the movie is mentioned along with its second-billed star, Douglas Fairbanks, Jr. Lowry, *October Ferry to Gabriola*, 12.
63 Stephen Spender's 1965 introduction to *Under the Volcano*, in which he praises Lowry's "camera eye," is typically cited as the origin of this discourse. Stephen Spender, introduction to *Under the Volcano* (Harper Perennial Modern Classics, 2007 [1965]), xiv.
64 Lowry to Clemens ten Holder, April 23, 1951, in Lowry, *Sursum Corda!*, 2:375.
65 Miriam Hansen, "Mass Production of the Senses," 61. On *Sunrise*'s relation to Fox's growth strategy in the late 1920s, see Robert C. Allen, "William Fox Presents Sunrise," *The Studio System*, ed. Janet Staiger (New Brunswick: Rutgers University Press, 1995), 127–139.
66 Gregory William Mank, *Hollywood Cauldron: 13 Horror Films from Hollywood's Golden Age* (Jefferson, NC and London: McFarland Classics, 2001), 122.
67 And studio-referential as well. The year before, the notoriously Anglophilic MGM released *The Barretts of Wimpole Street* (Sidney Franklin, 1935), produced by Irving Thalberg and starring Thalberg's wife Norma Shearer as Elizabeth and Fredric March as Robert.
68 Lowry, *1940 Under the Volcano*, 14–15.
69 Schatz, *The Genius of the System*, 22–23. The Office of the Coordinator of Inter-American Affairs (OCIAA; later the Office of Inter-American Affairs), established in August 1940, worked with the studios to develop positive relations between the US and Latin America during WWII. As the historian Pennee Lenore Bender observes, "During the five years that the OCIAA was active in film production and distribution it forged a direct relationship between several government agencies and all aspects of the motion picture industry and influenced Hollywood feature film and newsreel content that reached millions of viewers on both continents." Pennee Lenore Bender, "*Film as an Instrument of the Good Neighbor Policy, 1930s–1950s*," PhD diss., (New York University, 2002), 11–12. Thomas Doherty notes that the Office of War Information advised producers to help refute the Axis's assertion "that the American Government's policy with respect to Latin-American countries is camouflage for imperialism." Doherty, *Projections of War: Hollywood, American Culture, and World War II* (New York: Columbia University Press, 1993), 44.
70 "Kent, Balaban Lead Way in Latin American Drive," *Motion Picture Herald*, April 15, 1939, 13.
71 Jennifer Fay and Justus Nieland, *Film Noir: Hard-Boiled Modernity and the Cultures of Globalization* (London and New York: Routledge, 2010), 66.

72 Chris Ackerley and Lawrence J. Clipper, *A Companion to Under the Volcano* (Vancouver: University of British Columbia Press, 1984), 42.
73 Lowry, "Hollywood and the War."
74 Lowry to Cape, *Sursum Corda!*, 1:510.
75 In *Merton of the Movies*, the bumpkin Merton Gill stands in awe of the studio as a "microcosmos, a world in little, where one may ... behold, by walking a block, cities actually apart by league upon league of the earth's surface and separated by centuries of time." Wilson, *Merton of the Movies*, 56.
76 Lowry, "Hollywood and the War."
77 Lowry to Cape, *Sursum Corda!*, 1:507. On the politics of Lowry's figuration of Mexico as a fallen Eden, see Sharae Deckard, "'Perverse Paradiso': Malcolm Lowry and the Writing of Modern Mexico," *Paradise Discourse, Imperialism, and Globalization: Exploiting Eden* (New York and Oxford, UK: Routledge, 2010), 51–76.
78 Lowry to Clemens ten Holder, March 21, 1951, *Sursum Corda!*, 2:348. See also Lowry to Cape, *Sursum Corda!*, 1:511.
79 Lowry and Lowry, "Sort of Preface," 13, 16. Ruth Perlmutter draws similar attention to the Lowrys' insistence on appealing to multiple audiences. Ruth Perlmutter, "Malcolm Lowry's Unpublished Film Script of *Tender Is the Night*," *American Quarterly* 28, no. 5 (Winter 1976), 573.
80 Aldous Huxley, *Ape and Essence* (Chicago: Ivan R. Dee, 1992 [1948]), 12–13.
81 Eric Hodgins, "A Round Table on the Movies," *Life*, June 27, 1949, 103; Lowry and Lowry, "Sort of Preface," 6.
82 Lowry and Lowry, "Sort of Preface," 7.
83 Richard Fine, *James M. Cain and the American Authors' Authority* (Austin, TX: University of Texas Press, 1992), 97.
84 Dwight Macdonald, "Masscult and Midcult," *Partisan Review* 27, no. 2 (Spring 1960): 203–233. On the mainstreaming of modernism, Greg Barnhisel, *Cold War Modernists: Art, Literature & American Cultural Diplomacy* (New York: Columbia University Press, 2015), and Harris, *On Company Time*.

5 The Scenes of an Ending

1 William Miller, *The Book Industry: A Report of the Public Library Inquiry of The Social Science Research Council* (New York: Columbia University Press, 1949), 47.
2 Tino Balio, *Grand Design: Hollywood as a Modern Business Enterprise, 1930–1939* (Berkeley: University of California Press, 1995 [1993]), 73.
3 Justin Gautreau, *The Last Word: The Hollywood Novel and the Studio System* (Oxford, UK and New York: Oxford University Press, 2020), 147. This isn't to say, however, that movies produced during this era were perceived as credits to the industry. As Jurca observes of the four backstudio pictures included in the "Motion Pictures' Greatest Year" campaign of 1938, at least one major producer (Samuel Goldwyn) as well as trade papers and exhibitors worried

that such pictures as *Boy Meets Girl* and *The Affairs of Annabel* worked against Hollywood's best interests by satirizing the movie business and, in *Boy Meets Girl*'s case, lampooning the intelligence and taste of rural moviegoers. See Jurca, *Hollywood 1938*, 176–191.

4 "Queer People," *Time Magazine*, September 7, 1931, 35; Lester Cole, *Hollywood Red: The Autobiography of Lester Cole* (Palo Alto, CA: Ramparts Press, 1981), 98–101; J. E. Smyth, "Babylon Revisited," *Cineaste* 42, no. 2 (Spring 2018): 8.

5 Edna Ferber and George S. Kaufman, *Stage Door*, in *Kaufman & Co.: Broadway Comedies*, ed. Laurence Maslon (New York: Library of America, 2004 [1936]), 669.

6 Anne Kaufman Schneider and Laurence Maslon, "Stage Door," *George S. Kaufman*, www.georgeskaufman.com/play-catalogue/15-play-catalogue/library-of-america-collection/65-stage-door.html.

7 Miller, *The Book Industry*, 47.

8 Vera Caspary, *Laura* (New York: Feminist Press, 2005 [1942]), 106.

9 Raymond Chandler, *Farewell, My Lovely* (New York: Library of America, 1995 [1940]), 877.

10 On the long and winding road from MGM's 1934 purchase of *Postman*'s film rights to the adaptation's release in 1946, see Sheri Chenin Biesen, *Blackout: World War II and the Origins of Film Noir* (Baltimore: Johns Hopkins University Press, 2005), 96–123.

11 James M. Cain, *The Postman Always Rings Twice* (New York: Everyman's Library, 2003 [1934]), 12.

12 Dorothy Hughes, *In a Lonely Place* (New York: Feminist Press, 2003 [1942]), 61–62.

13 See, for instance, James W. Palmer, "*In a Lonely Place*: Paranoia in the Dream Factory," *Literature/Film Quarterly* 13 no. 3 (1985) and Dana Polan, *In a Lonely Place* (London: BFI Publishing, 1993).

14 Of the sale Hughes's literary agent Blanche Gregory said, "I thought it was such an obvious bet for Bogart that I couldn't have been more surprised when Mr. Bogart actually bought it!" Paul S. Nathan, "Books into Films," *Publishers Weekly*, December 25, 1948, 2493.

15 Michael Rogin observes a similar "inside joke at the expense of the studio system" in *Body and Soul* (Enterprise Productions, 1947), made by Hollywood Ten members Robert Rossen and Abraham Polonsky, where the gangster Roberts shares the surname of producer Bob Roberts. Rogin, *Blackface, White Noise*, 214.

16 Will H. Hays, *The Motion Picture in a Changing World: Annual Report to the Motion Picture Producers and Distributors of America, Inc.*, March 25, 1940, 15, Margaret Herrick Library, Academy of Motion Picture Arts and Sciences, https://digitalcollections.oscars.org/digital/collection/p15759coll11/id/11128/rec/1.

17 Donald Friede, "I Was a Hollywood Story Agent," *Writer's Digest*, May 1949, 23. For information on releases in 1949, see Figure 5.15.

18 "Brushoff 'Brainy' Bestsellers; Pix Depend on Originals, Mags," *Variety*, August 17, 1949, 5.

19 John Houseman, "Hollywood Faces the Fifties: Part I. The Lost Enthusiasm," *Harper's Magazine*, April 1, 1950, 56.
20 Manny Farber, "Movies Aren't Movies Anymore: The Art of the Gimp Takes Over," *Commentary*, January 1, 1952, 560.
21 "$100,000 Dollars for Novel," *Motion Picture Daily*, May 18, 1944, 2.
22 Schatz, *Boom and Bust*, 467.
23 A. P. Herbert, *The House by the River* (New York: Grosset and Dunlap, 1921), 12.
24 Compare *Variety*'s attitude to Franco Moretti's gloss of this moment in *The Third Man* as a testament "to the aura of legend surrounding the stream of consciousness, even outside avant-garde circles." Moretti, *Modern Epic*, 123.
25 "Novel Market Under Par for Screen; 64 Bought," *Motion Picture Herald*, January 21, 1948, 21; Eric Hoyt, *Hollywood Vault: Film Libraries before Home Video* (Berkeley: University of California Press, 2014), 115.
26 "Original Writers Writhe at Trend for Remakes, For Which They Get Nil," *Variety*, April 28, 1948, 1. It's important to note, however, that not all readaptations were remakes. As James L. West III notes, silent film and sound film rights were determined to be two different properties. Hence, Paramount's 1949 adaptation of *Gatsby* (Nugent, 1949) resulted from a new negotiation with Fitzgerald's estate. West, *American Authors*, 132.
27 See Hoyt, *Hollywood Vault*, especially chapter four, "Postwar Profit Centers (1940s)."
28 "SWG Wins Separation of Rights; Prods Agree to Talk IA Pay Boosts," *Variety*, February 14, 1951, 5, 55.
29 Grace Reiner, "Separation of Rights for Screen and Television Writers," *Los Angeles Lawyer* 28 (April 2001), 30.
30 From the vantage of 1972, in the midst of the American New Wave of personal films by the likes of Mike Nichols, Arthur Penn, and Bob Rafelson, Mankiewicz did one of the many things he so adeptly did with words: he took credit. In this case, he wanted to "'put into the record,' as presidents and lawyers say," that he had elaborated a theory of the auteur before the *Cahiers du Cinéma* firebrands and the "intra-critical haggling" of Sarris and Kael. Gary Cary and Joseph L. Mankiewicz, *More About All About Eve* (New York: Random House, 1972), 61–62.
31 See Jeff Menne, *Post-Fordist Cinema: Hollywood Auteurs and the Corporate Counterculture* (New York: Columbia University Press, 2019), 7–16.
32 Joseph L. Mankiewicz, "Film Author! Film Author!" *The Screen Writer*, May 1947, 27–28, my emphasis.
33 "Can Screenwriters Become Film Authors?: A Few Comments and Suggestions Concerning this Transition," *The Screen Writer*, June 1947, 25–36.
34 Gavin Lambert, *Nazimova: A Biography* (New York: Knopf, 1997), 357–389. See also Daniel Brown, "Wilde and Wilder," *PMLA* 119, no. 5 (2004): 1216–1230; Petra Dierkes-Thrun, *Salome's Modernity: Oscar Wilde and the Aesthetics of Transgression* (Ann Arbor: University of Michigan Press, 2011); and Lois Cucullu, "Wilde and Wilder Salomés: Modernizing the Nubile Princess from Sarah Bernhardt to Norma Desmond," *Modernism/modernity* 18, no. 3 (2011): 495–524.

35 See Vivian Sobchak, "'Surge and Splendor': A Phenomenology of the Hollywood Historical Epic," *Representations* 29 (Winter 1990): 24–49.
36 Charles Brackett, Billy Wilder, and D. M. Marshman, Jr., *Sunset Boulevard: The Complete Screenplay* (Los Angeles: University of California Press, 1999), 2.
37 On Wilder's secrecy, see Sikov, *On Sunset Boulevard*, 283. On Paramount's laissez-faire attitude, see Christensen, *America's Corporate Art*, 171: "As *Sunset Boulevard* would argue, in Hollywood only at Paramount were the directors and their stars more important than the studio—a hierarchy that was Paramount's brand identity."
38 Sikov writes that Wilder may instead have said "Go shit in your hat." Sikov, *On Sunset Boulevard*, 303. For the Production Code Administration's identification of *Sunset Boulevard*'s unhappy ending, see the *Sunset Boulevard* file in *History of Cinema*, series 1, *Hollywood and the Production Code Selected Files from the Motion Picture Association of America Production Code Administration Collection* (Woodbridge, CT: Primary Source Microfilm, 2006), reel 26.
39 Lillian Ross, *Picture* (New York: Da Capo Press, 2002 [1952]), 200.
40 Sir Joshua Reynolds, *Discourses on Art*, ed. Stephen O. Mitchell (Indianapolis, IN: Bobbs-Merrill, 1965 [1797]), 93.
41 Margaret Farrand Thorp, "The Motion Picture and the Novel," *American Quarterly* 3, no. 3 (1951): 195. André Bazin would unknowingly concur when he found that the Western, that most epic of archetypal Hollywood genres, had become "novelistic"—evidencing "originality of their characters, their psychological flavor, an engaging individuality"—under the direction of young filmmakers like Anthony Mann. Bazin, "The Evolution of the Western," *What Is Cinema?*, trans. Hugh Gray, vol. 2 (Berkeley: University of California Press, 1971), 155–156. Jeff Menne usefully reads against the grain Bazin's claim of the Western's novelization, finding that the psychologization of the cowboy is matched by a heightened interest in political economy, the latter a hallmark of the reflexive New Hollywood. As I have endeavored to show in this chapter, the usurpation of a sense of literariness is just as much a sign of Hollywood's new era. See Menne, *Post-Fordist Cinema*, 42.
42 The writing awards given by the Academy changed frequently up until 1957, when the distinction between Best Original and Best Adapted Screenplay was established. Between 1948 and 1957, a third award, Best Motion Picture Story, was given to honor the story (i.e., not the screenplay) conceived originally for the screen. That honor was eliminated in 1957 and implicitly incorporated into the awards that currently exist. See Tim Dirks, "Academy Awards: Best Screenplays and Writers," *Filmsite*, www.filmsite.org/bestscreenplays.html.
43 Philip K. Scheuer, "Moviemakers Get Tough in Tearing Apart Own Institution and Some of Society's Ills," *The Los Angeles Times*, December 24, 1950, C1+.
44 Saxe Commins to Joseph L. Mankiewicz, November 24, 1950, Random House collection, Box 295, Columbia University Rare Book & Manuscript Library.
45 "One-Man Studio," *Time Magazine*, June 12, 1950, 72.
46 Leo Rosten, "Mostly About Mankiewicz," *Reporter*, December 12, 1950, 40.
47 Sam Staggs, *All About* All About Eve (New York: St. Martin's Griffin, 2001), 8.

48 Bordwell, Staiger, and Thompson, *Classical Hollywood Cinema*, 3–12.
49 At least as Fox presented it in its exhibitors' catalogue, *Eve* was conceived more explicitly and fully as a Broadway-Hollywood hybrid:

> Once in the star's home she proceeds to ape her every gesture and eventually, after winning over the husband, succeeds in getting a hearing that results in an offer to her for a screen-test. She is besieged by reporters. She thought surely she was a star now—and proceeds to gloatingly tell the reporters how she had fooled New York's finest actress for months. She had never been out of Milwaukee where she was born! She had picked up the Norwegian accent from a waitress! Her father ran a restaurant! She had never married! She had saved for months to come to New York and work out a campaign to meet the star and her husband—and then to get on the stage.
>
> But, Eve's screentests are kaput. She doesn't screen well. Hollywood doesn't want her. Neither do her erstwhile friends whom she has made the laughingstock of Broadway. But, Eve insists they forgive her. How Eve gets her second chance and actually gets to Hollywood provides 'All About Eve' with a sensational climax—for she alters her original campaign and this time actually steals the husband-of[sic] another benefactor. Twentieth Century-Fox, *Dynamo* 24, no. 1 (April 1950), no page.

50 Joseph L. Mankiewicz, *All About Eve* (New York: Random House, 1951), 132.
51 Connor, *Studios after the Studios*, 11. Twenty years after the fact and burnishing the movie's legend, Mankiewicz would tell Gary Carey that though his model for Margo Channing was the eighteenth-century English actress Peg Woffington, "She was also Bette Davis. Also Mrs. Bellamy, Maggie Smith and Isabella Andreini, Mrs. Siddons and Joan Crawford, Modjeska, both Molière's wife and his mistress, Jessica Tandy, Laurette Taylor and Rachel, Zoe Caldwell, Sybil Thorndike, and yes, Tallulah [Bankhead]. Every woman for whom acting was identical with existence." Cary and Mankiewicz, *More About* All About Eve, 72–73.
52 See Szalay, *New Deal Modernism*, 237 and Cohan, *Hollywood by Hollywood*, 9.
53 Hodgins, "A Round Table on the Movies," 94, emphasis in the original.
54 Joseph L. Mankiewicz, "Joseph Mankiewicz Answers," *Motion Picture Herald*, August 6, 1949, 8.
55 "Skouras Spanks Manky," *Variety*, August 31, 1949, 3.
56 Kenneth Geist, *Pictures Will Talk: The Life and Films of Joseph L. Mankiewicz* (New York: Scribners, 1978), 151.
57 "Johnston Sounds Public Relations Keynote: 'Cease Intramural Feuds'; Name Depinet Permanent Chairman," *Variety*, August 31, 1949, 3.
58 "Results of Chi P.R. Powwow," *Variety*, September 7, 1949, 6.
59 Twentieth Century-Fox, *Dynamo*, n.p.
60 Mankiewicz, *All About Eve*, 135–136.
61 Mankiewicz, foreword to *All About Eve*, ix.
62 Cary and Mankiewicz, *More About* All About Eve, 105.
63 "'Scheduled Show' Test for 20th Pic," *Variety*, August 9, 1950, 3; John Belton, *Widescreen Cinema* (Cambridge, MA: Harvard University Press, 1992), 188. See also Peter Lev, *Twentieth Century-Fox: The Zanuck-Skouras Years, 1935–1965* (Austin, TX: University of Texas Press, 2013), 172, and Paul Young, *The Cinema Dreams Its Rivals* (Minneapolis: University of Minnesota Press, 2009), 137–192.

64 Twentieth Century-Fox, "We want you to see 'All About Eve' just the way we saw it," advertisement, *Boxoffice*, October 7, 1950, 15.
65 Raymond Williams formulated the concept of "flow," which has since become a keyword in television studies: "In all developed broadcasting systems the characteristic organization, and therefore the characteristic experience, is one of sequence or flow. This phenomenon, of planned flow, is then perhaps the defining characteristic of broadcasting, simultaneously as a technology and as a cultural form." Raymond Williams, *Television: Technology and Cultural Form* (London and New York: Routledge, 2004 [1974]), 86.
66 Peter Bogdanovich, *The Cinema of Alfred Hitchcock* (New York: Museum of Modern Art Film Library, 1963), 43; Linda Williams, "Discipline and Fun: Psycho and Postmodern Cinema," in *Reinventing Film Studies*, eds. Christine Gledhill and Linda Williams (Oxford, UK and New York: Oxford University Press, 2000), 362–363.
67 Bordwell, *Reinventing Hollywood*, 423–424.
68 Frank Krutnick, "A Living Part of the Class Struggle: Diego Rivera's *The Flower Carrier* and the Hollywood Left," in *"Un-American Hollywood," Politics and Film in the Blacklist Era*, eds. Frank Krutnick, Steve Neale, Brian Neve, and Peter Stanfield (New Brunswick, NJ and London: Rutgers University Press, 2007), 73.
69 E. H. Gombrich, "Reynolds's Theory and Practice of Imitation," *The Burlington Magazine for Connoisseurs* 80, no. 467 (February 1942): 45. On the synthesis of history painting and portraiture, Gombrich writes, "The two worlds of portraiture and of history, of realism and imagination are held in a perfect, if precarious, balance." On Reynolds's failure to synthesize his competing aesthetic concepts, see Günter Leypoldt, "A Neoclassical Dilemma in Sir Joshua Reynolds's Reflections on Art," *British Journal of Aesthetics* 39, no.4 (October 1999): 339: "Reynolds tries to go both ways: his aesthetics rests on pillars of objective beauty, which in turn are erected on the yielding foundations of idiosyncratic patterns of observer response, subject to constant change and cultural renegotiation."
70 George F. Custen, *Twentieth Century's Fox: Darryl F. Zanuck and the Culture of Hollywood* (New York: Basic Books, 1997), 333; Cary and Mankiewicz, *More About* All About Eve, 54.
71 William Hazlitt, "Mrs. Siddons," *Examiner*, June 16, 1816, qtd. in Heather McPherson, "Picturing Tragedy: Mrs. Siddons as the Tragic Muse Revisited," *Eighteenth-Century Studies* 33, no. 3 (Spring 2000): 401.
72 I have not been able to determine the provenance of either painting; they may have been painted for the occasion and modeled on Davis and Baxter (just as the portrait of Laura Hunt in Preminger's *Laura* was modeled on Gene Tierney). At least the Eve portrait seems to have remained in Fox's prop collection; it would reappear in Lucy Moore Hadley's bedroom in *Written on the Wind* (Universal-International, 1956).
73 Brackett, Wilder, and Marshman, *Sunset Boulevard*, 22.
74 See Elana Levine, *Her Stories: Daytime Soap Opera and US Television History* (Durham, NC and London: Duke University Press, 2020), 19–43.

75 Darryl Zanuck, qtd. in Belton, *Widescreen Cinema*, 77.
76 See Young, *Cinema Dreams Its Rivals*, 137–191.
77 John Houseman, "Battle over Television: Hollywood Faces the Fifties, Part II," *Harper's Magazine*, May 1, 1950, 51.
78 Mankiewicz, *All About Eve*, 202–203.
79 "'Scheduled Show' Test," 6.
80 James Savage, "Tower Ticker," *Chicago Daily Tribune*, November 10, 1950, 20.
81 In this sense, Eve prefigures Diana Christensen, Faye Dunaway's overtly allegorical figuration of television in Sidney Lumet and Paddy Chayefsky's *Network* (MGM, 1976).
82 "Mankiewicz at the end of *All About Eve* wishes to indicate that the central situation of the film is to be repeated, the ambitious young actress who has preyed upon the successful woman she admires is to be preyed upon in turn. He shows us the new aspirant trying on her idol's cloak before a triple mirror which multiplies to infinity her postures and her self-admiring glances. These are good beginnings but none of the symbolic objects is very deeply imbedded in the story." Thorp, "The Motion Picture and the Novel," 202.
83 Motion Picture Association of America, Inc, *1956 Annual Report*, 15, https://digitalcollections.oscars.org/digital/collection/p15759coll11/id/11758.
84 Eric Johnston, "Accomplishment of 1956 and a Look Ahead," *1956 Annual Report*, 3 https://digitalcollections.oscars.org/digital/collection/p15759coll11/id/11746/rec/6.
85 Knight observed that the escalating costs of productions have induced a need to defray risk by turning to presold properties. Arthur Knight, "The New Frankness in Films," *The Saturday Review*, December 19, 1959, 45.
86 Knight, "The New Frankness," 46.

6 Conclusion

1 At the start of *The Classical Hollywood Cinema*, Bordwell, Staiger, and Thompson admit that they chose their stopping point of 1960 "for reasons of history and of convenience." Although that year marked a point when, among other developments, most production companies had transferred their resources to television production, filmmaking technology had reached a "state of the art," and the international art cinemas presented an alternative to the classical style, 1960 was nonetheless a "somewhat arbitrary" endpoint (10). American commercial cinema never relinquished the continuity style it perfected in the late 1910s, Bordwell has contended, even if changing tastes and technological developments have promoted the development of what he calls "intensified continuity" (David Bordwell, "Intensified Continuity Visual Style in Contemporary American Film," *Film Quarterly* 55, no. 3 (2002): 16–28). For Douglas Gomery, the studio system persists, even as, from his point of view, the "Hollywood studio system is a misnomer": film production in Los Angeles had always been subsidiary to New York based corporate headquarters (*Hollywood Studio System*, 2).

2   In 1952, 368 domestic and foreign features were approved by the PCA, a number that approximates the ten-year average (378.6) and constitutes the median value in the range. The numbers are even more telling when isolating domestic features; 317 American-made movies were approved in 1952, which again constitutes the median and is nearly identical to the ten-year average (320.8). Motion Picture Association of America, Inc, *Annual Report 1956*, 17, https://digitalcollections.oscars.org/digital/collection/p15759coll11/id/11758.
3   Schatz, *Boom and Bust*, 337.
4   Ross, *Picture*, 259, my emphasis.
5   Ibid., 255.
6   Ibid., 268, my emphasis.
7   On "celebrities and personalities" as important subjects for the New Journalism and nonfiction novel, see John Hollowell, *Fact and Fiction: The New Journalism and the Nonfiction Novel* (Chapel Hill: University of North Carolina Press, 1977), 40–41.
8   Ralph Ellison, "The Shadow and the Act" (1949), in *Shadow and Act* (New York: Vintage, 1972), 276.
9   Ralph Ellison, "Change the Joke and Slip the Yoke" (1958), in *Shadow and Act*, 58.
10 Ralph Ellison, *Invisible Man* (Vintage International, 1995 [1952]), 1.
11 Ellison, "The Shadow and the Act," 276–277.
12 See, for example, Catherine Gallagher, "The Rise of Fictionality," in *The Novel*, ed. Franco Moretti (Princeton and Oxford, UK: Princeton University Press, 2006), 1:336–363.
13 Ellison, *Invisible Man*, 581.
14 Mark McGurl, *The Program Era: Postwar Fiction and the Rise of Creative Writing* (Cambridge, MA: Harvard University Press, 2011 [2009]), 49.
15 James Baldwin, *Go Tell It on the Mountain* (New York: Vintage, 2013 [1952]), 38.
16 Baldwin, *Go Tell It on the Mountain*, 39.
17 In an interesting act of self-citation and revision, Baldwin reuses in *The Devil Finds Work* the crucial phrase "she's uglier than mama! She's uglier than me!" Initially, in *Go Tell It on the Mountain*, the words appear in the midst of John Grimes's ecstatic conversion on the "threshing-floor" of his father Gabriel's storefront church; John uses them to refer to "a woman, very old and black … drunk, and dirty, and very old," the young man's allegorical vision of sin. In *The Devil Finds Work*, as Baldwin reflects on his youthful moviegoing, he attributes these words to himself as he points his mother to an "old, very black, and very drunk woman" as a way of explaining to his readers his cross-race, cross-sex identification with Davis in *20,000 Years in Sing Sing* (Michael Curtiz, Warners, 1932). This would lend support to the idea that Davis is the unnamed actress in *Go Tell It on the Mountain*. More importantly, it suggests the importance of Grimes's moviegoing to his incipient self-understanding and self-acceptance. As Baldwin would write two decades later, "I had discovered that my infirmity might not be my doom: my infirmity, or infirmities,

might be forged into weapons." James Baldwin, *The Devil Finds Work* (New York: Vintage International, 2011 [1976]), 7. On the significance of Davis to Baldwin, see Jane Gaines, *Fire and Desire: Mixed-Race Movies in the Silent Era* (Chicago and London: University of Chicago Press, 2001), 24–51.

18 On the essentially ironic nature of Joyce's epiphanies, see Peter K. Garrett, introduction to *Twentieth Century Interpretations of Dubliners: A Collection of Critical Essays*, ed. Peter K. Garrett (Englewood Cliffs, NJ: Prentice-Hall, 1968), 11–16.

19 James Baldwin, *The Fire Next Time*, in *The Collected Essays*, ed. Toni Morrison (New York: Library of America, 1998 [1962]), 301.

20 James Baldwin, "Everybody's Protest Novel," *Collected Essays*, 18.

21 Reviewing *Carmen Jones* (Otto Preminger, 1954), Fox's all-Black cast iteration of Bizet's opera *Carmen*, Baldwin follows Tyler's penchant for reading the fugitive gesture as the starting point of interpretation. In Pearl Bailey's turn as Frankie, played "with such a murderously amused disdain that one cannot quite avoid the suspicion that she is commenting on the film," Baldwin finds evidence that Fox's production "is controlled by another movie which Hollywood was studiously *not* making." In Baldwin's view, the impossibility of that movie, one that would faithfully represent Black life and which would actually attest to racial equality on and off the screen, gives the lie to the industry's self-congratulatory claims. James Baldwin, "Life Straight in De Eye: *Carmen Jones*: Film Spectacular in Color," *Commentary*, January 1, 1954, 74–75. On the affinities between Baldwin's thinking and later poststructuralist theories associated with *Cahiers du Cinéma* and *Screen*, see Ryan Jay Friedman, "'Enough Force to Shatter the Tale to Fragments': Ethics and Textual Analysis in James Baldwin's Film Theory," *ELH* 77, no. 2 (Summer 2010): 385–411.

22 McGurl, *The Program Era*, 366.

23 Leslie Fiedler, "The War against the Academy," *Wisconsin Studies in Contemporary Literature* 5, no. 1 (Winter-Spring 1964): 5.

24 Mary McCarthy, *The Groves of Academe* (New York: Mariner, 2002), 34.

25 Michael Trask, *Camp Sites: Sex, Politics, and Academic Style in Postwar America* (Palo Alto: Stanford University Press, 2012), 64–72.

26 Bruce Kawin, introduction to "Mythical Latin-American Kingdom Story," in *Faulkner's MGM Screenplays*, 430.

27 R. Monta, memo to John Houseman, March 26, 1952, *The Bad and the Beautiful*, Turner/MGM scripts, Margaret Herrick Library, Academy of Motion Picture Arts and Sciences, File B-163.

28 Christensen, *America's Corporate Art*, 152.

29 Larry Lockridge, *Shade of the Raintree, Centennial Edition: The Life and Death of Ross Lockridge, Jr., author of Raintree County* (Bloomington: Indiana University Press, 2014), 236, 269.

30 William York Tindall, "Many-Leveled Fiction: Virginia Woolf to Ross Lockridge," *College English* 10, no. 2 (November 1948): 71. Tindall's praise of *Raintree County*'s "value," understood as dependent "upon the amount of reality under control," resonates with Tindall's Columbia University colleague

Lionel Trilling's description of liberalism in *The Liberal Imagination*: "when we approach liberalism in a critical spirit, we shall fail in critical completeness if we do not take into account the value and necessity of its organizational impulse." The many-leveled fiction finds its political analogue in the many-leveled technocratic bureaucracy. Lionel Trilling, *preface to The Liberal Imagination: Essays on Literature and Society* (New York: New York Review of Books, 2008 [1950]), xx.

31 "Metro Seeks to Sell $1,000,000 Worth of Literary Properties," *Variety*, October 6, 1948, 15. MGM wouldn't sell the rights to *Raintree County*, however. It would be adapted in 1957 in a lavish, three-hour production, released to middling reviews, and would become most famous as the movie during which Montgomery Clift had the car accident that nearly killed him.

Index

Absalom, Absalom! (1936). *See* Faulkner, William
Academy of Motion Picture Arts and Sciences, 84, 163
adaptation
    as affront to the studio system's norms, 146–147
    as distinct from transmedial possibility, 27
    during the Transitional Era (1907–1917), 24
    as index of the studio system's stability, 143–146
    as key concern of The Formula (1924), 33
    studies, 8
    in the theory of remediation, 27–28
Adorno, Theodor W., 2, 101
Adventures of Tom Sawyer, The (1938), 84
Alger, Horatio, 45
All About Eve (1950), 185, 188, 230n49. *See also* Mankiewicz, Joseph L.; Twentieth Century-Fox; Zanuck, Darryl F.
    Academy Awards, 157, 176
    adapted from "The Wisdom of Eve" (Orr, 1946), 158, 161, 172
    as allegory of medium conflict, 164–166, 169–175
        Eve as figure for television, 169–175
        Margo as figure for cinema, 169
    classical style, 175
    difference from *Sunset Boulevard* (1950) and *In a Lonely Place* (1950), 160
    display of *Sarah Siddons as the Tragic Muse* (1784), 166–169
    dispute over authorship in, 163
    scheduled performance exhibition format, 164–166, 172
    as social problem film, 158
All That Heaven Allows (1955), 169
Allred, Jeff, 194–195n24
Amateur Gentleman, The (1926), 131. *See also* Lowry, Malcolm, *Ultramarine* (1933)
ambiguity, 120–121. *See also* commercial aesthetic
American Authors' Authority (AAA), 141–142. *See also* Cain, James M.

American Guide Series (Federal Writers' Project), 97
American Mercury, The, 81
An American Tragedy (1931) (film), 51
Anderson, Sherwood, 14, 18
Applause (1970), 164
Arbuckle, Roscoe ("Fatty"), 22
Arnold, Thurman, 64
Art of the Motion Picture, The (Jean Benoît-Lévy, 1946), 152. *See also* Mankiewicz, Joseph L., "Film Author! Film Author!" (1947)
Ashbery, John, 128
Association of Motion Picture Producers (AMPP), 33
auteur theory, 4, 141, 146, 152
Authors' League of America
    defense of literariness, 30
    origins in 1912, 25
    scuttling of American Authors' Authority, 142

backstudio picture (genre), 16, 34, 39, 58, 160
    historical variant, 86, 184
Bacon, Lloyd, 88
Bad and the Beautiful, The (1952), 185–189, 191
    and impossible adaptation, 186–189
Baldwin, James, 19–20
    Devil Finds Work, The (1976), 182
    Go Tell it on the Mountain (1953), 181–183
Ballard, Todhunter, 82
Bard College, 183
Barry, Iris, 84–85. *See also* Museum of Modern Art (MoMA) Film Department
Barrymore, Lionel, 60
Barthelmess, Richard, 14, 131
Barton, Ralph, 14, 16, 195n29
Battleground (1949), 188–189
Bazin, André, 229n41
Beery, Wallace, 55, 60, 66
Beetson, Fred, 144. *See also* Production Code Administration (PCA)
Belasco, David, 42, 45

236

Belfrage, Cedric, 97–100
    criticism of "super-liberalism", 99, 106
Bellamy, Ralph, 89
Belton, John, 164
Ben Hur: A Tale of the Christ (1880) (novel), 23–24
Benjamin, Walter, 101
Bennett, Whitman, 29, 31
Bennington College, 56
Bergman, Maurice, 83
Big Money, The (1936). *See* Dos Passos, John
Birth of a Nation, The (1915), 180, 202n72
Black Mask (pulp magazine), 82
Blackwell, Carlyle, 127. *See also* Tyler, Parker
Blanton, C. D., 120. *See also* late modern epic
Blind Alley (1939), 151. *See also Dark Past, The* (1948)
Blockade (1938), 84
Body and Soul (1925), 18
Bogart, Humphrey, 146–147, 167, 227n14
Bolter, Jay David, 27–28, 197n25. *See also* transmedial possibility, vis-à-vis remediation
Bombshell (1933), 39, 58, 70, 87, 184
Book of the Month Club, 190
Borderline (1930), 18
Bordwell, David, 3, 122, 160, 166. *See also Classical Hollywood Cinema, The* (1985)
Bourdieu, Pierre, 192n2
Bow, Clara, 86
box office poison, 83, 87. *See also* Brandt, Harry
Boy Meets Girl (1938) (film), 86, 88–89, 227n3
Boy Meets Girl (Bella and Samuel Spewack, 1935) (play), 88, 100, 104
Boyd, Ernest, 18
Boys in the Back Room, The: Notes on California Novelists (Wilson, 1941), 90–91, 94, 96, 101
Brackett, Charles, 153, 154. *See also Sunset Boulevard* (1950)
Brandt, Harry, 83, 88, 161
Breen, Joseph, 144, 186. *See also* Production Code Administration (PCA)
Brenon, Herbert. *See Great Gatsby, The* (1926) (film)
Brooks, Van Wyck
    America's Coming-of-Age (1915), 104, 108. *See also* West, Nathanael, *Day of the Locust, The* (1939)
    Flowering of New England, 1815–1865, The (1936), 108
    and "totalitarian cultural values", 108
Brown, Clarence. *See* Metro-Goldwyn-Mayer (MGM), *Intruder in the Dust* (1949)

Brown, Nacio Herb, 186. *See also Singin' in the Rain* (1952)
Browning, Elizabeth Barrett, 133. *See also Mad Love* (1935)
Browning, Robert, 133. *See also Mad Love* (1935)
Browning, Tod, 66, 69–70
Bruccoli, Matthew J., 41, 201n62. *See also* Fitzgerald, F. Scott
Bryher (Annie Winifred Ellerman), 18
Buell, Lawrence, 44–45
Bulletin (Authors' League of America), 25
Burke, Kenneth, 180, 220–221n20. *See also* Ellison, Ralph
Bush, W. Stephen, 24
Byron, Lord George Gordon, 5

Cabinet of Doctor Caligari, The (1920), 133
Cagney, James, 6, 88
Cahiers du Cinéma, 5, 146, 152
Cain, James M., 91
    Double Indemnity (1935), 141
    maturation of style, 81–82
    "Paradise" (1933), 81
    "Pastorale" (1928), 81
    Postman Always Rings Twice, The (1933) (novel), 81–82, 94, 141, 187
    anti-Hollywood sentiment, 145–146. *See also Postman Always Rings Twice, The* (1946) (film)
    "Taking of Montfaucon, The" (1929), 81
Caldwell, John Thornton, 4, 193n7
Camille: or, the Fate of a Coquette (1926), 14–20
Capote, Truman, 180
Capra, Frank, 110
Caspary, Vera, 145
Castle, Gregory, 102. *See also* modernist *bildungsroman*
Cerasulo, Tom, 11n4
Cerf, Bennett, 158. *See also* Mankiewicz, Joseph L.
Chandler, Raymond
    Big Sleep, The (1939) (novel), 66
    Farewell, My Lovely (1940), 145
Chaplin, Charlie, 14, 17–18, 124
Christensen, Jerome, 4, 6, 58, 86, 188, 193n7, 193n17
    Lord Byron's Strength (1993), 5, 193n14
    theory of corporate authorship, 4–8, 13
Citizen Kane (1941), 174, 185, 189
Classical Hollywood Cinema, The (1985), 3, 12, 24, 51, 82–83, 117
classical style, 3–4, 147. *See also All About Eve* (1950); *In a Lonely Place* (1950) (film); *Sunset Boulevard* (1950)
    conditions for allegorical transformation, 160

Clive, Colin, 133. *See also Mad Love* (1935)
Close Up (film journal), 19
Clune, Michael, 223–224n48
Cohan, Steven, 86
Cole, Lester, 69
Columbia Pictures, 3, 151
 eliminates story department, 151
 employment of James M. Cain, 81–82
 commercial aesthetic, 117–118
 Committee on the Sale of Original Material, 151–152
Confessions of a Nazi Spy (1939), 84
Connor, J. D., 4, 160, 177, 193n7
Conrad, Joseph, 107
Cooper, Gary, 110
Copyright Act of 1870, The, 197n27
Copyright Act of 1891, The, 197n27
Cowley, Malcolm, 180
Crane, Stephen, 178
Cummings, E. E., 86, 122

Dardis, Tom, 11n4, 65–66
Dark Past, The (1948), 151
Daumier, Honoré, 104, 109
Davies, Marion, 61
Davis, Bette, 163, 173, 182
Decherney, Peter, 23
Decline of the West (Spengler, 1918), 109
DeMille, Cecil B., 153–155
Denning, Michael, 95, 97, 98
Devil Finds Work, The (1976), 183. *See also* Baldwin, James
Dick, Philip K., 120
Didion, Joan, 180
Dies Committee, 91. *See also* the House Committee on Un-American Activities (HUAC)
Dinner at Eight (1933), 6, 7, 60
 as allegory of MGM's consistency, 60–61
dispositif, 10
Dmytryk, Edward, 145. *See also Murder, My Sweet* (1944)
Doctor X (1932), 135
Donen, Stanley, 184. *See also Singin' in the Rain* (1952)
Don'ts and Be Carefuls (1927), 33. *See also* Production Code, The
Dos Passos, John
 Big Money, The (1936), 98–99
 Manhattan Transfer (1925), 9, 21–22, 37–39, 45
Double Indemnity (1944) (film), 124
Douglas, Kirk, 185
Dragonwyck (1946). *See* Mankiewicz, Joseph L.
Drake, Frances, 133. *See also Mad Love* (1935)

Dreiser, Theodore, 14, 18
 An American Tragedy (1925), 50–51, 149
 "Real Sins of Hollywood, The" (1932), 51, 54
Dumas, Alexandre *fils*, 14, 18–20
Dunne, Philip, 152

Eaton, Mark, 199n46
Education of Henry Adams, The (Adams, 1907), 102
Eisenstein, Sergei, 51
Eliot, T. S., 118, 120, 122–123, 180
 on Henry James, 57
 "Tradition and the Individual Talent" (1919), 56–57
 Waste Land, The (1922), 113, 119, 125, 130
 assertion of authorial control in, 120
Ellison, Ralph, 19–20
 Invisible Man (1952), 119, 180, 181
 "Shadow and the Act, The" (1949), 181
Elsaesser, Thomas, 11n7
Emerson, John, 16
Empson, William, 1, 6, 7, 120
Esty, Jed, 103, 224n57

Famous Players-Lasky Corporation (FPL). *See also* Paramount Pictures
Farber, Manny, 142, 148
Faulkner, William, 12, 15, 68–69, 120, 164, 189
 Absalom, Absalom! (1936), 7, 59, 179
 corporate personhood of Sutpen's Hundred, 70–72, 74
 lawyer as flaw in Sutpen's Design, 77–80, 210n57, 210n58
 Overvoice as corporate expression of Sutpen's Hundred, 64, 74–77, 80–81
 punctuation as textual voice, 64
 Shreve McCannon's comic reduction of the novel's plot, 63
 Sutpen's "innocence" as lack of agency, 72–73
 "Art of Fiction, The" (*Paris Review* interview) (Jean Stein, 1956), 65–67, 69–70
 correspondence with Ben Wasson, 68
 "Golden Land" (1935), 79, 208n45
 "Louisiana Lou" (1933) (MGM assignment), 66
 maturation of style in the mid-1930s, 63–64
 "Mythical-Latin American Kingdom" unproduced MGM screenplay, 186
 Portable Faulkner, The (1946), 180
 Pylon (1935), 64, 67–68, 70, 73, 78–79
 Sound and the Fury, The (1929), 80
 "Turnabout" (1932), 77
 Wild Palms, The (1939), 81
Fay, Jennifer, 136, 137
Federal Art Project, 104

Fialkowski, Barbara, 124. *See also* Tyler, Parker
Fidelity Pictures. *See House by the River* (1950) (film)
Fiedler, Leslie
   on *Look Homeward, Angel* (Wolfe, 1929), 107
   "War against the Academy, The" (1964), 183
film noir, 145–146
Filmakers, The. *See* Lupino, Ida
Fine, David, 96, 97
Fine, Richard, 60, 197n17
Fitzgerald, F. Scott, 8, 11n4, 29, 147
   Beautiful and Damned, The (1922)
      mockery of transmedial possibility, 40–41
      part of Warners' "Screen Classics" campaign, 28
      sale of moving picture rights to Warners, 41
   correspondence with Harold Ober, 41–42
   correspondence with Maxwell Perkins, 44
   Great Gatsby, The (1925), 41–45
      sale of moving picture rights to Famous Players-Lasky, 23, 41, 201n62
      Tom Buchanan's intellectual fraudulence, 104–105
   Love of the Last Tycoon, The: A Western (1941), 55
      Aldous Huxley as model for screenwriter Boxley, 62
      debts to T. S. Eliot, 56–57
      Stahr's tragic incommensurability with his studio, 58–59
   notes on the "Thalberg system", 70
   Tender Is the Night (1934), 130, 140
   This Side of Paradise (1920), 41
   Trimalchio (draft of *The Great Gatsby*), 43
Fitzgerald, Frances Scott ("Scottie"), 46
Fitzgerald, Zelda, 46
Flesh (1932), 66
Foltz, Jonathan, 10, 213n43
Ford, Charles Henri, 122
Ford, John, 85
Forest Lawn cemetery, 62
Formula, The (1924), 17, 33, 44, 48, 50. *See also* Production Code, The
Foucault, Michel, 5
Fox, William, 132
Frankenstein (1931), 135
Freaks (1932), 135
Freed, Arthur, 184–186. *See also Singin' in the Rain* (1952)
Freund, Karl, 133. *See also Mad Love* (1935)
Friede, Donald, 147–148

Gable, Clark, 66
Garbo, Greta, 124

Gautreau, Justin, 143
Geertz, Clifford, 4
Gentleman's Agreement (1947), 121
Gentlemen Prefer Blondes: The Illuminating Diary of a Professional Lady (1925). *See* Loos, Anita
Gibbons, Cedric, 55
Gilbert, John, 86
Gleeson-White, Sarah, 195n26, 209n52
Go Tell it on the Mountain (1953). *See also* Baldwin, James
Goble, Mark, 10
Godden, Richard, 74, 206n29
Gold, Michael, 200n55
Golden Jubilee celebration (1939), 84–85
Goldwyn, Samuel, 3, 151
Gombrich, E. H., 4, 169
Gomery, Douglas, 3
Gone with the Wind (1939) (film), 82, 88, 144, 159, 175, 188–189
Goulding, Edmund, 6, 10
Goya, Francisco, 104, 109
Grahame, Gloria, 146
Grand Hotel (1932), 10, 55, 58, 60
Grapes of Wrath, The (1940) (film), 85
Grauman's Egyptian Theatre, 90, 110
Great Gatsby, The (1926) (film), 45–49. *See also* Fitzgerald, F. Scott, *Great Gatsby, The* (1925)
Great Train Robbery, The (1903), 85
Greed (1924), 51, 203n96
Green, Henry, 10
Greenblatt, Stephen, 192n2
Greer, Jane, 136
Griffith, D. W., 14, 90, 180, 202n72. *See also Birth of a Nation, The* (1915); *Intolerance* (1916)
Groves of Academe, The (McCarthy, 1952), 183–184
Grusin, Richard, 27–28, 197n25. *See also* transmedial possibility, vis-à-vis remediation
Gunga Din (1939), 82
Gunning, Tom, 23, 196n9

H. D. (Hilda Doolittle), 18
Hagen, Jean, 184. *See also Singin' in the Rain* (1952)
Hammett, Dashiell, 9, 95
Hampton, Benjamin, 85
Hand, Learned, 26
Hansen, Miriam, 116. *See also* vernacular modernism
Harlow, Jean, 58, 61
Harris, Donal, 7
Harrison, Louis Reeves, 24–25

Index

Harvard University, 63, 75, 104–107, 109, 189
Hawks, Howard, 58, 77
   friendship with William Faulkner, 66
Hawthorne, Nathaniel, 74
Hays, Will H., 16–17, 33
Hays Office. *See* Production Code
   Administration (PCA); Hays, Will H.
Hearst, William Randolph, 29, 31, 59, 61
Hecht, Ben, 88, 95, 105, 187
Hegeman, Susan, 37, 200n53
Hepburn, Katharine, 144
Hergesheimer, Joseph, 18
Hicks, Granville, 99
Himes, Chester, 69
History of the Movies, A (Hampton, 1931), 85
Hitchcock, Alfred, 166
Holden, William. *See Dark Past, The* (1948);
   Sunset Boulevard (1950)
Hollywood (1923), 16, 34
Hollywood Anti-Nazi League, 100
Hollywood Boulevard (1936), 86, 144
Hollywood Cavalcade (1939), 86, 89–90, 98, 110
Hollywood Hussars, 110
Hollywood novel (genre), 34–35, 39, 81
   modernist variant, 91–112
Hollywood Renaissance, 177
Hollywood studio system, 3–7
   discourse of maturation, 13, 84–86
   as group style, 3–4
   as industrial organization, 3
   reduction of story departments, 151
   as social world, 4
   turn from source material (1948–1953), 147–148
   turn to remakes, 151
   weakening norms of, 148
Hollywood-the-destroyer myth, 9
Hope of Heaven (John O'Hara, 1938), 94–95
Houghton Mifflin, 190
House by the River (1950), 149–150
House Committee on Un-American Activities (HUAC), 146
House of Strangers (1949), 162. *See also* Mankiewicz, Joseph L.
Houseman, John, 148, 172, 185
Howells, William Dean, 198n27
Hughes, Dorothy B., 146, 227n14
Hughes, Howard, 144
Hughes, Langston, 69
Huston, John, 153, 178–179, 184. *See also Picture* (Lillian Ross, 1952)
Huxley, Aldous, 12
   After Many a Summer Dies the Swan (1939), 54, 59, 61–63, 95, 214n43
   Ape and Essence (1948), 140–141

I Lost My Girlish Laughter (Jane Allen, 1938), 144
I Should Have Stayed Home (1938). *See also* McCoy, Horace
Im, Seo Hee, 59, 120. *See also* late modernism
In a Lonely Place (1950) (film), 146–147, 185, 189
   anticlassicism, 166–167
   Nicholas Ray as auteur, 146
   Santana Productions as auteur, 146–147
   similarity to *House by the River* (1950), 149
   similarity to *Sunset Boulevard* (1950), 153
In a Lonely Place (Hughes, 1947) (novel), 146
In the Sargasso Sea (Thomas Janvier, 1898), 107–108
industrial reflexivity, 4, 6–7, 13
institutions, 2–3, 6, 12
Intolerance (1916), 189
Intruder in the Dust (1949) (film), 189
Invisible Man, The (1933) (film). *See also* Ellison, Ralph, *Invisible Man* (1952)
Invisible Man, The (H. G. Wells, 1897). *See also* Ellison, Ralph, *Invisible Man* (1952)
Invisible Man (1952). *See also* Ellison, Ralph

Jackson, Robert, 203n103, 207n44
Jacobs, Lea, 203
Jacobs, Lewis: *The Rise of the American Film* (1939), 85
James, C. L. R., 64
Jameson, Fredric, 219n13, 221n22
Jannings, Emil, 114–115
Johnston, Eric, 162, 176. *See also* Motion Picture Association of America (MPAA)
Joseph Burstyn, Inc. v. Wilson (1952) (The *Miracle* decision), 1, 177–178
Joyce, James, 15, 63, 118, 150, 180, 183
   Portrait of the Artist as a Young Man, A (1916), 102–103, 111
   Ulysses (1922), 76, 121, 189
   assertion of authorial control in, 120
Jurca, Catherine, 4, 83, 88–89, 193n7, 226n3

Kalem Co. v. Harper Brothers (1911), 24–27
Kazan, Elia, 121, 173
Kazin, Alfred, 52
Keil, Charlie, 24
Kellman, Steven G., 8
Kelly, Gene, 184. *See also Singin' in the Rain* (1952)
Kenner, Hugh, 76, 103
Kenny, John M., 39–40, 44, 46
Knight, Arthur, 177
Knight, Eric, 94
künstlerroman, 102, 109, 131, 183. *See also* modernist bildungsroman

Index

La Dame aux camélias (Dumas *fils*, 1848), 14
   Hollywood adaptations, 16
Lacombe, Emile Henry, 27
Lady from Shanghai, The (1947), 174
Laemmle, Carl, 116
Lang, Fritz, 149. *See also House by the River*
   (1950) (film)
Lasky, Jesse, 22–25, 30, 42
Last Command, The (1928), 114–115, 138.
   See also Lowry, Malcolm, "Hollywood
   and the War"
late modern epic. *See also* Lowry, Malcolm;
   Tyler, Parker
   as distinct from modern epic (Franco
     Moretti), 119
late modernism, 59
Laura (1944) (film), 145, 166
Laura (Caspary, 1943) (novel), 145
Lazy River (1934), 66. *See also* Faulkner,
   William, "Louisiana Lou"
Le Jeune Européen (Pierre Drieu la Rochelle,
   1927), 102
Leave Her to Heaven (1945) (film), 148–149
Leave Her to Heaven (Ben Ames Williams, 1944)
   (novel), 148
Les Mains d'Orlac (Maurice Renard, 1920), 133.
   See also Mad Love (1935)
Les Misérables (Victor Hugo, 1862 tr. Isabel F.
   Hapgood), 109, 217n94. *See also* West,
   Nathanael, *Day of the Locust, The* (1939)
Lester, Bruce, 88
Letter to Three Wives, A (1949), 158, 161. *See also*
   Mankiewicz, Joseph L.
Levee, M. C., 33, 44. *See also* Formula, The
   (1924)
Lewis, Sinclair, 9, 14, 18
Lewton, Val, 185
Lindsay, Vachel, *The Art of the Moving Picture*
   (1915), 117
Lockridge, Ross, Jr., 189–191
Loew's Theatres Incorporated, 84. *See also*
   Metro-Goldwyn-Mayer (MGM)
Loney, Glenn, 197–198n27
Look Homeward, Angel (Wolfe, 1929), 105, 107
Loos, Anita, 16. *See also Camille: or, the Fate of a*
   Coquette (1926)
   But Gentlemen Marry Brunettes (1928), 17
   Gentlemen Prefer Blondes: The Illuminating
     Diary of a Professional Lady (1925), 14, 45
   global ambit, 15–16
   maximal transmedial possibility, 36–37
   Whole Town's Talking, The: A Farce in Three
     Acts (1923), 36
   widespread admiration of, 14–15
Lorre, Peter, 133, 137

Love's Crucifixion (1928), 131. *See also* Lowry,
   Malcolm, *Ultramarine* (1933)
Lowry, Malcolm, 180, 183
   1940 Under the Volcano, The, 128, 129, 136
   admiration of Joseph L. Mankiewicz, 141
   "cinematic" style, 132
   correspondence with Jonathan Cape, 128–130,
     139–140
   "Hollywood and the War" (1939), 113–115,
     119, 139
   In Ballast to the White Sea (1935–36), 131–132
   inspired by *Sunrise: A Song of Two Humans*
     (1927), 132
   interest in German Expressionism, 132
   October Ferry to Gabriola (1970), 128
   Tender Is the Night (with Margerie Lowry,
     1949) (screenplay), 140–141
   preface, 130–131, 140
   "Through the Panama", 218n4
   Ultramarine (1933), 131
   Under the Volcano (1947), 128–129, 189
     as an anti-*Ulysses*, 118, 129–130
     Laruelle's interpretation of *Las Manos de*
       Orlac, 137–139
     Las Manos de Orlac as emblem of
       Hollywood's global distribution, 133,
       135–136. *See also Mad Love* (1935)
     as late modern epic, 119–121
     similarity to *Out of the Past* (1947), 137
     superfluity of organizing systems, 129
   Voyage that Never Ends, The (uncompleted
     novel series), 140
Lowry, Margerie (née Bonner), 113, 130, 140–141
Luhmann, Niklas, 192n2
Luke, Keye, 133. *See also Mad Love* (1935)
Lupino, Ida, 153–154
Lurie, Peter, 207n43, 207–208n45

MacArthur, Charles, 88, 105
Macdonald, Dwight, 108, 142
Macpherson, Kenneth, 18
Mad Love (1935), 181
   as emblem of Hollywood's "commercial
     aesthetic" in *Under the Volcano*, 137–139
   as self-consciously "artistic" MGM product,
     133–135
Magic Mountain, The (Mann, 1924), 186
Magny, Claude-Edmonde, 9
Mahin, John Lee, 92, 105
   success in the "Thalberg system", 60, 77
Mailer, Norman, 180
Maltby, Richard, 118
de Man, Paul, 5
Manganaro, Marc, 120
Manhatta (1921), 17

242   Index

Mankiewicz, Herman J.
  Dinner at Eight (1933), 60
  "Herman J. Mankiewicz Fresh Air Fund for Writers", 52
Mankiewicz, Joseph L., 141, 169. *See also All About Eve* (1950)
  conflict with Spyros Skouras, 162–163
  correspondence with Bennett Cerf, 157–158
  disdain for exhibitors, 161
  Dragonwyck (1946) as allegory of desire for independence, 160–161
  "Film Author! Film Author!" (1947), 152–153, 160
  Fox's "gun for hire", 164
  literary aspirations for American film, 161–162
Mann, Denise, 4, 193
Mann, Thomas, 161, 186
Marion, Frances, 60
  success in the "Thalberg system", 60–61, 77
Marsh, Joss Lutz, 42
Marx, Sam, 66, 186
Maugham, W. Somerset, 14, 28
May Irwin Kiss (1896), 85
Mayer, Louis B., 6, 55, 62, 71, 144, 156, 178–179, 185, 188
  clash with Irving Thalberg, 57–58
McCarthy, Mary, 183
McCoy, Horace, 91
  I Should Have Stayed Home (1938), 7, 95–97, 101
  They Shoot Horses, Don't They? (1935), 82, 93–94, 96, 97
McGurl, Mark, 183, 192n2, 200n52
McLuhan, Marshall, 27, 119
  on *Magic and Myth of the Movies* (Tyler, 1947), 121
McWilliams, Carey, 110
Mencken, H.L., 14, 18, 35, 142
Menjou, Adolphe, 88
Menne, Jeff, 4, 229n41
Merton of the Movies (1924) (film), 34
Merton of the Movies (Harry Leon Wilson, 1922), 35, 45, 87, 226n75
Metro-Goldwyn-Mayer (MGM), 3, 5–8, 10, 12, 13, 39, 53, 58, 184. *See also Bombshell* (1933); *Dinner at Eight* (1933); Faulkner, William; Fitzgerald, F. Scott; Thalberg, Irving
  Ars Gratia Artis motto, 12, 55, 133
  Fortune profile (1932), 55, 67
  Intruder in the Dust (Faulkner, 1948), 180
  MGM Modernism defined, 60, 63
  semiannual novel award, 189, 190
  "Tiffany's of Hollywood", 5–6
Michaels, Walter Benn, 7, 52, 207n37

Micheaux, Oscar, 18
Mickey Mouse, 66
Mildred Pierce (1945) (film), 124
Miller, Patsy Ruth, 14, 105
  My Hollywood, When Both of Us Were Young (1988), 92
  That Flannigan Girl (1939), 92–94
Miller, William, 143, 177
Million and One Nights, A (Ramsaye, 1926), 85, 117
Minimum Basic Agreement of 1951 (MBA), 152
Minnelli, Vincente, 186. *See also Bad and the Beautiful, The* (1952)
Mitchell, Margaret, 188
Mitchum, Robert, 136
modernism, 7–13
  following Clement Greenberg, 8
modernist bildungsroman, 101–103
Molotov-Ribbentrop Pact, 113
Monogram Pictures, 3
Moore, Marianne, 122
Motion Picture Association of America (MPAA), 162, 176
Motion Picture Herald (trade newspaper), 110, 117, 161
Motion Picture Magazine (fan magazine), 48
Motion Picture Patents Company (Edison Trust), 24, 25, 143
Motion Picture Producers and Distributors of America (MPPDA), 3, 17, 33, 40, 44, 48, 50, 117
Motion Pictures' Greatest Year campaign (1938), 13, 83–84, 88–89, 162, 226n3
Moviegoer, The (Percy, 1961), 182
Movies are Better than Ever campaign (1950), 13, 162, 164
Movies March On!, The (1939), 85
moving picture rights, 1, 13, 147, 197n27. *See also* adaptation; transmedial possibility
  origins of, 23–27, 141
Moving Picture World (trade newspaper), 1, 24
Mr. Deeds Goes to Town (1936), 110
Mrs. Dalloway (Woolf, 1925), 128, 189
Mukařovský, Jan, 4
Murder, My Sweet (1944). *See also* Chandler, Raymond, *Farewell, My Lovely* (1940)
Murnau, F.W., 132. *See also Sunrise, A Song of Two Humans* (1927)
Murray, Simone, 23, 197n23
Museum of Modern Art (MoMA) Film Department, 84–85
Mutual Film Corp. v. Industrial Commission of Ohio (1915), 1, 177
myth. *See* late modern epic

Nathan, George Jean, 18
National Board of Review, 198n27
Native Son (Richard Wright, 1940), 10, 181–182
Nazimova, Alla, 17
  financially ruined by *Salomé* (1922), 153
Neilan, Marshall ("Mickey"), 90
neoclassical Hollywood, 177
neoclassical painting, 167–169
neo-naturalism, 12
New Criticism, The, 120
New Historicism, 5
New Journalism, The, 178
New Modernist Studies, 2, 8
New York Times, The, 21–22
New Yorker, The, 179
Nieland, Justus, 136–137
Ninotchka (1939), 82
Norris, Frank
  McTeague (1899), 51
  Octopus: A Story of California, The (1901), 51–52
North, Michael, 40
Nugent, Frank, 86

O'Brien, Pat, 88
O'Connor, Donald, 185. *See also Singin' in the Rain* (1952)
O'Hara, Frank, 128
Ober, Harold, 41. *See also* Fitzgerald, F. Scott
Of Human Bondage (1934). *See* Baldwin, James
Of Time and the River (1935). *See* Wolfe, Thomas
Office of Inter-American Affairs, 136
Office of the Coordinator of Inter-American Affairs, The, 225n69
Office of War Information (OWI), 13, 118, 225n69
On the Lot and Off (George Randolph and Lilian Chester, 1924), 34
Once in a Lifetime (Moss Hart and George S. Kaufman, 1930), 100
Orlacs Hande (1924), 133. *See also Mad Love* (1935)
Orr, Mary: "The Wisdom of Eve" (1946), 158, 172
Out of the Past (1947), 136
Outward Bound (1930), 131–132, 225n62. *See also* Lowry, Malcolm, *In Ballast to the White Sea* (1935–36)

Panic in the Streets (1950), 157
Paramount Pictures, 3, 7, 13, 16, 53, 84, 86
  as purchaser of motion picture rights, 22–23
  considers buying a publishing house, 29–30
  cosponsors First International Congress on Motion Picture Arts with the Authors' League of America, 30–31
  employment of James M. Cain, 81
  fame and infamy, 22
  Gentlemen Prefer Blondes (1928) (film), 36–37
  in *Manhattan Transfer* (1925), 22, 38–39
  Merton of the Movies (1924), 35
  monopolization of stars and stories, 25
  relation to Famous Players-Lasky Corporation, 21–23
Parker, Dorothy, 11n4, 93
Parsons, Louella, 107
Percy, Walker, 182
Perloff, Marjorie, 128
Photo Drama Motion-Picture Co., Inc. v. Social Uplift Film Corporation (1914), 26
Photoplay (fan magazine), 48, 195n28
Picture (Lillian Ross, 1952), 178–180
  next generation MGM Modernism, 179–180
  Singin' in the Rain (1952), 184
Picture-Play Magazine (fan magazine), 49
Pinky (1949), 121
Pirosh, Robert, 189. *See also Battleground* (1949)
Poe, Edgar Allan, 74, 181
  Narrative of Arthur Gordon Pym of Nantucket, The (1838), 181
Popular Front, the, 94
Postman Always Rings Twice, The (1946) (film), 146, 187, 190
postmodernity, 120. *See also* postmodernism
Pound, Ezra, 122
Poverty Row, 3, 82
Powell, Dick, 185
Preminger, Otto, 145, 166. *See also Laura* (1944) (film)
Princeton University, 104
Pringle, Aileen, 195n29
Production Code, the, 6, 17, 33, 117, 141, 143, 148, 156, 177
Production Code Administration (PCA), 3, 144, 148, 156, 178, 186
Program Era, The (2009). *See* McGurl, Mark
Promised Land: Notes for a History (Belfrage, 1938), 97–100
Proust, Marcel, 104

Queer People (Carroll and Garrett Graham, 1930), 100, 144

Raintree County (Lockridge, Jr., 1948), 189
Ramsaye, Terry, 85, 117
Random House, 76, 100, 102, 158, 164
Rapf, Harry, 58
Rappe, Virginia, 22
Rascoe, Burton, 32
ratings system, 177. *See also* Motion Picture Association of America (MPAA)

Index

Ray, Nicholas, 169. *See also In a Lonely Place* (1950) (film)
Rebel without a Cause (1955), 169
Recognitions, The (William Gaddis, 1955), 119
Red Badge of Courage, The (1951) (film), 178–180, 184. *See also Picture* (Lillian Ross, 1952)
Reed, Carol. *See Third Man, The* (1949)
Reid, Wallace, 22, 93
remediation, 27–28, 197n25. *See also* transmedial possibility
Republic Pictures, 3
    employment of Nathanael West, 82
Reynolds, Debbie, 184. *See also Singin' in the Rain* (1952)
Reynolds, Sir Joshua, 157, 166–169. *See also Sarah Siddons as the Tragic Muse* (1784)
Rivkin, Allen, 152
RKO Radio Pictures, 3, 85, 136, 145
Robeson, Paul, 14, 18–20
Rogin, Michael, 90
Romanticism, 5
Ross, Lillian. *See Picture* (Lillian Ross, 1952)
Ross, Stephen M., 64. *See also* Faulkner, William, *Absalom, Absalom!* (1936)
Rosten, Leo, 7, 79, 93, 107
    assessment of *All About Eve* (1950), 158
    Hollywood: The Movie Colony, The Movie Makers (1941), 85–86
Round Table on the Movies, A (*Life* magazine, 1949), 141, 161
Ryder, Albert Pinkham, 104

Salomé (1922), 153
Samson and Delilah (1949), 154. *See also Sunset Boulevard* (1950)
Sarah Siddons as the Tragic Muse (1784), 166–169, 172. *See also All About Eve* (1950)
    as medium allegory, 169
Saroyan, William, 91
Sarris, Andrew, 5, 152
Sartre, Jean-Paul, 37
Saturday Evening Post, 23
Savage, James, 173. *See also All About Eve* (1950)
scenario writing. *See* screenwriting
Schary, Dore, 153, 157, 178–180
    production of *Battleground* (1949), 189
Schatz, Thomas, 3
Schenck, Joseph, 16, 89
Schenck, Nicholas, 3, 179–180, 184, 188. *See also Picture* (Lillian Ross, 1952)
Schnee, Charles, 186. *See also Bad and the Beautiful, The* (1952)
Schulberg, B.P., 91

Schulberg, Budd, 11n4, 56
    "Literature of the Film: The Hollywood Novel" (1940), 91–92, 96
    What Makes Sammy Run? (1941), 91–92
Schulman Lardner, Silvia, 144. *See also I Lost My Girlish Laughter* (1938)
Screen Writer, The (trade newspaper), 152–153
Screen Writers Guild, 59–60, 69, 92, 141–142, 150–151
screenwriting
    early employment of writers, 29
    ennobled by Minimum Basic Agreement (1951), 151–152
    origins, 25
    relation to directing, 152
    subject of *Boy Meets Girl* (1938) (film), 88–89
    "Thalberg system", 60, 69
    topic in *In a Lonely Place* (1950) (film), 146
    topic in *Sunset Boulevard* (1950), 153–154
See, Sam, 122
Selznick, David O., 3, 7, 58, 84, 92, 144, 150, 185, 188
Selznick, Lewis, 86
Selznick-International Pictures, 84. *See also* Selznick, David O.
Sennett, Mack, 90
Seven Types of Ambiguity (Empson, 1930), 6
Shakespeare, William, 6, 41, 63, 125–127
Shawn, William, 179
Sheeler, Charles, 17
Singin' in the Rain (1952), 5, 184–185
Siraganian, Lisa: *Modernism and the Meaning of Corporate Persons* (2020), 7–8, 12–13, 52
Sirk, Douglas, 169
Skouras, Spyros, 162–163, 173
Smyth, J. E., 86
Son of Frankenstein (1939), 109
Souls For Sale (1923), 34
Spengler, Oswald, 109. *See also* West, Nathanael, *Day of the Locust, The* (1939)
Stage Door (1937) (film), 144
Stage Door (Edna Ferber and George S. Kaufman, 1936) (play), 144
Stagecoach (1939), 82
Staggs, Sam, 160
Stahl, John M., 148. *See also Leave Her to Heaven* (1945) (film)
Staiger, Janet, 3, 25, 160. *See also Classical Hollywood Cinema, The* (1985)
Stamp, Shelley, 24
Star is Born, A (1937), 7, 86–88, 92, 110, 144, 161
Star is Born, A (1954), 86
Stein, Gertrude, 122
Steinbeck, John, 85, 91
Stevens, Wallace, 122

Strand, Paul, 17
Stromberg, Hunt, 58
Studs Lonigan trilogy (James Farrell, 1932–1935), 103
Sundquist, Eric, 78. See also Faulkner, William, *Absalom, Absalom!* (1936)
Sunrise: A Song of Two Humans (1927)
    allegory of modernity, 132
    financed by Fox, 132
Sunset Boulevard (1950), 86, 153–157
    anti-classicism, 154–155, 166–167
    Best Original Screenplay Academy Award, 157
    Norma Desmond's adaptation of *Salomé*, 153
    Norma Desmond's untimeliness, 153–154
    Paramount's depiction of its own divorcement, 155–156
    "Untitled Love Story "as Joe Gillis's tragedy, 154
Szalay, Michael, 7

Talmadge, Constance, 46
Talmadge, Norma, 16
Taylor, Greg, 122
Technicolor, 84
Thalberg, Irving, 3, 6, 12, 62, 184–185
    clash with Louis B. Mayer, 57–58
    management of *Greed* (1924), 54
    as model for Fitzgerald's Monroe Stahr (1941), 55
    "Thalberg system" of screenwriting, 60
Third Man, The (1949), 150
Thompson, Hunter S., 180
Thompson, Kristin, 3, 160. See also *Classical Hollywood Cinema, The* (1985)
Thorp, Margaret Farrand, 83, 142, 174
    America at the Movies (1939), 84
    "Motion Picture and the Novel, The" (1951), 157
Three Caballeros, The (1944), 136
Tierney, Gene, 148, 160
Tindall, William York, 189
Townsend Amendment to the Copyright Act of 1909, 1, 24
Trader Horn (1931). See *Native Son* (Richard Wright, 1940)
Transitional Era of American cinema (1907–1917), 24
transmedial possibility, 13
    in contrast to adaptation, 27
    vis-à-vis remediation, 28
Trask, Michael, 184
Trip to Paramountown, A (1922), 16, 34
Turner, Lana
    in *The Bad and the Beautiful* (1952), 185
    in *The Postman Always Rings Twice* (1946), 146, 187

Twain, Mark, 41, 198n27
Twentieth Century (1934), 58
Twentieth Century-Fox, 3, 7, 84, 86, 136
    central producer system, 158
    desire to end double bills, 172–173
    employment of William Faulkner, 64, 66
    house style developed, 89
    Spyros Skouras's "Guarantee of Performance", 163–164
Tyler, Parker, 180, 183
    "Beyond Surrealism" (1935), 124–125
    "Cinematic Effects in a Long Poem" (1948), 124
    Granite Butterfly, The (1945), 122, 124–128
        "Author's Note on the Meaning of the Poem", 126
        inversion of *The Waste Land* (1922), 118, 125–126
        as late modern epic, 119–121
    "Hollywood as a Universal Church" (1950), 121–122
    Hollywood Hallucination, The (1944), 122–124, 127
    Magic and Myth of the Movies (1947), 122–124, 127
    Modern Things (1934), 122
        "Hollywood Dream Suite", 122–123
    "Ode to Hollywood" (1940), 124–125
    use of cellophane as emblem of techno-rationality, 126
    Young and Evil, The (with Charles Henri Ford, 1933), 122

Ulysses (1922). See Joyce, James
United Artists, 3, 46
United States v. Paramount Pictures, Inc. (1948), 1, 5, 83, 177
universal language metaphor, 116–117, 137
Universal Pictures, 3, 83–84, 95, 101, 116, 133, 151, 181
    employment of William Faulkner, 64, 66
Urgo, Joseph, 64, 203n103, 206n27. See also Faulkner, William, *Absalom, Absalom!* (1936)

Valentino, Rudolph, 122, 124
Vance, Louis Joseph, 30, 47
Variety (trade newspaper), 47, 65, 148, 150–151, 162, 172, 173
Vasey, Ruth, 219n12
Veidt, Conrad, 133, 137
vernacular modernism, 12, 189, 194
von Sternberg, Josef, 51
von Stroheim, Erich, 51

Wadlington, Warwick, 63
Walkowitz, Rebecca, 42

Wallace, Lew, 23
Walpole, Horace, 74
Wanger, Walter, 3, 58, 84–85
Warner Bros., 3, 6, 42, 84, 86, 163
  employment of William Faulkner, 66
  Screen Classics campaign, 28–29
  as the "studio of genres", 88
Was College Worth While? (John Tunis, 1936), 105–106. *See also* West, Nathanael, *Day of the Locust, The* (1939)
  reviewed by Conrad Aiken, 105–106
Wasserman, Lew, 176
Wasson, Ben. *See* Faulkner, William
Watson, Jay. *See* Faulkner, William, *Absalom, Absalom!* (1936)
Welles, Orson, 174, 185
Wells, Walter: *Tycoons and Locusts* (1973), 10, 94
West, Nathanael, 11n4, 105
  and the bildungsroman, 102
  Cool Million, A (1934), 102, 109
  correspondence with Edmund Wilson, 103
  Day of the Locust, The (1939), 82, 113, 183
    attack on the literati, 101–102
    correspondence with Malcolm Cowley about, 100
    mockery of Tod Hackett's Spenglerian worldview, 109–111
    the "Sargasso of the imagination", 101, 107–109, 139
    Tod Hackett as travesty of the "well-rounded man", 106–107
  "Impostor, The" (unpublished story), 215n63
  Miss Lonelyhearts (1933), 96, 100, 102
  practice of Dadaist appropriation, 108
  reflexive joking, 100
Wharton, Edith, 15

What Price Hollywood? (1932), 58
Whitney, John Hay, 84
Wiene, Robert, 133
Wilde, Oscar, 17–18, 45, 153
Wilder, Billy. *See Sunset Boulevard* (1950)
Wilkens, Matthew, 119, 181
Williams, Raymond, 231n65
Williams, William Carlos, 122
Willkie, Wendell, 220n17
Wilson, Edmund, 90–91, 94, 96, 101, 103
Wilson, Harry Leon, 34. *See also Merton of the Movies* (1922)
Wilson, Marie, 88
Wizard of Oz, The (1939), 82
Wolfe, Thomas, 103
Wood, Bethany, 200n52
Woolf, Virginia, 189
World War II, 13
Wright, Richard, 10
Wright, William Lord, 21, 32
Wuthering Heights (1939), 82

Yale University, 101, 103–104, 106, 109, 111
You Play the Black and the Red Comes Up (Eric Knight, 1938), 94

Zanuck, Darryl F., 60, 64, 107, 121, 148, 161
  belief in recreation as participation, 171. *See also All About Eve* (1950), as allegory of medium conflict
  called "One-Man Studio" by *Time* magazine (1950), 158
  founding of Twentieth Century Pictures, 89
  lack of formal education, 169
Zukofsky, Louis, 122
Zukor, Adolph, 1, 6, 22, 144

Printed by Printforce, United Kingdom